Praise for Mary L. Dudziak
Cold War Civil Rights

"This nuanced, scholarly appraisal of the relationship between foreign policy and the civil rights story offers a fresh and provocative perspective on twentieth-century American history."
—*Harvard Law Review*

"[This] book thoughtfully and thoroughly documents how ridiculous and hypocritical we appeared . . . by championing the ideals of freedom, democracy and economic equity around the world while at the same time shamelessly denying access to those very same principles to millions of Americans at home."
—Edward C. Smith, *Washington Times*

"An intelligent and informative book that is sure to become a staple of both civil rights and Cold War historiography."
—Steven F. Lawson, *American Historical Review*

"Meticulously researched and beautifully written, Mary Dudziak's book makes a spectacularly illuminating contribution to a subject traditionally neglected—the linkage between race relations and foreign policy: neither African-American history nor diplomatic history will be the same again."
—Gerald Horne, author of *Race Woman: The Lives of Shirley Graham Du Bois*

"This book reflects a growing interest among historians in the global significance of race. . . . It is accessible and will have multiple uses as an approach to civil rights history, as an examination of policy making, and as a model of how a study can be attentive to both foreign and domestic aspects of a particular issue. It is tightly argued, coherent, and polished, and it features some particularly fine writing."
—Brenda Plummer, author of *Rising Wind: Black Americans and U.S. Foreign Affairs, 1935–1960*

"This book is a *tour de force*. Dudziak's brilliant analysis shows that the Cold War had a profound impact on the civil rights movement. Hers is the first book to make this important connection. It is a major contribution to our understanding of both the Civil Rights movement and the Cold War itself. . . . Because it is beautifully written in clear, lively prose, and draws its analysis from dramatic events and compelling stories of people involved from the top level of government to the grass roots, it will be an outstanding book for both students and the general public. I recommend it with no hesitation and with great enthusiasm."
—Elaine Tyler May, author of *Homeward Bound: American Families in the Cold War Era*

COLD WAR
CIVIL RIGHTS

POLITICS AND SOCIETY IN
TWENTIETH-CENTURY AMERICA

SERIES EDITORS
William Chafe, Gary Gerstle, Linda Gordon,
and Julian Zelizer

A list of titles in the series appears at the back of the book

COLD WAR
CIVIL RIGHTS

RACE AND THE IMAGE OF AMERICAN DEMOCRACY

With a new preface by the author

Mary L. Dudziak

PRINCETON UNIVERSITY PRESS

PRINCETON AND OXFORD

COPYRIGHT © 2000 BY PRINCETON UNIVERSITY PRESS
PUBLISHED BY PRINCETON UNIVERSITY PRESS,
41 WILLIAM STREET, PRINCETON, NEW JERSEY 08540

IN THE UNITED KINGDOM: PRINCETON UNIVERSITY PRESS,
6 OXFORD STREET, WOODSTOCK, OXFORDSHIRE OX20 1TW
PRESS.PRINCETON.EDU

FIRST PRINTING, 2000
SECOND PRINTING, AND FIRST PAPERBACK PRINTING, 2002
PAPERBACK REISSUE, WITH A NEW PREFACE, 2011
PAPERBACK ISBN 978-0-691-15243-1

THE LIBRARY OF CONGRESS HAS CATALOGED THE
CLOTH EDITION OF THIS BOOK AS FOLLOWS

DUDZIAK, MARY L., 1956–
COLD WAR CIVIL RIGHTS : RACE AND THE IMAGE
OF AMERICAN DEMOCRACY / MARY L. DUDZIAK.
P. CM. —— (POLITICS AND SOCIETY IN
TWENTIETH-CENTURY AMERICA)
INCLUDES BIBLIOGRAPHICAL REFERENCES AND INDEX.
ISBN 0-691-01661-5 (alk. paper)
1. UNITED STATES–RACE RELATIONS–POLITICAL ASPECTS.
2. AFRO-AMERICANS–CIVIL RIGHTS–HISTORY–20TH CENTURY.
3. AFRO-AMERICANS–LEGAL STATUS, LAWS, ETC.–HISTORY–
20TH CENTURY. 4. RACISM–POLITICAL ASPECTS–UNITED
STATES–HISTORY–20TH CENTURY. 5. UNITED STATES–
POLITICS AND GOVERNMENT–1945–1989. 6. DEMOCRACY–
UNITED STATES–HISTORY–20TH CENTURY. 7. COLD WAR–
SOCIAL ASPECTS–UNITED STATES. I. TITLE. II. SERIES.

E185.61 .D85 2000
323.1'196073'09045–DC21   00-038515

BRITISH LIBRARY CATALOGING-IN-PUBLICATION
DATA IS AVAILABLE

THIS BOOK HAS BEEN COMPOSED IN GARAMOND

PRINTED ON ACID-FREE PAPER. ∞

PRINTED IN THE UNITED STATES OF AMERICA
10 9 8 7

Parts of this manuscript previously appeared in a different form in the following articles, and are republished with permission: "Desegregation as a Cold War Imperative," *Stanford Law Review* 41 (November 1988): 61–120; "Josephine Baker, Racial Protest and the Cold War," *Journal of American History* 81 (September 1994): 543–570; "The Little Rock Crisis and Foreign Affairs: Race, Resistance and the Image of American Democracy," *Southern California Law Review* 70 (September 1997): 1641–1716.

To Alicia

Abused and scorned though we may be
as a people, our destiny is tied up in the
destiny of America.

MARTIN LUTHER KING JR.
MARCH 31, 1968

Contents

Illustrations

Preface to the 2011 Edition

When I began the research project that would ultimately become *Cold War Civil Rights*, "America in the World" as a field in United States history did not exist. Many years later, a multiyear project on internationalizing American history is completed, there are many history courses in this area, and history departments train graduate students in this new field. The methodology of thinking globally about American history is embraced by more history teachers, with K–12 workshops in place around the country. And as so often happens with a methodological turn, just as this approach to conceptualizing U.S. history has been taking hold, another approach is emerging to destabilize it, as historians seek to transcend the way nations provide borders to historical subjects. Transnational history has much in common with internationalized American history, except perhaps the most fundamental point: whether retaining the nation as a historical frame illuminates more than it obscures.[1]

Along the way, this book continues to find new readers. For those of you who will be picking it up during the book's next decade, I thought it might be helpful to take up how a work that is part of a field that doesn't yet exist comes to be written. I will also discuss a couple of methodological issues, especially the question of whether the Cold War has been getting lost in studies of the Cold War and civil rights. What follows is simply the story of this book and this historian, rather than of the way the broader literature of related works emerged over time.[2] The rest of this edition remains unchanged, other than the correction of errors. If I had attempted more significant revisions, I am afraid that the result would have been a much longer and perhaps a different book.

* * * *

Robin Kelley once questioned the newness of internationalizing American history, since African American history has always been diasporic.[3] Kelley is right, of course, but, with a few exceptions, as a graduate student in the 1980s interested in civil rights history, I encountered little of this. My initial goal was to write a community-centered study. I wanted to understand how Topeka, Kansas, the home of *Brown v. Board of Education*, came to terms with its role in what was thought of as the American dilemma. I got interested in Topeka when I worked for the American Civil Liberties Union one summer during law school. The ACLU asked me to reconstruct the history of segregation in this community for ongoing school desegregation litigation in Topeka. The history of desegregation in Topeka is fascinating and complicated. The local school board voted to desegregate before the Supreme Court ruling in *Brown*. I decided that this should be my Ph.D. dissertation topic. Before long, I was well on my way toward finishing. But I got stuck on a problem, and I just couldn't finish until I figured it out.

When the Topeka school board voted to desegregate in 1953, the local press asked them why. "We feel that segregation is not an American practice," school board member Harold Conrad said.[4] This was a curious statement, in part because it expressed an understanding of what was "American" and defined a longstanding American practice as being outside the boundaries of American conduct. But the historical moment mattered to the use of this word. It meant something particular to characterize an act as "unAmerican" in 1953, during what we call the McCarthy era. This seemed to make it essential to get to the bottom of something I was curious about: Did it matter that *Brown* was decided during the McCarthy era? Did the two topics have anything to do with each other? I knew that civil rights activists were red-baited during this era. But was there something else going on?

Once I started to look for answers, I found connections all over the place. The Cold War context for *Brown* was apparent in the news stories when *Brown* was decided. The *Pittsburgh Courier*, for example, said of *Brown*: "this clarion announcement . . . will stun and silence America's Communist traducers behind the Iron Curtain." Another early clue was the Justice Department brief in *Brown* itself. An amicus curiae ("friend of the court") brief has a section explaining what interest the party filing the brief has in the case. According to the Justice Department, the interest of the United States in school segregation was that race discrimination harmed American foreign relations.[5]

Once I found these sources, if the Justice Department's files in *Brown* had been accessible, my topic might have retained a more domestic frame, as a history of ideas about desegregation during the McCarthy era. But the Justice Department is one of the worst at opening files to historians. Stymied, I turned to State Department records, since the *Brown* brief relied on a statement from Secretary of State Dean Acheson. I just wanted to see that side of the correspondence. And at this point in the story, pure luck intervened.

Serendipity is so often important to historical research, especially in the archives. I was fortunate to be doing research at a time when the National Archives was more fully staffed with experienced archivists who had the time to help researchers find material. And I was simply lucky to encounter Sally Marks (later Sally Kuisel), who was never disparaging about my rather profound ignorance.[6] With her help, I learned how to do diplomatic history research. I found the archival material that demonstrated the relationship between civil rights and U.S. foreign affairs. As I continued my work, I came to know Brenda Gayle Plummer and Gerald Horne, who had been writing in the area of race and international affairs and became sources of support and inspiration.[7] When charting a new path, connections like these are essential, for I also encountered stiff resistance. "You've taken something away from us," a senior colleague at my first law school teaching job told me. He was more melancholy than angry. A traditional liberal framing of civil rights history, in which white liberals aided the movement as the country embraced "simple justice" as a moral ideal, was part of his personal identity as a white, liberal, reform-minded lawyer.[8]

Years later, the question that had once stymied me resulted in this book. Along the way, a broader literature, both in race and international affairs, and in global approaches to U.S. history, developed, so that my book would have plenty of company on its shelf in the library. And, with some regret, I never went back to Topeka.

* * * *

Over the past decade, as the Cold War slips further into history, it has received new critical attention in works on American politics and culture. Important new scholarship has appeared, broadening our understanding of the relationship between international affairs and American civil rights. But sometimes it is hard to figure out just what work the Cold War is doing in works on the Cold War and civil rights.

The Cold War is a curious figure. Its definition is often left to the imagination. Yet at the same time it seems to act as an abstract but powerful historical actor. The Cold War, like some "hot" wars, is thought to *do* things in history. Sometimes the Cold War seems like atmosphere—it appears to be everywhere—or like a superhero—it can do anything. The Cold War is not usually invoked only as a simple temporal frame. Instead, it is a strange fusion—a historical era that is also a historical actor. Because of this, it seems important to nail down what we mean when we invoke the Cold War. By this I do not mean the debates about when the Cold War began and ended and who was at fault for what, but instead, when we view the Cold War as moving or enabling history in some way, *what is it* that is enabling the action?[9]

Sometimes the Cold War is domestic anticommunism without any direct connection to international relations. Sometimes Cold War foreign affairs are clearly in view, as in works on the relationship between civil rights and American public diplomacy. Sometimes the Cold War is an international relations problem that affects social conditions at the national or local level. Sometimes the Cold War is simply a backdrop or a climate system (as in the "Cold War climate") within which the narrative plays out. There are countless other formulations. These approaches are very different, but they are sometimes lumped together as if they are all about the same thing, since they are all about the Cold War. But when we say that the Cold War is having an impact, this is a causal argument. Being precise about what we mean by the Cold War, and how the Cold War is driving the action in the story, can help us identify what sort of historical evidence is needed to make the causal argument convincing. A foreign relations argument, for example, would require reliance on foreign relations sources. On occasion, climate systems can determine the course of history, but it is usually good to move beyond a meteorological approach to Cold War historiography.

So was the Cold War a good thing for American civil rights? A very smart historian once asked me that question, and has suggested in print that the answer in my book is yes.[10] Readers are welcome to use the evidence in the book in support of an argument like that—or its opposite—but you will find no such argument from me in these pages. Instead, the Cold War (and by this I mean the geopolitical Cold War, or Cold War–era U.S. foreign relations, and its domestic impact) narrowed the scope of civil rights discourse; undermined political activism and destroyed lives, as chapter 2 discusses; justified American intervention around the world, with devastating consequences; and fueled the creation of a national security state that continues to hamper American political possibilities. To say that the Cold War was "good" for the civil rights movement strikes me as like saying that Hurricane Katrina was good for the building trades in the Gulf Coast. That a devastating moment opens the door to particular opportunities does not mean that the devastation was "good" or that we would have wanted it to happen.

* * * *

Many years ago, I followed a question that took me off-track but then opened up what for me was a new way of thinking about history. At some point, this book's methodology will seem very old-fashioned, and scholars will turn to new approaches that have not yet been imagined. If there is a lesson in this book for that generation, perhaps it is that getting stuck is not a bad thing. Being truly puzzled can be the first step toward finding an answer. And when pursuing a lead, it is important to follow it wherever it takes you, even if the terrain is unfamiliar. Opening an unexpected door and finding a new world on the other side is, after all, one of the most exciting things about writing history.

Mary L. Dudziak
December 12, 2010

NOTES

1. The Organization of American Historians/New York University Project on Internationalizing the Study of American History (Thomas Bender, Director), *The LaPietra Report: A Report to the Profession* (September 2000), http://www.oah.org/activities/lapietra/final.html; *The Palgrave Dictionary of Transnational History,* Akira Iriye and Pierre-Yves Saunier, eds. (Hampshire, UK: Palgrave Macmillan, 2009), http://www.transnationalhistory.com/home.aspx.

2. Excellent overviews of this literature appear in Brenda Gayle Plummer, "The Changing Face of Diplomatic History: A Literature Review," *The History Teacher* 38 (May 2005): 385–400; Kevin Gaines, "A World to Win: The International Dimension of the Black Freedom Movement," *OAH Magazine of History* 20 (October 2006): 14–18; and Jeff Woods, "The Cold War and the Struggle for Civil Rights," *OAH Magazine of History* 24 (October 2010): 13–17.

3. Robin D. G. Kelley, "'But a Local Phase of a World Problem': Black History's Global Vision, 1883–1950," *Journal of American History* 86 (December 1999): 1045–1077.

4. Mary L. Dudziak, "The Limits of Good Faith: Desegregation in Topeka, Kansas, 1950–1956," *Law and History Review* 5 (Fall 1987): 376.

5. Mary L. Dudziak, *Cold War Civil Rights: Race and the Image of American Democracy* (Princeton: Princeton University Press, 2011), 99–102, 110.

6. Thomas Allen Schwartz, "In Memoriam: Sally M. (Marks) Kuisel," *Passport* 41 (April 2010): 50.

7. While they have written and edited many more books, essential to my early work were: Brenda Gayle Plummer, *Rising Wind: Black Americans and U.S. Foreign Affairs, 1935–1960* (Chapel Hill: University of North Carolina Press, 1996); and Gerald Horne, *Black and Red: W.E.B. Du Bois and the Afro-American Response to the Cold War, 1944–1963* (Albany: State University of New York Press, 1986).

8. My first publication in this area takes up the liberal paradigm and its limits: Mary L. Dudziak, "Desegregation as a Cold War Imperative," *Stanford Law Review* 41 (November 1988): 61–120.

9. The literature on Cold War historiography is, of course, vast. A starting point is the new three-volume compilation *The Cambridge History of the Cold War,* Melvyn P. Leffler and Odd Arne Westad, eds. (New York: Cambridge University Press, 2010). I expand on ideas about the way the Cold War is understood in *War·Time: An Idea, Its History, Its Consequences* (Oxford University Press, 2012).

10. Steven Lawson, review of *Cold War Civil Rights, American Historical Review* 107 (February 2002): 246–247.

COLD WAR
CIVIL RIGHTS

INTRODUCTION

All races and religions, that's America to me.

LEWIS ALLAN AND EARL ROBINSON,
"THE HOUSE I LIVE IN" (1942)[1]

Jimmy Wilson's name has not been remembered in the annals of Cold War history, but in 1958, this African American handyman was at the center of international attention. After he was sentenced to death in Alabama for stealing less than two dollars in change, Wilson's case was thought to epitomize the harsh consequences of American racism. It brought to the surface international anxiety about the state of American race relations. Because the United States was the presumptive leader of the free world, racism in the nation was a matter of international concern. How could American democracy be a beacon during the Cold War, and a model for those struggling against Soviet oppression, if the United States itself practiced brutal discrimination against minorities within its own borders?

Jimmy Wilson's unexpected entry into this international dilemma began on July 27, 1957. The facts of the unhappy events setting off his travails are unclear. Wilson had worked for Estelle Barker, an elderly white woman, in Marion, Alabama. He later told a Toronto reporter that he had simply wanted to borrow money from her against his future earnings, as he had in the past. As Wilson told the story, Barker let him into her home one evening, they had an argument, she threw some money on her bed and he took it and left. The coins would not be enough to cover the cost of his cab home. Barker told the police that his motives were more sinister. After taking the money she had dumped on her bed, she said he forced her onto the bed and unsuccessfully attempted to rape her.[2]

Wilson was prosecuted only for robbery, for the theft of $1.95. Over the objections of Wilson's attorney, Barker testified at trial about the alleged sexual assault. Wilson was quickly convicted by an all-white jury. Robbery carried a maximum penalty of death, and the presiding judge sentenced Wilson to die in the electric chair. When the Alabama Supreme Court upheld Wilson's sentence, news of the case spread across the nation. Because other nations followed race in the United States with great interest, the Wilson case was soon international news.[3]

Headlines around the world decried this death sentence for the theft of less than two dollars. The *Voice of Ethiopia* thought "it is inconceivable that in this enlightened age, in a country that prides itself on its code of justice, that, for the paltry sum of $1.95, a man should forfeit his life." An editorial in the Ghanaian *Ashanti Pioneer* urged that the underlying law be repealed. According to the paper, it was "the High, inescapable duty of every right thinking human being who believes in democracy as understood and practised on this side of the Iron Curtain to venture to bring it home to the people of Alabama." The Jimmy Wilson story was widely publicized in West Africa, prompting American businessmen to call the U.S. embassy in Monrovia to express their concern that Wilson's execution would undermine "American effort to maintain sympathetic understanding [of our] principles and government" in that part of the world.[4]

Petitions and letters of protest poured in. Hulda Omreit of Bodo, Norway, describing herself as "a simple Norwegian housewife," wrote a letter to the U.S. government. She wished "to express her sympathy for the Negro, Jimmy Wilson, and plead for clemency for him. It makes no difference whether he is black or white; we are all brothers under the skin." Six members of the Israeli Parliament sent a letter of protest. The Trades Union Congress of Ghana urged

American authorities "to save not only the life of Wilson but also the good name of the United States of America from ridicule and contempt." The Congress thought Wilson's sentence "constitutes such a savage blow against the Negro Race that it finds no parallel in the Criminal Code of any modern State." The Jones Town Youth Club of Jamaica was just one of the groups that held a protest in front of the U.S. consulate in Kingston. In one extreme reaction, the U.S. embassy in The Hague received calls threatening that the U.S. ambassador "would not survive" if Wilson were executed. After a story about the case appeared in *Time* magazine, someone in Perth, Australia, hung a black figure in effigy from the flagpole of the U.S. consulate. Above it was a sign reading "Guilty of theft of fourteen shillings."[5]

John Morsell, a spokesman for the National Association for the Advancement of Colored People (NAACP), thought that it would be "a sad blot on the nation" if Wilson were executed. The NAACP was worried about the international repercussions. According to Morsell, "We think the communists will take this and go to town with it." Sure enough, the communist newspaper in Rome, *L'Unita,* called Wilson's death sentence "a new unprecedented crime by American segregationists," while front-page stories in Prague appeared under headlines proclaiming "This is America." Even those friendly to the United States were outraged, however. A group of Canadian judges was disturbed about the sentence and passed a resolution conveying its "deep concern" to Alabama Governor James Folsom. The judges warned that "[i]f Alabama electrocutes Jimmy Wilson it will shock the conscience of the world." From St. Paul's Cathedral in London, Canon John Collins urged every Christian in Britain to protest the execution. The secretary of the British Labour Party thought it was unfortunate that "those who wish to criticize western liberty and democracy" had been given "such suitable ammunition for their propaganda."[6]

Before long, Secretary of State John Foster Dulles was involved in the case. The Congress of Racial Equality (CORE) had urged Dulles to intervene, calling the Wilson case "a matter of prime concern to the foreign relations of the United States." CORE warned that "if this execution is carried out, certainly the enemies of the

United States will give it world-wide publicity and thus convey a distorted picture of relations between the races in our country." A flood of despatches about the case from U.S. embassies around the world would make Dulles's participation inevitable.[7]

Secretary Dulles sent a telegram to Governor Folsom, informing him of the great international interest in the Jimmy Wilson case. Folsom did not need to be told that the world had taken an interest in Jimmy Wilson. He had received an average of a thousand letters a day about the case, many from abroad. The governor had "never seen anything like" it and was "utterly amazed" by the outpouring of international attention. He called a press conference to announce that he was "'snowed under' with mail from Toronto demanding clemency" for Wilson. Folsom told Dulles that he stood ready to "aid in interpreting the facts of the case to the peoples of the world." After the Alabama Supreme Court upheld Wilson's conviction and sentence, Governor Folsom acted with unusual haste to grant Wilson clemency. The reason he acted so quickly was to end what he called the "international hullabaloo."[8]

Jimmy Wilson's case is one example of the international impact of American race discrimination during the Cold War. Domestic civil rights crises would quickly become international crises. As presidents and secretaries of state from 1946 to the mid-1960s worried about the impact of race discrimination on U.S. prestige abroad, civil rights reform came to be seen as crucial to U.S. foreign relations.

During the Cold War years, when international perceptions of American democracy were thought to affect the nation's ability to maintain its leadership role, and particularly to ensure that democracy would be appealing to newly independent nations in Asia and Africa, the diplomatic impact of race in America was especially stark. The underlying question of whether the nation lived up to its own ideals had, of course, been raised before, and activists in earlier years had looked overseas for a sympathetic audience for their critique of American racism. Frederick Douglass sought support for the abolitionist movement in Great Britain, arguing that slavery was a crime against "the human family," and so "it belongs to the whole human family to seek its suppression." In 1893, Ida B. Wells traveled to England to generate support for the campaign against lynching. "The pulpit and the press of our own country remains silent on these continued outrages," she explained. She hoped that support from Great Britain would in turn "arouse the public sentiment of Americans."[9]

During World War I, NAACP President Morefield Story argued that since African Americans were risking their lives to make the world safe for democracy, the nation must "make America safe for Americans." W. E. B. DuBois took these ideas overseas when world leaders convened for the Paris Peace Conference. He hoped that international cooperation in a new League of Nations would provide a forum for the vindication of racial problems at home. "[W]hat we cannot accomplish before the choked conscience of America, we have an infinitely better chance to accomplish before the organized Public Opinion of the World."[10]

While World War I influenced civil rights activists' critique of American racism, it did not lead to extensive social change. The moment for broader change came after World War II, a war against a racist regime carried on by a nation with segregated military forces. During the war years the idea that a conflict inhered in American ideology and practice first gained wide currency.[11]

World War II marked a transition point in American foreign relations, American politics, and American culture. At home, the meaning ascribed to the war would help to shape what would follow. At least on an ideological level, the notion that the nation as a whole had a stake in racial equality was widespread. As Wendell L. Willkie put it, "Our very proclamations of what we are fighting for have rendered our own inequities self-evident. When we talk of freedom and opportunity for all nations the mocking paradoxes in our own society become so clear they can no longer be ignored."[12]

The war years became an occasion for a serious examination of what was called the "Negro problem" in America. The most detailed treatment of this issue came from Swedish sociologist Gunnar Myrdal and his team of researchers. In 1944, Myrdal published *An American Dilemma: The Negro Problem and Modern Democracy*. According to Myrdal,

[I]n this War, the principle of democracy had to be applied more explicitly to race. . . . Fascism and racism are based on a racial superiority dogma. . .and they came to power by means of racial persecution and oppression. In fighting fascism and racism, America had to stand before the whole world in favor of racial tolerance and cooperation and of racial equality.[13]

The contradictions between racism and the ideology of democracy were, for Myrdal, a quintessentially *American* dilemma. Myrdal thought that all Americans shared an "American creed," a belief in "ideals of the essential dignity of the individual human being, of the fundamental equality of all men, and of certain inalienable rights to freedom, justice and a fair opportunity." Racism conflicted with this creed. The conflict between racist thoughts and egalitarian beliefs created tension and anxiety, leading Myrdal to emphasize that this American dilemma inured "*in the heart of the American.*"[14]

The American dilemma was a moral dilemma, and yet its implications stretched far beyond guilty consciences. According to Myrdal, there was a strategic reason for social change. During the war years, the American dilemma had "acquired tremendous international implications." The "color angle to this War," meant that "[t]he situation is actually such that any and all concessions to Negro rights in this phase of the history of the world will repay the nation many times, while any and all injustices inflicted upon them will be extremely costly." American might would not be determined by military strength alone. "America, for its international prestige, power, and future security, needs to demonstrate to the world that American Negroes can be satisfactorily integrated into its democracy."[15]

Myrdal's concerns about the impact of American racism on the war effort were played out in Axis propaganda. Pearl Buck reported that "Japan. . .is declaring in the Philippines, in China, in India, Malaya, and even Russia that there is no basis for hope that colored peoples can expect any justice" from the U.S. government. To prove their point, the Japanese pointed to racism in the United States. According to Buck,

Every lynching, every race riot gives joy to Japan. The discriminations of the American army and navy and the air forces against colored soldiers and sailors, the exclusion of colored labor in our defense industries and trade unions, all our social discriminations, are of the greatest aid today to our enemy in Asia, Japan. "Look at America," Japan is saying to millions of listening ears. "Will white Americans give you equality?"[16]

In spite of these concerns, African Americans serving in the military in World War II were segregated and most often relegated to service units, not combat. A. Philip Randolph and many others mobilized against such wartime race discrimination. Civil rights groups capitalized on the nation's new focus on equality, and World War II spurred civil rights activism. The NAACP developed, for the first time, a mass membership base. As Brenda Gayle Plummer has written, during the war "[t]he NAACP internationaliz[ed] the race issue." A 1943 NAACP report suggested that race had become "a global instead of a national or sectional issue." The war had broadened people's thinking "with the realization that the United States cannot win this war unless there is a drastic readjustment of racial attitudes."[17]

The thinking that World War II was a war against racial and religious intolerance, and that the United States stood to gain from promoting equality at home was so widespread that Frank Sinatra even sang about it. The lesson of his short film *The House I Live In* was that racial and religious intolerance were "Nazi" characteristics. To be "American" was to practice equality, at least toward one's wartime allies. This Oscar-winning film ended with Sinatra singing, "all races and religions, that's America to me."[18]

As World War II drew to a close, the nation faced an uncertain future. Victory over fascism, a returned focus on the home front, the specter of a nuclear age—these joys and anxieties captured the nation. Yet more would be at stake in the postwar years. The purpose of the war would leave its victors with new obligations. And if the war was, at least in part, a battle against racism, then racial segregation and disenfranchisement seemed to belie the great sacrifices the war had wrought.[19]

This idea was captured by a military chaplain with U.S. Marine Corps troops at the Battle of Iwo Jima during the final months of the war. When the battle was over, Rabbi Roland B. Gittelsohn stood over newly dug graves on the island and delivered a eulogy. "Here lie men who loved America," he said.

> Here lie officers and men, Negroes and whites, rich and poor, together. Here no man prefers another because of his faith, or despises him because of his color. . . . Among these men there is no discrimination, no prejudice, no hatred. Theirs is the highest and purest democracy.

The equality these soldiers had found in death was, for Gittelsohn, at the heart of the war's meaning.

> Whoever of us lifts his hand in hate against a brother, or thinks himself superior to those who happen to be in the minority, makes of this ceremony, and of the bloody sacrifice it commemorates, an empty, hollow mockery. Thus, then, do we, the living, now dedicate ourselves, to the right of Protestants, Catholics and Jews, of white men and Negroes alike, to enjoy the democracy for which all of them have paid the price.[20]

There was an irony in the equality Gittelsohn found among the fallen soldiers, a point not mentioned in the chaplain's eulogy. The military forces that fought on Iwo Jima were racially segregated. Yet the limitations on the military's practice of equality did not dampen Gittelsohn's passionate argument that out of the carnage of the war came a commitment and an obligation to give democracy meaning across the divisions of race, religion and class.

> Too much blood has gone into this soil for us to let it lie barren. Too much pain and heartache have fertilized the earth on which we stand. We here solemnly swear: it shall not be in vain. Out of this will come, we promise, the birth of a new freedom for the sons of men everywhere.[21]

The commitment to democracy had been sealed in blood. And this "democracy" was more than a political system. It was an ideology, a set of beliefs about the nature and moral power of the nation. What remained to be determined was the way this ideological commitment to egalitarian democracy would be put into practice in the years after the war.

Following World War II, reconversion came to domestic life as well as the workplace. A renewed embrace of domesticity fueled a baby boom and a focus on consumption. Would the desire to return to normalcy mean a renewed embrace of racial norms of segregation, disenfranchisement, and subordination?[22] Paradoxically, international pressures would soon simultaneously constrain and enhance civil rights reform.

The inward turn of postwar American culture would have its limits, as the nation's political leaders soon warned that a new international threat loomed on the horizon. By 1947, the Cold War came to dominate the American political scene. As the Truman administration cast Cold War international politics in apocalyptic terms, "McCarthyism" took hold in domestic politics. If communism was such a serious threat world-wide, the existence of communists within the United States seemed particularly frightening. As the nation closed ranks, critics of American society often found themselves labeled as "subversive." Civil rights groups had to walk a fine line, making it clear that their reform efforts were meant to fill out the contours of American democracy, and not to challenge or undermine it. Organizations outside a narrowing sphere of civil rights politics found it difficult to survive the Cold War years.[23] Under the strictures of Cold War politics, a broad, international critique of racial oppression was out of place. As Penny Von Eschen has written, the narrowed scope of acceptable protest during the early years of the Cold War would not accommodate criticism of colonialism. Western European colonial powers, after all, were America's Cold War allies. For that reason, outspoken critics of colonialism found themselves increasingly under siege.[24]

Civil rights activists who sought to use international pressure to encourage reform in the United States also found themselves under increasing scrutiny. The strategic value of civil rights reform had given civil rights activists an important opportunity. Drawing upon international interest in race in America, following the war civil rights groups would turn to the United Nations. This new international forum, dedicated to human rights, might pressure the U.S. government to protect the rights of African Americans. However, to criticize the nation before an international audience and to air the nation's dirty laundry overseas was to reinforce the negative impact of American racism on the nation's standing as a world leader. It was seen, therefore, as a great breach of loyalty. As a result, just as the House Committee on Un-American Activities and the government's loyalty security program silenced progressive voices within the United States, through passport restrictions and international negotiations the long arm of U.S. government red-baiting silenced critics of U.S. racism overseas.[25]

In spite of the repression of the Cold War era, civil rights reform was *in part* a product of the Cold War. In the years following World War II, racial discrimination in the United States received increasing attention from other countries. Newspapers throughout the world carried stories about discrimination against nonwhite visiting foreign dignitaries, as well as against American blacks. At a time when the United States hoped to reshape the postwar world in its own image, the international attention given to racial segregation was troublesome and embarrassing. The focus of American foreign policy was to promote democracy and to "contain" communism, but the international focus on U.S. racial problems meant that the image of American democracy was tarnished. The apparent contradictions between American political ideology and American practice led to particular foreign relations problems with countries in Asia, Africa, and Latin America. The Soviet Union capitalized on this weakness, using the race issue prominently in anti-American propaganda. U.S. government officials realized that their ability to promote democracy among peoples of color around the world was seriously hampered by continuing racial injustice at home. In this context, efforts to promote civil rights within the United States were consistent with and important to the more central U.S. mission of fighting world communism. The need to address international criticism gave the federal government an incentive to promote social change at home.

Yet the Cold War would frame and thereby limit the nation's civil rights commitment. The primacy of anticommunism in postwar American politics and culture left a very narrow space for criticism of the status quo. By silencing certain voices and by promoting a particular vision of racial justice, the Cold War led to a narrowing of acceptable civil rights discourse. The narrow boundaries of Cold War–era civil rights politics kept discussions of broad-based social change, or a linking of race and class, off the agenda. In addition, to the extent that the nation's commitment to social justice was motivated by a need to respond to foreign critics, civil rights reforms that made the nation look good might be sufficient. The narrow terms of Cold War civil rights discourse and the nature of the federal government's commitment help explain the limits of social change during this period.

In addressing civil rights reform from 1946 through the mid-1960s, the federal government engaged in a sustained effort to tell a particular story about race and American democracy: a story of progress, a story of the triumph of good over evil, a story of U.S. moral superiority. The lesson of this story was always that American democracy was a form of government that made the achievement of social justice possible, and that democratic change, however slow and gradual, was superior to dictatorial imposition. The story of race in America, used to compare democracy and communism, became an important Cold War narrative.

American race relations would not always stay neatly within this frame. Racial violence continued to mar the image of the United States in the 1950s, even as the Voice of America heralded the Supreme Court's ruling that school segregation violated the Constitution. During the 1960s the civil rights movement and massive resistance in the South forced the federal government to devote more attention both to racial justice in the nation and to the impact of the movement on U.S. prestige abroad.

Out of this dynamic comes a rather complex story. Domestic racism and civil rights protest led to international criticism of the U.S. government. International criticism led the federal government to respond, through placating foreign critics by reframing the narrative of race in America, and through promoting some level of social change. While civil rights reform in different eras has been motivated by a variety of factors, one element during the early Cold War years was the need for reform in order to make credible the government's argument about race and democracy.

To explore this story, this study will take up civil rights history from a different standpoint than histories of civil rights activists and organizations and histories of domestic civil rights politics. The events that drive this narrative are the events that captivated the world. This focus on particular events and often on prominent leaders should not be seen as an effort to privilege a top-down focus as "the" story of civil rights history. The international perspective is not a substitute for the rich body of civil rights scholarship but another dimension that sheds additional light on those important and well-told stories. Looking abroad and then at home at the impact of civil rights on U.S. foreign affairs, we might more fully see the great impact of civil rights activists. It was only through the efforts of the movement that the nation and the world were moved to embrace the civil rights reform that emerged from this period of American history.[26]

The full story of civil rights reform in U.S. history cuts across racial groups. The U.S. policymakers in this study, however, saw American race relations through the lens of a black/white paradigm. To them, race in America was quintessentially about "the Negro problem." Foreign observers as well remarked that the status of "the Negro" was the paradigm for exploring race in America. Contemporary writers argue that the black/white paradigm renders other racial groups invisible. This limitation of vision affected the actors in this story, both U.S. policymakers and the international audience to which they were reacting. As a result, this history works within that narrowed conception of American race relations—not because race in America is a black/white issue, but because this study seeks to capture the way race politics were understood at a time when "the Negro problem" was at the center of the discourse on race in America.[27]

It will be the task of this volume to explore the impact of Cold War foreign affairs on U.S. civil rights reform. It brings together

Cold War history and civil rights history, helping us to see that federal government action on civil rights was an aspect of Cold War policymaking. Narratives of twentieth-century America have tended to treat civil rights and foreign relations as two separate categories, unrelated to each other. If developments in the history of international relations had a bearing on domestic policy, it might be as part of the background, but not as a player on the same stage. For that reason, attention to foreign relations may seem out of place in a study of civil rights reform. Yet as the United States emerged from World War II as a world power, looked to for leadership amid ensuing Cold War fears of a new global conflagration, domestic politics and culture were profoundly affected by events overseas. They were affected as well by the way local and national actors thought domestic events would impact the Cold War balance of power. The Cold War created a constraining environment for domestic politics. It also gave rise to new opportunities for those who could exploit Cold War anxieties, while yet remaining within the bounds of acceptable "Americanism."[28]

Chapter 1 explores the international reaction to postwar racial violence and race discrimination. Lynching and racial segregation provoked international outrage, and by 1949 race in America was a principal Soviet propaganda theme. These developments led the Truman administration to realize that race discrimination harmed U.S. foreign relations.

One way to respond to international criticism was to manage the way the story of American race relations was told overseas. Chapter 2 details U.S. government efforts to turn the story of race in America into a story of the superiority of democracy over communism as a system of government. The production of propaganda on U.S. race relations was one strategy. In addition, the government took steps to silence alternative voices, such as Paul Robeson's, when they challenged the official narrative of race and American democracy.

Ultimately the most effective response to foreign critics was to achieve some level of social change at home. Chapter 3 discusses Truman administration civil rights efforts, including its sustained reliance on national security arguments in briefs in the Supreme Court cases that would overturn the constitutional basis for Jim

Crow. In *Brown v. Board of Education* (1954), the U.S. Supreme Court held that school segregation, a particular target of foreign criticism, violated the U.S. Constitution. *Brown* powerfully reinforced the story of race and democracy that had already been told in U.S. propaganda: American democracy enabled social change and was based on principles of justice and equality.

Brown would not bring this story to closure, of course. Chapter 4 takes up the major challenge to the image of America abroad during Eisenhower's presidency. Massive resistance to school desegregation in Little Rock, Arkansas, threatened to undermine the narrative of race and democracy carefully told in U.S. propaganda. As Little Rock became a massive worldwide news story, and as his leadership was questioned at home and abroad, Eisenhower was forced to act. Although the crisis in Little Rock would be resolved, in later years Little Rock remained the paradigmatic symbol of race in America and served as the reference point as Presidents Kennedy and Johnson faced civil rights crises of their own.

President Kennedy hoped to put off addressing civil rights so that civil rights initiatives would not interfere with his other domestic proposals and especially with his foreign affairs agenda. As chapter 5 illustrates, however, events in the early 1960s conspired to frustrate Kennedy's efforts to control the place of civil rights on his overall agenda. Ambassadors from newly independent African nations came to the United States and encountered Jim Crow. Each incident of discrimination reinforced the importance of race to U.S. relations with Africa. Sustained civil rights movement actions, and the brutality of resistance to peaceful civil rights protest, came to a head in Birmingham, Alabama, in 1963. As Bull Connor's violent treatment of protesters became a subject of discussion among African heads of state, the diplomatic consequences of discrimination and the importance of more extensive social change were underscored.

President Kennedy's support for a civil rights bill in 1963 was celebrated internationally. His assassination led many nations to question whether federal support for civil rights reform would continue. Foreign leaders looked to President Johnson to maintain continuity—not only in U.S. foreign affairs but also in U.S. civil rights policy. Chapter 6 details the role of civil rights in international perceptions of Johnson's presidency. During the Johnson years the role of foreign relations in U.S. civil rights politics changed significantly. The passage of important civil rights legislation convinced many foreign observers that the U.S. government was behind social change. The narrative of race and democracy seemed to have more salience. Yet just as new questions surfaced about urban racial unrest, the focus of international interest in U.S. policy shifted. As American involvement in Vietnam escalated, the Vietnam War eclipsed domestic racism as a defining feature of the American image abroad.

Cold War Civil Rights traces the emergence, the development, and the decline of Cold War foreign affairs as a factor in influencing civil rights policy by setting a U.S. history topic within the context of Cold War world history. The Cold War was a critical juncture in the twentieth century, the "American Century." For this century, characterized by the emergence of the United States as a global power, it makes sense to ask whether the expansion of U.S. influence and power in the world reflected on American politics and culture at home. Following the transnational path of the story of race in America, we see that the borders of U.S. history are not easily maintained. An event that is local is at the same time international. "Foreign" developments help drive domestic politics and policy. American history plays out in a transnational frame. The international context structures relationships between "domestic" actors. It influences the timing, nature, and extent of social change. This suggests that an international perspective does not simply "fill in" the story of American history, but changes its terms.[29]

CHAPTER 1

Coming to Terms with Cold War Civil Rights

[T]he colour bar is the greatest propaganda gift
any country could give the Kremlin in its
persistent bid for the affections of the coloured
races of the world.

OBSERVER (CEYLON, 1949)[1]

One shot could have killed George Dorsey, but when he and three companions were found along the banks of the Appalachee River in Georgia on July 25, 1946, their bodies were riddled with at least sixty bullets. Many white men with guns had participated in this deed. Yet the ritual that produced the deaths of two "young Negro farmhands and their wives" required more than mere killing. The privilege of taking part in the executions, the privilege of drawing blood in the name of white supremacy, was to be shared.[2]

George Dorsey had recently returned to Georgia after five years of service in the United States Army. His mother received his discharge papers within days of his death. Dorsey survived the war against fascism to die in a hail of bullets on an American roadside. His crime was to be African American, and to be in the wrong place at the wrong time.[3]

Dorsey died in the company of his wife, Mae Murray Dorsey, and his friends Roger and Dorothy Malcom. Roger Malcom had been arrested after stabbing a white man during a fight. Bailed out by a wealthy white farmer, J. Loy Harrison, the Malcoms and the Dorseys took a ride from Harrison, who told them he wanted them to work his fields. When Harrison's car came upon a wooden bridge over the Appalachee River, he noticed a car on the far side, blocking the way. Another car drove up from behind, and Harrison reported: "One of the men came out, put a shotgun against the back of my head and said, 'All of you put 'em up.' "[4]

Someone pointed at Roger Malcom, saying, "There's the man we want." But both Malcom and George Dorsey were bound with ropes "expert like," and dragged from the car. It appeared that the women would be spared. Then one woman began "cussing like everything and called out one of the men's name whom she evidently recognized." The leader of the group stopped and said, "Hold everything." He picked four men, telling them, "Go back and get them." The women were then pulled, shrieking, from the car. Harrison was asked, "You recognize anybody here?" He answered "No," the same answer he would give investigators later when asked whether he could identify participants in this crime.[5]

The Dorseys and the Malcoms were lined up. Harrison could hear the mob's leader say " 'One, two, three,' and then boom. He did that three times. There were three volleys." Shots were fired after the four had fallen. "It looked like it was a rehearsed affair," the head of the Georgia Bureau of Investigation would later say. When the sheriff came upon the scene later that day, "the upper parts of the bodies were scarcely recognizable because of the mass of bullet holes." As one reporter later put it, "nothing in the undertaker's art could put back the faces of Roger Malcom or Mae Dorsey."[6]

This crime was, in some ways, unremarkable. Its pattern was familiar: African American man detained by police, then released, then killed with companions by a white mob. So many had met gruesome deaths in this way that what distinguished the Monroe killings was not their brutality. It was the attention bestowed upon them.[7]

So many hundreds of letters and telegrams protesting the Monroe murders poured in to the U.S. Justice Department that attorney general Tom Clark held a press conference to answer them. "These crimes," the attorney general said, "are an affront to decent Americanism. Only due process of law sustains our claim to orderly self-government." Clark called upon "all our citizens to repudiate mob rule and to assist the authorities to bring these criminals to justice. The lives and liberties of none of us are safe when forces of terror operate outside the laws of God and man." To some, the lynching of a black veteran was part of a chilling postwar turn in American race relations. According to Oliver Harrington, former war correspondent for the *Pittsburgh Courier,* "The Georgia lynchings were only part of the highly organized conspiracy to 'put the returned Negro veteran in his place.' "[8]

While the investigation into the murders was stymied, demonstrators marched in front of the White House. This horrible crime was not a burden for Georgia alone to bear. The nation as a whole had a stake in its resolution. As fifty members of the National Association of Colored Women marched in front of the White House, their picket signs spoke to the nation's role in achieving racial justice. "America, our home, let it be known that lynching must cease," proclaimed one. "Where Is Democracy?" asked another. The press in other nations asked the same question, as this incident was widely covered overseas. The Monroe lynching was the lead story in an article on "Position of Negroes in the USA" in the Soviet publication *Trud.* The August 1946 story mentioned the incident as just one example of "the increasing frequency of terroristic acts against negroes" in the United States. The U.S. embassy in Moscow found this story to be "representative of the frequent Soviet press comment on the question of Negro discrimination in the United States."[9]

In Monroe, in spite of offers of thousands of dollars of reward money for identifying those involved in the killings, a tight-lipped white community protected its own. Meanwhile relatives stayed away from the funeral they had carefully prepared for George Dorsey and Dorothy Malcom, his sister, out of fear of more violence.[10]

Two days after the killings, Senator William F. Knowland, Republican of California, introduced an account of the events into the

National Association of Colored Women delegates from across the nation picket the White House in July 1946 to protest the lynching of four African Americans in Georgia. (UPI/ CORBIS-BETTMANN)

George Dorsey's coffin was draped in an American flag in honor of his military service at funeral services for Dorsey and his sister, Dorothy Malcom, lynched July 25, 1946, outside Monroe, Georgia. (UPI/CORBIS-BETTMANN)

Congressional Record. "[N]othing that we can do here today can bring back the lives of those people," he said. "But by what we do here today we can show, or at least speak out and say that such things must not continue in the United States of America." Knowland urged the attorney general to place "the full power of his office" behind efforts to solve the crime, "because this is not merely a blot upon the escutcheon of a single local area, but this and this sort of thing is a blot upon the entire United States of America."[11]

The idea that racism was "a blot" on the nation was to become a very familiar theme. In the years following World War II, a wave of violence swept the South as African American veterans returned home. Lynchings and beatings of African Americans, sometimes involving local law enforcement officials, were covered in the media in this country and abroad. The violence spawned protests and demands that the federal government take steps to alleviate that brutality and other forms of racial injustice.

In one incident during the summer of 1946, Sergeant Isaac Woodard was beaten with a nightstick and blinded in both eyes by the chief of police in Aiken, South Carolina. Woodard had been on his way home after three years of military service. The police chief was indicted for the incident but was then acquitted "to the cheers of a crowded courtroom." Also that summer, Macio Snipes, the only African American in his district in Georgia to vote in a state election, was killed at his home by four whites. These incidents, the Monroe, Georgia, lynchings, and other race-based violence fueled African American protest. Demonstrations were held and thousands of letters of protest were sent to President Truman and the attorney general demanding federal action. In one protest action, close to four hundred members of the National Association of Colored Women marched on the White House, maintaining a picket line for over a week.[12]

In response to the lynchings, civil rights, religious, labor, and other groups formed the National Emergency Committee Against Mob Violence. The committee met with President Harry S. Truman on September 19, 1946, to call for federal government action to ensure that lynchers were prosecuted. During the meeting, Walter

White of the NAACP described acts of violence to Truman, including the blinding of Isaac Woodard. Truman "sat with clenched hands through the recounting" and said that he was shocked at how bad things were. Following the meeting, he set up a presidential committee to study the problem of racial violence and discrimination, and to make recommendations for federal policy.[13]

Harry Truman would come to be seen as a president who put civil rights firmly on the nation's agenda. When Truman assumed the presidency after Roosevelt's death in April 1945, people on both sides of the civil rights issue had seen reasons for encouragement. As a border-state senator, Truman's nomination as vice-president had been supported by the South. When he became president, southerners assumed he would be sensitive to southern-style race relations. Nevertheless, Truman's record on civil rights in the Senate was considered good enough by the NAACP that an editorial in *The Crisis* remarked that he was "entitled to a chance to add to that record as President."[14]

When he became president, Truman's sensibilities on race were mixed. He would use racist language in private when referring to African Americans. At the same time, however, in a private letter to an old friend he wrote of his personal commitment to civil rights reform. Truman's friend asked him to moderate his position on civil rights, but the president criticized his friend's "antebellum proslavery outlook" and called to mind recent acts of brutality. "When a Mayor and a City Marshall can take a negro Sergeant off a bus in South Carolina, beat him up and put out one of his eyes, and nothing is done about it by the State Authorities, something is radically wrong with the system," he wrote. "I can't approve of such goings on and I shall never approve of it, as long as I am here . . . I am going to try to remedy it and if that ends up in my failure to be reelected, that failure will be in a good cause."[15]

On matters of civil rights policy, as far as the NAACP was concerned, Truman did well in an early test. An important issue in domestic civil rights politics in 1945 was the establishment of a permanent Fair Employment Practices Commission (FEPC) that would protect racial and religious minorities from discrimination by government agencies and government contractors. Roosevelt had established an FEPC by executive order in 1941 in response to A. Philip Randolph's call for African Americans to march on Washington. Legislation to establish a permanent FEPC had been introduced in Congress, but Roosevelt had not pushed the matter. In contrast, upon the urging of NAACP executive secretary Walter White, Truman intervened with the House Rules Committee where the bill was mired, urging that it was "unthinkable" to abandon the principle the FEPC was based on. And when Truman found Congress uncooperative on the issue, he continued to keep the FEPC alive through executive orders. The FEPC's effectiveness was seriously hampered, however, because without authorizing legislation, it had no enforcement powers, and because Congress refused to grant more than token funding.[16]

Increasing pressure on Truman to address race discrimination coincided with an impending presidential campaign. Truman's advisors believed the African American vote would be important in the 1948 election. In order to court African American voters away from Progressive Party candidate Henry A. Wallace and Republican Thomas E. Dewey, a Truman campaign strategy memo recommended that Truman should "go as far as he feels he could possibly go in recommending measures to protect the rights of minority groups." Otherwise, the memo warned, the African American vote would go Republican. Truman's advisors believed that his position on civil rights need only involve election-year posturing, not tangible results. The strategy assumed that the administration "will get no major part of its own program approved." Consequently, its tactics would be "entirely different than if there were any real point to bargaining and compromise. Its recommendations . . . must be tailored for the voter, not the Congressman; they must display a label which reads 'no compromises.' " The advisors predicted that a pro–civil rights posture would not jeopardize Truman's southern support. "As always, the South can be considered safely Democratic. And in formulating national policy, it can be safely ignored."[17]

This strategy was right on two counts: the African American vote was of great importance in the '48 election, and it could not be earned without a strong pro–civil rights position. Truman miscalculated on the South, however. In keeping with his aides' recommendations,

Truman called for civil rights legislation that had no chance of passage. Southern politicians reacted by threatening to break with the Democratic Party if the nominating convention chose Truman and adopted a pro–civil rights plank. When both occurred, southerners formed the States' Rights Party and nominated segregationist Strom Thurmond as their presidential candidate. The party's platform denounced "totalitarian government" and advocated racial segregation. While Thurmond had no chance of winning the election, the State's Rights Party hoped to deprive Truman of enough votes to throw the election into the House of Representatives.[18]

Southern protest made it clear that a pro–civil rights posture could be politically risky. Truman downplayed the issue, depending on his audience. The African American vote, however, remained a priority. Consequently, although he appeared at a segregated white college, Truman also became the first president to speak in Harlem. Before the Harlem audience he promised to work for the achievement of equal rights "with every ounce of strength and determination that I have." Truman also took concrete steps to further civil rights during the campaign. He issued executive orders desegregating the military and establishing a Fair Employment Board in the Civil Service Commission to review complaints of race discrimination in employment in the executive branch.[19]

Though the polls predicted otherwise, Truman defeated Dewey by a surprising margin of electoral votes. The popular vote in key states was close, however, and some have argued that African Americans, particularly in urban areas in the North, provided the president with the margin of victory. In many areas, including Harlem, Truman received a greater proportion of the African American vote than Roosevelt had in 1944. While many groups could claim responsibility for the outcome in a close election, African American voters were an indispensable part of the electoral majority that put Truman over the top.[20] To pursue those voters, in the context of the election, Truman advocated civil rights reform.

Apart from electoral politics and pressure from civil rights activists, the Truman administration had another reason to address domestic racism: other countries were paying attention to the problem. Newspapers in many corners of the world covered stories of racial discrimination against African Americans. When nonwhite foreign dignitaries visited the United States and encountered discrimination, it led to serious diplomatic consequences. And as tension between the United States and the Soviet Union increased in the years after the war, the Soviets made effective use of U.S. failings in this area in anti-American propaganda. Concern about the effect of U.S. race discrimination on Cold War foreign relations led the Truman administration to adopt a pro–civil rights posture as part of its international agenda to promote democracy and contain communism.

Following World War II, anything that undermined the image of American democracy was seen as threatening world peace and aiding Soviet aspirations to dominate the world. In 1947, in an address before a joint session of Congress, President Truman warned the nation of the threatening environment of the Cold War. "At the present moment in world history nearly every nation must choose between alternative ways of life," he said. "The choice is too often not a free one." Nations were divided between a way of life "distinguished by free institutions, representative government, free elections, guarantees of individual liberty, freedom of speech and religion, and freedom from political oppression," and a way of life that "relies upon terror and oppression, a controlled press and radio, fixed elections, and the suppression of personal freedoms." The gravity of the situation made this a "fateful hour," and it placed upon the United States a new responsibility. "The free peoples of the world look to us for support in maintaining their freedoms. If we falter in our leadership, we may endanger the peace of the world— and we shall surely endanger the welfare of this Nation."[21]

Truman's speech was "greeted with rapture" by members of Congress. His approach to international relations, what would be called the Truman Doctrine, informed U.S. foreign policy for many years. Anticommunism would not be limited to foreign affairs, however. With the communist threat now perceived in global, apocalyptic terms, scrutiny of how domestic policies affected the struggle against world communism became a priority. The most direct way in which this manifested itself was the concern about communist "infiltration" in American government. On March 21, 1947, only nine days after his Truman Doctrine speech, the president signed an executive order creating a loyalty program for federal employees that required a loyalty investigation for federal employment. According to the order, "complete and unswerving loyalty" on the part of federal employees was of "vital importance," and therefore the employment of "any disloyal or subversive person constitutes a threat to our democratic processes."[22]

In this atmosphere, many other government policies were evaluated in terms of whether they served or undercut the more central U.S. mission of fighting communism. In June 1947, for example, Congress passed the Taft-Hartley Act over Truman's veto. The act required officers of labor unions to sign affidavits indicating that the officer was not a Communist Party member and did not "believe in, and is not a member of or supports any organization that believes in or teaches, the overthrow of the United States Government by force or by any illegal or unconstitutional methods." A union whose officers refused to sign such an affidavit could not take advantage of protection for unions under the National Labor Relations Act. Motivated by the fear that communist infiltration in the public schools would poison fragile young minds, many states adopted loyalty oath requirements for public school teachers. The U.S. Supreme Court upheld a New York State loyalty oath statute in 1952, based on findings that communists "have been infiltrating into public employment in the public schools of the State. . . . As a result, propaganda can be disseminated among the children by those who teach them and to whom they look for guidance, authority and leadership."[23]

In the area of civil rights, anticommunism figured prominently on both sides of the debate. Segregationists argued that efforts to abandon racial segregation were communist-inspired and would undermine the fabric of American society. According to Wayne Addison Clark, "Realizing the vulnerability of racial segregation as a social system, southerners most intent on pressing white supremacy consistently promoted the notion that only alien forces bent on social upheaval would challenge the racial status quo. Large segments of the population in the Deep South, including educated whites, accepted this explanation as the primary force behind resistance to white supremacy."[24]

While efforts to change American society during the Cold War were usually viewed as "un-American," the NAACP cast its efforts at racial reform as part of the struggle against communism. According to NAACP executive director Roy Wilkins, "the survival of the American democratic system in the present global conflict of ideologies depends upon the strength it can muster from the minds, hearts and spiritual convictions of all its people." He argued that "the Negro wants change in order that he may be brought in line with the *American* standard . . . which must be done not only to preserve and strengthen that standard here at home, but to guarantee its potency in the world struggle against dictatorship."[25]

As the United States held itself out as the leader of the free world, the nation opened itself up to criticism when its domestic practices seemed to violate the nation's principles. Race discrimination, in particular, was America's "Achilles heel." Robert E. Cushman, a Cornell University professor and member of the President's Committee on Civil Rights, explained the problem in a January 1948 *New York Times* magazine article. Following World War II, he argued,

> the nation finds itself the most powerful spokesman for the democratic way of life, as opposed to the principles of a totalitarian state. It is unpleasant to have the Russians publicize our continuing lynchings, our Jim Crow statutes and customs, our anti-Semitic discriminations and our witch-hunts; but is it undeserved?

Cushman thought that Americans "cannot deny the truth of the charges; we are becoming aware that we do not practice the civil liberty we preach; and this realization is a wholesome thing."[26]

International scrutiny of American race discrimination increased in the postwar years. U.S. diplomatic posts frequently reported to the State Department about foreign reactions to racial matters in the United States. In December 1946, for example, the American consulate in Suva, Fiji Islands, reported that the *Fiji Times & Herald* published an article entitled "Persecution of Negroes Still Strong in America." According to the Fiji paper, "the United States has within its own borders, one of the most oppressed and persecuted minorities in the world today." In the southern states, "hundreds of thousands of negroes exist today in an economic condition worse than the out-and-out slavery of a century ago." Treatment of African Americans was not merely a question of race discrimination; "it is frequently a question of the most terrible forms of racial persecution."[27]

The article described the 1946 Monroe, Georgia, lynchings. "This outrage," the article noted, followed Supreme Court action invalidating Georgia voting restrictions. "The decision gave the negro the legal right to vote but [Georgia Governor] Talmadge challenged him to exercise it. He also flung a defiance to the Court itself and asked the voters of his State to back him up, which they did." According to the paper, "very few negroes dared to vote, even though the country's highest tribunal had found them entitled to. Most of those who did, or tried to, were badly mauled by white ruffians." The article noted that federal antilynching legislation had been proposed in the past, and "further attempts are certain in the next Congress." The article also discussed other instances of discrimination, such as the Daughters of the American Revolution's refusal to allow opera singer Marian Anderson to perform in Constitution Hall.[28]

The *Fiji Times & Herald* was not entirely critical, however. Reporting that a recent dinner honoring African American journalists had brought together African Americans and white southerners, the paper concluded that "the point is that the best culture of the south, in America, is opposed to the Bilbo-Talmadge anti-negro oppression and seems today more than ever inclined to join with the north in fighting it." Efforts against racial intolerance had particular consequences in the United States, for "there cannot be, on the basic tenants [sic] of Americanism, such a thing as second class citizenship." The issue also had broader implications, however. "The recognition and acceptance of the concept of a common humanity should, and must, shatter the longstanding bulwarks of intolerance, racial or otherwise, before anything entitled to call itself true civilization can be established in America or any other country."[29]

The American consul in Fiji was unhappy with the *Times & Herald* article, which he saw as "an indication of certain of the anti-American and/or misinformation or propaganda now carried" in the paper. A response to the article seemed appropriate and necessary.

"If and when a favorable opportunity occurs, the matter of the reasonableness or justification in the publication of such biased and unfounded material, obviously prejudicial to American prestige throughout this area, will be tactfully broached to the Editor and appropriate government officials."[30]

In Ceylon, American embassy officials were concerned about what they considered "Asian preoccupation with racial discrimination in the United States." Ceylon newspapers ran stories on U.S. racial problems picked up from Reuters wire service. In addition, a Ceylon *Observer* columnist focused on the issue, particularly the seeming contradiction of segregation in the capital of American democracy. In his article, Lakshman Seneviratne quoted *Time* magazine as saying, "in Washington, the seated figure of Abraham Lincoln broods over the capital of the U.S. where Jim Crow is the rule." According to Seneviratne, in Washington "the colour bar is the greatest propaganda gift any country could give the Kremlin in its persistent bid for the affections of the coloured races of the world, who, if industrialized, and technically mobilized, can well dominate, if domination is the obsession, the human race." How could the embassy combat such criticism? At this point American diplomats chose to point a finger in the other direction. Why should Ceylonese criticize the United States when that nation was plagued with prejudice of its own? American embassy officials planned to put together a brief description of "the 'caste system' as it exists in Ceylon today."[31]

In China, the media focused on the effect of U.S. race discrimination on the nation's leadership in postwar world politics. Shanghai's *Ta Kung Pao* covered the May 2, 1948, arrest of U.S. Senator Glen Taylor for violating Alabama segregation laws. At the time, Taylor was the vice-presidential running mate of Progressive Party candidate Henry A. Wallace. On May 2, 1948, Taylor, who was white, attempted to use the "colored entrance" to a Birmingham, Alabama, church where he was scheduled to speak to a meeting of the Southern Negro Youth Congress. As the paper reported it, a police officer stationed at the door informed Taylor that "[t]his was the colored entrance." Taylor responded that "it did not make any difference to me and started in." Five officers then arrested Taylor, who sustained minor injuries in the process. "[They] treated me very rough—anything but gentlemanly," he later said. "God help the ordinary man." Although Taylor violated the Birmingham segregation law, he was only charged with disorderly conduct, circumventing a challenge to the city law.[32]

Criticizing Taylor's arrest, the Chinese paper noted that "the Negro problem is a problem of U.S. internal politics, and naturally, it is unnecessary for anybody else to meddle with it." However, the issue had international ramifications.

> We cannot help having some impressions of the United
> States which actually already leads half of the world and
> which would like to continue to lead it. If the United
> States merely wants to "dominate" the world, the atomic
> bomb and the U.S. dollar will be sufficient to achieve
> this purpose. However, the world cannot be "dominated"
> for a long period of time. If the United States wants to
> "lead" the world, it must have a kind of moral superiority
> in addition to military superiority.

According to the paper, "the United States prides itself on its 'liberal traditions,' and it is in the United States itself that these traditions can best be demonstrated."[33]

The American consul general in Shanghai believed that the *Ta Kung Pao* editorial "discusses the Negro problem in the U.S. in a manner quite close to the Communist Party line." The consul general preferred an editorial in the *China Daily Tribune* that cast American race discrimination as a problem generated by a small minority who were acting against the grain. According to that paper, "Prejudice against people of color seems to die hard in some parts of the United States despite all that President Truman and the more enlightened leaders of the nation are doing to ensure that race equality shall become an established fact."[34]

Attention to problems of U.S. race discrimination sometimes focused on matters in the courts. State or federal court decisions that overturned discriminatory practices had favorable consequences for foreign relations. For example, when the California Supreme Court overturned that state's antimiscegenation statute in 1948, the *Ma-*

nila Chronicle called the action "an answer to the prayer of Filipinos now residing in San Francisco, California." According to the paper, there were "not enough women among the Filipinos there. So the laborers have been forced to seek life partners from among the whites." In commenting on the story, the chargé d'affaires in the American embassy in Manila noted that

> "color" feeling, stimulated by hearsay and/or fact of discrimination in the United States, is an ever-present catalyst among Filipinos. Therefore, it may be readily understood that the action of the Supreme Court of California, seemingly being evidence of concrete progress in eliminating racial discrimination, is important in dispelling or mitigating "color barrier" psychology and its concomitant, the tendency to formation of "color", racial or "Asia for the Asiatics" groupings.

The *Manila Chronicle* story was "fairly representative of Philippine opinion" on this matter.[35]

During the Truman years, in no country was the focus on American race relations of greater importance than in India. Chester Bowles discovered in 1951, early in his tenure as U.S. ambassador to India, that "the number one question" in Asia about the United States was "about America's treatment of the Negro." Bowles took Indian concerns very seriously because he believed India to be of great strategic importance to the United States.[36]

Indian newspapers were particularly attuned to the issue of race discrimination in the United States. According to the American consul general in Bombay, "the color question is of intense interest in India." Numerous articles with titles like "Negro Baiting in America," "Treatment of Negroes a Blot on U.S.," and "Untouchability Banished in India: Worshipped in America" appeared in the Indian press. The American consul general thought that the latter article was "somewhat typical of the irresponsible and malicious type of story on the American Negro which appears not too infrequently in segments of the Indian press." This rather dramatic article was written by Canadian George T. Prud'homme, described as a "communist writer." The story was illustrated with photographs of a chain gang and of a "Negro youth, worn out by hard labour and

tortured by man's [in]humanity to man," and "Waiting for Death."
According to Prud'homme, "the farther South one travels, the less
human the Negro status becomes, until in Georgia and Florida it
degenerates to the level of the beast in the field."[37]

Prud'homme's article described the history of American racial
practices, including the history of the Ku Klux Klan and the denial
of voting rights through poll taxes and discriminatory voter registration tests. It was a shameful story, and a contrast to the U.S. government's efforts to present American democracy as a shining example
for the world. Instead, Prud'homme suggested that U.S. treatment
of African Americans "strangely resembles the story of India under
British domination." The "only bright spot in this picture" was provided by individuals like a white Baptist pastor who was committed
to racial equality. But the minister told Prud'homme, "If one of us
fights for true democracy and progress, he is labeled a Communist. . . . That is an effective way of shutting him up."[38]

Soviet propaganda about American racial problems was equally
harsh. A *Tass* article distributed in India claimed that "American
imperialism destroyed the largest section of the native population of
North America and doomed the survivors to a slow death." The
same story found "the fate of Negroes" to be "equally tragic. . . .
America's soil is drenched in the blood and sweat of Negro toilers."[39]

U.S. officials in India felt that Indian criticism of American racial
practices was somewhat ironic since India had a caste system. As the
American consul in Madras put it, "an oft-repeated answer by the
recent Consul General at this post to questions about the 'color
problem' in the United States was 'Yes, it's almost as bad as it is in
India.' This often caused such embarrassed confusion that the subject was immediately dropped."[40]

Criticism of American racism came from Europe as well. The
British press covered postwar racial tension in the South and Ku
Klux Klan activity, giving particular attention to scheduled executions of African Americans. For example, in 1946, Charles Trudell
and James Lewis Jr., both fourteen years old, were sentenced to death
in Jackson, Mississippi, for murdering their white employer. By January 16, 1947, the U.S. embassy in London had received three hundred and two communications protesting the death sentences.

Forty-eight of those were petitions with several hundred signatures. In addition, three members of the House of Commons sent a telegram to President Truman, urging him to "protect basic human rights by intervening" to stop the executions. Petitions were also sent to the British secretary of state for foreign affairs, requesting his intervention, and the matter was discussed in the House of Commons. The secretary declined to become involved because the death sentences were "a matter of United States domestic policy in which it would not be proper for His Majesty's Government to intervene" and because the case was pending in the U.S. Supreme Court. The convictions and sentences were affirmed by the Mississippi Supreme Court, and the U.S. Supreme Court declined to review the cases. In spite of the attention given to the cases, Mississippi Governor Fielding Wright denied clemency.[41]

In Europe, according to U.S. Senator William Benton, the "Communist-inspired press and radio" carried the same themes. In addition to oppression of African Americans, "Italy is told about discrimination against Italians; Slavic countries are told that the Slavs hold a very low place on the 'American racial ladder.' " A characteristic twist to these stories was illustrated by a January 17, 1950, Bucharest radio report that "Joe Louis is forced to take up boxing activities again because racial laws hinder his finding other means of livelihood."[42]

European reporting on the "American Negro Problem" was so widespread that it was the subject of a July 1950 article in the NAACP publication *The Crisis*. James W. Ivy analyzed more than five hundred clippings from the press of ten European countries. "Black Tragedy in the United States is No Myth" stated the headline of one Swiss paper, while other European papers carried stories under headlines such as "Odor of Burning Flesh," "Lincoln or Lynch?" and "Is the Negro a Man?" The European press was also interested in African American politics and culture. In addition to accounts of racism, the periodicals printed biographical sketches of Ralph Bunche, Paul Robeson, Lena Horne, and others.[43]

Ivy found that European criticism of American race relations was often quite harsh. For example, Georges Duhamel wrote in *Ici Paris* that "this great nation which has taken such a delight in lecturing Europeans on colonialism and the duties of the white race early simplified its problems by exterminating the Indians." As Ivy put it, "our segregation, our mob violence, and our Dixiecrats contribute grist to the European mills of anti-Americanism. To preach democratic equality while making distinctions of color and race strikes Europeans as bizarre, if not perverse."[44]

Ivy felt that the "preoccupation of the European press with the American Negro and his problems" had emerged in the postwar period, partly in response to racial segregation among U.S. servicemen stationed in Europe during World War II. "Even the European man in the street sensed the incongruity of a 'democratic equality' that condemned Negroes to service battalions and segregated outfits." In addition, European intellectuals resented American "meddling in Continental affairs."[45]

Reports by American embassy staff on foreign press coverage of racial problems in the United States poured in through the Truman years. Embassy reporting usually contained information on the political leanings of the publication, particularly whether it tended to be "anti-American" and/or "leftist." While coverage would cross political boundaries, embassy officials often thought that the "leftist" media was more "critical and unfriendly to the United States," while other writers showed "some understanding." When criticism came from a source perceived as leftist, the writer's motive was often called into question. When embassy officials found critical coverage of U.S. race discrimination in politically conservative publications, however, they were less likely to assume that the writer was biased. In one example, Helen Vlachos, a writer for *Kathimerini*, a prominent conservative Greek newspaper with the highest circulation of all Athens daily papers, noted, "America has its Achilles heel and . . . the heel is quite black!" Following a trip to the American South, the writer felt that she understood "the bitter answer of a small Negro boy who, when asked by his teacher what punishment he would impose upon Adolph Hitler, said: 'I would paint his face black and send him to America immediately'!" According to K. L. Rankin, the chargé d'affaires at the American embassy in Athens, Vlachos's writing on the United States had generally been "well disposed with respect to the American people and their institutions and in harmony with the basically friendly attitude the author has always shown toward the United States." Accordingly, "her comments . . . should therefore be regarded, not as stemming from any anti-American bias, but as the author's frank reaction to what she regards as a deplorable situation." Rankin noted that Vlachos's views were "being widely read and discussed by educated Athenians, the overwhelming majority of whom share her feelings in the matter."[46]

In a world divided by Cold War, it was frightening to see the Soviet Union capitalize on America's "Achilles heel." Soviet propaganda exploited U.S. racial problems, arguing that American professions of liberty and equality under democracy were a sham. The U.S. embassy in Moscow took notice of this issue in 1946, reporting that a number of articles that year "may portend stronger emphasis on this theme as [a] Soviet propaganda weapon." In August 1946, the U.S. embassy in Moscow sent the State Department a translation of an editorial from the periodical *Trud* that was "representative of the frequent Soviet press comment on the question of Negro discrimination in the United States." Soviet reporting did not require extensive research. The *Trud* article was based on information the Soviets had gathered from the "progressive American press." It described lynchings and poor labor conditions for African Americans in the South.[47]

According to *Trud*, American periodicals had reported "the increasing frequency of terroristic acts against negroes," including "the bestial mobbing of four negroes by a band of 20 to 25 whites" in July 1946 in Monroe, Georgia. In another incident, near Linden, Louisiana, "a crowd of white men tortured a negro war veteran, John Jones, tore his arms out and set fire to his body. The papers stress the fact that the murderers, even though they are identified, remain unpunished." U.S. census figures indicated that three-quarters of African Americans lived in the South. In the southern "Black Belt," "the negroes are overwhelmingly engaged in agriculture, as small tenant-farmers, share-croppers and hired hands. Semi-slave forms of oppression and exploitation are the rule." African Americans were denied economic rights because of the way the legal system protected the interests of the landowners upon whose property sharecroppers and tenant farmers labored. In addition, "the absence of economic rights is accompanied by the absence of social rights. The poll tax, in effect in the Southern States, deprives the overwhelming majority of negroes of the right to vote."[48]

Trud observed that "the movement for full economic, political and social equality is spreading among the negro population," but that "this movement has evoked exceptional fury and resistance." "Particularly great efforts" had been made by "the reaction" during recent primary elections in the South, resulting in "unbridled terror directed against the negroes . . . to keep the negro masses from participating in the elections . . . and to crush the liberation movement among the negroes at its root." According to the paper, "the progressive public opinion of the USA is indignant at the baiting of negroes, and rightly sees in this one of the means by which reaction is taking the offensive against the working people."[49]

The *Trud* story was one example of an increasing tendency of the Soviet Union to exploit American racial problems. By 1949, this issue had become so prominent that the U.S. embassy in Moscow reported that "the 'Negro question,'[was] [o]ne of the principal Soviet propaganda themes regarding the United States." According to the embassy, "[T]he Soviet press hammers away unceasingly on such things as 'lynch law,' segregation, racial discrimination, deprivation of political rights, etc., seeking to build up a picture of an America in which the Negroes are brutally downtrodden with no hope of improving their status under the existing form of government." *Pravda* reported that there were "mass Negro pogroms" in the United States, while Soviet radio claimed that "our Constitution was written by representatives of exploiting classes and does not truly guarantee civil rights."[50]

A U.S. embassy official believed that Soviet preoccupation with the American "Negro problem" "serves political ends desired by the Soviet Union and has nothing whatsoever to do with any desire to better the Negro's position." The "Soviet press seizes upon anything showing the position of the US Negro in a derogatory light while ignoring entirely the genuine progress being made in America in improving the situation." The writer felt that his point was "graphically revealed" by the way Ralph Bunche, a United States representative in the United Nations, was treated in the Soviet media. Although Bunche's name was mentioned frequently in conjunction with his role in the UN, in that context his race was not mentioned. He was identified by race, however, when Bunche announced that " 'Jim Crow' practices in Washington had been one of the contributing factors in his decision to decline the offer of an appointment as an Assistant Secretary of State." In addition, "the Moscow newspapers passed over in silence Dr. Bunche's speech at Fisk University in May when he asserted that the democratic framework of society in the United States offers the greatest hope to the American Negro."[51]

Senator William Benton warned his U.S. Senate colleagues that Soviet propaganda on American civil rights was most vigorously used in the "critical periphery," the areas "where the Cold War is raging most fiercely." According to Benton, "These sensitive areas, where the fate of mankind may be decided, are in Latin America, in Germany, and the Slavic countries of Europe, among the dark-skinned nations of Africa and southeast Asia, and among the yellow skinned peoples on the Asiatic mainland and the nearby island areas." He thought that "by far the most active use of the civil rights issue" was in the Far East, including China and India.[52]

For Senator Benton, U.S. Ambassador to India Chester Bowles, and many U.S. diplomats, race discrimination undermined the nation's prestige abroad, threatening its Cold War leadership. If other nations, and particularly nonwhite peoples, were to have faith in democracy, the United States would need to reassure them that American democracy was not synonymous with white supremacy.

Race discrimination in the United States was not only directed at American citizens. When nonwhite foreign dignitaries visited the country, they were often subjected to similar treatment, and incidents of discrimination against visiting foreigners would generate a highly critical reaction against U.S. racism in their home country. In 1947, for example, Mohandas Ghandi's physician was barred from a restaurant during a visit to the United States. A story about the incident was carried in every newspaper in his hometown of Bombay.[53]

In November 1947, François Georges, Haiti's secretary of agriculture, traveled to Biloxi, Mississippi, to attend a conference he had been invited to by the National Association of Commissioners, Secretaries and Directors of Agriculture. Unaware that Georges was black, the Biloxi Buena Vista Hotel had confirmed a reservation for him. Upon his arrival, Georges was informed that for "reasons of color" he would not be able to stay in the hotel with others attending the conference but would be offered separate accommodations. There was some dispute regarding the nature of the separate accommodations. According to one source, they were "servants' quarters which had not been prepared to receive guests." According to the manager of the Buena Vista, the accommodations consisted of "one of our attractive guest cottages which are very much in demand with our regular guests located immediately adjacent to the hotel." Georges was informed that his meals during the conference would be served in his rooms, rather than in the hotel restaurant with other guests. Indignant, he left without attending the conference. He later told a U.S. embassy official in Haiti, "You can see how I would not wish to visit your country soon again."[54]

The Haitian ambassador to the United States lodged a complaint with the secretary of state regarding the incident. According to the ambassador, Georges had accepted the invitation to attend the conference in the belief that "it would afford one more occasion for setting forth how much his country is determined to furnish its cooperation in all circumstances for strengthening the solidarity among the democratic nations anxious to see the establishment in the world of a just and lasting peace based on the principles of justice and equality." The ambassador found Georges's treatment out of step with such principles. He concluded that, "considering the unfavorable repercussions produced on opinion by incidents of this kind, the Haitian Government would be disposed to decline all invitations to congresses and conferences which are to take place in States where its delegates would be exposed to slights not to be endured by the representatives of a sovereign and friendly country."[55]

Although some Haitian newspapers initially "thought [it] better not to mention" the Biloxi incident, on November 17 *La Phalange* reprinted a *Miami Herald* article reporting the Haitian ambassador's protest of the discrimination against Georges. Other papers followed with editorials the next day. According to a U.S. embassy airgram, "Popular Socialist *La Nation* begins its attack on [the] United States with reference to recent accusations made by its readers to [the] effect [that] this newspaper was too pro-Soviet and anti–United States." According to *La Nation*,

> [T]he ardent defenders of American democracy now have before their eyes the brutal fact of what this democracy is. . . . Can a civilized people call the treatment of which our minister has been a victim other than barbaric; can serious people still speak of American democracy? Can the Americans themselves speak of Pan-American solidarity when among themselves they make a fierce discrimination between the peoples of the Americas?

The editorial concluded that "the Negro of Haiti understands that the word democracy in the United States has no meaning."[56]

In contrast to the *La Nation* indictment of American democracy, the U.S. embassy reported that *Le Nouvelliste* "place[d] [the] onus on ignorance and backwardness in [the] Southern states." That paper noted that other states, such as New York, prohibited race discrimination. Nevertheless, Southern racism was a "hideous disgusting fact that constitutes shame for any country as civilized as [the] United States." The Biloxi incident "reenforces [sic] the unhappy opinion which is held throughout the world of the stupid color prejudice which is rotting certain Southern states of the United States."[57]

The U.S. embassy in Haiti responded to this incident by apologizing and advising Haitians that they should contact the State Department before accepting invitations from nongovernment organizations in the future. Meanwhile, the international implications of the event were not lost on a New York import-export company. Robert P. Holt, vice-president of Gillespie & Company, wrote to Secretary of State George C. Marshall that "at a time when the vast problems of international relationship not only presuppose but require the utmost tact, it is to be deplored that an incident of this nature should have occurred, but even more so that those on the ground apparently should have been unable to mitigate the effect if not the circumstances."[58] If international relations and international trade were to proceed unfettered, the United States would have to handle such incidents more effectively. If race discrimination could not go away, at the very least it must be handled with more foresight and tact.

Discrimination against foreign nationals could at times provoke more than outrage. In January 1945, Pan American Airways refused to allow a Jamaican journalist to eat in its Miami airport public restaurant. The *Kingston Daily Gleaner* reported the incident and the matter was discussed in the Jamaican Council. Councillor Wills O. Isaacs stated that "any nation which indulges in racial discrimination . . . is a nation that is devoid of any real culture and any real decency." He argued that "if these people cannot respect the people of this country and place them on an equal footing with the people of America, then as far as I am concerned I would not allow one Pan American plane to fly over this country at all." Councillor E. H. Fagan agreed. "If we are to get anywhere as a coloured people," he argued, "let us get it in our cranium that Jamaicans as a whole are coloured people, and in common with the big majority of coloured people all over the world it is time for us to talk out loud whenever acts of discrimination are practised against us. We find that the Americans do not care anything about us." In reporting on the incident to the secretary of state, however, the American consul in Kingston dismissed Isaacs by noting that he "has definite leftist tendencies."[59]

Even when foreign persons of color were not subject to discrimination, they did not necessarily leave the States with a positive impression. As one Indian visitor put it,

> American racialism is not logical. Non-American non-whites on their visit to the States are accorded a kind of "honorary" white status which is embarrassing to them and the source of considerable justified grievance to colored nations. Instances are not uncommon of Negroes donning a turban or an English accent to escape the prejudice which as American citizens they are made to suffer.[60]

* * *

American vulnerability on the race issue gave civil rights activists a very effective pressure point to use in advocating for civil rights reform. Civil rights organizations relied on the argument that race discrimination harmed U.S. interests in the Cold War. At the same time, they effectively brought international pressure to bear on the Truman administration. The United Nations provided a convenient forum for African American leaders to present their grievances before an international audience. It also provided an environment in which critics of the United States would have an opportunity to focus attention on the country's weaknesses.

In February 1946, the United Nations Commission on Human Rights was established. The commission was charged with preparing "proposals, recommendations and reports concerning a) an international bill of rights; b) international declarations or conventions on civil liberties, the status of women, freedom of information and similar matters; c) the protection of minorities; d) the prevention of discrimination on the grounds of race, sex, language or religion." The work of the Subcommission on the Prevention of Discrimination and Protection of Minorities would create the greatest difficulty for the United States. State Department officials recognized this prior to the subcommission's first meeting. Dean Rusk wrote in a November 4, 1947, memorandum that the

> first session of the Subcommission is a very important one to the United States, principally because it deals with a very difficult problem affecting the internal affairs of the United States. United States problems concerning relationships with minority groups have been fully treated in the press of other countries. This Subcommission was established on the initiative of the U.S.S.R., and there is every indication that that country and others will raise questions concerning our domestic problems in this regard.[61]

Rusk was right. However, the most powerful critique of U.S. racism presented before the United Nations came not from the Soviets but from African Americans. In June 1946, the National Negro Congress filed a petition seeking "relief from oppression" for American blacks. The organization expressed "profound regret that we, a section of the Negro people, having failed to find relief from oppression through constitutional appeal, find ourselves forced to bring this vital issue, which we have sought, for almost a century since emancipation, to solve within the boundary of our country to the attention of this historic body." The group sent a copy of the petition to President Truman. Although the United Nations did not act upon the petition, it reinforced international scrutiny of American race discrimination.[62]

On October 23, 1947, the NAACP filed "An Appeal to the World," a petition in the United Nations protesting the treatment of blacks in the United Sates. The petition denounced U.S. race discrimination as "not only indefensible but barbaric." It claimed that racism harmed the nation as a whole. "It is not Russia that threatens the United States so much as Mississippi; not Stalin and Molotov but Bilbo and Rankin; internal injustice done to one's brothers is far more dangerous than the aggression of strangers from abroad." The consequences of American failings were potentially global. "The disenfranchisement of the American Negro makes the functioning of all democracy in the nation difficult; and as democracy fails to function in the leading democracy in the world, it fails the world." W. E. B. DuBois, the principal author of the petition, said that the purpose behind the appeal was to enable the United Nations "to prepare this nation to be just to its own people." [63]

The NAACP petition "created an international sensation." According to Walter White, the NAACP was

> flooded with requests for copies of the document, particularly from nations which were critical of the United States, including Russia, Great Britain, and the Union of South Africa. It was manifest that they were pleased to have documentary proof that the United States did not practice what it preached about freedom and democracy. But it was equally apparent that Russia, Great Britain, and the Union of South Africa were morally afraid that acceptance of the appeal on behalf of American Negroes and action on the document would establish a precedent giving the United Nations authority in those countries.[64]

The petition received extensive coverage in the American and foreign media. Meanwhile, Attorney General Tom Clark remarked, "I was humiliated . . . to realize that in our America there could be the slightest foundation for such a petition." Although Eleanor Roosevelt, a member of the board of directors of the NAACP, was also a member of the American delegation to the United Nations, she refused to introduce the NAACP petition in the United Nations out of concern that it would harm the international reputation of the United States. According to DuBois, the American delegation had "refused to bring the curtailment of our civil rights to the attention of the General Assembly [and] refused willingly to allow any other nation to bring this matter up; if any should, Mr. [sic] Roosevelt has declared that she would probably resign from the United Nations delegation." [65]

The Soviet Union, however, proposed that the NAACP's charges be investigated. On December 4, 1947, the United Nations Commission on Human Rights rejected that proposal, and the United Nations took no action on the petition. Nevertheless, the *Des Moines Register* remarked that the petition had "accomplished its purpose of arousing interest in discrimination." Although the domestic press reaction was generally favorable, the West Virginia *Morgantown Post* criticized the NAACP for "furnishing Soviet Russia with new ammunition to use against us." DuBois responded to similar criticism from southern journalist Jonathan Daniels, a member of the United Nations Subcommission on Discrimination and Protection of Minorities, by stating that "the NAACP is not 'defending Russia' or anybody else; it is trying to get men like Mr. Daniels to stand up and be counted for the decent treatment of Negroes in America."[66]

U.S. diplomats around the globe were concerned about the effect of domestic race discrimination and of propaganda on U.S. racial problems on the anti–United States or pro-Communist leanings of other nations. In a confidential memorandum to the State Department regarding "Dutch Attitudes Toward American Racism," Robert Coe of the American embassy, The Hague, reported on a "casual conversation" between an unnamed embassy officer and a Dutch Foreign Ministry official. According to Coe, the Dutch official had remarked that the Netherlands is very unreceptive to anti-American propaganda, whether it emanates from Communist sources or from right-wing colonial die-hards. However, he added that the opponents of American policies possess one propaganda theme which is extremely effective throughout Europe and even more effective in Asia—criticism of American racial attitudes.[67]

According to the memorandum, the Dutch official was "well-informed about American politics and the American culture generally," but, nevertheless, "he himself had never been able to understand the American point of view toward negroes and other minority groups, and that the point of view was extremely difficult for friends of America to explain, let alone defend." The Dutch official's "knowledge of America" had

> convinced him that America has made real progress in eliminating the worst aspects of racism, and he agreed that the nature and extent of American racial feeling has been grossly exaggerated by the Communists. However, he said that, in his opinion, the actual situation is sufficiently bad to provide a very solid foundation for the fabulous structure of lies which the Communists have built up.

There was a solution to this problem, however. The Dutch official suggested that the "United States information program should devote a major portion of its facilities and energies to a campaign aimed at counteracting the impression which so many people have of American racial suppression."[68]

If the nation could not eradicate the conditions that gave rise to foreign criticism, it could at least place them "in context." It could weave them into a story that led ultimately to the conclusion that, in spite of it all, America was a great nation. Rehabilitating the moral character of American democracy would become an important focus of Cold War diplomacy.

CHAPTER 2

Telling Stories about
Race and Democracy

These neighbors in a housing project, like
millions of Americans, are forgetting whatever
color prejudice they may have had; their children
will have none to forget.

U.S. INFORMATION SERVICE,

THE NEGRO IN AMERICAN LIFE (ABOUT 1950)[1]

In 1947, Public Affairs Officer Frederick C. Jochem wrote an article
for a Rangoon, Burma, newspaper, with the approval of the U.S.
consul general in Rangoon. The article, entitled "Negro Problem,"
politely suggested that the Burmese did not have all the facts on the
issue of race in the United States It began:

A Burmese friend was astonished the other day when I told
him that a Negro had just been appointed to a professorship
in my university back home. We were discussing the "Negro
problem" in America, and it turned out that a number of
facts and viewpoints that I take for granted are surprising
news in Burma.[2]

Among the facts unknown to the Burmese was the statistic that "more than fifty Negroes now hold major teaching posts in prominent American universities." The students and nearly all faculty at the institutions were "black as the proverbial ace of spades." That many of these schools were the product of enforced racial segregation was a detail Jochem failed to mention to his friend. Black colleges, instead, provided evidence of the availability of higher education to African Americans. Jochem thought that "there is still a 'Negro problem' in the United States," particularly in the South. However, he saw race prejudice as an understandable phenomenon in light of the nation's history of slavery. "Of course there is prejudice against Negroes, because for the first few generations of their life in America nothing was done to educate or train them, and the heritage of ignorance, and all that goes with it, persists." In spite of this legacy, Jochem was hopeful.

> [S]ome of the best people in the North and South are working constantly to improve the position of the Negro everywhere in the United States. . . . The goal is now to realize, to the letter, and in every one of the 48 states, the provisions of the fourteenth and fifteenth amendments which abolish all legal distinctions between individuals.[3]

Jochem's article was one of countless efforts by the U.S. government to tell its side of the story of race in America. International criticism of U.S. race discrimination could not be left unanswered. American embassies did their part to address racial difficulties by cooperating with the State Department in an effort to present what they considered to be a more balanced perspective on the issue. Organized U.S. government efforts to disseminate favorable information about the United States to other countries represented one method of doing so. During World War II, the Roosevelt administration increasingly recognized the value of print and broadcast media in U.S. government efforts to influence international opinion. By 1948, the Cold War increased the perceived importance of such efforts. In some government circles fears were expressed that America was losing an unequal war of propaganda in which the Soviet Union and its satellites routinely misrepresented and distorted American ideals and actions. The federal government needed to respond by disseminating the "truth" to counteract such communist propaganda.[4]

The United States Information Service (USIS) prepared materials that placed American race relations in the best possible light for dissemination overseas. Such propaganda on race during the Cold War can be seen as part of an effort to hide the nation's blemishes as the government tried to portray American democracy as a model for the world. Yet of equal interest are stories the government would *tell* about the American past, including sins that were purposefully exposed. The best-developed presentation of the government position on race appeared in *The Negro in American Life*, a pamphlet produced by the USIS in 1950 or 1951. This pamphlet revealed, rather than concealed, the nation's past failings, and it did so for the purpose of presenting American history as a story of redemption. In this story, democracy as a system of government was the vehicle for national reconciliation. The telling of a shameful story became an avenue for Cold War argument. Democracy, not totalitarian forms of government, it argued, provided a context that made reconciliation and redemption possible.[5]

The pamphlet's simple cover opened to reveal the photograph of an elementary school classroom. Sixteen white students and one African American student were visible in the picture, along with an African American teacher. The caption read, "In New York, a Negro teacher teaches pupils of both races." These are not the only school-children in the opening pages, however. In a much smaller picture in the upper right-hand corner of the page was a photograph of what was called "A new school for farm children." In front of the building was a large group of children, all of whom appeared to be African American. "Education and progress for the Negro people move together," the caption explained. "Thousands of new rural schools, like the one above, provide free education in the South."[6]

While the photos of happy children may have reassured some readers, the widespread knowledge of American race discrimination meant that racism and segregation could not go without comment. Unable to avoid the most glaring troubles of the past, which were well known to foreign critics, *The Negro in American Life* instead turned that history into an advantage. Given how bad things were in the past, the pamphlet argued, isn't it amazing how far we've come?

According to *The Negro in American Life*, the "cardinal cause" of American racial prejudice was the nation's history of slavery. That history was presented as an unfortunate part of the American past. The reader was told that during the colonial period "enlightened men vigorously opposed the slave trade," but "farmers and plantation owners accepted slavery as the answer to their ever growing need for cheap labor." At this time, "use of cheap or slave labor was the way of the world." Some had "moral qualms" about slavery, but they "could be persuaded to accept the notion that Negroes—strange men from Africa—were something less than human. And so there began in the United States a theory of racial inferiority which became a key tenet in support of slavery and, later, of economic and social discrimination." From this theory of inequality, "a divided society was built upon the assumption of white superiority. In some places it became a serious crime to educate a Negro. To treat a Negro as an equal was heresy. The Negro who challenged his slave status did so at risk of life." In the late eighteenth century, when the nation was formed, some American leaders were cognizant of the contradiction between slavery and American democratic ideals, but nevertheless accommodated slavery's continued existence in order to foster national unity.[7]

The reader of *The Negro in American Life* might have been shocked not only by the hypocrisy of slavery in a nation that claimed to embrace freedom and individual liberty but also by the fact that it was portrayed so starkly in a U.S. government publication. In educating the reader about slavery, the pamphlet also impressed the reader that openness and a free exchange of information and ideas were features of American government. In learning from the U.S. government about slavery, the reader may have felt that she had experienced democracy in action.

The discussion of slavery had another, and more central, rhetorical function, however. By setting forth the history of the evil slave past, and contrasting past with present, the pamphlet asked the reader to marvel at the progress that had been made. The reader was asked not to view American race relations in isolation. Rather, "it is against this background that the progress which the Negro has made and the steps still needed for the full solution of his problems must be measured." With the shameful past as a benchmark, race relations in the early 1950s could certainly be seen as an improvement.[8]

Over the previous fifty years, since the beginning of the twentieth century, progress for "the Negro" had occurred in all areas "at a tremendous pace." Such change was the result of efforts by African American and white citizens and was supported by government efforts. However, the government did not make "fundamental changes in human attitudes by commands from a central source" or attempt to "alter psychology by fiat." Such efforts would be counterproductive, for "pressures driven underground by legal means are not really eliminated but smolder, only to manifest themselves later." The problem of racial prejudice ultimately could not be eradicated through law, for it was "essentially a question of evolving human relations."[9]

Using a combination of fact and, at best, aspiration, the pamphlet presented a rather rosy picture of the contemporary conditions of life for the Negro in American life. "Some Negroes are large landholders; some are wealthy businessmen," it stated. "Negroes work in banks, public utilities, insurance companies, and retail stores. They are physicists, chemists, psychologists, doctors, metallurgists. Nearly 200,000 own farms averaging seventy-eight acres in size." The pamphlet acknowledged that "much remains to be done," because the average income of white Americans was still "substantially better than that of Negroes." However, "the gap is closing."[10]

"The most significant index of over-all Negro progress," was education. Education lifted up "the Negro," giving him the status to overcome other forms of discrimination.

> As long as he is ignorant and illiterate, the Negro is unqualified for the better jobs; without the improved income which comes from better jobs, he is handicapped in finding better housing; poor housing breeds disease and crime and discouragement. Given education, he is enabled to speak up for his

rights; he increases the prestige of his community and his own self-respect and is able thereby to develop friendly face-to-face relations with the white population.

Most important, the pamphlet continued, "he achieves real cultural status and the sense of social responsibility which exerts continual and inexorable pressure against the web of discrimination which confines him." Education, therefore, made "the Negro" more worthy of equal treatment, and made him more likely to insist on his rights.[11]

There had been significant improvement in education for "the Negro." Drawing from census data, the pamphlet reported that 51 percent of African Americans of school age were attending school in 1900. In 1950, the proportion had jumped to 90 percent. It was in college education, however, where the greatest progress had been made, with 128,000 African Americans attending college at the time the essay was written. Further, "in 1948 there were more Negro students enrolled in and graduated from colleges than were enrolled in and graduated from high schools in 1920." In addition, "more than seventy northern colleges number Negro professors among their faculties; in addition there are some sixty-eight Negro colleges and universities, most of which are situated in the South."[12]

As to the effect of these enrollment increases, the figures meant that

in the first instance, an important gain in economic status. Not long ago, nearly all Negro boys and girls had to earn a living at an early age. They mean that ever increasing numbers of Negroes are being trained as professors, writers, engineers, lawyers, and doctors. They mean that an army of community leaders and spokesmen for the Negro cause is being developed. They mean that the Negro is well on the way to equal opportunity in the field of education.

The essay went on to suggest that increased education would be effective in combating prejudice. "The Negro," it appeared, had to be well educated to overcome stereotyping. Another benefit of the growth of a black professional class would be the enlightenment of whites. "The large number of educated Negroes, and their journalists and novelists, have made the white community keenly aware of the cruel injustice of prejudice." At the turn of the century, "the majority of whites, northern as well as southern, were unabashed in their estimate of the Negro as an inferior. . . . Today, there is scarcely a community where that concept has not been drastically modified."[13]

The Negro in American Life celebrated the great strides that had been made in the area of legal rights, due largely to the efforts of the NAACP. In 1949, "among the year's most outstanding legal efforts were the *McLaurin* and *Sweatt* cases, which established the rights of Negroes to higher education on a nonsegregated basis." Further, "since the war, in cases prosecuted by the NAACP, the Supreme Court has declared unenforceable by law leases which exclude Negroes from renting homes; *it has ruled against segregation in public transportation and in public education.*" The Court's public education cases were the *McLaurin* and *Sweatt* cases, yet the pamphlet reads as if the Court had done something more. *McLaurin* and *Sweatt* only held that segregation at the University of Texas Law School and the University of Oklahoma School of Education did not provide equal treatment to African American students. The cases did not address the separate-but-equal formula that still governed most other educational settings, especially elementary and secondary education. Yet approximately four years before *Brown v. Board of Education, The Negro in American Life* seemed to declare that school segregation across the spectrum was unlawful. In doing so, the pamphlet went beyond merely placing a positive gloss on the facts. It left readers with the impression that the Supreme Court had already outlawed all public school segregation.[14]

From *The Negro in American Life*, we see the image of gradual and progressive social change which was described as the fulfillment of democracy. Through education and enlightened participation by all in electoral politics, equality was "nurtured." This was contrasted with the "authoritarian measures" used when the North sought to *impose* equality on the South after the Civil War. The equality achieved now under the "new reconstruction" would be more lasting.

An integrated classroom and an integrated housing project (facing page) embody the image of "The Negro in American Life," circa 1950, as projected in U.S. propaganda. (Chester Bowles Papers, Manuscripts and Archives, Yale University Library)

To reinforce this point, the final picture in the pamphlet had the following caption: "These neighbors in a housing project, like millions of Americans, are forgetting whatever color prejudice they may have had; their children will have none to forget."[15] The optimism in this document might have seemed uplifting, inspiring, something to reach for. In embracing the optimistic vision in *The Negro in American Life,* the reader would hold onto, as well, a carefully crafted image of American democracy: a nation so open it could acknowledge its faults, a nation that had sinned but was on the road to redemption, a nation where politics reflected the will of the people, and where the people were sufficiently good that, at least in time, they willed for the right things.

Even with the help of materials such as this, by the early 1950s U.S. officials came to realize that their information programs were inadequate on the difficult question of "the Negro problem." Much attention was paid to educating embassy personnel, as well as visiting lecturers, about how to respond to queries about U.S. race relations,

and to locating speakers who could address the issue more effectively. While the United States hoped that, with the help of an improved information program, other countries would rally behind the flag of democracy and would perceive communism as the most important threat to world peace, many Asian and African countries did not view the conflict between the superpowers as their primary concern. According to a 1952 report on the status of U.S. propaganda efforts, "In South and Southeast Asia, anti-colonialism and associated racial resentments have been far more important elements in the psychological situation than anti-communism." The United States attempted to shape its propaganda accordingly, finding that approaches that focused on matters of local concern were more effective in "underdeveloped" nations "where the memory or actuality of domination by the white man is a far greater psychological reality than the Soviet menace."[16]

State Department and American embassy officials recognized that African Americans themselves would be most effective in countering negative international opinion. Consequently, the State Department sponsored trips by African Americans to speak on the "Negro Problem" in the United States. Max Yergan, a founder and executive secretary of the Council on African Affairs, an organization that attempted to gain American support for anticolonial movements in Africa, traveled to Africa on such a trip in 1952. The American consul in Lagos, Nigeria, made sure he received ample exposure. An advance story on Yergan's visit was sent by the USIS to the Lagos press and radio, where it received "substantial play." Notice of a scheduled speaking engagement was carried in all local newspapers, as requested by an American information officer. Following Yergan's July 17, 1952, speech, the USIA sent out a special press release with the title "Yergan Says Trend in U.S. Race Relations is Toward Full Civil Rights for Negroes."[17]

Yergan's value as a State Department–sponsored speaker was not merely that he could speak from personal experience and claim that his family enjoyed "ever-expanding rights and privileges which his grandfather, a Negro slave, could only dream of." He also spoke against communism. As the US/A reported it, in Yergan's view,

a testimony to the progressive direction of American race relations . . . was that Negroes in the United States have as a group rejected communism as a "sinister force" interested in exploiting their position in America for the designs of a foreign power. "Every communist is a potential traitor to his country, . . . and my people in America have chosen to cast their lot with democracy, because they believe it offers them the opportunity to achieve full equality."[18]

Two members of the audience challenged Yergan's characterization of communism, asking "1) if the Communists were not the leading fighters for full civil rights for Negroes? and 2) if the Communists had made promises to the American Negro and broken them, had not the American Constitution done the same thing?" In response, "Dr. Yergan called upon his own bitter experience with Communists to answer the questions negatively."[19]

According to the American vice-consul in Lagos, the reaction to Yergan's visit was generally favorable. Nevertheless, Yergan was criticized in editorials in two local papers. According to the *West African Pilot*,

> Any honest inquirer after truth pondering over the monivations [sic] of Dr. Max Yergan urging the African to shun the vices of "Communism and its agents as one shuns poison" will only surmise: "We have heard this before." For, in the grim days of the battle against the forces of Nazism and Fascism, Africans were warned too to shun Nazism and Fascism as one shuns poison all because at the time we were—all lovers of freedom—engaged in a battle to guarantee freedom in order that free men may continue to learn freedom.

The paper concluded that, "for the African, no less [than for] the Negro in the United States of America, two world wars have brought no dramatic changes in status. . . . Daily we grapple with the forces of imperialism, projected by the democracies who condemn Communism ever so much."[20]

The American vice-consul believed that the author of the *Pilot* editorial had a "personal axe to grind" because of an argument he and Yergan had "over the merits of Africans taking sides in the cold war." In the vice consul's view, the paper attempted to smear Yergan by publishing a photograph of him with former officials of the Council on African Affairs. With Yergan in the photograph were "convicted Communist Dr. Hunton and the controversial Dr. W. E. B. Du Bois."[21]

When Jay Saunders Redding took a State Department–sponsored speaking tour of India in 1952, he felt that Indians spoke more freely to him than to white Americans. "Dozens of Indians told me that I was 'one of them;' that (obviously, because of my color) I looked like a 'Madrassi,' or a 'Bengali,' that they felt 'immediately at home' with me." He reported that "most of the Indians met me with their guards consciously lowered and free of the reticence with which (some of them told me) they meet other Westerners. I think that in general my Indian friends and acquaintances told me the truth."[22]

The truth about America, as Indians saw it, was that the nation was imperialistic, and its foreign aid was a tool of imperialism. Redding's contacts also believed that "American policy is opposed to the 'liberation and rise' of the colored peoples of the world, and that the treatment of Negroes in America is a home demonstration of this. The color question is linked with imperialism." He continued, "America, the belief is, is prejudiced against non-whites and that prejudice, long documented in the disabilities under which Negroes suffer in the U.S., is now being expressed in American world policy. My Indian acquaintances contrasted the American billions given or loaned to Europe with the few millions disbursed in the East."[23]

Redding felt that the Indians he met showed "an understandably great ignorance of the actual facts of race relations in America and there is a strong tendency, which among Communists amounts to determination, not to be set right on the facts." Among the questions he was asked were: "Isn't it true that the Haitian Ambassador to the U.S. must live in a ghetto in Washington?" "Aren't Negroes prohibited public education in America?" "Weren't American citizens of Japanese descent interred in slave labor camps in America during the war?" "Why has no colored person ever held high office in America?" Are . . . "Negroes in America lynched for looking at white women?" Redding's response to such questions was hampered by the fact that people in the audience often had copies of a United Nations genocide petition prepared by Civil Rights Congress documenting hundreds of incidents of racially motivated violence in the United States. After Redding had given an account of U.S. race relations, undoubtedly with a positive gloss, a questioner held up a copy of the petition, *We Charge Genocide* and said, "what you say does not convince us in the face of this."[24]

Further evidence of U.S. racism was the lack of African American personnel in U.S. embassies. Redding was asked, "Isn't it unusual for your Government to send you (a Negro) out here? It is the general feeling in India that Negroes in your Foreign Service are conspicuous by their absence." Redding reported that the question was "in line with the thinking that Negroes (and also Jews) in America, no matter what their abilities, are not only looked down upon but purposefully kept down." U.S. embassy personnel believed that Redding's report on Indian reactions to race in America was "overly pessimistic," but they were still concerned. One officer thought that the matter should be pursued, for if Redding were "even 50% right, it is of fundamental political significance for the future of this country."[25]

Redding's overall impressions regarding Indian concern with U.S. racial problems were mirrored in reports filed by Roving Cultural Affairs Officer Clifford Manshardt on a 1952 speaking tour. At the top of a list of typical questions he was asked was "Do negroes have equal opportunities for education in the U.S.?" The question was asked "over and over again." Indians also wanted to know "how many Negroes were lynched in the U.S. last year?" and "what race does America hate most?"[26]

U.S. Ambassador to India Chester Bowles followed up on the implication of Redding's report that it would be helpful to hire African American Foreign Service officers. In a January 1953 letter to the director general of the Foreign Service, he concluded an account of staffing needs with a discussion of a problem that he said had concerned him for some time. Bowles requested to have "top notch Negro Foreign Service Officers" assigned to India. He explained that "Indians, particularly those outside official circles in the capital, will open up much more freely to an American Negro than they will to others. It will also, of course, help us to combat to a certain extent the feeling in India about the Negro problem in the U.S."[27]

Many felt that efforts at cultural exchange paid off, and praise for such programs went beyond the U.S. diplomatic corps. Supreme Court Justice William O. Douglas thought that a speech by African American attorney Edith Sampson "created more good will and understanding in India than any other single act by any American." Speaking in New Delhi in 1949, Sampson told her audience that she would not tolerate criticism of the United States for its civil rights record because, in the previous eighty years, African Americans had advanced further "than any similar group in the entire world."[28]

The State Department also sponsored trips by Indians to the United States. When Indians returned home and defended American culture, however, they made themselves vulnerable to attack. After a trip to the United States, C. P. Ramaswamy Iyer said that "the spirituality of Americans should not be overlooked by those who emphasize American materialism." The paper *Cross Roads* ridiculed Iyer, noting that many Indians were visiting the United States and, upon returning, "dutifully pay back their hosts by lauding to the skies the American way of life." The *Cross Roads* depiction of American culture was represented in a cartoon published alongside the article. According to the U.S. embassy in New Delhi, the cartoon showed "a Negro hanging from a tree, on which sits 'Uncle Sam' as a vulture." A later issue of the paper quoted from a New York *National Guardian* report that two African Americans had been executed, indicating that that was "evidence of American spirituality."[29]

Efforts at cultural exchange could backfire when foreign persons of color experienced American-style race discrimination. Students from other nations often came to the United States in search of educational opportunities not available in their countries. In March 1950, the Carnegie Corporation released a report of a study it conducted of 410 African students studying in the United States. The students had been attracted to the United States by the wide range of courses offered at American colleges. According to the report, the students were "shocked and embittered" by the widespread racism they encountered. Rigid racial segregation in the South created "an undesirable atmosphere" for the students, but the South was not the only problem. Students reported that they were "very much embittered by the treatment they received . . . in New York," and that they "saw little to distinguish segregation in the South from discrimination in the North." Because the students would return as future leaders in their native countries, such experiences would not aid future relations with African nations.[30]

In spite of the efforts to address racial issues, a 1952 report on U.S. information programs concluded that "efforts to counteract communist exploitation of the race relations problem in the United States have not been fully successful."[31] The impact of race discrimination on U.S. prestige abroad was so entrenched that ultimately more would be required to overcome it. And propaganda on race would be more effective once greater social change gave the American government a better story to tell.

Propaganda was only one of the avenues for constructing a narrative about race in America for foreign audiences. People in other nations developed their understandings of American race relations from all the information they received. African Americans traveling abroad could bear witness to the character of American equality. Reporting on personal experiences, their statements had a significant impact.

Because of this, the U.S. government took a keen interest in the international travels of African Americans, particularly celebrities and political figures. Individuals who would say the right thing, from the perspective of the government, could find their travel and international contacts facilitated, directly or indirectly, by the State Department. Talking about progress, and embodying black middle-class status, helped reinforce the message conveyed by U.S. information programs. The only difficulty was that not all African Americans believed that the federal government was doing all it could to achieve racial equality. Not all had faith in the inevitability of American justice.

When critics of U.S. race discrimination traveled overseas, they posed a powerful challenge to the government's narrative of race in America. The story of progress could be protected if these challenges were contained.

Paul Robeson and W. E. B. DuBois, among others, found that their ability to travel overseas was curtailed in the early 1950s. Robeson through song and DuBois through political organizing generated international interest in American racial problems. As far as the U.S. government was concerned, however, the nation had enough of a foreign relations problem from international media coverage of events at home. It didn't help matters when people went out of their way to generate foreign interest in race discrimination in the United States. Consequently, when Robeson and DuBois criticized U.S. racism abroad, the State Department confiscated their passports, effectively denying them access to an international audience.

Robeson was perhaps the most prominent target of Cold War travel restrictions. His troubles began not long after a speech he delivered at the Congress of World Partisans for Peace in Paris in 1949. He reportedly said that United States government policy was "similar to that of Hitler and Goebbels" and that it was "unthinkable" that African Americans would go to war against the Soviet Union. According to Martin Duberman, Robeson's statements were misquoted. Still, Robeson was widely denounced in the American press and by African American leaders. Rioting at a Robeson concert in Peekskill, New York, was widely covered in the international media. Though the rioters included Ku Klux Klan members, Robeson was blamed for this international embarrassment because his friendliness toward the Soviet Union was perceived to have caused the disturbance.[32]

Robeson continued to speak out. In 1950 he criticized President Truman's decision to send troops to Korea, arguing that "if we don't stop our armed adventure in Korea today—tomorrow it will be Africa." At this point, the State Department and the FBI took action. The State Department issued a "stop notice" at all ports to prevent Robeson from leaving the country. J. Edgar Hoover sent out an urgent call to FBI agents to find Robeson. Robeson was asked to surrender his passport, but he refused, leading the State Department to inform the Immigration and Naturalization Service that Robeson's passport was invalid and that he should not be allowed to leave the country. State Department officials indicated that the reason for their action was that "Robeson's travel abroad at this time would be contrary to the best interests of the United States." His "frequent criticism of the treatment of blacks in the United States should not be aired in foreign countries," they explained. "It was a family affair."[33]

The State Department also barred Robeson from entering Canada, where a passport was not required, leading Robeson to host a concert at the Peace Arch at the Canadian border. While well attended by Canadians, this concert and others failed to draw the American crowds expected, and blacklisting seriously interfered with Robeson's ability to perform and to earn a living within the United States for many years. His international popularity meant that he was always a big draw abroad, but without a passport Robeson was exiled by his own country from his international audience.[34]

Travel abroad by lesser-known civil rights activists also caught the eye of the State Department. William Patterson's actions in 1951 were thought to be particularly incendiary. As chairman of the Civil Rights Congress (CRC), Patterson helped draft a petition claiming that the United States had committed genocide against African Americans, and he personally delivered the petition to the United Nations Committee on Human Rights in Geneva, Switzerland. While many felt that genocide was too strong a charge, Patterson and others found support for their efforts in the language of the U.N. Convention on Genocide. According to that document, "genocide" was defined as killing, causing serious bodily or mental harm, and other actions directed at a group "with intent to destroy, in whole or in part, a national ethnical, racial or religious group." Punishable acts included "complicity in genocide," as well as genocide itself. Ratifying states agreed to punish any of their citizens who committed genocide, "including public officials responsible for genocidal policies."[35]

The bulk of the Civil Rights Congress's lengthy petition consisted of documentation of 153 killings, 344 other crimes of violence against African Americans, and other human rights abuses committed in the United States from 1945 to 1951. Ninety-four individuals signed the petition. Among them was W. E. B. DuBois, the person behind the NAACP's 1947 U.N. petition, "An Appeal to the World." The CRC petition claimed:

> Out of the inhuman black ghettos of American cities, out of
> the cotton plantations of the South, comes this record of
> mass slayings on the basis of race, of lives deliberately warped
> and distorted by the willful creation of conditions making for
> premature death, poverty and disease. It is a record that calls
> aloud for condemnation, for an end to these terrible

injustices that constitute a daily and ever-increasing violation of the United Nations Convention on the Prevention and Punishment of the Crime of Genocide.

According to the Civil Rights Congress, African Americans "suffer from genocide as the result of the consistent, conscious, unified policies of every branch of government." The petition continued:

It is our hope, and we fervently believe that it was the hope and aspiration of every black American whose voice was silenced forever through premature death at the hands of racist-minded hooligans or Klan terrorists, that the truth recorded here will be made known to the world; that it will speak with a tongue of fire loosing an unquenchable moral crusade, the universal response to which will sound the death knell of all racist theories.

The petition was filed with an international body because "history has shown that the racist theory of government of the U.S.A. is not the private affair of Americans, but the concern of mankind everywhere."[36]

The Civil Rights Congress called upon the United Nations "to act and to call the Government of the United States to account." The consequences for the United States related not only to internal human rights matters but also to its posture in international politics.

We believe that the test of the basic goals of a foreign policy is inherent in the manner in which a government treats its own nationals and is not to be found in the lofty platitudes that pervade so many treaties or constitutions. The essence lies not in the form but rather, in the substance.[37]

According to the petition, American genocide had important consequences for world peace.

This genocide of which your petitioners complain serves now, as it has in previous forms in the past, specific political and economic aims. Once its goal was the subjugation of American Negroes for the profits of chattel slavery. Now its aim is the splitting and emasculation of mass movements for peace and democracy, so that a reaction may perpetuate its control and continue receiving the highest profits in the entire history of man. That purpose menaces the peace of the world as well as the life and welfare of the Negro people.

Ending genocide against African Americans "will mean returning this country to its people. It will mean a new growth of popular democracy and the forces of peace."[38]

The Civil Rights Congress petition immediately found an international audience. In India, for example, *Blitz*, described as a procommunist paper, enthusiastically covered the story. The paper celebrated the efforts of CRC leader William Patterson. It reported that Patterson characterized the petition as illustrating the "shocking and inhumane butchery and physical destruction of the colored American citizens under the patronage of the American government." A *Tass* bulletin distributed in India also covered the petition in an article entitled "Crimes of American Racists." According to the United States Information Service (USIS) in New Delhi, the article said that the petition exposed " 'criminal' activity by the American authorities and terroristic organizations seeking to perpetuate the 'national oppression and slave-like condition' of the 15,000,000 Negroes in the U.S."[39]

William Patterson hoped that the petition would help "internationalize" civil rights efforts. For Patterson, the struggle for black liberation was global. American racism was manifested both in its toleration of racial brutality at home and in its support for colonial regimes abroad. The movement to overturn racial oppression was also global. Patterson drew support from labor and communist groups worldwide. This international support and the leverage of the United Nations would give momentum and create pressure for civil rights reform at home. Unfortunately for Patterson, his efforts to internationalize the civil rights movement ran directly counter to U.S. government efforts to create and sustain an image overseas of a progressive and just nation.

The State Department did not look favorably upon the Civil Rights Congress's efforts. After Patterson submitted the petition in Paris, the U.S. embassy in Paris asked him to surrender his passport.

Patterson refused, but his passport was seized when he returned to the United States. The *New York Times* reported that "the State Department said that further travel by Mr. Patterson would not be in the 'best interest of the United States.' " Patterson had broken the unwritten rule of Cold War civil rights activism. He had aired the nation's dirty laundry overseas. Patterson had also run afoul of other Cold War norms: he was active in a left-of-center organization, and worse, he openly associated with members of the Communist Party. The CRC itself was on the attorney general's list of subversive organizations. The organization was under constant pressure from anti-communists in the federal government, so that eventually, according to Gerald Horne, it "seemed . . . to be in business in order to defend itself." As with the NAACP petition, the United Nations would take no action on the Civil Rights Congress petition.[40]

Louis Armstrong was one of many African Americans tapped by the State Department for travel abroad. Armstrong's cancellation of a State Department–sponsored trip to the Soviet Union led to angry public reaction and to government concern. During the crisis over the desegregation of Central High School in Little Rock, Arkansas, in the fall of 1957, Armstrong said that "the way they are treating my people in the South, the government can go to hell." Were he to go to the Soviet Union, and "The people over there ask me what's wrong with my country, what am I supposed to say?" Armstrong later added, "The Government could go to the devil with its plans for a propaganda tour of Soviet Russia." Many harshly criticized Armstrong's angry words. In Armstrong's FBI file for that year was an anonymous letter stating "Louis 'Satcho' [sic] Armstrong is a communist, why does State Dept. give him a passport?" While Armstrong's passport was not seized, the FBI recorded the episode and continued to collect information on his activities. In the eyes of the federal government, Armstrong had spoken out of turn under the etiquette of Cold War race politics. Domestic problems were to be shielded from outside ears. And the discourse on civil rights was bounded by the terms of Cold War liberalism. Some level of liberal activism would be tolerated, but only if articulated in a way that did not challenge the democratic order. Armstrong's offense was that he seemed unwilling to defend the nation against communist critics. Patriots were supposed to close ranks.[41]

Outside the borders of the United States, other African Americans found themselves under surveillance. After moving to France, Richard Wright formed an organization concerned with racism in Paris that would examine the hiring practices of American businesses abroad. Its meetings were infiltrated, and reports on Wright's activities were placed in his FBI file. FBI interest in James Baldwin, also living in Paris, was heightened when he considered writing a book about the FBI. Acceptable activists included such people as NAACP executive secretary Walter White. After White had traveled on behalf of the government to settle disputes involving African American soldiers during World War II, and after the NAACP had passed a resolution excluding communists from its membership, White had earned the credentials to criticize, within the walls of the White House, racial violence and segregation. When sent abroad, however, he would emphasize racial progress in the United States and argue that persons of color had nothing to gain from communism.[42]

Entertainer Josephine Baker presented a somewhat different problem. Relegated to stereotyped black vaudeville roles in the United States, Baker left for Paris in the 1920s and found stardom. After experiencing racial discrimination on a return trip to the United States, Baker used her international prominence to call attention to American racial practices when she traveled throughout the world. Since she was no longer a U.S. citizen by the early 1950s, the government could not withhold her passport and directly restrict her international travels. Instead, more creative means would be employed to silence her.[43]

The red-baiting of Baker had its origin, in part, in a run-in with New York gossip columnist Walter Winchell. After Baker protested discrimination at New York's exclusive Stork Club and Winchell's refusal to come to her aid, Baker became the subject of an FBI investigation. Winchell wrote to FBI Director J. Edgar Hoover asking him to check up on allegations that Baker was a communist. The FBI began collecting derogatory information about Baker, paying close attention to the question of whether she was sympathetic to communism. In fact, Baker preferred to distance herself from the left and was praised for this move by the staunchly anticommunist *Counterattack* magazine. Her brother, Richard Martin, found irony in the allegation that the glamorous Baker was a communist. "Imagine Josephine a communist," he said. "When you think of the way they dress in Moscow."[44]

More threatening than Baker's questioning of race discrimination within U.S. borders was her propensity to raise the issue overseas. On September 25, 1952, during a Latin American tour, Baker gave a lecture about U.S. race discrimination in Uruguay. According to the acting public affairs officer (PAO) at the U.S. embassy in Montevideo, "Before an audience of approximately 200 Uruguayans," Baker "stated that she felt impelled by God and her deep religious feelings to fight discrimination by stressing this problem in talks to people wherever she goes." Baker began by criticizing racial practices in South Africa and then turned to a lengthy discussion of race discrimination in the United States. The PAO described Baker as a "staunch crusader for the elimination of racial and religious discrimination throughout the world," and he thought that her objective was "a most worthy one." Nevertheless, he was concerned about her activities because "[h]er remarks concerning racial discrimination in the United States are wholly derogatory, thus presenting a distorted and malicious picture of actual conditions in the United States." The embassy officer's claim that Baker's account was distorted stemmed from the fact that she did not mention that progress was being made. "Not once was any mention made of what the American people have done and are doing to eliminate racial and religious discrimination." He was also concerned because Baker's message had an effect. "It was evident that the spectators were impressed by her analysis of the status of the negroes in the United States."[45]

Baker was "devoting as much time as her artistic schedule will permit" to her campaign against discrimination. According to the embassy officer, she would "undoubtedly . . . continue to misrepresent the United States with respect to the negro problem." Consequently, the officer thought that the State Department would be "interested in following her campaign" and that "the Department might find it advisable to prepare special material to counteract her activities."[46]

Baker's impact in Montevideo was muted by limited local press coverage. The U.S. embassy seems to have had a hand in this. Baker later commented that "Upon my arrival in Montevideo, the press was very kind to me, but after my speeches, only one newspaper dared to publish my discourse, and they told me that they had received a friendly visit from the American Embassy requesting them not to publish it."[47]

Although the State Department was alarmed at Baker's harsh critique of American race relations, her notion of social change was not very radical. Baker's underlying philosophy was that education and respectful interaction among persons of different races and religions would overcome prejudice. Baker believed that "there is only one race and that is the human race." Differences between people were a result of the different circumstances in which they had lived. Baker believed that such differences must be understood and respected.[48]

The State Department became increasingly concerned about Baker's actions when she traveled to Argentina the following month. In most other contexts, the U.S. government was concerned with communist or left-wing criticism. In Argentina, race in the United States was instead an anti-American tool of the right-wing Peronistas. Baker's statements about race discrimination were given "dramatic play" by most Buenos Aires newspapers. Baker also escalated the rhetoric in her critique of the United States, reportedly comparing American racism to the Holocaust. According to the evening paper *Critica*, Baker believed that "Negroes throughout the world entirely rightly are looking upon the United States in the same way the Jewish people pointed a short time ago to the land where they had been sentenced to extinction."[49]

News of Baker's appearances quickly found its way to Washington. Acting Assistant Secretary of State Ben Brown thought that it was very unfortunate that Baker was "permitting herself to become the tool of foreign interests which are notoriously unfriendly to the United States and which are only interested in the causes which she sponsors in so far as they can be made to embarrass the United States." The State Department was upset about the effect of Baker's speeches in Argentina. According to an internal memo on Baker's activities, "her work was welcomed in Argentina by the Peronistas who had been making much of the discrimination issue in their propaganda against the U.S." One staff member suggested that the State Department should do something "to counteract the effects of her visit. One of the most effective ways to my mind would be to have one or two outstanding negro intellectuals make trips through the southern part of the hemisphere." The USIS staff began to consider such a strategy involving people like Ralph Bunche, Walter White, and Jackie Robinson. Meanwhile, Congressman Adam Clayton Powell publicly denounced Baker, arguing that she was "guilty of deliberate distortion and misrepresentation of the situation in the United States."[50]

In planning a strategy to counter Josephine Baker, the State Department and USIS acted carefully. One staff member felt that they should not "immediately rush in with our big cannon (like Bunche) just because La Baker has a 'running off at the mouth.' " The staff member suggested instead that the USIS send embassy public affairs officers information on Baker "for confidential background use." Before anyone was selected for a lecture tour, the USIS would make sure he or she was likely to say the right thing. Though one staff member suggested Walter White, he wasn't sure "what kind of an impression or what kind of a line Walter White, Pres. of the National Assn. for the Advancement of Colored People, would take with a foreign audience, but this might be investigated." The Harlem Globetrotters had been to Buenos Aires, but this staff member didn't "recall that one single line was printed indicating that they believe the racial question is improving in the U.S." The Globetrotters were popular and would probably be returning to Argentina, so he wondered whether one of them could "speak out on the progress [the] U.S. is making on the racial question."[51]

Although they had different ideas about strategy, the USIS staff was unanimous on one point. As one individual put it, "[N]aturally we should avoid any appearance of having sent someone to 'offset' J. Baker." According to another, "[T]o put ourselves on the defensive in this case could serve to weaken our arguments. We should do nothing to directly refute Baker's charges." A third person noted that such a cautious approach was "in keeping with the Depart-

William Patterson, Paul Robeson, and Robeson's attorney, James Wright, leave the Washington, D.C., federal district court after Robeson's challenge to his passport denial was rejected on August 16, 1955. (UPI/CORBIS-BETTMANN)

ment's policy to avoid doing things which draw attention to the fact that we have a problem in connection with the negro."[52]

While the State Department planned a propaganda response to Baker, embassy personnel also took steps to silence and discredit her. Baker found it increasingly difficult to perform in Latin American countries. She was unable to travel to Peru in December 1952 because that country denied her request for a visa. A representative of the theater in Lima, Peru, where Baker was scheduled to perform told the local press that Baker's contract had been canceled because she insisted on using her performances not just for artistic purposes but also to express her views about racial inequality. A scheduled trip to Colombia was called off for the same reasons. According to Baker, her Bogotá appearances were canceled when she refused to make a written commitment to refrain from making speeches against racial discrimination while in that city.[53]

In early February 1953, Baker was scheduled to appear in Havana, Cuba. The American embassy in Havana, concerned about

Josephine Baker holds a one-woman protest outside a Havana, Cuba, radio station, February 15, 1953. When she criticized American racism in Latin America the entertainer found her contracts canceled and conditions placed on visas requiring that she not engage in political activities. (UPI/CORBIS-BETTMANN)

what it called "further anti-American activity," urgently cabled the State Department for background information on Baker. The staff wanted to know about her "anti-American statements," recent cancellations of appearances in Peru and Colombia, quotes from African American newspapers criticizing Baker, and personal data, including the fact that she had given up her U.S. citizenship. The information supplied included the fact that Baker had been married three times (it was actually four), and that two of her husbands were white.[54]

Embassy officers then contacted Goar Mestre, who owned the theater where Baker was scheduled to perform, and local newspapers. As the U.S. embassy reported it, embassy personnel

> informally outlined to Mr. Mestre and to certain newspaper people that Miss Baker had given statements to the Argentine press highly uncomplimentary to the United States. The idea was planted discreetly that Miss Baker might use the Cuban press, particularly its communistic elements, as a further sounding board for her accusations of the mistreatment of Negroes in the United States.[55]

Baker did not arrive in Cuba in time for her scheduled performances but sent a wire requesting a later date. Rather than being rescheduled, her performances were canceled. As Mestre explained, "[W]e know that Josephine Baker has terrific drawing power, but we can't keep adjusting our business to her." As an embassy officer put it, Baker's tardiness "may well have provided her Habana employers with just the legal loophole they needed to 'get out from under' a ticklish situation."[56]

Baker showed up in Havana anyway. She blamed American influence for her contract cancellations, claiming that Teatro América had canceled a scheduled performance because the theater was afraid of losing its U.S. film franchise. Though Baker's other engagements in Havana had been canceled, an advertising agency scheduled a February 11 appearance for her on a popular television show. The agency did not seek approval from Goar Mestre, who was also the president of the television station, however, and Mestre ordered his doorman to bar Baker from entering the television studio. When she arrived on February 11 for an afternoon rehearsal, she was not allowed to enter. As the U.S. embassy reported it, "[A]damant, Miss Baker, costume over her arm, stood outside the gate from 3:00 p.m. to 9:30 p.m. in an apparent effort to elicit sympathy. 'Cabaret Regalias' went on the air without her."[57]

After much effort, Baker finally was able to arrange an appearance in Cuba. On February 16, she opened a one-week run at the Teatro

Campoamor, described in an embassy despatch as "a down-at-the heels theater which last year was a burlesque house." The embassy reported that "there was no indication she . . . used the Campoamor stage for political purposes." Baker was warned not to. At 4:30 the afternoon after her opening, Baker was taken into custody by the Cuban military police. They filed no charges against her, but they interrogated her for three hours about her political and social views. The military police reported that "the questioning was in response to a suggestion by the U.S. Federal Bureau of Investigation that Miss Baker might be an active Communist." Baker was photographed and fingerprinted. The military police asked her to sign a stenographic report of her interrogation, but she refused. She later wrote in an autobiography that the statement would have had her admit to "being paid by Moscow and indulging in subversive activities." When she was fingerprinted, "the word 'Communist' was marked beneath my picture." As the embassy put it, Baker was warned to "stick to her art and refrain from any voicing of political views at the Campoamor." She was released in time for her evening appearance.[58]

Baker's visit to Cuba had far less of an artistic and political impact than she would have liked. After she left the country, the American embassy in Cuba concluded that "Miss Baker's visit to Cuba must be considered of little value to her cause." The embassy also felt that Baker had done little harm. "All in all, Miss Baker's influence on Cuban Negroes may well be appraised as negligible. The Negro press ignored her, and Negro societies made no fuss over her." The embassy reported that a Cuban newspaper editor "explained to an Embassy officer that the attitude of the Cuban Negro toward the United States has changed radically in the last few years and that the Cuban Negro is now aware that real progress is being made in the United States toward the elimination of racial discrimination."[59]

After her visit to Cuba, Baker planned to appear in Haiti. This created a more delicate problem for the State Department because Haiti was a black country. In anticipation of her visit, Mauclair Zéphyrin, Haitian minister of the presidency and acting minister for foreign relations, telephoned the American chargé d'affaires. Zéphyrin expressed the fear that Baker might use her visit to create trouble between the United States and Haiti, and he wanted to know the chargé's views on the subject. At this point the chargé told Zéphyrin that "he did not see how he could restrict Miss Baker's freedom of speech nor how he could properly comment on the advisability of the visit." He told Zéphyrin that Josephine Baker's visit was a problem the Haitian government would have to handle.[60]

Minister Zéphyrin then wrote to Baker's agent in New York, informing him that Baker "was welcome to Haiti but should clearly understand that she was not to embarrass the Haitian Government by anti-American remarks which would disturb the excellent relations between the American and Haitian Governments." The letter notwithstanding, the U.S. embassy public affairs officer reported to the State Department that "in spite of the good intentions of the Haitian Government," the American embassy could "expect unpleasant and embarrassing publicity which will tend to counteract much positive effort which has been made in the past by American officials in Haiti to better relationships." Even though the embassy was likely "to see many of its 'friends' brought under the spell of Miss Baker and considerable encouragement to Anti-Americanism, it does not appear possible for the Embassy to take a firm stand against her proposed visit."[61]

Secretary of State John Foster Dulles would not tolerate the impending damage to U.S. prestige in Haiti. Upon receiving an account of the situation, he contacted the embassy in Port-au-Prince regarding background information on Baker the department was sending to the embassy. The material contained information about Baker's change of citizenship and the fact that, according to Dulles, "her activities have been widely denounced by prominent negroes and by the negro press in the United States." Dulles said that the embassy was authorized to make the information available to the Haitian acting foreign minister. Subsequent communications involving the embassy about Baker's trip remain classified for national security reasons. Whatever transpired, Josephine Baker's trip to Haiti never happened.[62]

Clearly frustrated in her efforts to appear in Latin America and the Caribbean, Baker could not turn to the United States as an alternative market for her performances. According to a December 10,

1954, FBI internal memorandum, the commissioner of the Immigration and Naturalization Service had taken a "personal interest in the case of Josephine Baker and has directed that INS obtain sufficient information with which to order her exclusion from the U.S." The INS requested that FBI files be reviewed to ensure that "all pertinent derogatory information" had been forwarded to the INS. On January 21, 1955, the *New York Herald Tribune* reported that Josephine Baker was detained by the INS at a New York airport where she had stopped en route from Paris to Mexico City. She was held for four hours before being allowed to depart. The INS gave no explanation for its actions. Baker's literal exclusion from the United States capped government efforts to exclude her from the discourse on race relations in America. Although the FBI ultimately concluded that Josephine Baker was not "pro-communist," but, in their words, "pro-Negro," they continued to pass derogatory information about her to the State Department and other agencies for several years.[63]

Josephine Baker's saga is, in some ways, simply a global counterpart to the red-baiting that was so pervasive within U.S. borders during the early Cold War years. More can be drawn, however, from this particular episode and other efforts to manage the impact of African Americans overseas. The degree of effort put into quieting this cultural figure underscores the importance to Cold War international politics of maintaining control over the narrative of race and American democracy. As other nations seized on stories of U.S. race discrimination, they questioned how the United States could argue that its form of government was a model for the world when American democracy accommodated racial oppression. The persistence of racial problems in the United States meant that race had to be addressed. The legacy of discrimination could not be denied, so through carefully prepared propaganda and through coaching well-chosen speakers, the USIS and embassy personnel tried to manage the narrative of race and democracy. By acknowledging past problems and emphasizing reforms, the story of race in America was told as a story of progress. Because American democracy was the site for this progress, it was argued democracy was a model of government that enabled peaceful social change. The world was focused on race in America, and so the story of American race relations became an important Cold War narrative. The U.S. government did its best to turn a liability into an advantage. A history of oppression became a narrative of progress toward the inevitable goal of greater social justice.

The image of America projected in *The Negro in American Life*, the classic example of the narrative of race and democracy, would be hard to sustain in the face of criticism by Paul Robeson, William Patterson, Josephine Baker, and others perceived to be more authentic voices on the topic of American racial justice. For that reason, silencing Robeson, Patterson, Baker, and other critics can be seen as part of the broader effort to safeguard the image of America, and maintain control over the narrative of race and democracy.

In spite of U.S. efforts to tell a progressive story about race in America, the counternarrative of racial oppression continued to make headlines. The news took its toll. The impact of race on foreign relations greatly troubled Chester Bowles as he neared the end of his first tenure as U.S. ambassador to India. Bowles stressed the importance of race to foreign relations in a 1952 speech at Yale University.

> A year, a month, or even a week in Asia is enough to convince any perceptive American that the colored peoples of Asia and Africa, who total two-thirds of the world's population, seldom think about the United States without considering the limitations under which our 13 million Negroes are living.

Bowles believed that most Asians and Africans were "convinced that, solely because of their color, many Americans are denied a full share in the life of the richest nation on earth, and in their ears this conviction gives our claim to world leadership a distinctly hollow ring." Bowles asked his audience, "[C]an any of us say they are wrong?"[64]

Chester Bowles believed that more was required than information programs. American society ultimately had to change. "A great majority of Americans now accept the idea that discrimination is wrong and must be ended," he argued. "The remaining differences are over the timing and the method." Yet Bowles questioned how much time remained. "Since the end of World War II our country, somewhat reluctantly, has advanced to the center of the world stage. . . . With such leadership the world comes to know more about us, both good and bad."[65]

"How much does all our talk of democracy mean, if we do not practice it at home?" Bowles asked. "How can the colored peoples of Asia be sure we are sincere in our interest in them if we do not respect the equality of our colored people at home?" It would be easier to answer these questions "if we have a better answer from home. I can think of no single thing that would be more helpful to us in Asia than the achievement of racial harmony in America." This issue was of such importance, Bowles would later write, that "of one thing I am certain. I have not exaggerated. It is impossible to exaggerate."[66]

CHAPTER 3

Fighting the Cold War
with Civil Rights Reform

It is in the context of the present world
struggle between freedom and tyranny that the
problem of race discrimination must be viewed.

BRIEF FOR THE UNITED STATES AS AMICUS CURIAE,
BROWN V. BOARD OF EDUCATION (FILED 1952)[1]

American embassies scattered throughout the world tried to do their
part to salvage the tarnished image of American democracy. They
used the tools available to them: speakers and news stories that
would cast American difficulties in the best light possible. Meanwhile, in Washington, the Truman administration could take more
affirmative, less reactive steps. President Truman and his aides
sought change in the domestic policies and practices that fueled
international outrage.

In 1947, Truman's President's Committee on Civil Rights issued
a report that highlighted the foreign affairs consequences of race
discrimination. The committee's report, *To Secure These Rights*, argued that there were three reasons why civil rights abuses in the
United States should be redressed: a moral reason—discrimination
was morally wrong; an economic reason—discrimination harmed

the economy; and an international reason—discrimination damaged U.S. foreign relations. According to the report,

> Our foreign policy is designed to make the United States an enormous, positive influence for peace and progress throughout the world. We have tried to let nothing, not even extreme political differences between ourselves and foreign nations, stand in the way of this goal. But our domestic civil rights shortcomings are a serious obstacle.

The committee stressed that "we cannot escape the fact that our civil rights record has been an issue in world politics. The world's press and radio are full of it." Countries with "competing philosophies" had stressed and distorted American problems. "They have tried to prove our democracy an empty fraud, and our nation a consistent oppressor of underprivileged people."[2]

To support this argument, the committee report quoted a letter from Acting Secretary of State Dean Acheson to the chairman of the Fair Employment Practices Commission (FEPC). According to Acheson,

> [T]he existence of discrimination against minority groups in this country has an adverse effect upon our relations with other countries. We are reminded over and over by some foreign newspapers and spokesmen, that our treatment of various minorities leaves much to be desired. . . . Frequently we find it next to impossible to formulate a satisfactory answer to our critics in other countries.
>
> An atmosphere of suspicion and resentment in a country over the way a minority is being treated in the United States is a formidable obstacle to the development of mutual understanding and trust between the two countries. We will have better international relations when these reasons for suspicion and resentment have been removed.

Because he thought it was "quite obvious" that race discrimination interfered with foreign relations, Acheson wrote that the State Department had "good reason to hope for the continued and increased effectiveness of public and private efforts to do away with these discriminations."[3]

Why was the acting secretary of state advocating civil rights reform? Perhaps State Department officials argued that race discrimination harmed foreign relations simply because they thought that argument would be useful to civil rights reform at home, not because they thought there was any substance to it. Perhaps Acheson was seeking to further a domestic civil rights agenda, not to protect U.S. foreign policy interests. The State Department's preoccupation with American race discrimination during the early Cold War years and the volume of diplomatic cable traffic on the issue would seem to belie that point. More importantly, it was simply not Dean Acheson's job to focus on purely domestic matters. As a State Department official, he was charged with furthering American foreign policy interests, not domestic policy. Acheson's own philosophy was that moral imperatives should not drive foreign policy, so it would be ironic if he used his position at the State Department to further views about the morality of racial practices at home. For these reasons, it is unlikely that Dean Acheson, along with other American diplomats, was a closet civil rights activist crafting an argument, for the purpose of furthering a social change agenda at home, that race discrimination harmed U.S. foreign relations.[4]

The President's Committee on Civil Rights took the impact of race discrimination on U.S. foreign relations very seriously. The committee report stressed, however, that "the international reason for acting to secure our civil rights now is not to win the approval of our totalitarian critics. . . . [T]o them our civil rights record is only a convenient weapon with which to attack us." Instead, "we are more concerned with the good opinion of the peoples of the world." Maintaining U.S. prestige abroad would help safeguard democracy in other lands.

> Our achievements in building and maintaining a state dedicated to the fundamentals of freedom have already served as a guide for those seeking the best road from chaos to liberty and prosperity. But it is not indelibly written that democracy will encompass the world. We are convinced that our way of

life—the free way of life—holds a promise of hope for all people. We have what is perhaps the greatest responsibility ever placed upon a people to keep this promise alive. Only still greater achievements will do it.

The consequences were stark, for the future was uncertain. The committee emphasized that "*the United States is not so strong, the final triumph of the democratic ideal is not so inevitable that we can ignore what the world thinks of us or our record.*"[5]

President Truman, trying to lead the free world through the dangers of the Cold War, made this message his own. The president repeatedly emphasized the importance of civil rights to U.S. foreign affairs. On February 2, 1948, he delivered a special message to Congress, outlining several civil rights initiatives. Truman told Congress that the "position of the United States in the world today" made civil rights "especially urgent." According to the president, "The peoples of the world are faced with the choice of freedom or enslavement." The United States was promoting human rights with the goal of preserving world peace. The nation had to protect civil rights at home to be effective and to strengthen the nation. "We know that our democracy is not perfect," he said, but democracy offered "a fuller, freer happier life" than totalitarianism.

> If we wish to inspire the peoples of the world whose freedom is in jeopardy, if we wish to restore hope to those who have already lost their civil liberties, if we wish to fulfill the promise that is ours, we must correct the remaining imperfections in our practice of democracy.[6]

Truman urged Congress to enact civil rights laws that would establish a permanent civil rights commission, outlaw lynching, and protect the right to vote, among other proposals. Congress did not pass civil rights legislation while Truman was in office, however. Truman's relations with Congress were sufficiently strained that he did not have great success with any of his domestic legislative proposals. On civil rights, his prospects were particularly bleak because of the hold of Southern Democrats on key Senate committee chairmanships. Truman had greater latitude to act on civil rights when he could act alone. For that reason his greatest civil rights accomplishments were things within executive power: the issuance of executive orders and the involvement of the Justice Department in landmark desegregation litigation.[7]

One of President Truman's most important civil rights accomplishments was initiating desegregation of the armed services. Discrimination and segregation in the military were particularly galling to people of color who risked their lives to protect the nation yet were not treated equally even during their military service. When troops traveled to foreign lands, other nations were directly exposed to American racial practices. During World War II, U.S. segregation followed American troops overseas, creating an awkward situation for their foreign hosts. In September 1942, Winston Churchill was asked in the House of Commons to politely ask U.S. military authorities in Britain "to instruct their men that the colour bar is not the custom in this country and that its non-observance by British troops or civilians should be regarded with equanimity." The British government was unable to avoid responding to this problem. Although conflict arose when some British residents encouraged a code of conduct reminiscent of the mores of the American South, Christopher Thorne has written that "a greater danger appeared to lie in the very warmth of the welcome which many people were ready to give to these soldiers—a response which threatened to conflict with the patterns of behaviour and expectations brought over with them by white Americans." The warm welcome created resentment on the part of white American troops. The British had their own race issues, particularly their hold on colonial subjects. Yet because of their "growing material dependence on the U.S.A. and the perceived need to retain her cooperation after victory," the British found themselves unable to respond to criticism of empire by pointing out racism in Alabama.[8]

NAACP executive secretary Walter White thought it was "perilous" to transport American racism overseas during the war. "I have seen bewilderment in the eyes of brown, yellow and black peoples in the Pacific at the manifestations of race prejudice by some American whites, not only against American Negro servicemen but against the natives whose aid we need *now* in winning the war, and whose friendship we will need *after* the war if we are to have peace." Racism gave the enemy an effective propaganda weapon, White argued.

> The Japanese eagerly capitalize on these incidents and on race riots, lynchings and segregation in the United States. They utilize the anti-Negro rantings of congressmen like Rankin and of senators like Bilbo in filibustering against a Fair Employment Practices Committee. In Guam I saw a poster which has been put up all over the Island during the Japanese occupation which read, "Fight on to Asia with Asia's own. Drive out the imperialist, aggressive American. The sole purpose of the white peoples of the earth is to exploit colored people."

White warned that "[n]one can yet tell how deep such roots have sunk into the thinking of the one billion colored peoples of the Pacific, Asia and Africa who constitute with colored peoples in other parts of the world two-thirds of the earth's population."[9]

Waging the Cold War would require military strength. Military preparedness would be one line of defense against Soviet aggression. Although the armed forces were the nation's physical line of defense against Soviet aggression, they were also a source of the nation's moral failure, for American forces in the postwar years continued to be segregated.

Racial segregation in the armed forces came under fire in the report of Truman's President's Committee on Civil Rights. There was strong sentiment on the part of the committee that segregation in the armed services should be eliminated as quickly as possible. Committee member James Carey spoke of the "paradox of massing an army in World War II to fight for the Four Freedoms, and in engaging in that work they segregate people on the basis of race." Channing Tobias insisted that the committee call for immediate desegregation, rather than gradualism. "Segregation is wrong wherever it exists," he argued, "but when our Government holds up before its citizens the Constitution, with the Bill of Rights, saying to every man that he is a citizen and appealing to him for loyalty in peace and war on that basis, then I don't think we have any right to permit the pattern that has grown up in any section of the country to dominate the national policy."[10]

In spite of this sentiment, A. Philip Randolph was concerned that a proposed Universal Military Training Program would continue to perpetuate patterns of segregation in the armed services. On December 28, 1947, he wrote to President Truman protesting the proposal as "a great threat to Negro youth and the internal stability of our nation. Segregation becomes all the more important when the United States should be assuming moral leadership in the world." Randolph threatened that African Americans would refuse to serve in a Jim Crow army. "Negro youth will have no alternative but to resist a law, the inevitable consequences of which would be to expose them to un-American brutality so familiar during the last war." According to Randolph, "So long as the American government attempts to sponsor any program of Jim Crow, its aspiration to moral leadership in the world will be seriously impaired."[11]

This sentiment would come, as well, from ordinary citizens. Mr. and Mrs. Irvin Dagen wrote President Truman urging him to "use all the power you have to abolish . . . undemocratic segregation of ANY kind" in the armed services. "We feel that one of the most effective, firm, and noticeable ways in which we can show the rest of the world we believe in democracy is to practice such a virtue . . . at home. We believe this will still Russian propaganda against us for this gross injustice in this country."[12]

On February 2, 1948, in his special message to Congress on civil rights, President Truman announced that he had "instructed the Secretary of Defense to take steps to have the remaining instances of discrimination in the armed services eliminated as rapidly as possible." Truman called for reinstitution of the draft in March 1948, but the legislation passed by Congress did not address segregation, and the army intended to continue it. Randolph organized the Committee Against Jim Crow in Military Service to pressure President Truman to act. If Truman did not desegregate the military, the committee would "work in the big East Coast cities on behalf of a campaign of civil disobedience, nonregistration and noninduction." On March 22, 1948, at a meeting with the president at the

White House, Randolph warned Truman that "Negroes would not shoulder a gun to fight for democracy abroad while they were denied democracy here." He reiterated his call for civil disobedience later that month in testimony before the Senate Armed Services Committee.[13]

Then, on July 26, 1948, Truman issued Executive Order 9981. The order stated that it was "essential that there be maintained in the armed services of the United States the highest standards of democracy, with equality of treatment and opportunity for all those who serve in our country's defense." Under the order, it was "the policy of the President that there shall be equality of treatment and opportunity in the armed services without regard to race, color, religion or national origin." This policy was to be implemented "as rapidly as possible, having due regard to the time required to effectuate any necessary changes without impairing efficiency or morale." The order did not specifically mention desegregation, however, and provided no deadline by which "equality" should be accomplished.[14]

The timing of Truman's order—in the middle of the 1948 election campaign—lends support to the argument of many historians that a principal motive behind the action was political. The order came shortly after the Democratic Party convention. The Democrats adopted a strong civil rights party platform; prompting southern Democrats to walk out and form their own Dixiecrat Party. The departure of the Dixiecrats meant that Truman would have to look elsewhere for electoral support. This reinforced the importance of the black vote to his campaign. In light of political motives, Bernard Nalty suggests that the order resulted from "a marriage of politics and principle," as Truman stood to gain politically from an action that, Nalty believes, Truman thought was morally right.[15]

In an effort to maintain as broad a political base as possible, Truman was silent on civil rights for much of the campaign to avoid alienating critics of his civil rights stance. When he appeared in Harlem on October 29—the first major presidential candidate who had done so—Truman emphasized his accomplishments. The president told the crowd that when Congress had not enacted civil rights legislation, he had turned to executive orders. His actions served the need for equality and also safeguarded democracy. "Today the democratic way of life is being challenged all over the world. Democracy's answer to the challenge of totalitarianism is its promise of equal rights and equal opportunities for all mankind." Maintaining a hold on the black vote as well as other critical constituencies, Truman went on to win the 1948 election by the narrowest of margins.[16]

Publicly and privately, the president persistently stressed the importance of civil rights reform to the nation's Cold War foreign relations. Michael Sherry has written that "[c]ivil rights leaders, and Truman himself on occasion, did also invoke morality and justice, but national security was the dominant rationale" for civil rights reform. It was also "the most persistent." While domestic politics and principle surely played a role in Truman's decision to desegregate the military, safeguarding the nation's overseas image, an important theme throughout Truman's presidency, was also a critical factor.[17]

In spite of the desegregation order, racism in the armed forces continued to be an issue. Congressman Jacob Javits of New York drew attention to the problem on January 12, 1950, by calling for a congressional investigation. According to Javits, race discrimination continued, and "[n]othing could be more useful . . . to the Communist propagandists in the 'cold war.'" Javits had been to Europe, where he had been repeatedly questioned about American racial practices in many areas, including the military. He reported that "[t]he Communist propagandists in Western Germany and Western Europe seek to build up the alleged evils and to magnify them, but there is enough to them to damage us seriously in the cold war." In Asia and Africa the problem was "even worse." The "fall" of China exacerbated this crisis, for now China was another source of anti-American propaganda. As Javits put it, "With Communist China as a propaganda base, segregation and discrimination on grounds of race, creed or color in the United States can be used to win tens of millions to the Communist cause." The problem of discrimination had become, at least in part, "a question . . . relative to the foreign policy of the United States."[18]

A turn in the Cold War finally led to meaningful racial integration in the army. In June 1950 North Korean troops invaded South Korea. Hoping to contain communism, Truman sent U.S. troops to

Korea to attempt to push back North Korean forces. The war would ultimately expand into an unsuccessful effort to liberate North Korea. This long and bloody "police action" required a substantial commitment of U.S. troops. When American units needed reinforcements, American commanders came to realize that attempts to maintain segregation were interfering with military objectives. It was ultimately the imperatives of wartime that led military leaders to assign reinforcements without regard to race.[19]

Equality in service meant equality in death. The casualties of the Korean War would achieve the democracy at last that Chaplain Gittlesohn had imagined on Iwo Jima during World War II. "White men and Negroes alike, Protestants, Catholics and Jews," their guns held the line at the Cold War's periphery. These integrated troops fulfilled the promise of U.S. propaganda. Their bodies held the line in the battle for the hearts and minds of the people of the world.

Congress took up the issue of the effect of discrimination on U.S. foreign relations, but with less success. When legislation to create a permanent Fair Employment Practices Commission to combat race discrimination in employment under federal defense contracts was before the Senate in May 1950, Democratic Senator William Benton of Connecticut argued that the bill was essential to national security. Benton spoke with authority, since he had previously served as assistant secretary of state in charge of public affairs. In that capacity, he said that it had been his "unhappy responsibility to study how Communist propaganda twisted and distorted our civil-rights problems in the channels of world communication." As an American delegate to UNESCO, he "saw how our unsolved civil rights problems hampered our efforts and our prestige in reaching out— gropingly as it were—for the hearts and the minds of men." It was not only "Sovietized" minds and the minds of Asians and Africans that Americans could not reach, but Europeans and Central and South Americans as well.[20]

Benton argued that civil rights problems had "enormous but little understood worldwide impact." He cautioned that "it can be a great and tragic mistake for us if we underestimate this weakness of ours in this highly dangerous world. . . . It is impossible to exaggerate how sensitive other countries are to the question of civil rights in America, and how much single instances of discrimination are magnified in their eyes."[21]

Senator Richard B. Russell of Georgia responded that he was confused by Benton's argument. He did not understand why the Senate "should pass the bill because of the Communists' propagandizing a state of affairs that does not exist in this country." On the one hand, senators were urged to support the Marshall Plan because communists opposed it. "Now we are told that we must pass the FEPC bill because the Communists are in favor of it. That is somewhat confusing." Benton argued that passage of the FEPC legislation would be a great blow to communist propaganda, and that failure to pass it would be exploited by the communists as evidence of American racial prejudice. Russell then countered that the communist *Daily Worker* "has claimed credit for originating the whole idea of the FEPC legislation, and has supported it constantly since the first day it was introduced in this body." While Benton tried to focus on the issue of Soviet propaganda and its effectiveness, Russell remained unconvinced. His position was "that we cannot believe anything which comes out of Russia and that any of us who believes anything that comes from Russia is very foolish."[22]

Senator Russell turned the Cold War argument on its head. In a political and cultural climate steeped in anticommunism, arguing that civil rights reform would be a capitulation to communists, who themselves must clearly be pursuing ulterior motives to undermine American society, proved to be a very effective strategy. Anticommunism was more important to Congress than civil rights. For that reason, casting a red taint on a civil rights bill was an effective way to derail it.

Benton's argument did not seem to go very far with the rest of the Senate. When he finally yielded the floor, a quorum call revealed that only twenty-two members, less than a quorum, had heard him out. The FEPC legislation ultimately failed to pass. Representative Vito Marcantonio, the bill's chief sponsor in the House, assailed the Democrats, the Republicans, and the President, arguing that "everybody wants civil rights as an issue but not as a law." *New York Times* columnist Arthur Krock blamed President Truman for this defeat, arguing that in failing to push the Democratic leadership in the House to bring the legislation up for a vote, Truman preserved the issue of civil rights as a 1950 campaign issue without accomplishing civil rights reform. Even if he had been a more active supporter of civil rights legislation, however, Truman might not have had much success in getting his programs through Congress.[23]

Desegregation of the military is often thought of as Truman's principal civil rights accomplishment. Of great significance as well, however, was the Truman administration's participation in the landmark desegregation cases leading up to *Brown v. Board of Education*. Although *Brown* itself was decided in 1954, when Dwight D. Eisenhower was president, it was Truman's Justice Department that initiated the government's participation in the legal battle to overcome Jim Crow. The Justice Department's most important brief in *Brown* itself was filed in December 1952, during the last weeks of Truman's presidency. The decision to participate in these cases was made at the highest levels of the Truman administration, at times involving the president himself.[24]

In amicus curiae, or "friend of the court," briefs in civil rights cases, the Truman administration stressed to the Supreme Court the international implications of race discrimination and at times focused on the negative impact on U.S. foreign relations that a prosegregation decision might have.[25] In terms of its consequences for American prestige, a Court decision rendering segregation unconstitutional was potentially of the greatest symbolic value. Change emanating from a Supreme Court interpretation of the Constitution would show that the principle of racial equality was already there in the governing document of American democracy. This would show that, as Gunnar Myrdal had suggested, it was a principle waiting to be realized as Americans perfected their practice of democracy.

The Truman administration's involvement in high-profile desegregation cases was a new practice. The United States was not a plaintiff or defendant in these cases. The Justice Department filed amicus curiae briefs to inform the Court of important interests at stake beyond those presented by the parties to the cases. Previously, the Justice Department had filed amicus briefs only in cases where the United

States had a concrete interest at stake. The cases leading up to *Brown v. Board of Education* did not involve a concrete federal interest. Instead, the federal government was interested in the abstract concept of justice at stake in these cases, and in the well-being of the plaintiffs. Why was the Justice Department filing briefs to vindicate the interests of one of the parties? In brief after brief, the Justice Department argued that crucial national interests were also implicated. The segregation challenged in these cases damaged U.S. prestige abroad and threatened U.S. foreign relations. In the context of heightened Cold War tensions, the stakes in these cases were very high.[26]

The Truman Justice Department began its participation as amicus curiae in civil rights cases with a restrictive covenant case, *Shelley v. Kraemer*. In Shelley, whites sold residential property to African Americans in violation of a covenant among landowners prohibiting sales to nonwhites. State supreme courts in Missouri and Michigan had ruled that the covenants were enforceable. The question in *Shelley* was whether judicial enforcement of the covenants constituted "state action" violating the Fourteenth Amendment rights of the African Americans who purchased the property. The Justice Department argued that state court action was "state action" and therefore that when state courts enforced racially restrictive covenants they violated the Fourteenth Amendment.[27]

According to Solicitor General Philip Perlman, the Justice Department brief filed in the restrictive covenant cases was "the first instance in which the Government had intervened in a case to which it was not a party and in which its sole purpose was the vindication of rights guaranteed by the Fifth and Fourteenth Amendments." In previous civil rights cases, the solicitor general participated when the litigation involved a federal agency and when the question in the case concerned the supremacy of federal law. A different sort of federal interest was involved in the restrictive covenant cases. According to Perlman, racially restrictive covenants hampered the federal government "in doing its duty in the fields of public health, housing, home finance, and in the conduct of foreign affairs." The brief for the United States in *Shelley v. Kraemer* relied on the State Department's view that "the United States has been embarrassed in the conduct of foreign relations by acts of discrimination taking place in this country." To support this argument, the brief quoted at length from the Dean Acheson letter relied on in *To Secure These Rights*.[28]

Although not addressing the international implications of the case, the Supreme Court agreed with the result sought by the Justice Department. The Court ruled that enforcement of restrictive covenants in state courts constituted state action violating the rights of African Americans to equal protection of the laws. Private agreements to exclude African Americans from housing were therefore not enforceable by state courts. The *Shelley* decision was celebrated by civil rights supporters in the U.S. and abroad. The decision was heralded by an Indian newspaper as "another victory in the battle for civil rights that is now going on in America."[29]

In 1949 the Justice Department filed a brief in *Henderson v. United States*, a case about segregation in railroad dining cars. Because the legal foundation for Jim Crow, *Plessy v. Ferguson*, was also a case about railroad segregation, *Henderson* held the potential to overturn this icon of racial oppression. In *Henderson*, the Justice Department took a position contrary to the Interstate Commerce Commission (ICC) regarding the validity of segregation under the Interstate Commerce Act's equal treatment requirement. The ICC had ruled that the Southern Railway Company's practice of providing separate seating behind a curtain in dining cars for African American passengers did not violate the statute. The Justice Department's position on appeal was, first, that dining car segregation was unlawful under the Interstate Commerce Act, and, second, that if it was authorized, this segregation violated the Fourteenth Amendment.[30]

As in *Shelley*, the government argued that the case had implications for U.S. foreign relations. The *Henderson* brief elaborated more fully on the problem. The Justice Department told the Court of the "frequent and caustic" foreign press coverage of U.S. race discrimination. The brief bolstered its argument with examples from Soviet publications and critical statements about U.S. race discrimination made in United Nations proceedings. It quoted from recent statements made by representatives of other governments in a United Nations subcommittee meeting that "typify the manner in which racial discrimination in this country is turned against us in the international field." For example, a representative of the Soviet Union had commented, "Guided by the principles of the United Nations Charter, the General Assembly must condemn the policy and practice of racial discrimination in the United States and any other countries of the American continent where such a policy was being exercised." Similarly, the representative from Poland "did not . . . believe that the United States Government had the least intention to conform to the recommendations which would be made by the United Nations with regard to the improvement of living conditions of the coloured population of that country."[31]

In one example of the foreign press, the brief quoted an article from *The Bolshevik* that claimed that

> the theory and practice of racial discrimination against the negroes in America is known to the whole world. The poison of racial hatred has become so strong in post-war America that matters go to unbelievable lengths; for example a Negress injured in a road accident could not be taken to a neighbouring hospital since this hospital was only for "whites."

A story in the *Soviet Literary Gazette* titled "The Tragedy of Coloured America," stated,

> It is a country within a country. Coloured America is not allowed to mix with the other white America, it exists within it like the yolk in the white of an egg. Or, to be more exact, like a gigantic ghetto. The walls of this ghetto are invisible but they are nonetheless indestructible. They are placed within cities where the Negroes live in special quarters, in buses where the Negroes are assigned only the back seats, in hairdressers where they have special chairs.[32]

Through its reliance on United Nations statements and the Soviet press, the *Henderson* brief hammered home the point that racial segregation hampered the U.S. government's fight against world communism.

There was another turf upon which the battle for democracy waged: the home front. The *Henderson* brief raised the specter of

African American radicalism. "The apparent hypocrisy of a society professing equality but practicing segregation and other forms of racial discrimination furnishes justification and reason for the latent urge to rebel, and frequently leads to lasting bitterness or total rejection of the American creed and system of government." However, the brief emphasized that African American protest was not tied to the Communist Party. The brief drew from the testimony of baseball player Jackie Robinson, who had appeared before the House Committee on Un-American Activities. Robinson testified:

> Just because Communists kick up a big fuss over racial discrimination when it suits their purposes, a lot of people try to pretend that the whole issue is a creation of Communist imagination.
>
> But they are not fooling anyone with this kind of pretense, and talk about "Communists stirring up Negroes to protest," only makes present misunderstanding worse than ever. Negroes were stirred up long before there was a Communist Party, and they'll stay stirred up long after the party has disappeared—unless Jim Crow has disappeared by then as well.[33]

The clear implication was that while African American protest was not directly tied to communism, racial injustice added to discontent among African Americans and, if not remedied, could lead them to reject American democracy. Equality was a safeguard against domestic subversion. Racial segregation threatened the government's ability to maintain its role as a leader of the free world and to govern peacefully at home.

In *Henderson*, the Supreme Court ruled that railroad dining car segregation violated the Interstate Commerce Act because it was unequal treatment. Since segregation violated a federal statute, the Court did not need to decide whether segregation in interstate travel was unconstitutional and whether *Plessy v. Ferguson* should be overturned.[34]

In the same year as the *Henderson* case, the Justice Department participated for the first time in cases challenging school segregation. The department argued that *McLaurin v. Oklahoma State Regents for Higher Education* and *Sweatt v. Painter* were of "great importance" to the nation because "they test the vitality and strength of the democratic ideals to which the United States is dedicated." In *McLaurin*, the University of Oklahoma had admitted an African American student, G. W. McLaurin, to its graduate program in education after he successfully challenged Oklahoma's segregation statutes in federal district court, but McLaurin was segregated within the university. He was assigned to a separate table in the library, a separate row in the classroom, and a separate table in the cafeteria. The NAACP argued that this different treatment on the basis of race violated the equal protection clause of the Fourteenth Amendment. *Sweatt* involved a challenge to racial segregation at the University of Texas Law School. Heman Marion Sweatt was denied admission to the law school because he was African American. When a state trial court found that the university's action violated the Fourteenth Amendment, the state responded by quickly opening a separate black law school. There were great differences between the schools in libraries, faculties, and other resources. The question before the Supreme Court was whether the legal education provided at the black school was equal to that provided to whites at the University of Texas.[35]

The U.S. brief in *Sweatt* and *McLaurin* stressed again that race discrimination was "the greatest unsolved task for American democracy." This time the Justice Department urged the Supreme Court to consider the foreign policy repercussions the Court's ruling in the cases might have.

> The Court is here asked to place the seal of constitutional approval upon an undisguised species of racial discrimination. If the imprimatur of constitutionality should be put on such a denial of equality, one would expect the foes of democracy to exploit such an action for their own purposes. The ideals embodied in our Bill of Rights would be ridiculed as empty words, devoid of any real substance.

The consequences of such a ruling would be stark, extending far beyond the cases, and affecting the American way of life.

> It is in the context of a world in which freedom and equality must become living realities, if the democratic way of life is to survive, that the issues in these cases should be viewed. In

these times, when even the foundations of our free institutions are not altogether secure, it is especially important that it again be unequivocally affirmed that the Constitution of the United States, like the Declaration of Independence and the other great state papers in American history, places no limitation, express or implied, on the principle of the equality of all men before the law.

The brief then noted again the specific foreign policy implications of U.S. race discrimination that the Justice Department had previously outlined in the *Henderson* brief.[36]

In *Sweatt* and *McLaurin,* the Supreme Court again sided with the Justice Department and the NAACP. In important rulings that significantly eroded the separate-but-equal doctrine, the Court found that segregation at the University of Texas Law School and the University of Oklahoma School of Education denied the African American plaintiffs equal treatment. The Court found that the plaintiffs' very isolation from white students meant that the education provided to them was unequal. Isolating them from white classmates denied Heman Sweatt and G. W. McLaurin the equality guaranteed them by the Fourteenth Amendment. The Court, however, declined to reconsider directly the constitutionality of segregation itself.[37]

Segregation in the District of Columbia was an issue in the next series of crucial desegregation cases before the Court. While racial discrimination in southern states and throughout the nation had been the subject of foreign criticism, segregation in the District of Columbia was particularly embarrassing and was often a special focus of international attention. If segregation only existed in particular areas of the country, it would have been easier for the federal government to characterize it as a regional phenomenon, as something at odds with generally accepted American practices. As long as the seat of the federal government was segregated, however, any claims that segregation was not a widespread national practice seemed hollow. The District of Columbia was "the window through which the world looks into our house." If the United States were to clean up its international image, Washington was the place to begin.[38]

President Harry S. Truman receiving the report of his President's Committee on Civil Rights, October 29, 1947. The report argued that one important reason the nation needed to make progress on civil rights was that race discrimination harmed U.S. foreign relations. (UPI/CORBIS-BETTMANN)

George McLaurin was able to attend the University of Oklahoma School of Education but was segregated within the school. Here he attends class in an anteroom, separated from his white classmates, October 16, 1948. In McLaurin's Supreme Court challenge, the Justice Department argued that discrimination like this harmed the international image of American democracy. (UPI/CORBIS-BETTMANN)

Segregation in the District was at issue in *Bolling v. Sharpe*, a companion case to *Brown v. Board of Education*. *Brown* challenged the constitutionality of racial segregation in public schools in cases from the states of Kansas, South Carolina, Virginia, and Delaware. The NAACP argued that state school segregation violated the equal protection clause, even if other conditions in the schools were equal. Because the federal government was responsible for District of Columbia schools, in *Bolling* the NAACP argued that school segregation in the District violated the due process clause of the Fifth Amendment, which applied to the federal government.[39]

The school desegregation cases were consolidated, and the Justice Department filed one amicus brief arguing that school segregation in all five cases was unconstitutional. The brief emphasized the embarrassment of race discrimination in the nation's capital. "[F]oreign officials and visitors naturally judge this country and our people by their experiences and observations in the nation's capital; and the treatment of colored persons here is taken as the measure of our attitude toward minorities generally." The brief quoted President Truman's statement that "the District of Columbia should be a true symbol of American freedom and democracy for our own people, and for the people of the world." However, the President's Committee on Civil Rights had found that the District of Columbia was "a graphic illustration of a failure of democracy." The brief quoted at length from the Committee's report describing the segregation of African Americans in Washington:

> The shamefulness and absurdity of Washington's treatment of Negro Americans is highlighted by the presence of many dark-skinned foreign visitors. Capital custom not only humiliates colored citizens, but is a source of considerable embarrassment to these visitors. . . . Foreign officials are often mistaken for American Negroes and refused food, lodging and entertainment. However, once it is established that they are not Americans, they are accommodated.[40]

Beyond concerns about the District of Columbia, the implications of the school cases were very broad. Discrimination in public school systems raised "questions of the first importance in our society. For racial discriminations imposed by law, or having the sanction or support of government, inevitably tend to undermine the foundations of a society dedicated to freedom, justice, and equality." Under the "rule of law" embodied in the U.S. Constitution, every arm of government "must treat each of our people as an *American*, and not as a member of a particular group classified on the basis of race or some other constitutional irrelevancy."[41]

Racial segregation interfered with the Cold War imperative of winning the world over to democracy, for

> the existence of discrimination against minority groups in the United States has an adverse effect upon our relations with other countries. Racial discrimination furnishes grist for the Communist propaganda mills, and it raises doubts even among friendly nations as to the intensity of our devotion to the democratic faith.[42]

To document this claim, the Justice Department devoted nearly two pages of the brief to a lengthy quotation from Dean Acheson, who was now secretary of state. Acheson expanded upon his earlier statement on race discrimination. Now he argued that the problem had worsened.

> [D]uring the past six years, the damage to our foreign relations attributable to [race discrimination] has become progressively greater. The United States is under constant attack in the foreign press, over the foreign radio, and in such international bodies as the United Nations because of various practices of discrimination against minority groups in this country. As might be expected, Soviet spokesmen regularly exploit this situation in propaganda against the United States, both within the United Nations and through radio broadcasts and the press, which reaches all corners of the world. Some of these attacks against us are based on falsehood or distortion; but the undeniable existence of racial discrimination gives unfriendly governments the most effective kind of ammunition for their propaganda warfare.[43]

World attention to U.S. discrimination was of increasing concern to the State Department, because

> the hostile reaction among normally friendly peoples, many of whom are particularly sensitive in regard to the status of non-European races, is growing in alarming proportions. In such countries the view is expressed more and more vocally that the United States is hypocritical in claiming to be the champion of democracy while permitting practices of racial discrimination here in this country.[44]

School segregation, in particular, had been "singled out for hostile foreign comment in the United Nations and elsewhere. Other peoples cannot understand how such a practice can exist in a country which professes to be a staunch supporter of freedom, justice, and democracy." The secretary of state concluded that "racial discrimination in the United States remains a source of constant embarrassment to this Government in the day-to-day conduct of its foreign relations; and it jeopardizes the effective maintenance of our moral leadership of the free and democratic nations of the world."[45]

With this clear statement of the national security implications of the cases before the Court, the Justice Department brought its discussion of the interest of the United States to a close, and the brief turned to a more conventional constitutional argument. The centrality of the Cold War imperative to the government's posture on segregation was then reemphasized in the brief's closing paragraphs. The brief concluded by reiterating the notion that race discrimination "presents an unsolved problem for American democracy, an inescapable challenge to the sincerity of our espousal of the democratic faith." An affirmance of constitutional principles "in these days, when the free world must conserve and fortify the moral as well as the material sources of its strength, . . . is especially important." The final statement in the brief consisted of a quote from President Truman:

> If we wish to inspire the people of the world whose freedom is in jeopardy, if we wish to restore hope to those who have already lost their civil liberties, if we wish to fulfill the promise

that is ours, we must correct the remaining imperfections in our practice of democracy.

We know the way. We need only the will.[46]

The NAACP referred to the Cold War argument, although briefly, when the *Brown* case was reargued in 1953. It stressed that the "survival of our country in the present international situation is inevitably tied to resolution of this domestic issue." Meanwhile the significance of the pending *Brown* litigation was not lost on foreign critics of American racism. In December 1952, a prominent Amsterdam newspaper pointed to the pending cases as a "dynamic development of the handling of the negro problem in the United States." Referring to Gunnar Myrdal's definition of the "American Dilemma" as "the divergence between the American credo and American practice," the paper believed that "the fact that the Washington Court deals with this problem, indicates that the bridge between credo and reality is nearing its completion."[47]

In *Brown* and *Bolling*, the Supreme Court, adopting the position the Justice Department had been urging since *Henderson*, ruled that racial segregation violated the Constitution. The Court emphasized the "importance of education to our democratic society." Education was "required in the performance of our most basic public responsibilities, even service in the armed forces." It was "the very foundation of good citizenship." Because "in these days, it is doubtful that any child may reasonably be expected to succeed in life if he is denied the opportunity of an education," where a state provided public education, it is "a right which must be made available to all on equal terms." Relying on social science data detailing the harmful effects of segregation on schoolchildren, the Court concluded that "separate educational facilities are inherently unequal."[48]

Making national security arguments in civil rights cases would seem an odd thing for the Justice Department to do. The cases would presumably turn upon the Justices' reading of the Constitution and of the cases interpreting it. The Justice Department briefs were filed with a Court that had been focused for some time on questions of national security. During World War II, the Court regularly interpreted the Constitution in light of wartime necessities, foreign and domestic. For example, for a time the Court allowed schools to expel children who failed for religious reasons to salute the flag, arguing in 1940 that "national unity is the basis of national security." When the Court reversed itself in 1943, it argued that suppression of religious liberty was a step down the road to totalitarianism. National security had required the denial of a right but later served as the basis for its protection. In perhaps the most dramatic line of wartime individual rights cases, the Court upheld aspects of the program to relocate Japanese Americans to internment camps. Justice Harlan Fiske Stone, often a champion of minority rights, wrote in *Hirabayashi v. United States* that "distinctions between citizens solely because of their ancestry are by their very nature odious to free people whose institutions are founded upon the doctrine of equality." Yet Stone wrote the Court's majority opinion upholding a curfew requirement as applied to Japanese American citizens. According to Stone, "[w]e cannot close our eyes to the fact, demonstrated by experience, that in time of war residents having ethnic affiliations with an invading enemy may be a greater source of danger than those of a different ancestry." When Japanese Americans were ordered from their homes and sent to what Justice Owen Roberts called America's concentration camps, the Court majority in *Korematsu v. United States* acknowledged that this was a hardship, but "hardships are part of war."[49]

In the wartime cases, the Court's assessment of the requirements of national security and the correct balance between security and liberty came not simply from the facts of the cases and the briefs before the Court but also from what members of the Court felt that they knew about the world. In *Hirabayashi*, the Court dared not "close its eyes" to what it thought to be the danger of ethnic ties. During the Cold War, as well, members of the Court would draw upon their own understanding of the world in assessing new questions of national security. In *Dennis v. United States*, a 1951 case upholding the prosecution of Communist Party members for subversive activities, Justice Felix Frankfurter suggested in a concurring opinion that the Court was not limited to the facts presented by the parties. "We may take judicial notice that the Communist doctrines which these defendants have conspired to advocate are in the ascendency in powerful nations who cannot be acquitted of unfriendliness to the institutions of this country." The perceived threat of communism was a necessary backdrop to the case. To understand the "meaning of the menace of Communism," Frankfurter turned to the architect of containment himself, George F. Kennan, and quoted at length from an essay Kennan had published in the *New York Times* magazine.[50]

In these cases the Court was explicit about something that surely happens as a matter of course. Members of the Court bring to each case their understanding of the world and the same hopes and fears about the future that grip other mortals. Unable to step out of their own cultural and political moment, members of the Court operated during the Cold War within an environment shaped by Cold War tensions. They applied the law to the world they knew.[51] Within their world, national security was at risk, and national security would be enhanced by racial equality. In *Korematsu*, national security required discrimination; in *Brown*, national security required equality. The Justice Department hammered home in *Brown* an argument that any reader of American newspapers would already have been familiar with. The function of the briefs, therefore, was not to introduce to the Court a new idea but to underscore its role in the cases, and to emphasize the Court's responsibility. The briefs were a call to arms to enlist the Court in a project it was already engaged in: safeguarding national security in the Cold War.

The *Brown* opinion itself does not directly invoke national security and does not contain explicit Cold War rhetoric. It would, of course, be somewhat impolitic of the Court to suggest that the decision was motivated not by a dispassionate reading of the Constitution but rather by a concern about how others viewed the morality of the American form of government. *Brown* would be a more effective Cold War tool by suggesting that racial equality was simply an American constitutional principle.

There does not appear to be direct evidence that members of the Supreme Court discussed the impact of racial segregation on Cold War foreign relations in their deliberations in *Brown*, but the Justices were well aware of this issue. Justice William O. Douglas, in particular, addressed the impact of race discrimination on American prestige abroad in his writings. When Douglas went to India in 1950, the first question asked of him at his first press conference in New Delhi was "Why does America tolerate the lynching of Negroes?" In his 1951 book, *Strange Lands and Friendly People*, he wrote about the importance of Asian "color consciousness." Douglas found that in India "this color consciousness is a major influence in domestic and foreign affairs. The treatment of colored peoples by other nations is an important consideration in the warmth of India's relations to the outside world." As a result, Douglas wrote, "the attitude of the United States toward its colored minorities is a powerful factor in our relations with India."[52]

Douglas believed that a speech by Edith Sampson, an African American attorney from Chicago, "created more good will and understanding in India than any other single act by any American." Speaking in New Delhi in 1949, Sampson told her audience that she would not tolerate criticism of the United States for its civil rights record because, in the previous eighty years, African Americans had advanced further "than any similar group in the entire world." Douglas's sense of the significance of Sampson's speech was in keeping with his view that in the battle for Asia's allegiance, "it is ideas that will win, not dollars." He wrote that goodwill between peoples was ultimately of most importance to the Cold War struggle for the allegiance of other nations. "Neither wealth nor might will determine the outcome of the struggles in Asia. They will turn on emotional factors too subtle to measure. *Political alliances of an enduring nature will be built not on the power of guns or dollars, but on affection.*"[53]

An account of Douglas's later Himalayan trek reflects increasing concern about communist influence in Asia. He observed among the people "a race and color consciousness that is a dominant and often overriding factor in basic policy issues." In July 1951 in Peshawar, Pakistan, a man Douglas described as a "Mongol prince" told him that the Soviet Union would prevail over the United States in the battle for Asia in part because the United States was not viewed as an advocate of social justice. "America has the wealth and the military power," he told the Justice. "Russia has the ideas."[54]

Chief Justice Earl Warren saw things the same way. He agreed with Justice Douglas that the Cold War was a war of ideas, and he thought that the judiciary had a role to play in this battle. Justice Warren told the judges of the Fourth Circuit Court of Appeals in June of 1954 that the world needed "a sense of justice instead of a sense of might." He suggested that the American conception of justice "separates us from many other political systems of the world." If the judiciary would uphold the ideals of American justice, "you and I can make our contribution to justice at home and peace in the world." Later that year in a speech at the American Bar Association, Warren stressed that

> [o]ur American system like all others is on trial both at home and abroad. The way it works; the manner in which it solves the problems of our day; the extent to which we maintain the spirit of our Constitution with its Bill of Rights, will in the long run do more to make it both secure and the object of adulation than the number of hydrogen bombs we stockpile.

A peaceful world, he argued, "will be accomplished through ideas rather than armaments; through a sense of justice and mutual friendships rather than with guns and bombs and guided missiles." American ideals were central in the "contest for the hearts and minds of people." Chief Justice Warren's understanding of the importance of *Brown* to U.S. foreign relations would be illustrated most dramatically when President Eisenhower sent him on a goodwill tour of India in 1956. It was because Warren was the author of *Brown* that his mere presence was thought to promote good relations with that nation.[55]

Other members of the Court traveled extensively abroad in the years before *Brown v. Board of Education.* Spending time overseas during a period when American race discrimination was a prominent source of news headlines, these Justices could not have helped but recognize the international concern over American civil rights abuses. Members of the Court were also concerned about the impact of their opinions on a broader audience and so were well aware of the importance of the concern expressed by the Justice Department that an opinion by the Court upholding segregation would have negative implications for foreign relations. Justice Hugo Black once cautioned that airing "dirty linen" in Supreme Court opinions was unwise, particularly when " 'softer blows' yielded the same results without displaying ugly facts that enemies abroad could use 'to do us harm.' "[56]

When *Brown v. Board of Education* was decided, the opinion gave the U.S. government the counter to Soviet propaganda it had been looking for, and the State Department and U.S. information programs wasted no time in making use of it. Within an hour after the decision was handed down, the Voice of America broadcast the news to Eastern Europe. An analysis accompanying the "straight news broadcasts" emphasized that "the issue was settled by law under democratic processes rather than by mob rule or dictatorial fiat." The *Brown* broadcast received "top priority on the Voice's programs" and was to be "beamed possibly for several days, particularly to Russian satellites and Communist China." As the Voice of America put it: "[I]n these countries . . . the people would know nothing about the decision except what would be told them by the Communist press and radio, which you may be sure would be twisted and perverted. They have been told that the Negro in the United States is still practically a slave and a declassed citizen."[57]

The rosy picture of racial equality celebrated in the U.S. government's coverage of *Brown* seemed to fulfill a promise that had already been made in official government materials on race in America that were disseminated overseas. *Brown* was an essential and long-overdue affirmation of the story of race and American democracy that the government had already promoted abroad.

The *Brown* decision had the kind of effect on international opinion that the government had hoped for. Favorable reaction to the opinion spanned the globe. On May 21, 1954, for example, the president of the Municipal Council of Santos, São Paulo, Brazil, sent a letter to the U.S. embassy in Rio de Janeiro celebrating the *Brown* decision. The municipal council had passed a motion recording "a vote of satisfaction" with the ruling. It viewed *Brown* as "establishing the just equality of the races, essential to universal harmony and peace." The council desired that "the Consul of that great and friendly nation be officially notified of our desire to partake in the rejoicing with which the said decision was received in all corners of the civilized world."[58]

Newspapers in Africa gave extensive coverage to the decision. According to a dispatch from the American consul in Dakar, *Brown* was "greeted with enthusiasm in French West Africa although the press has expressed some slight skepticism over its implementation." *Afrique Nouvelle*, a weekly paper that was a "highly vocal opponent of all racial discrimination," carried an article under the headline "At last! Whites and Blacks in the United States on the same school benches." According to the consul, *Afrique Nouvelle* was concerned that there would be

> "desperate struggles" in some states against the decision but expresses the hope that the representatives of the negroes and the "spiritual forces" of the United States will apply themselves to giving it force and life. The article concludes by saying that "all the peoples of the world can salute with joy this measure of progress."

According to the dispatch, "other editorial comment has been similar and the news has been prominently featured in all papers received by the Consulate General since the decision was made." The American consul was pleased with this response. "[W]hile it is, of course too soon to speculate on the long range effects of the decision in this area," he wrote, "it is well to remember that school segregation more than any other single factor has lowered the prestige of the United States among Africans here and the overall results, therefore, can hardly fail to be beneficial."[59]

Not all reaction to *Brown* was enthusiastic. In South Africa, the decision "elicited general public interest, but little articulate reaction." According to the U.S. embassy in Cape Town, "[M]ost South African Whites are segregationists and, though they may see some similarity in America's color problem, regard their own racial situation as having no true parallel elsewhere. Their interest in the decisions, then, would be very academic."[60]

In India, where substantial attention was paid to American racial problems, Carl Rowan would not face the usual inquiries on his 1954 speaking tour in that country because the *Brown* decision had dampened criticism. He wrote that "at least five people in USIS and the Embassy told me I could expect less heat on the race question than previous visitors, because USIS, the Voice of America and other agencies had done a thorough job of publicizing the May 17, 1954, decision of the United States Supreme Court declaring racial segregation in public schools to be unconstitutional." When Chief Justice Earl Warren arrived in India in October 1956, his reputation had preceded him. According to the vice-chancellor of Delhi University, Warren "rose to fame in 28 minutes of that Monday afternoon as he read out his momentous decision outlawing racial segregation in American public schools."[61]

It is not surprising that Justice Warren's Indian hosts were fully aware of *Brown*. According to an August 1954 National Security Council Report, the U.S. Information Agency "exploited to the fullest the anti-segregation decision of the U.S. Supreme Court." *Brown* "was of especially far-reaching importance in Africa and India." In Africa, for example, the report noted that "the decision is regarded as the greatest event since the Emancipation Proclamation, and it removes from Communist hands the most effective anti-American weapon they had in Black Africa." To take advantage of the ruling, "[a]rticles on the decision were placed by the Agency in almost every African publication, and its post in Accra published a special edition of the American Outlook for distribution in British West Africa and Liberia." Throughout the Near East, South Asia, and Africa, "the initial effort is being followed up with reports of how the decision is being put into effect."[62]

A report on end-of-the-year activities also noted that desegregation stories were continuing to be emphasized in India and Africa. The impact of *Brown* in India came as a great relief. As a State Department document noted in 1956, "Criticism of the United States because of color discrimination practices . . . has markedly declined in recent years, partly as a result of the Supreme Court decisions in the school segregation cases."[63]

Although the initial decision to participate in *Brown* had been made by the Truman administration, the Republican National Committee (RNC) was happy to take credit for it. On May 21, 1954, the RNC issued a statement that claimed that the decision "falls appropriately within the Eisenhower Administration's many-frontal attack on global Communism. Human equality at home is a weapon of freedom. . . . It helps guarantee the Free World's cause." President Eisenhower himself was less enthusiastic, however, and he repeatedly refused to endorse *Brown* publicly.[64]

Newspapers in many parts of the United States celebrated *Brown* as affirming democratic principles. According to the *New York Herald Tribune*, the decision "squared the country's basic law with its conscience and its deepest convictions." Others considered the decision's foreign policy benefits to be of central importance. The *San Francisco Chronicle* believed that "great as the impact of the antisegregation ruling will be upon the states of the South in their struggle to make the physical and intellectual adjustment which it requires, still greater, we believe, will be its impact on South America, Africa and Asia, to this country's lasting honor and benefit." The paper believed that "to the vast majority of the peoples of the world who have colored skins, [*Brown*] will come as a blinding flash of light and hope" that "presents a new picture of America and puts this Nation in a new posture of justice." As the *Pittsburgh Courier* saw it, "[T]his clarion announcement will . . . stun and silence America's Communist traducers behind the Iron Curtain. It will effectively impress upon millions of colored people in Asia and Africa the fact that idealism and social morality can and do prevail in the United States, regardless of race, creed or color."[65]

Throughout the South, many newspapers called for calm. In North Carolina, the *Charlotte News* urged that "somehow, the South must keep the sweep of human history in proper perspective, must apply its intelligence coolly and dispassionately, and must find the resources for giving all its children equality of education." Many southern politicians, however, were less magnanimous. Governor Herman Talmadge of Georgia, who had promised that "there will never be mixed schools while I am governor," claimed that the decision "has reduced our Constitution to a mere scrap of paper." Governor James F. Byrnes of South Carolina was "shocked" at the decision but called for whites and blacks to "exercise restraint and preserve order." Although most Alabama public officials "met news of the high court's ruling with a calm wait and see attitude," one state legislator claimed, "we are going to keep every brick in our segregation wall intact." Some southerners, however, welcomed the decision. According to the *Atlanta Daily World*, "local leaders and educators" in Atlanta viewed *Brown* "as a giant step forward for democracy at home and abroad." A member of the Atlanta Board of Education proclaimed that *Brown* had "given an effective and resounding reply to the Communist criticism of our treatment of our minority group."[66]

Anticommunism in the South cut both ways. Robert Patterson, a founder of the first White Citizens Council, thought that the "dark cloud of integration" was communist-inspired. He protested "the Communist theme of all races and mongrelization" and promised that, if southerners worked together, "we will defeat this communistic disease that is being thrust upon us."[67]

The Justice Department had argued that segregation had to be abandoned because of its use in Soviet propaganda. This sort of argument was too much for Governor Herman Talmadge. In his 1955 book *You and Segregation*, Talmadge claimed that "for over a decade now, the American people have been undergoing . . . vicious and dangerous 'brain-washing' " directed by international communists. "Stop and think for a moment," he urged.

> How many times have you read in your newspapers and magazines or heard over the airwaves this question:
> "What will Russia say if our government does this?"
> How many times have you read or heard this: "What will the Reds say if we don't do this?" or "What will the Communist newspaper *Pravda* print about the United States because we do this or that?" In some instances we have shaped our national policy by trying to please the Communists.

Talmadge thought that "too many things are being done in our country and by our country because we keep looking back over our shoulders at the Communists. Who cares what the Reds say? Who cares what *Pravda* prints?" He claimed that "only one group stands to gain" from the "attacks on the Bill of Rights" that *Brown* represented. "That group is the Communist party and its fellow travelers."[68]

As Talmadge's segregationist polemic suggested, U.S. actions taken to dismantle racial segregation were motivated, in part, by what *Pravda* printed. This was not, as Talmadge suggested, because the U.S. government was procommunist, but because it was anti-communist. The simple reality of American race discrimination, and the impact of its use in communist propaganda abroad, meant that the United States could not leave these charges unanswered and still succeed with its Cold War international agenda.

Although *Brown* was heralded as a great advance, significant segregation remained in the nation's schools. The Supreme Court appeared satisfied, for the time being, with abstract pronouncements about equality. When *Brown* was decided in 1954, the Court announced the formal legal principle that racial segregation in public education violated the Fourteenth Amendment, but the Court put off the question of how the denial of equal rights might be remedied. In 1955, the Court ruled in *Brown v. Board of Education II* that lower courts should fashion relief in a way that led to desegregation "with all deliberate speed." The lower courts, in taking up *Brown II*, interpreted it as an indication that delaying school desegregation was appropriate. As a result, the rights upheld in *Brown* remained abstract rights. The Supreme Court then stayed out of the business of defining and enforcing the rights in *Brown* for several years. Although the Court would extend *Brown's* desegregation principle to other areas, in the school cases the Court, for the most part, remained silent.[69]

Some actual change had been needed to give the State Department and information programs something more convincing to work with. Although *Brown II* required no immediate, concrete steps to implement *Brown's* nonsegregation principle, American diplomats could still point to the formal right to equality established in *Brown*, and argue that change was at hand.

Following *Brown*, the world kept a close eye on U.S. race relations, but the perspective had changed for the better. In Madras, India, for example, the American consul reported that "South India interest in the progress of racial desegregation in the United States has been keen ever since the Supreme Court's decision." The Montgomery bus boycott and white resistance to Autherine Lucy's attempt to enroll at the University of Alabama were prominently covered in newspapers in that region, but the coverage reflected "the hope of most South Indians that the conflict will be resolved quickly and relatively painlessly, in compliance with the ruling of the Supreme Court."[70]

While incidents such as the Lucy case continued to captivate foreign audiences, criticism would at times be tempered with discussions of American constitutionalism. For example, an editorial in the Swiss paper *La Sentinelle* expressed outrage over acquittals in the lynching of fourteen-year-old Emmett Till in Mississippi but also praised a Florida judge who sentenced a white man to life in prison for the rape of an African American woman. This difference was attributed to "United States federalism." The paper believed that American racism existed in particular regions of the country where "habit and tradition are so deep rooted that nothing (short of a Federal law) could change such revolting trial ethics." While most stories on the Till case blistered with indignation, another Swiss paper "balanced" its coverage with a reference to *Brown*.[71]

The continuing reality of racial brutality in the American South kept American race discrimination on the pages of the foreign press, but the framework provided by *The Negro in American Life*, capped by *Brown v. Board of Education*, provided a counternarrative to Soviet exploitation of this American dilemma. National policy was said to endorse ever burgeoning equality. The basic charter of the nation embraced equal rights for all. Yet the very document that provided the foundation for the value of equality, the American Constitution, also protected freedom to dissent. Expression of racial animosity was therefore a sign of the strength, not the weakness, of the nation. America was sufficiently sure of herself that she could tolerate the free expression of dissent even as she encouraged her people on the path toward racial enlightenment.

American constitutional change, the Voice of America had proclaimed in announcing *Brown*, illustrated the superiority of democratic process over communist oppression. *Brown* and the image of American democracy it projected were thought to be of the utmost importance in a world torn by Cold War animosities. Any threat to that image was a threat to U.S. national security. Although the

American image was battered after *Brown* by the Autherine Lucy case and the murder of Emmett Till, these events would be eclipsed by a direct threat to *Brown* and to the carefully crafted image of *The Negro in American Life*. The place would be Little Rock, Arkansas, where the opening of school in 1957 precipitated a crisis within the city that would reverberate around the world.

CHAPTER 4

Holding the Line in Little Rock

Little Rock has unfortunately become a symbol of
Negro-White relations in the United States.

AMERICAN CONSULATE, LOURENÇO MARQUESZ, MOZAMBIQUE
TO DEPARTMENT OF STATE, SEPTEMBER 30, 1957[1]

The school year would not begin easily in Little Rock, Arkansas, in 1957. On September 4 of that year, nine African American students tried to enroll at Little Rock's Central High School. Their admission had been ordered by a federal district court. However, just two days earlier, Arkansas Governor Orval Faubus declared that the students' enrollment threatened "imminent danger of tumult, riot and breach of the peace and the doing of violence to persons and property." He proclaimed a state of emergency and ordered the Arkansas National Guard into service. These troops surrounded Central High School on September 4 and turned the students away as they tried to enter the school.[2]

What transpired that day would capture the attention of the international media and of President Dwight D. Eisenhower. School desegregation in Little Rock was no longer a local or state issue, but a critical national problem.[3]

As the *Arkansas Gazette* reported it,

> The first Negro applicant to try to enroll at Little Rock Central High School . . . , Elizabeth Eckford, 15, was twice blocked from entering the grounds, walked calmly down two blocks then sat out 35 minutes of vocal abuse while waiting for a bus to go home. . . . When she approached Guardsmen at the corner they drew together and blocked her entrance to the sidewalk.[4]

Eckford was harassed in front of television cameras as "a crowd of 200 saw her and rushed to the scene." A white woman, Grace Lorch, ultimately came to her defense and boarded a bus with Eckford, taking her away from the scene. Seven of the nine students arrived together and, on orders of the governor, were also turned away.[5]

Governor Faubus was something of a latecomer to resistance. Little Rock had a reputation as a progressive southern community, and Faubus had been thought of as a moderate. In contrast to Georgia Governor Herman Talmadge, Faubus had given no speeches of defiance after *Brown* was decided. Instead, he gave African Americans a role in the state Democratic leadership during the 1954 gubernatorial campaign. In addition, there was progress, albeit with mixed success, toward desegregation in other communities in Arkansas after 1954. Faubus's most direct statements on school desegregation prior to Little Rock were to declare the issue a local one, to be handled by local school boards.[6]

As school prepared to open in 1957, however, Faubus announced his "prayerful" decision to call in the troops. "They will act not as segregationists or integrationists," he pledged, "but as soldiers called to active duty to carry out their assigned tasks." Their duty was to maintain order, but, Faubus continued, it would not be possible to maintain order "if forcible integration is carried out tomorrow in the schools of this community."[7]

A school desegregation plan had been developed by the Little Rock school board. As did many other communities, Little Rock set about exploring how it might implement *Brown v. Board of Education* immediately after that decision was handed down. Community support for compliance with *Brown* was evident when the school board was reelected after the desegregation plan was announced. With desegregation set to begin with the opening of the 1957–58 school year, however, the opposition became more active and vocal. Mrs. Clyde D. Thomason, a member of a Little Rock mothers' committee opposed to desegregation, filed suit in state court in August 1957, seeking an injunction against the plan. Based on unsubstantiated testimony by Governor Faubus of an increase in gun sales in the Little Rock area, the state court issued an injunction on August 29. The school board then turned to the federal district court. As fate would have it, the case came before a nonsouthern judge. Judge Ronald N. Davies from South Dakota was sitting by designation in federal district court in Arkansas. Judge Davies ordered desegregation to go forward. When Faubus called out the National Guard on September 2, the school board returned to the district court. Judge Davies noted that "[t]he chief executive of Little Rock has stated that the Little Rock police have not had a single case of inter-racial violence reported to them and that there has been no indication from sources available to him that there would be violence in regard to this situation" and denied the school board's petition to delay desegregation.[8]

As the crisis deepened, the federal government was drawn in. Judge Davies called upon U.S. Attorney General Herbert Brownell to investigate allegations that African American students had been denied admission to Central High. President Eisenhower ultimately found himself involved in the crisis as well. While Faubus telegraphed the president complaining of federal interference and concerns that his phone lines were being tapped by federal agents, Little Rock Mayor Woodrow Wilson Mann urged Eisenhower to become more involved. Eisenhower's response to Faubus was to emphasize that "when I became President, I took an oath to support and defend the Constitution of the United States. The only assurance I can give you is that the Federal Constitution will be upheld by me by every legal means at my command."[9]

For the next three weeks, desegregation in Little Rock was at an impasse. As school went on at Central High, the "Little Rock Nine" stayed home, unable to pass through the national guardsmen still surrounding the school.[10] The Little Rock crisis was to become a defining moment. It was not the first civil rights event in Eisenhower's presidency to capture widespread international attention. Following the 1954 *Brown* decision, Emmet Till's brutal murder in 1955 had outraged the world, the 1955–56 Montgomery bus boycott had focused international media attention on civil rights protest, and Autherine Lucy's attempt to cross the color line at the University of Alabama in 1956 had become a civil rights crisis with international impact. Little Rock, however, was a crisis of such magnitude for worldwide perceptions of race and American democracy that it would become the reference point for the future. Later presidents, facing crises of their own, would try their best to avoid "another Little Rock." Foreign commentators would judge American progress by how far the nation had come from Little Rock. If slavery had been the benchmark against which American racial progress had been measured in the past, Little Rock provided a new measure, as the Cold War required more of the leader of the free world.

When school first opened in September 1957, the *Arkansas Gazette* had expressed its confidence that "the world will see that we are lawabiding people."[11] The world would, unfortunately, draw a different lesson from Little Rock.

On September 11, the people of Little Rock learned that even Secretary of State John Foster Dulles was concerned about the difficulties in their city. The *Arkansas Gazette* quoted Dulles as saying that the Little Rock crisis, along with school desegregation battles elsewhere in the South, "are not helpful to the influence of the United States abroad." The *Gazette* reported that "Radio Moscow has been chirping happily about the troubles of integration," and the Little Rock crisis was a particular subject of its attention. President Eisenhower later described the situation in his memoirs. He wrote that Faubus's "outrageous action" in Little Rock

> called to my mind the first act of the Rodgers and Hammerstein musical *South Pacific* in which the hero, a Frenchman, mistakenly calls the heroine's American hometown "Small Rock." Before September 1957, that line was meaningless to

foreign audiences. Thereafter, no one anywhere would miss the point: the name of Little Rock, Arkansas, would become known around the world.

According to Eisenhower, "Overseas, the mouthpieces of Soviet propaganda in Russia and Europe were blaring out that 'anti-Negro violence' in Little Rock was being 'committed with the clear connivance of the United States government.' "[12]

Coverage of the Little Rock crisis had blanketed the international media beginning with the incidents of September 4. Elizabeth Eckford's trials appeared on front pages around the world. The London *Times*, the *Times of India*, the *Tanganyika Standard*, the *South China Morning Post*, and many other papers carried stories virtually every day for the entire month of September. According to the U.S. embassy in Brussels, Little Rock "has been followed in the Belgian press with far greater interest than any other American domestic issue in recent years. The more dramatic aspects of the case, including photographs of beatings and other violence, have usually been given greater prominence in the press than leading local or foreign news articles." International coverage of the crisis was so noteworthy to U.S. newswriters that there was widespread coverage in U.S. papers of the coverage abroad.[13]

On September 6, for example, the *Times of India* carried a story on its front page under the title "Armed Men Cordon Off White School: Racial Desegregation in Arkansas Prevented." That same day the front page of the *Tanganyika Standard* declared, "Troops Stop Negroes Going to School." "Little Rock Troubled" proclaimed a page-one headline in the *East African Standard*, followed by a front-page story the next day: "Eisenhower Intervenes as School Bars Negroes." The *Egyptian Gazette* repeatedly placed Little Rock in the context of school desegregation struggles elsewhere in the American South. The paper's September 5 front-page story outlining the facts of the exclusion of the Little Rock Nine from school was tempered with news of successful school desegregation efforts in Van Buren and Ozark, Arkansas, and Louisville, Kentucky.[14]

The September 4, 1957, edition of the London *Times* described Eisenhower's reaction to the Little Rock crisis with some skepticism:

Questions about the action taken by the state government in Arkansas brought forth from the President only a restatement of the axioms on which he has based his own "gradualist" approach to the problem. "You cannot change people's hearts merely by laws," he observed, and the Supreme Court's ruling in 1954 therefore had caused "emotional difficulties" for both sides. Southerners, he implied, were genuinely frightened by what they thought would lead to "a mongrelization of the races."

Difficult though the problem might be, he added, "We are going to whip it in the long run by Americans being true to themselves, and not by law"—a comment that seems to be as wide of the real issue as was Polonius's advice. Who is to say that the southerners—who see in attempts to integrate their schools a threat to the whole social fabric of their communities, and who try to prevent it by every means—are not being true to themselves?[15]

International papers often commented on the international attention itself. According to the *Montreal Star*, "The world watches Negroes in the United States going to Southland schools under the muzzles of loaded rifles, just ninety-four years after the Emancipation Proclamation was signed by another Republican, Abraham Lincoln." In London, the *Times* spoke of "the lonely, isolated negro children whose pictures have touched and shamed millions, in the United States and abroad." Student organizations and other groups around the world also registered their support for the Little Rock Nine and their opposition to Faubus's actions.[16]

Dutch papers noted that Little Rock harmed American prestige. In Stockholm, Sweden, *Svenska Dagbladet* wrote that the events in Arkansas "will be watched with concern throughout [the] Western world." If the federal government did not take a strong stand, it would pose a serious threat "not only to President Eisenhower's personal prestige but also to [the] position of [the] U.S. in [the] eyes [of the] free world." According to the *Irish Times*, the crisis had "given Communist propagandists the text for innumerable sermons to coloured peoples everywhere." The Swiss press expressed dismay over the "incalculable harm done" by Little Rock to the "Occidental position throughout [the] non-European world."[17]

At home, the impact of the Little Rock crisis on world opinion was widely understood. Harry S. Ashmore wrote in 1958 that Little Rock "has become a symbol that arouses strong emotions among people everywhere in the world." The crisis "was about as handy a package as the Russians have had handed them since they set out to woo the colored peoples of the earth." William Ross of Brooklyn, New York, wrote to Governor Faubus that he was "furnishing the Communists with priceless propaganda material and hurting our standing with Asian and African countries."[18]

It was a short step, in the consciousness of 1950s Americans, from international criticism to Cold War implications. U.S. editorial writers and political figures regularly noted the negative impact Little Rock was thought to have on the nation's standing in the Cold War. The Soviet Union's extensive use of Little Rock in anti-American propaganda—often simply republishing facts disseminated by U.S. news sources—reinforced the concern that Little Rock redounded to the benefit of America's opponents in the battle for the hearts and minds of peoples around the world.[19]

For example, *Komosomolskaya Pravda* carried a Little Rock story under a banner headline declaring "Troops Advance Against Children!" According to the *Current Digest of the Soviet Press*, related articles were accompanied by photographs including "[a] photo of the national guard unit in Little Rock directing a Negro girl away from the high school." The Soviet paper *Izvestia* suggested that "[r]ight now, behind the facade of the so-called 'American democracy,' a tragedy is unfolding which cannot but arouse ire and indignation in the heart of every honest man." The tragedy was that in the southern states of the United States

> fascist thugs of the Ku Klux Klan are organizing a savage hunt for Negro children because the latter plan to sit in the same classrooms with white boys and girls. National guard soldiers and policemen armed to the teeth bar Negro children from entering the schools, threaten them with bayonets and tear-gas bombs and encourage hooligans to engage in violence with impunity.[20]

Careful, the Walls Have Ears
September 11, 1957. (Reprinted with permission from *Arkansas Democrat-Gazette*)

In Little Rock, "troops in full battle dress, armed with rifles with unsheathed bayonets and with tear-gas bombs, surrounded the high school to 'defend' it against nine Negro children who wished to study there." These circumstances raised questions about the American form of government.

The patrons of Governor Faubus . . . who dream of nooses and dynamite for persons with different-colored skins, advocates of hooliganism who throw rocks at defenseless Negro children—these gentlemen have the audacity to talk about "democracy" and speak as supporters of "freedom." In fact it is impossible to imagine a greater insult to democracy and freedom than an American diplomat's speech from the tribu-

Right into Their Hands

September 11, 1957. Editorial cartoons around the nation expressed concern that the world was listening in on the school desegregation crisis in Little Rock and that the crisis provided communists with an effective propaganda weapon. (Reprinted with permission from *Oakland Tribune*)

nal of the U.S. General Assembly, a speech in which Washington was pictured as the "champion" of the rights of the Hungarian people.

Izvestia believed that "the events in the U.S. South cannot remain a matter of indifference. The tale of the American racists, who abuse human dignity and stoop to the level of animals, must be told." Since the United States promoted democracy abroad, it was "even more impossible to remain silent when these gentlemen attempt to act as the world's mentors."[21]

Americans were well aware of the existence of such coverage. Drawing upon this widespread understanding, a political cartoon in the September 7 *Minneapolis Star* suggested that the "Three 'R's" in Arkansas were "Race Hate," "Rights Denial," and "Red Propaganda Boost."[22]

Governor Faubus's actions were seen to be such a strong aid to the Soviet propaganda machine that *Confidential* magazine suggested that the governor's role might actually be part of a communist plot and the governor a communist agent. "The Commies Trained Gov. Faubus of Arkansas," declared a full-page headline framing a photo of the governor. According to the article,

> When Governor Orval Faubus of Arkansas openly defied the government of the United States on the school integration issue, he handed to the Communists the handsomest gift they could possibly have received from any American. Four-fifths of the people of the world are colored. All over the world—in Asia and Europe, in Africa and the Middle East—the Communists have invoked the name of Little Rock to tell colored people that the United States is a land of lynching and repression. . . . [T]hanks to Faubus' actions and the Red propaganda that plays upon them, no American can travel abroad without being asked by every foreigner about Little Rock.

For *Confidential*, these circumstances naturally led to the question, Was Faubus "unwittingly playing a pro-Communist game? Or is he deliberately aiding the Soviet propaganda machine?"[23]

The state of Arkansas had its own suspicions of communist influence, which culminated in a hearing held before the Special Education Committee of the Arkansas Legislative Council in December 1958. State Attorney General Bruce Bennett told the committee that the hearings would prove that Little Rock was one of the "predetermined trouble areas . . . designated officially by the Communist Party many years ago to be developed for trouble purposes." He argued that "from 1928 to 1958 an intensive communist conspiracy climaxed in Little Rock, and . . . the purpose of these incidents is to attract and use the Negro—not to help the Negro." The NAACP had been heavily involved in promoting school desegregation in the city, and Bennett believed that "[m]any of the officials of this organization both local and national, have an almost incredible tie-in with Communist and Communist front organizations." Local organizer Daisy Bates and legal director Thurgood Marshall were among the NAACP leaders singled out for their allegedly subversive connections.[24]

U.S. embassies around the globe sent dispatches to the State Department detailing the international impact of events in Little Rock. In Copenhagen, the U.S. embassy telegraphed the State Department that the mission was "embarrassed over heavy local press play and general Danish reaction [to the] Little Rock race problems." In Lourenço Marques, Mozambique, the American consul warned that the crisis had "unfortunately become a symbol of Negro-White relations in the United States." He believed that "[o]ur moral standing has been very considerably damaged and . . . any pretension of an American to advise any European Government on African affairs . . . would be hypocrisy." In the Netherlands, the Dutch reportedly reacted to Little Rock with "quiet indignation," while some saw in Little Rock "the well-worn analogy between Hitlerian methods and the activities of American racists." The fact that many thought there was "very little difference between the two" was "what hurts America in the eyes of the world." In São Paulo, Brazil, a legislator took the United States to task in the legislative assembly.

> The so-called American democracy has been able by means of the world press to hold itself out as a standard for other peoples but we, the Brazilians, will always reject racial fights and never will agree that any restriction may be imposed on a Brazilian whatever his origin simply because he was born with a black skin.[25]

According to the U.S. embassy in Paramaribo, Surinam, press reports had led to "an open reinforcement of suspicions about some of the moral emphasis which the United States places on world affairs problems." As a result of Little Rock "[t]he reporting officer has heard more volunteered negative criticism in the last week about race matters in the United States than he has in the year he has been here." According to the officer, this was "not helpful to our national standing in Surinam."[26]

Not all nations were critical. The U.S. embassy in Bonn reported that Germans did not feel it was their place to cast aspersions on the United States, and press coverage, with the exception of "tabloids and east zone press" was not sensationalized. "Persecution and extermination of millions of Jews do not permit us [to] blame Americans or report with indignation events [in] Arkansas." The U.S. embassy in South Africa reported that "[t]he effect of Little Rock, of course was to confirm to South African 'Apartheid' supporters—most white South Africans—that the forces against integration were gaining in the United States." In South Africa, a nation "caught up in their own apartheid policy," whites "appear to derive some inner consolation and a feeling of greater support for their own ideas out of incidents such as Little Rock."[27]

As the world looked on, governor Faubus dug in. On September 10, the Governor received a summons ordering him to appear in federal court and "show cause why he should not be charged with contempt." Faubus then let President Eisenhower's staff know that he was looking for a way out. Eisenhower and Faubus met at Eisenhower's vacation retreat in Newport, Rhode Island, on September 14. In private, Eisenhower stressed the importance of a peaceful resolution of the crisis and told Faubus that he wished to avoid embarrassing him publicly. When the meeting ended, the president believed that he had received an assurance from Governor Faubus not to violate the orders of the court.[28]

As Faubus returned to Arkansas, the foreign and domestic press published smiling photos of the governor and the president. Eisenhower believed, and the nation hoped, that the men had come to an agreement that would end the impasse. Yet within a couple of hours, plans for a joint statement started to unravel. Faubus later insisted that "he would remove the guardsmen only on condition that the Justice Department recommend a delay in desegregation pending a Supreme Court test of the state's interposition law." In spite of this clear defiance, Eisenhower remained reluctant to intervene.[29]

As the Arkansas National Guard continued to encircle Central High, the London *Times* reported the president's "deep disappointment that voluntary means had not been found to comply with the court's orders" yet noted that "many people feel that a greater exertion of authority by the President might have avoided a head-on collision in the courts."[30] The *Times* blamed Faubus's personal ambition and desire for reelection to a third term for the crisis in Little Rock. Yet the paper commented that moderates in Arkansas were angry about "the part President Eisenhower is playing in this bitter controversy—or rather not playing." There was "a feeling of helplessness—of betrayal almost—among moderates, who feel that there is no one but the President who can speak clearly and strongly for them. The sour joke is current: 'If President Eisenhower were alive all this wouldn't have happened.' "[31]

The pressure on Faubus from the president was followed by a federal court order. On September 20, Judge Davies enjoined Governor Faubus from interfering with desegregation. If Faubus wanted to call in the troops, "the proper use of that power in this instance was to maintain the Federal Court in the exercise of its jurisdiction . . . and not to nullify it."[32]

Faubus responded to the court order by withdrawing the National Guard, then promptly leaving town. At the Southern Governors' Conference at Sea Island, Georgia, Faubus told a reporter that he expected violence if integration were attempted. Back in Little Rock, Mayor Mann urged residents to be calm.[33]

The morning of September 23, 1957, came to be known as "Black Monday" in Little Rock. *Sacramento Bee* reporter Relman Morin described a "frightening sight." Eight African American students had walked calmly into school that morning as the city police held back the crowds surrounding Central High. Momentarily distracted by a diversion, the crowd soon realized that the students had entered the school, and mayhem broke loose. The crowd had already beaten three "Yankee" reporters for *Life* magazine and four African American reporters whom they believed had intentionally created a diversion to enable the students to enter the school. Now the crowd battled the police.[34]

Concerned that growing crowds would be even more threatening to the safety of the students by the end of the school day, the mayor, the school superintendent, and the assistant police chief decided to remove them in the middle of the day. As one of the African American students, Melba Pattillo Beals, remembered it, the students were hurried down a dark passageway to the basement of the school. There they got into two cars driven by frightened white men. "Listen to your driver's instructions," the assistant police chief warned the students. "Your lives depend on it." The students were ordered to put their heads down, and the cars sped past the crowds and beyond the reach of rocks and sticks hurled in their direction. The students made it safely home.[35]

From his Newport retreat, President Eisenhower decided that the time had come for action. He issued a proclamation finding a "wilful obstruction of justice" in Little Rock and commanding those engaged in obstruction of justice to cease and desist. The president thought that "every right-thinking citizen will hope that the American sense of justice and fair play will prevail in this case. It will be a sad day for this country—both at home and abroad—if school children can safely attend their classes only under the protection of armed guards."[36]

The following day, crowds surrounded the school, and the Little Rock Nine waited at home. Mayor Mann sent the president a telegram saying that "[t]he immediate need for federal troops is urgent." He warned that the "[s]ituation is out of control and police cannot disperse the mob." Mann urged, "I am pleading to you as President of the United States in the interest of humanity law and order and because of democracy world wide to provide the necessary federal troops within several hours." By this time, for Eisenhower, "the question had become not whether to act, but what force I should use to insure execution of the court's order." Eisenhower decided to rely on federal troops, and by that afternoon, five hundred paratroopers from the 101st Airborne Division were stationed in the city. Another five hundred arrived later in the day. Armed with bayonets, the troops ringed Central High School on the morning of September 25. From the perspective of Governor Faubus and his supporters, the "occupation" of Little Rock had begun.[37]

Only two months before, in July 1957, Eisenhower had told reporters, "I can't imagine any set of circumstances that would ever induce me to send Federal troops . . . into any area to enforce the orders of a federal court."[38] What had caused the president to change his mind so dramatically?

Paratroopers from the 101st Airborne Division escort nine African American students into Central High School in Little Rock, Arkansas, September 25, 1957. (UPI/CORBIS-BETTMANN)

Eisenhower's decision to act was not based on support for desegregation. He was not a supporter of court-ordered desegregation or of the *Brown* decision itself. Eisenhower communicated his feelings about the desegregation cases to Chief Justice Earl Warren while the cases were pending. He invited Warren to a dinner at the White House. Following the meal, Warren later wrote, Eisenhower took him by the arm, and "as we walked along, speaking of the Southern states in the segregation cases, he said, 'These are not bad people. All they are concerned about is to see that their sweet little girls are not required to sit alongside some big overgrown Negroes.' " Justice Warren felt that President Eisenhower's lack of support for *Brown* contributed to the resistance to the decision. He believed that "much of our racial strife could have been avoided" if the president had stood up for the principal of equality. The nation seemed to agree with Justice Warren's assessment. According to a 1955 Gallup Poll, one of the main criticisms of Eisenhower's leadership was that he "encourages segregation." When *Brown* was decided, Eisenhower was asked whether he had "any advice to give the South as to just how to react to the recent Supreme Court decision banning segregation." The president responded, "Not in the slightest." He thought that South Carolina Governor James Byrnes "made a very fine statement when he said let us be calm, and let us be reasonable, and let us look this thing in the face." As for his own role, Eisenhower said, "The Supreme Court has spoken, and I am sworn to uphold the Constitutional process in this country. And I am trying—I will obey it."[39]

Notwithstanding his lack of enthusiasm for *Brown*, Eisenhower became deeply involved in managing the Little Rock crisis. He was concerned, in part, with the threat the crisis posed for the rule of law. As Eisenhower described it in his memoirs, "[t]hat situation, if a successful defiance of federal court orders continued, could lead to a breakdown of law and order in a widening area." Eisenhower was also angry with Governor Faubus, who he felt had defied him. But the breakdown of law and order and the management of an insubordinate governor were not all that was at stake. In addition, Eisenhower wrote, "around the world it could continue to feed the mill of Soviet propagandists who by word and picture were telling the world of the 'racial terror' in the United States." It was a mix of factors, domestic and international, that led to Eisenhower's extraordinary action in Little Rock.[40]

The president's top aides emphasized the international impact of the Little Rock crisis. The U.S. ambassador to the United Nations, Henry Cabot Lodge, wrote President Eisenhower that:

> Here at the United Nations I can see clearly the harm that the riots in Little Rock are doing to our foreign relations. More than two-thirds of the world is non-white and the reactions of the representatives of these people is easy to see. I suspect that we lost several votes on the Chinese communist item because of Little Rock.[41]

Secretary of State John Foster Dulles was "sick at heart" over the Little Rock crisis. On September 24, 1957, as President Eisenhower was returning to Washington to deliver his public address on Little Rock, Dulles put in a call to Attorney General Herbert Brownell. As the two exchanged concerns about Little Rock, Dulles told Brownell that "this situation was ruining our foreign policy. The effect of this in Asia and Africa will be worse for us than Hungary was for the Russians." Dulles thought that "there should be an awareness of the effect of all this." Brownell indicated that he had taken Eisenhower "the USIA report which mentioned the use Nasser and Khrushchev were making of it." He believed that President Eisenhower "was very alert to this aspect." In addition "[t]here has been considerable in the papers since then." Brownell believed that Secretary Dulles's "part of the problem would not be solved" by Eisenhower's decision to send in the troops, "although firm action would certainly help a lot." According to records of the phone call, the men "discussed the seriousness of the situation at some length." Brownell asked Dulles to look over a draft of the president's speech, which Dulles agreed to do.[42]

Later in the day, Dulles called Eisenhower with suggestions to "put in a few more sentences in this draft speech emphasizing the harm done abroad." Dulles dictated the following statement to the president's secretary:

It would be difficult to exaggerate the harm that is being done to the prestige and influence, and indeed to the safety, of our nation in the world. Our enemies are gloating over this incident and using it everywhere to misprepresent [sic] our nation. We are portrayed as a violator of the standard of conduct which the peoples of the world united to proclaim in the Charter of the United Nations whereby the peoples re-affirmed "faith in fundamental human rights and in the dignity and worth of the human person" and did so "without distinction as to race, sex, language, or religion."

According to the draft language, Eisenhower would "beg the people of Arkansas to erase the blot upon the fair name and high honor of our nation." This was a time when the nation "faces the gravest of peril" from enemies abroad, and "patriotism cannot be reconciled with conduct which injures grievously our nation."[43]

The president returned to Washington to take his case to the nation. He hoped that speaking "from the house of Lincoln, of Jackson and of Wilson" would best convey his sadness and "the firmness with which I intend to pursue this course." Eisenhower's televised address drew heavily upon Dulles's suggestions. He reminded the nation of the Supreme Court's ruling in *Brown*. "Our personal opinions about the decision have no bearing on the matter of enforcement," he suggested. "[T]he responsibility and authority of the Supreme Court to interpret the Constitution are very clear." Many southern communities had begun the process of desegregation and in doing so had "demonstrated to the world that we are a nation in which laws, not men, are supreme." The president regretted that "this truth—the cornerstone of our liberties—was not observed" in Little Rock. Because of resistance to court-ordered desegregation in that city, "both the law and the national interest demanded that the President take action."[44]

According to the president,

A foundation of our American way of life is our national respect for law. In the South, as elsewhere, citizens are keenly aware of the tremendous disservice that has been done to the people of Arkansas in the eyes of the nation, and that has been done to the nation in the eyes of the world.

This situation had perilous implications.

> At a time when we face grave situations abroad because of the hatred that Communism bears toward a system of government based on human rights, it would be difficult to exaggerate the harm that is being done to the prestige and influence, and indeed to the safety, of our nation and the world.
>
> Our enemies are gloating over this incident and using it everywhere to misrepresent our whole nation. We are portrayed as a violator of those standards of conduct which the peoples of the world united to proclaim in the Charter of the United Nations.[45]

The president called upon the citizens of Arkansas to put an end to obstruction of the law in their state.

> If resistance to the Federal Court orders ceases at once, the further presence of Federal troops will be unnecessary and the City of Little Rock will return to its normal habits of peace and order and a blot upon the fair name and high honor of our nation in the world will be removed.
>
> Thus will be restored the image of America and of all its parts as one nation, indivisible, with liberty and justice for all.[46]

Ending with the exact language of the last words of the Pledge of Allegiance, Eisenhower appealed to patriotism. Little Rock was not simply an internal dispute: the nation, the national image, and national security were at stake. Patriotism required that the needs of the nation be placed ahead of sectional loyalties.

Secretary Dulles was pleased with the president's speech. But as Attorney General Brownell had suggested, Dulles's "part of the problem" was not yet solved, and Little Rock's impact on U.S. foreign affairs continued to be felt.[47]

The president's address to the nation was also an address to the world, and it was widely covered in the international press. Eisenhower's actions were widely and favorably viewed as safeguarding the image of democracy. In the Netherlands, the independent newspaper *Algemeen Dagblad* announced that "Eisenhower's airborn troops again are bearers of democracy's banner on which [is] inscribed [the] words 'human rights,'" just as they had been during World War II. The largest newspaper in Wales praised Eisenhower for demonstrating "the ultimate political courage." In Brazil, the Bahia state legislature passed a motion approving of the president's action. In Hong Kong, the *South China Morning Post* found Eisenhower's action to be "firm and decisive." It was "an answer both to legal quibblers and to the lawless few whose conduct unjustly exposed Americans as a whole to new propaganda blasts from the Kremlin." On September 30, the *Egyptian Gazette* ran a story devoted to a commentary in the British *Observer.* That paper called Eisenhower's actions "belated but strong" and claimed that although a crisis like Little Rock could not happen in Britain, "it could happen in Kenya or Central Africa where the British Government has certain rights and duties comparable" to the U.S. government's relationship to the State of Arkansas.[48]

According to a front-page editorial in the Luxembourg paper *Tageblatt,* Eisenhower had "save[d] not only a principle but the soul of a country which, if it had permitted the situation in Little Rock to continue, could no longer have laid claim to being the leader of the free bloc." Although Little Rock had made a "deep impression" on the Portuguese in Mozambique, the one "ray of light" was Eisenhower's stand, demonstrating "a determination to see to it that American democracy is no farce." Eisenhower's action was seen as upholding the rule of law and maintaining the principles laid down by the Supreme Court. According to an editorial in the Brazilian *Diario de Noticias,* "the drastic step of the American President will not surprise those who know the respect for law in that country and the part which the Supreme Federal Tribunal plays in the structure of American political life."[49]

Political parties of all kinds came out in support of Eisenhower. In Uganda, the secretary general of the United Congress Party asked the American consul to "convey to the President and the people of the United States the sincere appreciation of the United Congress

Party of Uganda for the President's sustained efforts and firm stand on the question of enforcing the Ruling of the Supreme Court against segregation in American schools." Even communist leaders could find favor with Eisenhower's action. Costa Rican Communist Party leader Manuel Mora Valverde suggested that "[n]ot every man . . . would have dared to take the step taken by Eisenhower. . . . I am of the personal opinion that Mr. Eisenhower is worthy of admiration as a man, even though he continues to be the President of an imperialist power." There were, of course, dissenters. In China, the *People's Daily* thought that the "U.S. government did not really intend to protect black people's rights, but to hoodwink the public domestically and abroad."[50]

U.S. officials tried to put the best face possible on the nation's handling of the Little Rock crisis. AFL-CIO President George Meany, U.S. delegate to the United Nations General Assembly's Social and Humanitarian Committee, told that committee that the Little Rock crisis was "only one episode in a peaceful revolution which had been going on for several years." In response to widespread criticism in France, Secretary Dulles sent a telegram to the U.S. embassy in Paris on September 30 with the text of a statement that embassy personnel could use in reporting on Little Rock. The statement stressed that

> there is one essential point to be drawn from the events at Little Rock: that is, that the full force of the United Government [sic], both moral and physical, has been directed to enforcing the law and order and to ensure the carrying out of the decision of the Supreme Court. Although we deplore the events themselves and make no RPT no effort to excuse those who have caused them, it nevertheless has appeared to me worthy of note here that our national authority is being used to ensure the education of children, in dramatic contrast to the uses to which Soviet armed might was put last year in Hungary.[51]

Although many saw a foreign affairs boost from Eisenhower's actions, Georgia Senator Herman Talmadge drew upon international affairs in quite a different way. "We still mourn the destruction of the sovereignty of Hungary by Russian tanks and troops in the streets of Budapest," he said. "We are now threatened with the spectacle of the President of the United States using tanks and troops in the streets of Little Rock to destroy the sovereignty of the state of Arkansas." Senator Richard Russell of Georgia called the action "totalitarian." "Our founding fathers . . . would turn over in their graves" upon hearing of it, he insisted. Similarly, Senator James O. Eastland of Mississippi considered the action an attempt to "destroy the social order of the South" and thought that "[n]othing like this was ever attempted in Russia."[52]

As Orval Faubus would have it, his own vision of democracy was implicated by the Little Rock crisis. In an address that was nationally broadcast while federal troops ringed Central High, the governor asked, "In the name of God whom we all revere, in the name of liberty we hold so dear, in the name of decency which we all cherish, what is happening in America?" Faubus claimed that federal intervention in Little Rock had resulted in a denial of constitutional rights to the people of Arkansas.[53]

The dispute between Eisenhower and Faubus about the meaning of democracy paralleled a debate about the nature of the U.S. system of government in the international press. What was the nation's true nature? Was the face of democracy represented by Orval Faubus and the white women and men who screamed and struggled with authorities upon hearing the horrifying news that African American students had entered Central High School? Or was the face of democracy that of President Eisenhower, the general who had helped lead the Allies through World War II and who now seemed poised to lead his nation through another important test?

The intensity of the international media coverage of Little Rock finally declined in October 1957, and observers drew lessons from the crisis. In the Netherlands, *De Maasbode* believed that the Little Rock crisis "must be seen as one of last violent convulsions of [a] system and mentality that is [a] thing of past."[54]

According to *Hindustan Times* reporter Michael Owen, the furor over Little Rock has had repercussion all over the world, causing a further denigration of American democratic stock in Asia and once again posing the old question that if this is how America feels towards those whose pigmentation of skin is not the shade of their own, that if the Governor of a comparatively unimportant state can defy the Supreme Court of the nation, then what exactly are the real feelings of Americans towards Asians, brown, black or yellow?[55]

In Indonesia, Owen wrote, one newspaper asked "whether Governor Faubus should not be hauled before the Un-American Activities Committee for alienating half of the world from the U.S." In Japan, Owen reported, "a conservative citizen of some prominence raised the question: 'If Americans can regard Negroes as inferior, how do they really regard Asians?' "[56]

Owen believed that Eisenhower's actions did not "appreciably mitigate the international effects of the affair." The president's statements had not "[r]esulted in reassuring Asia that their ingrained suspicion that the shape of American democracy is in reality only 'skin-deep,' is unfounded." He felt that "[t]he periodical occurrence of episodes like that at Little Rock are not only subversive to international concord and understanding but also serve to drive more and more Asians to the conclusion that there cannot be, at least not in this sorry generation, any real meeting ground between Occident and Orient."[57]

Meanwhile, President Eisenhower had difficulty deflecting attention from Little Rock. The *South China Morning Post* reported that on October 3, "Reporters attempting to question the President on Foreign Affairs had a difficult time at to-day's 28-minute press conference because of the intense pre-occupation of most correspondents over the situation in Little Rock. . . . Out of 17 questions asked at the press conference, 13 concerned the Little Rock situation."[58]

As Central High settled into an extraordinary school year under military guard, Arthur Larson, director of the U.S. Information Agency (USIA), suggested to the president that he send an open letter to the Central High School students. In Larson's view, "the students themselves are the best source of hope in this situation."

Larson thought that Eisenhower should encourage students to act in a "democratic manner that does justice to our proud heritage." Such efforts would mean that "the good name of Arkansas . . . could be held up for all to admire. At the same time you would help to show the world that freedom and equality not only are enshrined in our laws but also dwell in the hearts of our people." In this and other instances, Eisenhower declined to follow his staff's advice to appeal personally to members of the Little Rock community.[59]

As a semblance of order, if not tranquillity, descended at last on Little Rock, the military presence declined. The 101st Airborne would leave the city by early November, and the Arkansas National Guard deployment was decreased by four-fifths. The remaining troops would patrol Central High School for the rest of the school year. Then, during the summer of 1958, the future of integration in Little Rock was placed, again, in the hands of the courts. On June 20, 1958, District Judge Harry J. Lemley, who had replaced Judge Davies, ordered that desegregation be postponed for two-and-a-half years. Judge Lemley agreed with the school board, which had sought the postponement, that the students' education suffered under the difficult conditions Central High had endured that school year. According to Judge Lemley, the difficulties in Little Rock

> did not stem from mere lawlessness. . . . Rather, the source of
> the trouble was the deep seated popular opposition in Little
> Rock to the principle of integration, which, as is known, runs
> counter to the pattern of southern life which has existed for
> over three hundred years. The evidence also shows that to
> this opposition was added the conviction of many of the peo-
> ple of Little Rock, that the Brown decisions do not truly rep-
> resent the law.

Providing a "breathing spell" in Little Rock was, in Lemley's view, an appropriate exercise of the court's discretion and consistent with the Supreme Court's requirement in *Brown v. Board of Education II* of desegregation "with all deliberate speed." [60]

Many reacted with outrage and disappointment to the district court's ruling. Maurice H. Goodenough of Clichy-sous-Bois,

France, expressed his views directly to Judge Lemley. "Those who welcome that kind of publicity can thank you for having put Little Rock back on the front pages of the world's newspapers," he wrote the judge.

> Last fall, here in France, the population was literally "lapping up" their daily portion of Little Rock. They were following it with the same interest they give to their national sports, and I assume that other peoples around the globe were doing the same. Little Rock had become America's entry in an international exhibit.
>
> You must be very ignorant of where America is in relationship to time and space; if not, you must be willfully seeking the loss of America's prestige and position, with its ultimate disasterous [sic] consequences.[61]

Civil rights leaders A. Philip Randolph, Lester B. Granger, Reverend Martin Luther King Jr., and Roy Wilkins sent a joint statement to President Eisenhower claiming that Judge Lemley's decision had "shocked and outraged Negro citizens and millions of their fellow Americans. This opinion is being construed, rightly or wrongly, as a green light to lawless elements in their defiance of Federal authority." They felt that "[t]he process of peaceful advancement toward equality of citizenship for all Americans" had "reached a critical turn." Resistance to civil rights reform had "assumed a significance beyond the question of racial justice, important as that is. The welfare of the whole country is involved." The nation faced important internal and external concerns. Among the people, there was "a pattern of calloused disrespect for law. Moral values have been corrupted. Mob violence has emerged as an instrument to maintain the status quo." Basic constitutional liberties were threatened, and politicians at all levels had disobeyed the law. Externally,

> It is no secret that the foreign relations program of our nation has been hampered and damaged by the discriminatory treatment accorded citizens within the United States, solely on the basis of their race and color. In our world-wide struggle to strengthen the free world against the spread of totalitarianism,

we are sabotaged by the totalitarian practices forced upon millions of our Negro citizens.[62]

The statement called for "a clear national policy and a program of implementation" to eradicate racial segregation. They urged the president to direct the Justice Department to file a brief supporting desegregation in an appeal from the Lemley decision and to take other steps to ensure that, throughout the nation, "the law will be vigorously upheld with the total resources at [the president's] command."[63]

While the NAACP prepared an appeal of the district court order, Orval Faubus avowed his opposition to "integration by force" and was overwhelmingly reelected to an unprecedented third term as governor of Arkansas. Faubus explained his July 29 victory in the Democratic primary, which assured his November reelection, as "a condemnation by the people of illegal Federal intervention in the affairs of the state and the horrifying use of Federal bayonets in the streets of an American city and in the halls of a public school." Just over two weeks later, noting the governor's involvement in encouraging opposition to the court ordered integration plan, the court of appeals reversed Judge Lemley's postponement. According to the court,

> The issue plainly comes down to the question of whether
> overt public resistance, including mob protest, constitutes suf-
> ficient cause to nullify an order of the Federal court directing
> the board to proceed with its integration plan. *We say the
> time has not yet come in these United States when an order of a
> federal court must be whittled away, watered down, or shame-
> fully withdrawn in the face of violent and unlawful acts of indi-
> vidual citizens in opposition thereto.*[64]

As the opening of the school year neared and the Supreme Court took up the Little Rock case, one reporter found that "[t]he situation at Little Rock looks infinitely more dangerous today than it did a year ago." Relman Morin wrote that "[s]entiment has crystallized. Resistance to desegregating Central High School . . . has become truly massive." It was "a tense moment in the history of the South and the whole nation."[65]

* * *

In spite of the alarm over Little Rock's impact on international opinion, when foreign opinion was surveyed it appeared at first glance that in Western Europe the survey results were not much worse than before. A November 1957 report found that "opinions of race relations in the U.S. are highly unfavorable, but apparently have not become materially more so as a result of Little Rock." Compared to April 1956, there were no great changes when survey respondents were asked, "From impressions you have received from any sources, would you tell me your opinion of the treatment of Negroes in the U.S.[?]" According to the report, "[t]hat the Little Rock happenings have apparently had no major effect in worsening opinion of the treatment of Negroes in the U.S. . . . may be owing to the fact that America's standing in the area of race relations was already in a very depressed state prior to the Arkansas desegregation incidents, and hence not readily susceptible to further decrease."[66] Discrimination against Autherine Lucy at the University of Alabama "was an international *cause célèbre* in early 1956 and . . . in all probability did much to lower U.S. standing in the race area to the very unfavorable levels" found in April 1956. In other words, European opinion could not go down because it was already so low. The figures were quite discouraging. In Norway, 82 percent of respondents had a bad opinion or a very bad opinion of the way the United States treated African Americans. In Great Britain, France, and West Germany, the percentages were 66 percent, 65 percent, and 53 percent, respectively. In Italy, only 34 percent had a bad or very bad opinion of U.S. race relations, but only 12 percent had a good or very good opinion.[67]

According to the report, the lack of significant change in these numbers did not mean that Little Rock had not had an effect. "The absence of any general decline . . . does not preclude the possibility, of course, that the Little Rock happenings have had considerable effect in confirming and solidifying already held unfavorable attitudes." Such an occurrence was "rather strongly suggested" by the survey results.[68]

A favorable overall opinion of the United States persisted despite these highly negative views about race. The report suggested that this may have been due in part to the respondents' belief that, over the previous decade, "on balance Negroes in the U.S. have been drawing closer to equality with whites." There were policy implications from these survey results. The more favorable views about the improvement of racial conditions over time "underscore the value of making every effort to place recent racial developments in a broader perspective" in the projection of America abroad.[69] This broader perspective, reflected in documents such as *The Negro in American Life*, could present racial change as a gradual, democratic process and America as being on a trajectory toward ever greater equality.

The USIA took on the task of developing a strategy for responding to international criticism. The director of planning for the agency described its approach in a September 24, 1957, memorandum for a staff report for the president:

> As the Soviet propagandists step up their attacks on "racial terror" in the United States following recent developments in Little Rock, USIA media are attempting to minimize the damage by summarizing anti-integration events on a factual basis, supplying facts whenever possible to balance adverse sensational items, quoting editorials and official statements which indicate steady determined progress toward integration, and informally suggesting to friendly editors possible constructive treatment.

The report noted that "USIS posts in all areas reported heavy but reasoned coverage of the Little Rock episode" through the previous week. "News photos were particularly damaging to U.S. prestige." The foreign relations crisis was continuing. "Agency officials are apprehensive that this week's violence in Little Rock will have serious adverse public reaction abroad."[70]

For its response, the State Department prepared "Talking Points to Overcome Adverse Reaction to Little Rock Incident." The document was "intended for guidance on a world-wide basis." The first strategy recommended was to place the Little Rock crisis "in perspective." To do that, U.S. officials could suggest that "[t]he events at Little Rock are widely misunderstood and misinterpreted. Distressing as they are, they arise from the force and strength of the

American people's insistence upon complete equality. They measure, in a sense, the sweeping and basic character of one of the most important reforms in our history." The talking points stressed that "marked progress toward integration" had been achieved "in most parts of the country; it will inevitably spread throughout our entire nation." Unrest was perpetrated by a "small minority." It was the "basic nature of the American people" to be law abiding. Finally, "[t]he President's intervention has demonstrated the determination of the American people and the effectiveness of the American system in preserving the rights of the individual under law." Overall, "tremendous strides have been made in removing racial barriers in the US."[71]

Another way to put Little Rock in perspective was to talk about the difficulties other nations faced. "The problems we are experiencing are not unique to the US," the talking points emphasized. "These situations result from the effort of free societies to maintain and expand the freedom and equality of the individual," and were "not be confused with those tragic disturbances that arise through the efforts of certain other nations to repress human liberty." Ultimately, Little Rock provided an opportunity to compare Cold War adversaries.

> In the US, national authority is being used not to suppress individual equality and freedom but to uphold them. In the Little Rock incident national authority has been invoked to maintain equal rights of a minority. In the Soviet Union national authority has been repeatedly invoked to suppress the rights of minorities.[72]

A USIA pamphlet on school desegregation, *The Louisville Story,* was distributed before Little Rock news broke, and it provided a useful counter to Little Rock. The American consulate in Port Elizabeth, South Africa, found these materials "most welcome." After distributing copies of the pamphlet, the *Port Elizabeth Evening Post* published a story comparing Little Rock with Louisville in just the way the consulate had hoped. According to the paper, "There is trouble in Arkansas," but "let us keep eruptions like this . . . affair in perspective. Let us not be misled by news of such transitory happenings into believing that the vast programme for the removal of the schools colour bar in the United States is not progressing very well." The *Post* believed that "[t]he truth about the 'desegregation' programme in the United States is that it is making surprisingly smooth progress and already is far advanced." To put Little Rock in perspective, the paper described desegregation in Louisville. The Louisville story was "told in a happy, illustrated brochure recently published by the United States Information Service." It highlighted "the great change achieved in only three years in the United States, since the Supreme Court ruled that to keep the children apart in tax-supported schools was a denial of equal opportunity and, therefore, unconstitutional." In spite of this "balanced" coverage, the American consulate reported that South African blacks remained "somewhat shocked" over Little Rock but "realized that the events at Little Rock were counter . . . to U.S. national policy."[73]

USIS staff in different countries supplied news media with materials on race in the United States that could result in coverage American officials were more comfortable with. As one American consulate put it, "Through friendly contacts with the local editors and others, we can, through judicious selection of materials, bring our point of view to bear in different situations." American efforts at spin control had their successes. In Rio de Janeiro, the U.S. embassy reported that "[s]everal papers frontpaged USIS photos showing peaceful integration elsewhere." According to a report concerning U.S. efforts in Africa, Nigerians "were willing to accept our explanation that Little Rock was not all of the US, nor was it typical of America." USIS material was also distributed in Australia to good effect. It was used by prominent radio and television commentators. "The effort was particularly effective in Sydney where a commentator who had previously been critical reversed his stand."[74]

The USIA described its efforts to provide "perspective" on Little Rock in a semiannual report to Congress. The agency's strategy was to present the crisis "in the context of the significant advances of our Negro population as well as the general development of integration in the public schools." The agency "supplied facts and photographs on typical integrated schools" for use in Voice of America broadcasts and newsreels. Overseas officers organized discussions with "distinguished American Negro personalities." For example, singer Marian Anderson discussed American race relations during a concert tour in Asia. As might be expected, the agency reported to Congress, the source of its appropriations, that its efforts had been successful. "Reports from posts abroad indicate that this consistent, factual handling of the racial question contributed substantially to the generally restrained and well-balanced reaction to the Little Rock story overseas." While there had been communist-inspired sensationalism, "the main body of responsible foreign newsmen and officials described the general situation accurately and referred to Little Rock as an episode in a period of social change."[75]

A reprieve from Little Rock coverage would come, but not quite the way American officials would have hoped. On October 4, 1957, the Soviet Union launched the Sputnik satellite, rushing dramatically ahead of the United States in the space race. For Americans, the idea of a Soviet spaceship circling overhead led to a crisis in national confidence and, ultimately, a renewed commitment to improving education as well as accelerating the space race itself. Internationally, Sputnik, following Little Rock, was a second blow to U.S. prestige. In Genoa, Italy, news of Sputnik "crowded out Little Rock coverage." The American embassy reported that Sputnik had had a "greater and more adverse impact upon local attitudes and United States prestige." Sputnik and a subsequent Soviet spacecraft "for the time being overshadowed Little Rock and other U.S. racial news items" in South Africa as well.[76]

When the initial shock of Sputnik had subsided, the task of rehabilitating America's image remained. The double blow to U.S. prestige in Arkansas and in the heavens made the task all that much more compelling. As had been the case with *Brown*, strong federal government action would always provide the greatest benefit. Rather than spending their efforts placing negative news "in context" and attempting to divert the world's attention from racial incidents, meaningful government action gave the USIA and other government officials something worth reporting. In the Little Rock crisis, helpful action came first in Eisenhower's order to send in the troops. It came again in the form of a definitive Supreme Court ruling in *Cooper v. Aaron.*[77]

* * *

When the school year ended at Central High in June 1958, Melba Pattillo took her schoolbooks into the backyard of her home, placed them in a pile, and set them on fire. The flames consuming her schoolwork could not take away the searing memories of her difficult year, and the sixteen-year-old girl stared into the flames, wondering if she could go back the next fall. Eight of the nine African American students had made it through the school year. Minnijean Brown was expelled when, fed up with constant harassment by white students, she retaliated. "One Nigger Down, Eight to Go" read cards distributed by white high school students who supported segregation. At the end of the year, a measure of victory could be felt as Ernest Green, the lone senior in the group, became the first African American student ever to graduate from Central High School.[78]

While the summer provided a respite for the students, the political and legal conflict over integration at Central High continued. Governor Faubus called the state legislature into a special session on August 26, just two days before the U.S. Supreme Court was to hear the Little Rock case. The legislature passed a series of bills that gave the governor broad latitude to oppose desegregation. As historian Tony Freyer has put it, "the central purpose of most of the measures was to establish a legal basis for closing any public schools under court order to desegregate and to transfer public funds to private, segregated institutions."[79]

Because the opening of the school year in Little Rock was set for the following Monday, the Supreme Court acted without delay. On Friday, September 12, the day after oral arguments, the Court issued a per curiam order unanimously affirming the judgment of the court of appeals, thereby reinstating the original district court order to enforce desegregation in Little Rock. A full opinion would follow on September 29.[80]

In Arkansas, the Court's order prompted Governor Faubus to put his signature to the legislation passed during the summer's special session. One statute granted him authority to close public schools "whenever the Governor shall determine that such action is necessary in order to maintain the peace against actual or impending domestic violence . . . because of integration of the races in any school of the district." Faubus called for a local referendum in Little Rock, as provided for under the new law, and on September 27 the vote was 19,470 to 7,561 in favor of closing the schools rather than desegregating. High school would not open in Little Rock that fall.[81]

On September 29, two days after the Little Rock referendum rejecting its judgment, the Supreme Court issued its opinion in *Cooper v. Aaron*. The opinion was written by Justice William Brennan, but it was signed by all nine members of the Court. Having all members of the Court sign the opinion together reinforced the strength of their unanimity behind the principles articulated in the case.[82]

The Court saw the case as raising "questions of the highest importance to the maintenance of our federal system of government." According to the Court, "[t]he constitutional rights of respondents are not to be sacrificed or yielded to the violence and disorder which have followed upon the actions of the Governor and Legislature. . . . [L]aw and order are not here to be preserved by depriving the Negro children of their constitutional rights." The Court unanimously reaffirmed its holding in *Brown* that segregated schools violated the Fourteenth Amendment's equal protection clause.

> The principles announced in [*Brown*] and the obedience of
> the States to them, according to the command of the Constitution, are indispensable for the protection of the freedoms
> guaranteed by our fundamental charter for all of us. Our constitutional ideal of equal justice under law is thus made a living truth.[83]

The Court's strong statement in *Cooper* helped reinforce the point the USIA and U.S. embassy staffs had been emphasizing for so long. *Cooper* illustrated the working of American constitutionalism, and it preserved the argument that racial equality was an American ideal. While *Brown* had proclaimed that the tenets of American democracy embodied in the Constitution were fundamentally inconsistent with racial segregation, *Cooper* rescued that principle from the threat of extinction posed by massive resistance.

The Supreme Court ruling in *Cooper v. Aaron* was widely covered in the international press. The London *Times* described it in detail, noting that the Court had "virtually exploded the Little Rock school case in a shining opinion which indirectly disposed of all attempts in the south to evade the desegregation law." The paper also covered the continuing difficulties in Little Rock in detail but blamed the problems on Governor Faubus, who "needed an issue if he were not to be out of office at the end of his second term."[84] The paper carried stories about Little Rock on a daily basis for much of September 1958, but the articles appeared on the interior pages. The impression left by the *Times*'s coverage was that continuing racial tensions in the South were attributable more to individual actors, such as Faubus, than to the sanctioning of racism by the American government.

As the start of the school year approached in the fall of 1958, the *South China Morning Post* in Hong Kong had expressed skepticism about President Eisenhower's commitment to desegregation, criticizing the president's lack of support for *Brown*. In the aftermath of *Cooper*, however, Eisenhower was no longer the focus of concern. The paper instead highlighted a speech in Hong Kong by Dickinson College political science professor Donald Flaherty, who argued that continuing difficulties were the product of American federalism. Speaking at a Rotary Club luncheon, Flaherty told his audience that the Little Rock crisis was "related to the U.S. system of government," and "there was always the possibility of strife between the national government and one or more of the state governments under the federal system." Flaherty believed that "complete integration would be accomplished gradually. If this could be done peacefully . . . then the federal system of government would have achieved something of major importance." The *Times of India* carried a lengthy analysis of federalism and desegregation by American journalist Anthony Lewis, who also argued that conflict over desegregation was a product of American federalism.[85]

In many other countries, the press highlighted *Cooper*, then covered continuing difficulties sporadically and off the front page. Little Rock schools were closed. Massive resistance had taken hold in the community, but these circumstances did not precipitate a foreign affairs crisis.[86]

Social change in the Little Rock crisis was both dramatic and dramatically limited. President Eisenhower's strong stand in sending in federal troops was a clear statement that the federal government stood behind federal law. It showed, as well, that regardless of his personal views, the president was committed to upholding the Supreme Court's judgments. Yet when school reopened in Little Rock in the fall of 1959, Jefferson Thomas was the lone African American student in attendance at Central High. At Little Rock's Hall High School, three African American students were enrolled and 730 whites. By the spring of 1960, five African Americans could be counted among Central's student body of 1,515. The following year, eight more African American students were assigned to these schools. In spite of these tiny numbers, Central and Hall were now regarded as desegregated schools.[87]

The small numbers of African American students at Little Rock high schools did not reflect a reluctance of African American parents to send their children to these schools. Rather, Little Rock had adopted a student-assignment process benignly called a "Pupil Placement Law." Compared with the resistance measures of 1958, the Arkansas pupil placement law was quite dispassionate. The purpose of the act appeared on its face to have nothing to do with desegregation, but rather with the need for flexibility and selectivity in student assignments. The legislature determined that "any general or arbitrary reallocation of pupils heretofore entered in the public school system according to any rigid rule of proximity of residence or in accordance solely with request on behalf of the pupil would be disruptive to orderly administration." When a student wished to be reassigned, a parent or guardian was required to file a petition with the school board on behalf of the individual child. A hearing would then be held to determine the appropriateness of the transfer. The statute identified a long list of criteria relevant to pupil placement decisions, including "[a]vailable room and teaching capacity . . . ; the suitability of established curricula for particular pupils; the adequacy of the pupil's academic preparation . . . ; the scholastic aptitude and relative intelligence or mental energy or ability of the pupil; the psychological qualification of the pupil . . . ; the psychological effect upon the pupil of attendance at a particular school; . . . the home environment of the pupil," and on and on. The one factor that spoke directly to the context of desegregation in Little Rock was the fact that in deciding whether a transfer was appropriate the school board could take into consideration "the possibility of breaches of the peace or ill will or economic retaliation within the community."[88]

Bureaucratizing the process meant that racial integration was minimized. School boards now had a cumbersome process that by itself would delay integration. They could use a long list of facially neutral criteria as a basis for refusing individual requests by African American students to attend white schools. As NAACP Legal Defense Fund lawyer Jack Greenberg put it, "violence and physical obstruction having failed, bureaucracy in the form of pupil assignment laws became the principal means of fighting integration." The Supreme Court nevertheless allowed such plans to stand. There would be no drama attending the Court's handling of this important issue. The lack of fanfare would not cause this issue to go unnoticed. To white southerners, the path was clear: bureaucratization could accomplish most of what overt resistance had not.[89]

This lesson took hold in the South, yet the lesson was lost in Africa and Asia. The international press did not notice the pupil placement cases, perhaps because these cases did not undermine the formal and abstract principle of racial equality articulated in *Brown* and reaffirmed in *Cooper*. As a result, the bureaucratization of segregation did not pose a threat to America's democratic image. There is no indication that the federal government was concerned with the impact of pupil placement plans on foreign affairs, even though it was clear that these plans would undermine efforts to integrate public schools. National policy projected overseas continued to be framed in the broad outlines of *Cooper* and *Brown*.[90]

In spite of its minimal impact on actual school desegregation, the Supreme Court ruling in *Cooper* remained of tremendous significance in another arena. *Cooper* safeguarded the basic principle of *Brown* in the face of massive resistance. *Cooper* emphasized the supremacy of federal law and the role of the Court in defining federal constitutional principles. In so doing, the Court protected the idea of a rule of law. Individual rights could not be taken away by mob violence. By upholding the basic principles of U.S. constitutionalism, the Court protected the image of democracy. *Cooper* upheld the principle that American democracy functioned to protect individual rights and that racial equality was a value the courts would defend. Because of *Cooper*, the narrative of race and democracy in *The Negro in American Life* would still have salience.

Measured, at least, by the degree and pace of integration, it may be that *Cooper* succeeded more in maintaining democracy's image than in actually desegregating the schools. From the perspective of President Eisenhower, the core interests at stake in Little Rock had more to do with federal authority and foreign affairs than with racial equality. Having established those broad principles, the president and his administration withdrew their presence from the continuing struggle. To the extent that safeguarding the image of America was behind Eisenhower's involvement, he got what he needed with *Cooper v. Aaron*. At this juncture, the Cold War imperative could be addressed largely through formal pronouncements about the law. More substantive social change would await another day.

CHAPTER 5

Losing Control in Camelot

The shortest line between America and Addis
Ababa is now a straight wire from Alabama.

AMERICAN EMBASSY, NIAMEY,

TO DEPARTMENT OF STATE, MAY 21, 1963[1]

On June 26, 1961, Malick Sow of the African nation of Chad was
on his way to Washington. The first ambassador to the United States
from this newly independent nation, Ambassador Sow planned to
present his credentials to President John F. Kennedy. The ambassador's drive from New York, the site of the United Nations, to Washington, D.C., took him along Route 40 through Maryland. Sow
stopped along the highway for gas. Hoping to ease a headache, he
also stopped in at a diner for a cup of coffee. What happened in the
diner would not make Sow feel better but would instead create a
headache for the Kennedy Administration of an entirely different
sort. The ambassador was refused service. This diner did not serve
blacks.[2]

Ambassador Sow was one of many African diplomats discriminated against on Route 40 and elsewhere in the United States. Such
incidents were more than embarrassing to the diplomats and to the
Kennedy administration. They threatened U.S. relations with an
important new bloc of independent nations. Sow himself felt

"deeply hurt" by this incident. While he did not wish to "involve his country in any scandal," the ambassador did tell U.S. State Department representatives that "situations like this make it very difficult for African diplomats to leave New York and Washington, and that they make normal relations between the United States and African countries very strained."[3]

John F. Kennedy was elected president in 1960, "the Year of Africa." Between January and November of that year, seventeen African nations achieved independence. A total of twenty-five former colonies on the continent had now been liberated. Eight more would follow while Kennedy was in office.[4] Africans were particularly attuned to U.S. racial problems. As a result, State Department officials were greatly troubled by the implications of discrimination for U.S. national security. One concern—a motivating issue since the late 1940s—was how race discrimination in the United States would affect Cold War alignments. Would race discrimination make it less likely that African and Asian nations would ally themselves with the United States and against the Soviet Union? There were practical consequences for United Nations politics as well. Would race discrimination make it more difficult for the United States to gain support for its positions in the UN from African and Asian nations? Would that affect the usefulness of the UN as a forum for the nation to further its interests in the global community?

While the impact of domestic racial issues on the nation's diplomatic interests was of concern during the Truman and Eisenhower years, the issue took on even greater importance during the Kennedy administration. "[R]acism and discrimination . . . had a major impact on my life as secretary of state," noted Dean Rusk. "Stories of racial discrimination in the United States and discriminatory treatment accorded diplomats from the many newly independent countries of the old colonial empires began to undermine our relations with these countries." The relationship between civil rights and Cold War foreign affairs was so well understood at this time that leaders sometimes felt the need to stress that civil rights reform was motivated by other objectives as well. As Democratic National Committee Deputy Chairman Louis Martin would stress, "[L]et it be clear, in our own hearts and minds, that it is not entirely because of the Cold War, not merely because of the economic waste of discrimination, that we are committed to achieving true equality of opportunity. The basic reason is because it is right."[5]

The Year of Africa was also the year of the Greensboro, North Carolina, lunch counter sit-ins. The civil rights movement entered a new phase as activists increasingly used the tactic of nonviolent civil disobedience to challenge segregation and to direct attention to their struggle. The movement would be very effective in keeping worldwide attention focused on civil rights in the United States.[6]

Just as the movement entered a new phase, the early 1960s brought a new era in Cold War politics, both domestic and international. Overseas, the Cold War intensified in 1960 as the Soviets shot down an American U-2 plane over Soviet airspace. President Eisenhower had given his word that the United States was not sending reconnaissance flights over the Soviet Union, and he was caught in a lie. Cold War tensions increased in Kennedy's first year in office when the United States engaged in a failed attempt to overthrow Cuban leader Fidel Castro in the Bay of Pigs. During the 1962 Cuban missile crisis, American leaders and the American public worried that the world had come too close to nuclear war. Only one year later President Kennedy would shift course, edging toward détente with the Soviets and proposing a nuclear test ban treaty.[7]

At home, McCarthyism had been repudiated. Led by a progressive Supreme Court, the nation entered a period of greater tolerance of the right to dissent. Critics of the U.S. government had their passports restored. W. E. B. DuBois used his renewed freedom to travel to leave the United States and spend his last years in Ghana. Newer voices in the civil rights movement found that criticizing the United States overseas might have consequences, but losing one's passport was much less likely to be one of them.[8]

During the early 1960s, the civil rights movement no longer seemed bounded within the framework imposed during the McCarthy era. Activists still invoked the idea of American democracy in their rhetoric, and the icons of American democracy in their protest. Yet critiquing the nature of American democracy led to fewer federal consequences, at least on the surface. Red-baiting of the movement continued, but often behind the scenes. The consequences of protest at the hands of state authorities in the South, the Klan, and the forces of massive resistance remained, of course, as brutal as ever.[9]

As the movement broadened and shifted to the left, the federal government found itself needing to listen to new voices, to harsher critics. A posture of reluctant engagement characterized President Kennedy's response to the movement during the first two years of his presidency, until in 1963, when he embraced civil rights and appeared to make that cause his own.

Although John F. Kennedy took steps to court African American voters during the 1960 campaign, civil rights reform was not a high priority for the new president as he entered office. Kennedy's own aides considered him rather uninterested in civil rights. Harris Wofford, Kennedy's advisor on civil rights during the 1960 presidential campaign, was later asked whether, at that time, he "had any feeling . . . that the President had a particular interest in the problem of civil rights or did he recognize it as a political problem?" Wofford answered, "the latter." Wofford felt that during this period "civil rights was not a high priority for Kennedy." Instead, "his chief concern then and very possibly . . . to the end of his life, was foreign policy and peace and relations with the Soviet Union." According to Wofford, such issues "always seemed to be the dominant issues for him."[10]

During the campaign, Kennedy realized that he had "a problem" with African American voters. Although weak on civil rights, Kennedy had made a name for himself in another area that many black voters cared about: African affairs. He had harshly criticized Eisenhower's lack of support for Algerian independence in 1957. During the campaign, Kennedy courted the black vote by drawing upon his record of support for African independence. According to Richard D. Mahoney, "[t]he strategy was to use concern for Africa as a means of wooing American blacks without alienating Southern whites." This was "a minor classic in political exploitation of foreign policy."[11]

Harris Wofford had drafted many of Kennedy's speeches on Africa, and Kennedy turned to him to help with civil rights. Carrying out Wofford's advice, Kennedy promised to end discrimination in federal housing programs "with the stroke of a pen," since that action could be taken by executive order. However, at the end of his first year in office, with no order in sight, civil rights activists sent thousands of pens to the White House to pressure Kennedy to fulfill his promise. The administration had a civil rights agenda, but its priorities were not always the priorities of the movement. The Justice Department decided to focus its civil rights efforts on voting rights. As Kennedy aide Arthur Schlesinger put it, voting was perceived as "the keystone in the struggle against segregation." Also, the vote "did not incite social and sexual anxieties" in the way that integration did. As a result, "[c]oncentrating on the right to vote . . . seemed the best available means of carrying the mind of the white South." Yet civil rights leaders were dissatisfied with Kennedy. According to Carl Brauer, "in his first year in office, President Kennedy had done little that regular Southern Democrats could not tolerate." Facing an election year, liberal Democratic senators urged the president to back civil rights legislation in 1962, but the president declined. The justification for his stance on civil rights in the face of increasing pressure from the civil rights movement and from some members of his own staff and party was that moving forward on civil rights legislation would jeopardize his other initiatives in Congress.[12]

Recognizing that Kennedy's priorities were elsewhere, civil rights leaders argued that civil rights reform was crucial to the president's objectives for economic growth and foreign policy. In a confidential memorandum to the president, Roy Wilkins and Arnold Aaronson of the NAACP suggested:

> As the criterion by which our democratic professions are measured in many parts of globe, civil rights is and will increasingly be an important aspect of our foreign relations. And without progress on civil rights, we shall be unable to achieve the full utilization of our manpower resources so indispensable to accelerated economic growth. Action on civil rights, therefore, cannot be postponed pending the accomplishment of other foreign and domestic goals but, being inseparable from them, must proceed simultaneously with them.

Civil rights was therefore not a distraction from the president's other objectives. Instead, it was "the third leg of the stool."[13]

Wilkins and Aaronson argued that more would be required of Kennedy than his predecessors. "The world-wide movement of colored people for emancipation and self-determination has given a momentum to the civil rights cause in our own country—a momentum that will accelerate rapidly in the months and years ahead." Because of that, "[t]he pace of our government's civil rights effort must be accelerated," not only because it was just, but also "to avoid increased frustration, bitterness, tension and strife." The nation needed a civil rights "breakthrough."[14]

A Kennedy administration "breakthrough" on civil rights would be some time in coming. In the meantime, one way to improve the nation's standing overseas was to send Peace Corps volunteers to Africa and other parts of the world. As Elizabeth Cobbs Hoffman has suggested, "At the top of the Peace Corps' list of implicit goals was to show skeptical observers from the new nations that Americans were not monsters." The nation's bad press on civil rights could be ameliorated through one-on-one contact with American volunteers.[15]

The year before Kennedy took office, the civil rights movement took an important turn. On February 1, 1960, four African American college students held a sit-in at the segregated lunch counter at Woolworth's in Greensboro, North Carolina. The North Carolina protest inspired others, and by August 1961 more than seventy thousand people had participated in sit-ins and more than three thousand had been arrested. Student involvement in the sit-ins and other movement activity was a catalyst behind the founding of the Student Nonviolent Coordinating Committee (SNCC) in April 1960. Encouraged by Ella Baker of the Southern Christian Leadership Conference (SCLC), students created their own organization, which would be a major force in the civil rights movement. The civil rights movement was developing a broader base and was increasingly turning to the tactic of nonviolent civil disobedience.[16]

In May 1961, the Congress of Racial Equality (CORE) planned to use direct action to challenge segregation in interstate bus travel. The Supreme Court had ruled that segregation was unlawful in interstate transit, and in 1960 that ruling was extended to interstate busses and terminals. In spite of federal law, however, interstate bus travelers were still segregated in southern states. CORE planned to have an interracial group ride together on a nonsegregated basis to test compliance with the Court's rulings. It was called the Freedom Ride.[17]

Thirteen Freedom Riders departed from Washington, D.C. on May 4 on two Trailways busses. Their destination was New Orleans. The Freedom Ride encountered resistance along the way. Tensions heightened when the riders arrived in Alabama. Outside Anniston, one bus was firebombed. In Anniston and Birmingham, riders were brutally attacked by mobs. Rider Walter Bergman suffered permanent brain damage, and many others required medical care for beating injuries and smoke inhalation. The riders were committed to continuing their journey, but no bus drivers would take them. With Justice Department help, the Freedom Riders instead flew to New Orleans.[18]

Hoping to prove to the world that violence would not stymie civil rights protest, SNCC sent in reinforcements. On May 20, SNCC members continued the Freedom Ride from Birmingham to Montgomery. President Kennedy thought he had assurance from Alabama Governor John Patterson that the riders would be protected, but a mob of a thousand met the riders and savagely beat them. Justice Department aide John Siegenthaler was attacked and knocked unconscious in the melee. Martin Luther King Jr. then came to the city, addressing a mass meeting that itself became the target of violence. President Kennedy was forced to act, and sent six hundred federal marshals to the scene.[19]

A weak and battered James Zwerg, interviewed from his hospital bed, told a nationwide television audience that the ride would go on. "We will continue the Freedom Ride, . . . no matter what happens. We'll take hitting, we'll take beating. We're willing to accept death." The riders would keep coming until they could ride free of segregation, "just as American citizens."[20]

President Kennedy was angered by the Freedom Riders' persistence. As biographer Richard Reeves put it, the president was upset in part because the violence against the riders was "exactly the kind of thing the Communists used to make the United States look bad around the world." He told civil rights advisor Harris Wofford, "Stop them! Get your friends off those buses!" Kennedy felt that the movement was "embarrassing him and the country on the eve of the meeting in Vienna with Khrushchev." He was preparing for his first presidential trip overseas, and he hoped to draw the world's attention away from the disaster at the Bay of Pigs and establish himself as a confident and accomplished world leader. The Freedom Riders interfered with these objectives. According to Wofford, Kennedy "supported every American's right to stand up or sit down for his rights—but not to ride for them in the spring of 1961."[21]

Kennedy had reason to be concerned with the overseas impact of the violence against the Freedom Riders, for the international reaction to these events was harsh. The USIA later reported that "[a]ssessed in terms of its impact on the American image abroad, the Alabama racial incident was highly detrimental." Worldwide news accounts "presented a stark picture of developments in Alabama even though conscious distortion in free world reporting was limited and efforts to present some balance or at least exercise some restraint were common in most areas of the world." Some regions of the world—Western Europe, India and parts of Southeast Asia—applauded Kennedy's action and discussed American racial progress, but still the USIA reported that editorial comment suggested that the incident "had dealt a severe blow to U.S. prestige which might adversely effect its position of leadership in the free world as well as weaken the overall effectiveness of the Western alliance."[22]

The *Pakistani Observer* suggested that "[t]he race riots in Alabama seem to out-Little Rocked [sic] Little Rock." The Moroccan *Al Fair* thought that these incidents were "compromising the U.S. position of world leadership," yet believed that Kennedy administration action would address this problem. The *Ghanaian Times* suggested that "[s]urely the Negro problem on the earth as well as the plight of oppressed peoples in Africa and elsewhere demand much more serious attention and consideration than the sending of a man to the moon." Reports from Moscow first characterized the events as indicative of the American "way of life" and later emphasized their impact on U.S. standing around the world. Meanwhile, the USIA reported that "Chinese Communist wireless files to all parts of the world reflect a business-like effort on the part of Peking propagandists to sharpen the tools of their craft in a blunt exploitation of racial tensions in the United States." Peking accounts "bore down

President John F. Kennedy and Nigerian Prime Minister Sir Abubakar Tafawa Balewa at the White House following talks between the two leaders, July 27, 1961. When African leaders traveling in the United States encountered race discrimination, it led to embarrassing diplomatic problems for the Kennedy administration. (UPI/CORBIS-BETTMANN)

hard on the theme that rampant racism has 'exposed' the savage nature of American freedom and democracy."[23]

According to the USIA, of even more concern than the media reports were "the largely unvoiced private views of the masses of 'colored' peoples throughout the world who are known to be hyper-sensitive on the question of racial discrimination." The agency felt

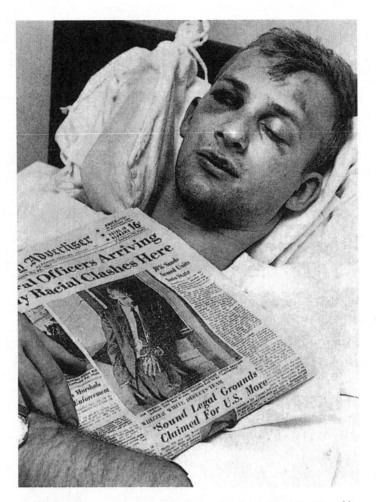

Freedom Rider James Zwerg, recovering in a Montgomery, Alabama, hospital bed, caresses a newspaper with front-page coverage of his brutal beating, May 20, 1961. The civil rights movement made effective use of the media, broadening national and international support for civil rights reform. (UPI/CORBIS-BETTMANN)

that "[r]eliable reports . . . suggest that racial incidents in the U.S. frequently are seen as a general reflection of what they believe to be the superior or, at best, condescending attitude which the 'whites' have toward the 'non-whites.'" Resentment about racism "feeds upon U.S. racial incidents and may well be a much stronger force in shaping their response to the West over the long-haul."[24]

The president's concerns about the impact of these incidents on the Vienna talks were echoed in the London *Daily Telegraph*: "It is a pity that the Russians and Chinese in their endless efforts to foster hatred of America, who have made great play with the disturbances at Little Rock, should have another opportunity on the eve of the President's meeting with Khrushchev." Other papers thought that Kennedy had displayed courage in intervening in Alabama, and in the words of the London *Daily Express*, had "proven to an anxious world that the Kennedy brothers are as ready to defend the ideals of individual liberty within the borders of the United States as they are to act outside. . . . On the eve of perhaps the most vital personal confrontation in post-war history . . . between President Kennedy and Mr. Khrushchev, that is an incalculable contribution not only to American prestige but to Western unity."[25]

Ultimately, the Kennedy administration handled the crisis in a manner that helped minimize mob violence and negative headlines, but without protecting federal rights. Following negotiations between the administration and Mississippi's governor, when the Freedom Ride arrived in Jackson, Mississippi, on May 24, police officers were on hand and kept the peace. The officers directed the riders from the bus, through the waiting rooms, and into paddy wagons. The riders were arrested, convicted of breach of the peace, and sentenced to sixty-seven-day jail terms. The federal government did not intervene.[26]

The Freedom Rides provided an early and dramatic example for the Kennedy administration of the way that civil rights movement activities, coupled with violent southern white reaction, created civil rights crises that demanded federal government attention. President Kennedy could not fully define the place of civil rights in his administration's overall agenda. He could not control the nature and timing of the issues. Civil rights crises would periodically demand the president's attention and concern. Because federal rights were at stake, because law and order demanded it, because it had an impact on his image as a national leader, because it harmed U.S. prestige abroad, Kennedy would find himself increasingly involved in civil rights.

As Kennedy's first year in office drew to a close, the administration took stock of its accomplishments. Achievements on the civil rights front were included on a draft list of "Major Foreign Policy Measures Taken by the Kennedy Administration." The administration's foreign policy activity including encouraging "the orderly evolution of desegregation in the United States. This has had a favorable effect overseas. Progress in the fields of civil rights and education have been noteworthy."[27] It was clear that the Kennedy administration's foreign affairs objectives would be enhanced by civil rights reform.

In September 1962, the University of Mississippi in Oxford handed the Kennedy administration a civil rights crisis that would resonate even more forcefully overseas then the Freedom Rides had done. James Meredith, a resident of Mississippi, applied to the university and was rejected solely because he was African American. Meredith sued the university, and in June 1962 the Fifth Circuit Court of Appeals ruled that Meredith's exclusion was unconstitutional. After the U.S. Supreme Court declined to review the case, Mississippi Governor Ross Barnett responded that the state would "not surrender to the evil and illegal forces of tyranny." Ultimately, with Barnett recalcitrant and mobs on campus protesting Meredith, Kennedy sent in federal marshals. Through the night of September 30, a battle raged between troops and demonstrators. Two people were killed, including a French reporter, and hundreds were wounded. The next morning, with troops in control of the campus, Meredith was registered.[28]

The violence in Oxford and the federal role in managing the crisis were widely followed overseas. Although dramatic racial conflict harmed the nation's image abroad, the Meredith incident, like Little Rock before it, also provided an opportunity for demonstrating the federal government's resolve. In England, the Manchester *Guardian* noted that "[i]n the world outside Mississippi's long night has already done serious damage to America's name." Yet along with many international commentators, the *Guardian* believed that the federal government's role was "proof that the killers and rioters are not a portent but a remnant." In Sweden, the *Stockholms-Tidningen* thought that "[t]here is hardly to be found a corresponding example in the world of a Government so powerfully protecting the rights of a minority. In the midst of tragedy, this is a victory for American democracy and for the ideas upon which it rests." In contrast, however, a survey of university students in Bogotá reported that the crisis damaged U.S. prestige abroad and undermined the president's standing.[29]

Even in Africa, many critics of the United States found reasons to praise Kennedy's actions. The USIA reported the "[n]oteworthy . . . fact that some African sources exemplified by Sudan, Ghana, and Libya, often critical of the United States in the past and particularly so when racial incidents occur, have not in this case launched attacks on America but have instead praised the federal action." In Nigeria, Kenya, and Ethiopia, newspapers had "displayed considerable understanding of the difficulties faced by the American government with this problem." In Kenya, the *Daily Nation* thought that "the words 'Little Rock' and 'Oxford, Mississippi' should be considered . . . as a vindication of American democracy." According to the paper, "In each case we have seen the federal authorities, working through the channel of the decisions of the Supreme Court, pursuing honestly and fearlessly a policy aimed at eradicating the taint of racialism from American life." The coverage in some African newspapers, however, was searing. The Moroccan *La Nation* saw Meredith as "a symbol as he enters the university between a double hedge of armed soldiers. Let us wish that his name remains that of the last American to be wounded in heart and flesh because he is a Negro." The local press in Katanga argued that "[t]he United States is incapable of establishing a multiracial society in their own country" and suggested that it was time to consider sending a United Nations delegation "to the United States to protect the rights of black American citizens."[30]

The former governor general of India was impressed by President Kennedy's handling of the Mississippi crisis. He told U.S. Ambassador Chester Bowles that "as far as he knows this is the first time in the history of the world that any nation has ever demonstrated so dramatically its respect for law. Where else, he asked, could we expect to see a government throw thousands of men and huge resources behind the application of a single individual to enter a university because the law said he had a right to be there." Such reactions convinced Bowles that the United States had now dramatized that racial discrimination was illegal and that the federal government was committed to opposing it. Bowles believed that the Meredith situation could be "a turning point not only in our struggle against segregation in this country, but in our efforts to make the people of Asia, Africa and Latin America understand what we are trying to do."[31]

The international impact was not lost on members of the administration. As Arthur Schlesinger put it,

> President Kennedy's action had a profound effect around the world, most of all in Africa. As the delegate from Upper Volta put it in the UN General Assembly, segregation unquestionably existed in the United States, but what is important is that the Government of the United States did not make an institution of this. It does not praise the policy. On the contrary, it energetically fights it. For one small Negro to go to school, it threatens governors and judges with prison . . . it sends troops to occupy the University of Mississippi.

In Schlesinger's view, the administration's actions in Mississippi had concrete foreign relations benefits. "Three weeks after Oxford, Sékou Touré and Ben Bella were prepared to deny refueling facilities to Soviet planes bound for Cuba during the missile crisis." The lesson was clear. The nation's world leadership and security were enhanced by efforts to secure civil rights at home.[32]

Although federal action at the University of Mississippi was widely praised, the overall impact of this crisis remained troubling. Assessing worldwide press coverage, the USIA noted that the restrained editorial comment was "overshadowed by the massive news reporting on the incident. Despite the factual nature of news coverage based primarily on Western wire services, the vivid portrayal in news reports and wire photos of the more sensational aspects of the incident—such as rioting and bloodshed—may well have left a more lasting impression of the less palatable aspects of the racial situation in the U.S." Moderate editorial comment could not overcome visceral news reporting on the actual events. The USIA's concerns bore themselves out in a subsequent 1962 report, which found that "[r]acial prejudice is the chief blemish on the image of the American people abroad, even among the majority of citizens of non-Communist nations who hold the United States in high esteem."[33]

USIA reports detailing the widespread international media coverage of the Mississippi crisis crossed the president's desk, and he was concerned about Mississippi's impact on the U.S. image abroad. Kennedy had been critical of Eisenhower's handling of the Little Rock crisis. As Richard Reeves put it, he had hoped "there would be no photo opportunities on his watch that would embarrass the United States all over the world." In the aftermath of the Mississippi crisis, Kennedy wondered how Mississippi compared with Little Rock. How did the world react to his administration's handling of the crisis, compared to the reaction to Eisenhower's action in Little Rock? The USIA responded with a detailed report on the international reaction to the crisis at Ole Miss. The lessons to be drawn from it were clear. Definitive federal action in civil rights crises would have a positive effect on the nation's image abroad. A more passive civil rights stance might serve the president's interest in not alienating the South before the 1964 election and in keeping his other legislative priorities from getting sidetracked by a congressional battle over civil rights. An active posture, however, would better serve U.S. foreign affairs.[34]

If things remained quiet, this trade-off could be avoided, at least for a time. With the Mississippi crisis over, the Kennedy administration might have hoped for a breathing spell. Yet as long as discrimination and disenfranchisement plagued the nation, the image of democracy would be at risk. And the rank and file of the civil rights movement did not shy away from protest actions out of fear of harming the nation's image abroad. Instead, the movement questioned the truth of American rhetoric. As protest actions met with violent resistance, the movement kept the gaze of the international media focused on race in America.

* * *

A particularly awkward and persistent problem for the administration was discrimination against black foreign diplomats. Troubling incidents occurred with increasing frequency as UN delegates from newly independent nations came to the United States. Dean Rusk recalled one incident:

> Early in the Kennedy years a black delegate to the United Nations landed in Miami on his way to New York. When the passengers disembarked for lunch, the white passengers were taken to the airport restaurant; the black delegate received a folding canvas stool in a corner of the hangar and a sandwich wrapped with waxed paper. He then flew on to New York, where our delegation asked for his vote on human rights issues.[35]

Rusk believed that incidents like this were "a severe barrier to cordial relations with many foreign states." The State Department Protocol Office tried to handle difficulties faced by foreign diplomats, but Rusk quickly discovered that the problems were deep-seated and "depended on racial progress throughout Washington and indeed the entire country. We could not expect an African diplomat to gain privileges and services denied black Americans. Nor could we expect him to display his diplomatic passport every time he wanted to eat or get a haircut." For these reasons, as well as, Rusk said, "the simple rightness of the cause," the State Department worked on antisegregation efforts, throwing "its full weight behind the Civil Rights Acts of 1964 and 1965, and especially legislation dealing with public accommodations."[36]

A source of particular concern was Maryland's Highway 40, the route taken by many diplomats on the drive from the United Nations in New York City to the nation's capital. Time after time, when African diplomats stopped for a bite to eat, they were refused service at Maryland restaurants. Such incidents upset the diplomats and often generated a hostile press reaction in their home country. The implications of discrimination for U.S. relations with these countries concerned Kennedy administration staffers. As Chester Bowles remarked,

Now you have some 20 new nations in Africa. You have, of course, all the new nations of Asia. The UN has grown from 50 nations in the last few years to a hundred. They are all coming to the United States because the UN is here and because they look on this as a country of great promise. . . . And they come here and, of course, some of them get into all kinds of difficulties with some of our own ways of doing things. And they go home, a lot of them, pretty upset individuals.[37]

Upon hearing of these incidents, President Kennedy's initial reaction was that African ambassadors shouldn't be driving on Highway 40. They should fly. "It's a hell of a road," he said. "I used to drive it years ago, but why would anybody want to drive it today when you can fly? Tell these ambassadors I wouldn't think of driving from New York to Washington. Tell them to fly!" According to Harris Wofford, Kennedy's reaction led State Department officials to wonder whether the president was behind their efforts to end discrimination on Route 40. Still, as Carl M. Brauer notes, because Kennedy "wanted to improve America's image in the Third World and because he had served as chairman of a Senate subcommittee on Africa, Kennedy came to office disposed to be especially sensitive to this problem."[38]

The seriousness of the problem required a systematic response. The administration established a new program within the State Department Protocol Office. The Office of Special Protocol Services, and its director Pedro Sanjuan, worked on long-term solutions to the problem of race discrimination against foreign diplomats. While Sanjuan was charged with handling the vast array of difficulties foreign diplomats encountered throughout the country, a particular focus of his work was Route 40. When a bill prohibiting discrimination in public accommodations was introduced in the Maryland state legislature, Sanjuan testified in favor of the bill on behalf of the Department of State. Federal government involvement in state legislative action would seem to be a great breach of federalism. Sanjuan acknowledged that some people might wonder "why the Department of State is interested in what may appear to some to be an internal matter within the State of Maryland." He recast his appearance as "a request by the Department of State for the assistance of the State of Maryland in insuring the success of the foreign policy of the United States." The State Department strongly supported the bill because it would "eliminate a source of embarrassment that greatly damages our relations with not only the neutral nations of the world, but many nations which are stoutly with us in the fight for freedom." The importance of civil rights to U.S. foreign relations seemed to take precedence over the usual boundaries between state and federal authority.[39]

Sanjuan drew an analogy between this request for assistance and the U.S. government's appeal to private industry to help by building better weapons during World War II. This time the war was a Cold War, and the weapons required were different. "GIVE US THE WEAPONS TO CONDUCT THIS WAR OF HUMAN DIGNITY," he urged. "The fight for decency against Communism is everyone's war in America." After an initial setback, the Maryland public accommodations bill was passed by the state legislature in January 1963.[40]

The impact of race in America on international politics came to a head in the spring of 1963 in Birmingham, Alabama. On May 3, more than a thousand African American children and teenagers embarked on a civil rights march. Birmingham's jails were already filled with protesters, so it was Police Commissioner Eugene "Bull" Connor's objective to deter the demonstrators without arresting them. To do that, he used fire hoses. The strength of the city's high-pressure hoses knocked down protesters. Water guns were backed up by police dogs that lunged at demonstrators.[41]

The police tactics did not deter Birmingham's determined civil rights movement, but they had a profound impact that Connor may not have contemplated. Dramatic photographs in newspapers throughout the country captured the nation's attention, focusing concern on the need for civil rights reform. News coverage throughout the world underscored international concerns about racial injustice in America.[42]

On May 14, 1963, the USIA reported that the Soviet Union had "stepped up its propaganda on Birmingham over the weekend to campaign proportions, devoting about one fifth of its radio output to the subject." This propaganda was more extensive than during the Meredith dispute. In most other countries, with the exception of African nations, "coverage has been unexpectedly moderate and factual, except in the Communist and leftist press." Nevertheless, "the damaging pictures of dogs and fire hoses have been extremely widely used." In Lagos, Nigeria, for example, "substantial improvement over [the] past two years in Nigerian public understanding of progress in U.S. race relations is being rapidly eroded by reports, photographs and TV coverage from Alabama. Growing adverse local reactions [are] in marked contrast [to the] situation at [the] time [of the] Meredith case when [the] strong stand [of the] Federal Government [was] widely understood and applauded." In Kenya, police dogs and fire hoses were featured on television, and front page newspaper stories featured headlines such as: "Riots Flare in U.S. South—Infants Sent to Jail." The nation also took a "heavy beating in Ghana over Birmingham." The U.S. embassy in Accra reported that the United States had "definitely lost ground" due to the crisis.[43]

When trouble began in Birmingham, as John Walton Cotman put it, initially "President Kennedy did not take the lead in promoting civil rights" in that city. "Prior to May 3rd the President made no discernable attempt to confront the clear pattern of Bill of Rights violations, systematic abuse of police authority and police brutality. . . . President Kennedy was cautious and conservative," Cotman argues, "only acting when forced to by political crisis."[44]

Following the May 3 demonstrations, Kennedy called a meeting of his top advisors. According to Burke Marshall, the reason for the meeting was that Birmingham "was a matter of national and international concern at the time because of the mass of demonstrations." The administration was under pressure to take action, yet the course of federal involvement was unclear. As Marshall remembered it, "the pictures of the police dogs and fire hoses going throughout the country stirred the feelings of every Negro in the country, most whites in the country, and I suppose particularly colored persons throughout the world. And all of that emotion was directed at President Kennedy. 'Why didn't he do something?' " The concern about Birmingham's impact led the administration to play a key role in resolving the crisis. Kennedy dispatched Marshall to the city, and Marshall helped manage negotiations that led to an agreement between the SCLC, the local government, and the business community. Under the pact, steps would be taken to desegregate facilities in large department stores, redress employment discrimination, and release jailed civil rights demonstrators.[45]

Yet once Birmingham had focused the world's attention on racial brutality in America, resolving problems on the local level would not fully resolve the crisis. As with so many civil rights crises in the 1960s, Birmingham required a global, as well as a local, response.

In Addis Ababa, Ethiopia, the diplomatic consequences of discrimination reached a particularly dramatic level. African leaders had gathered in that city for an historic moment of an entirely different kind. On May 22, 1963, Emperor Haile Selassie of Ethiopia convened the Conference of African Heads of States and Governments. Gathered together were heads of state and other representatives of all but two independent African nations.[46] This was a moment, Selassie told the assembled leaders, "without parallel in history."

> We stand today on the stage of world affairs, before the audience of world opinion. . . . Africa is today in mid-course, in transition from the Africa of Yesterday to the Africa of Tomorrow. . . . The task on which we have embarked—the making of Africa—will not wait. We must act to shape and mould the future and leave our imprint on events as they pass into history.[47]

The task before this body was to chart the future of African politics. Out of the meeting would come the Organization of African Unity. It was Selassie's hope that this gathering, and the foundation it laid, would ultimately bear fruit in the formation of a unified Africa, operating as a political body like the United States of America or the Soviet Union.[48]

Over the next few days, African leaders worked together to produce a series of resolutions embodying their common goals and aspirations. As they did so, the focus of their deliberations strayed far from the shores of Africa. These heads of state believed that their own interests were implicated in a dramatic conflict many miles away.

The news of Birmingham was fresh in the minds of African leaders as they gathered in Addis Ababa. On the second day of the conference, Prime Minister Milton Obote of Uganda released an open letter to President Kennedy protesting the treatment of African American demonstrators in Birmingham.

> The Negroes who, even while the conference was in session, have been subjected to the most inhuman treatment, who have been blasted with fire hoses cranked up to such pressure that the water could strip bark off trees, at whom the police have deliberately set snarling dogs, are our own kith and kin. The only offences which these people have committed are that they are black and that they have demanded the right to be free and to hold their heads up as equal citizens of the United States.[49]

These matters were relevant to African leaders, for "the tasks before us of effecting closer union of African states both in the political and economic fields necessarily include the emancipation of the people of dark races, and . . . colonialism and race discrimination are one of the fundamental issues for the future of our civilization." Obote believed that "[n]othing is more paradoxical than that these events should take place in the United States and at a time when that country is anxious to project its image before the world screen as the archtype of democracy and the champion of freedom." Africans, who had "borne the white-man's burden for . . . centuries, . . . feel that our own freedom and independence would be a mere sham if our black brethren elsewhere in Africa and in the United States still remain in political, social and economic bondage." Obote told President Kennedy that "the eyes and ears of the world are concentrated on events in Alabama and it is the duty of the free world and more so of the countries that hold themselves up as the leaders of that free world to see that all of their citizens, regardless of the colour of their skin, are free."[50]

According to the U. S. embassy in Addis Ababa, the idea for this critique of the United States came from an "American Negro black

Muslim representative, resident [of] Cairo," who had "been very active in lobbying among journalists and delegates to [the] conference against racial discrimination in [the] US." Accordingly, this episode may be an example of the increasing effectiveness of African American efforts to use international pressure as leverage for social change at home.[51]

African leaders engaged in a lengthy discussion of Birmingham and debated the proper way to express concern over the incidents in their joint resolutions. The Reuters news agency reported that, in its original form, a resolution on Birmingham had said "it 'could lead to a break in relations' between the United States and African countries." According to reports, some delegations objected, "and in the end all agreed on substitution [of] the word 'deterioration' for 'break.'" According to Agence France-Presse, some delegates suggested that other nations be "black-listed" as well. "It was then realized that the resolution would lose its value if it mentioned a long list of states." The result was a milder resolution that mentioned only the United States. The French wire service called it a "well-balanced plan adopted after long debate," and a "painful compromise."[52]

In its final version, the resolution indicated that the conference:

> *Expresses* the deep concern aroused in all African peoples and governments by the measures of racial discrimination taken against communities of African origin living outside the continent and particularly in the United States of America. *Expresses* an appreciation for the efforts of the Federal Government of the United States of America to put an end to these intolerable mal-practices which are likely seriously to deteriorate relations between the African peoples and governments on the one hand and the people and government of the United States of America on the other.[53]

The State Department's reaction was that the resolution on discrimination was "appreciably better from our standpoint, than the preliminary proposal." According to a State Department memorandum for the White House, U.S. Ambassador to Ethiopia Edward M. Korry thought it was "as good an outcome as possible." The adoption of the watered-down version "was a remarkable tribute to the United States Government, considering the depth of African feeling about the Alabama incidents." This achievement was "tangible evidence of the international impact of local incidents, and in the context of our African relations reinforces the wisdom of Federal policy." From the State Department's perspective, the federal government's role in resolving the Birmingham crisis had concrete and beneficial effects on U.S. foreign relations. This perspective was reinforced in post–Addis Ababa correspondence with African leaders. For example, President Nyerere of Tanganyika wrote to Kennedy that he "appreciated your efforts in connection with the reinvigorated demand by the Negro Citizens of America for full equal rights." Nyerere had confidence that Kennedy would "find a solution which gives justice to all American citizens. In doing so you will be making a great contribution to the cause of non-racialism throughout the world."[54]

There was another reason for the turnabout in Addis Ababa. President Youlou of the Congo had written to Kennedy on the eve of the conference. Knowing that Birmingham would be on the minds of participants in the meeting, Youlou noted that "[c]ertainly you can measure better than anyone else the repercussions which the events in Birmingham are having in Africa." However, Youlou would not support a reaction to Birmingham at Addis Ababa. He had argued against UN intervention in his own country, and he believed that problems in Africa could be solved without the involvement of those outside the continent. "This is the same argument I shall give to those who would like to see me take a position on the events in Alabama," Youlou wrote. "I believe that the American Negroes are Americans, and that, at the present stage of your difficulties, they do not yet have any aspiration for national independence. It is your government that either will or will not be able to keep them in the United States, or else make foreigners of them. But it is, first of all, *among Americans* that the solution must be sought." President Kennedy's response to Youlou after the conference noted his pleasure that the resolution on discrimination in the United States mentioned the progress made by the government to abolish segregation. He also indicated that he appreciated Youlou's "concern that any intervention in African affairs by non-Africans might encourage a counterreaction involving the United States' own affairs." Each nation, it was clear, had an interest in handling its domestic matters on its own.[55] Now that the Congo was independent, that nation's leaders shared with Kennedy an interest in national sovereignty. The desire to avoid foreign interference in their own domestic difficulties led some African leaders to soften their criticism of the United States.

A crisis was averted in Addis Ababa. No "break" in United States–African relations was contemplated. Yet following the meeting much work remained to be done. Secretary of State Dean Rusk sent a circular on race and foreign relations to all American diplomatic and consular posts. Rusk emphasized that the Kennedy administration was "keenly aware of [the] impact of [the] domestic race problem on [the] US image overseas and on achievement [of] US foreign policy objectives." Rusk felt that "[t]here should be no illusions as to [the] seriousness of [the] situation." Foreign reaction to race in the U.S. was a "source of great concern. Evidence from all parts of [the] world indicates that racial incidents have produced extremely negative reactions." The reaction of African heads of state at Addis Ababa was just one example illustrating the "depth of emotional feeling" throughout the world. Such incidents suggested that "we have a certain amount of time before our racial problem will impinge even more seriously upon our policies and objectives."[56]

"Under these circumstances," Rusk continued, "we recognize there is no effective substitute for decisive action on [the] part of [the] United States Government. This will include [a] special Presidential message to Congress today, Administration-backed legislation, and [a] continued series of positive Federal actions throughout [the] country."[57]

Rusk's concerns were emphasized in a June 1963 speech by USIA Deputy Director Donald Wilson to the Women's National Democratic Club in Washington. According to Wilson, Birmingham "opened a new era in race relations." Due to the efforts of the civil rights movement, international attention given to U.S. race relations would be sustained. "We are no longer coping with isolated incidents. Where the span between a Little Rock and an Oxford could be marked by months and years, now we are wit-

Firefighters bear down on civil rights demonstrators who had tried to seek refuge in a doorway, Birmingham, Alabama, May 3, 1963. Photographs of Police Commissioner Bull Connor's brutal tactics blanketed the world's press. (UPI/CORBIS-BETTMANN)

The harsh treatment of civil rights protesters in Birmingham was a subject of discussion at the first meeting of the Organization of African Unity, Addis Ababa, Ethiopia, May 23, 1963. (UPI/CORBIS-BETTMANN)

nessing a massive effort throughout the nation, and there will be no long pauses which allow us to slip into apathy." A State Department analyst put it this way: "This movement is watched from abroad not always tolerantly, not always patiently—the picture of a dog attacking a Negro, of a police officer pinning a Negro woman to the ground—these pictures have a dramatic impact on those abroad who listen to our words about democracy and weigh our actions against those words."[58]

The difficulty of managing this problem was magnified by the fact that the civil rights movement sought to use international concern to increase pressure on the Kennedy administration for civil rights reform. As State Department analyst Richard N. Gardner put it, "The American Negro himself has made the link between the international and domestic problems." For example, James Baldwin quoted one African American as saying, "At the rate things are going here, . . . all of Africa will be free before we can get a lousy cup of coffee." Baldwin added, "What is demanded now, and at once, is not that Negroes continue to adjust themselves to the cruel racial pressures of life in the United States but the United States readjust itself to the facts of life in the present world."[59]

The need for positive federal action presented itself yet again when Alabama Governor George Wallace stood in the schoolhouse door to block the integration of the University of Alabama. On May 21, 1963, a federal district judge had ordered the university to admit two African American students to its summer session. At his inauguration earlier in the year, Wallace had pledged "Segregation now! Segregation tomorrow! Segregation forever!" in front of television cameras and a crowd of reporters from around the world. Now, he stood behind a line drawn in front of the doorway of the university administration building, decrying the "unwelcome, unwanted and force-induced intrusion . . . by the central government." With careful planning, and the president's order to federalize the Alabama National Guard, the students were quietly registered later that day. Still, Wallace and southern defiance had an important moment in the spotlight. A need to respond helped motivate President Kennedy to take a step his advisors and civil rights activists had been urging for some time. On the evening of June 11, 1963, Kennedy delivered an impassioned plea for civil rights reform before a nationwide television audience.[60]

Administration officials were also concerned about continuing civil rights demonstrations. As Robert Kennedy put it, "street demonstrations" were likely to continue. "The result is that someone is very likely to get hurt. It's bad for the country. It's bad for us around the world." Civil rights legislation would enable the Justice Department to bring suit to enforce civil rights, and that would "get this into court and out of the street."[61] Placing civil rights problems in a manageable judicial forum would help accomplish one of the president's objectives: avoiding photo opportunities that embarrassed the nation overseas.

President Kennedy responded by calling for landmark civil rights legislation, explaining his course of action in a televised address to the nation. It was the president's most dramatic and heartfelt statement on civil rights. Kennedy asked all Americans to examine their conscience on the subject of race discrimination. The nation had been founded upon the principle of equality, he noted.

> Today we are committed to a worldwide struggle to promote and protect the rights of all who wish to be free. And when Americans are sent to Viet-Nam or West Berlin, we do not ask for whites only. It ought to be possible, therefore, for American students of any color to attend any public institution they select without having to be backed up by troops.[62]

Kennedy called civil rights "a moral issue . . . as old as the scriptures and . . . as clear as the American Constitution." He believed that "[t]he heart of the question" was "whether we are going to treat our fellow Americans as we want to be treated." While Kennedy presented the issue as a question of morality, its resolution would protect the freedom of all Americans, for "this Nation . . . will not fully be free until all its citizens are free."[63]

> We preach freedom around the world, and we mean it, and we cherish our freedom here at home, but are we to say to the world, and much more importantly, to each other that

this is a land of the free except for the Negroes; that we have no second-class citizens except Negroes; that we have no class or cast [sic] system, no ghettoes, no master race except with respect to Negroes?[64]

The president described an ambitious civil rights agenda that would depend upon more than congressional action, executive branch enforcement efforts, and court orders. Kennedy called upon "every American in every community across our country" to join together in a national commitment to equality.[65]

The following week, President Kennedy appeared before a joint session of Congress and urged that body to take up the fight. If Congress did not act on civil rights, the consequences would be widespread, he argued. Legislative inaction would result in "continued, if not increased, racial strife—causing the leadership on both sides to pass from the hands of reasonable and responsible men to the purveyors of hate and violence, endangering domestic tranquility, retarding our Nation's economic and social progress and weakening the respect with which the rest of the world regards us."[66]

Kennedy's civil rights speech marked a critical shift. No longer holding civil rights at arm's length, the president seemed to embrace it. What had led to this dramatic turnabout? Carl Brauer has written:

> Intellectually Kennedy had long believed in the principle of racial equality, but the disturbing events of the spring added an emotional dimension to that belief. . . . With Birmingham, American race relations seemed to be entering a period of crisis, yet the federal government lacked the necessary tools to deal with it. Thousands of blacks were taking to the streets to demand their rights—rights no federal law guaranteed. When local authorities proved obdurate and arrested or repulsed the demonstrators, a situation was created that both soiled America's reputation abroad and bred violence and extremism among blacks at home.

In Brauer's view, the most important factor was Kennedy's "perception of himself as a decisive leader." Birmingham "fostered an atmosphere in which he could only weakly respond to events rather than direct and shape them. It cast him in a weak and defensive position when his personality and view of the Presidency called for decisive leadership and a measure of control over events."[67] President Kennedy's strengthened commitment to civil rights came at a time when international criticism was heightened and the goodwill developed from the Meredith affair had been undermined. If Kennedy's sense of himself as a leader was at stake, then surely his sense of himself as a world leader, as well as a national leader, was implicated.

As Jennifer See has illustrated, the drama of Kennedy's June 11 civil rights speech was enhanced by the fact that it was part of a broader political moment. The speech followed by just one day a critical address on foreign relations that he delivered at American University. In that speech, the president hoped to move public opinion in favor of détente to help generate political support for a proposed nuclear test ban treaty. As he would on civil rights, Kennedy asked Americans to examine their consciences on peace, the Soviet Union, and the Cold War as well. "[E]very thoughtful citizen who despairs of war and wishes to bring peace, should begin by looking inward," he said. The prospect of nuclear war was so horrendous that Cold War adversaries had a mutual interest in getting past their differences, and pursuing peace. While earlier presidents hoped to save the world for democracy, Kennedy thought that "we can at least make the world safe for diversity." Because no nation could survive a nuclear holocaust, the United States and the Soviet Union had a mutual interest in peace and in arms control.[68]

The Nation commented that the president had let "two genii out of their respective bottles on successive days": civil rights and the Cold War. *Newsweek* writer Kenneth Crawford called it the "politics of courage."[69]

While he spoke most directly to the American people, the target audience for President Kennedy's address on civil rights was much broader. The speech was distributed to all American diplomatic posts with directions from the secretary of state and the president himself regarding how the speech should be used, and why this issue was of such importance.[70]

World reaction to the speech was highly favorable. U.S. Ambassador to Ethiopia Edward M. Korry wrote to President Kennedy about the "quick turnaround in attitudes" that his civil rights statements had caused in Ethiopia. Emperor Haile Selassie thought the statements were "masterpieces." In addition to Ethiopian royalty, "student leaders, the up-and-coming educated middle bureaucrats and the younger Army elite" discussed Kennedy's actions "without trace of the sensitivity that reportedly characterized their remarks in years gone by." Korry sent the president an *Ethiopian Herald* editorial that called him "the Abraham Lincoln of the Democratic Party" and lauded the fact that the U.S. government, "in the person of John F. Kennedy, has at long last come out in defence of the Constitution." Predictably, in the Soviet Union, the speech was virtually ignored, as Soviet broadcasting continued a barrage at an unprecedented level, criticizing racism in America as an inevitable consequence of capitalism and as an illustration of "the hypocrisy of US claims to leadership of the free world."[71]

All eyes then turned to Congress and the effort to pass civil rights legislation. During the Kennedy administration, the public battleground over civil rights reform was more focused on Congress than on the courts. This was not because the courts were unengaged in racial equality during the early 1960s. The Supreme Court handed down important rulings protecting the rights of civil rights organizations and activists, among other areas. The defining *public* battleground had shifted from the courts to Congress in part because the movement demanded rights beyond what the courts were likely to provide. Discrimination by seemingly private parties—restaurant, hotel, and gas station owners, for example—was discrimination the Supreme Court considered a matter of state, not federal, concern. Federal rights to equal protection of the laws only came into play when the state itself practiced discrimination. Private discrimination, in contrast, was not a matter of federal constitutional concern.[72]

The discrimination against African diplomats on Route 40 and against African American students at Greensboro lunch counters was not discrimination at the hands of the state. As a result, based on an understanding of federalism and individual rights dating back to the 1880s, this was discrimination that the courts, acting alone, would not redress. To remedy this problem, the civil rights movement, supporters of civil rights in Congress, and, ultimately, President Kennedy himself, set their sights on a new civil rights bill. In what would later become the Civil Rights Act of 1964, Congress relied on its expansive power to regulate private activities that had an impact on interstate commerce. Because discrimination in private businesses was thought to harm the economy, Congress could outlaw it under the Commerce Clause.[73]

Because of its importance in resolving the kinds of civil rights crises that so often blanketed the world's press in the early 1960s, the civil rights bill was closely followed overseas, and developments in the courts received much less attention. Even though the principal civil rights front, at least in the eyes of foreign observers, was in Congress, the Constitution continued to play a role in the way federal obligations were understood. Over and over again, federalism played a crucial role in the rhetorical strategy to explain to foreign audiences that continuing racial injustice in the United States did not mean that the American political system was unjust.

Many members of Congress were anxious to pass a civil rights bill and were well aware of the diplomatic importance of such action. While the USIA kept the president informed of the details of the overseas reaction to Birmingham, members of Congress did not need USIA briefings to be aware of the international uproar over this particular civil rights crisis. The foreign press reaction to Birmingham was a story in American newspapers. Senator Jacob Javits of New York inserted into the *Congressional Record* news stories about the foreign press. Javits was concerned about the foreign affairs impact of Birmingham. He thought that "the propaganda value of what has happened can only help those who are opposed to our free institutions, and is unfortunately a forceful incentive to them in propagating communism in Africa, Asia and Latin America." While Javits thought that the executive branch had failed in its responsibilities in Birmingham, he also believed that Congress had a crucial role to play in resolving civil rights crises. "[T]he role of Congress is as vital as the role of the executive department," he argued, and Congress had "failed signally" to meet its responsibilities. "The national interest will not let us wait; we had better get at it now."[74]

When the Kennedy administration's civil rights bill came before the Senate Commerce Committee, the president asked Secretary of State Dean Rusk to lead off the administration's testimony with a discussion of the impact of discrimination on U.S. foreign affairs. In the desegregation cases, it had been the Justice Department's job, relying on State Department evidence, to educate the Supreme Court about the foreign relations consequences of discrimination. When the civil rights bill came before Congress, the secretary of state himself took on the task of explaining to members of Congress the national security implications of their votes on civil rights.[75]

The Civil Rights Act of 1963, as proposed by the Kennedy administration, would address a range of problems. Proposals included enabling the Justice Department to bring school desegregation lawsuits, creation of an Equal Employment Opportunity Commission, some protection of the right to vote, and authority to deny federal funding to programs that discriminated on the basis of race in hiring. Of particular interest to the secretary of state was Title II of the bill, which prohibited discrimination in public accommodations. Lobbying on behalf of the civil rights bill was an extension of State Department efforts to address the embarrassment that discrimination in housing, restaurants, theaters, and hotels had caused the administration. As Pedro Sanjuan had stressed, there was only so much the federal government could do to protect foreign diplomats from discrimination when American persons of color were segregated. If the public accommodations section became law, a foreign passport would not be a prerequisite to equal treatment.[76]

As a result of incidents like Birmingham, Rusk believed that race relations in the nation as a whole in the 1960s "had a profound impact on the world's view of the United States and, therefore, on our foreign relations." He told the Commerce Committee that the "primary reason why we must attack the problems of discrimination" was not foreign affairs but because racism was "incompatible with the great ideals to which our democratic society is dedicated. If the realities at home are as they should be, we shan't have to worry about our image abroad." All was not as it should be, however, and as a result, "racial discrimination here at home has important effects on our foreign relations." Racial and ethnic discrimination existed elsewhere in the world, he told the senators.

> But the United States is widely regarded as the home of democracy and the leader of the struggle for freedom, for human rights, for human dignity. We are expected to be the model. . . . So our failure to live up to our proclaimed ideals are noted—and magnified and distorted.[77]

International developments had crystallized this issue's importance. According to Rusk, decolonization was "[o]ne of the epochal developments of our time." "The vast majority of these newly independent peoples are nonwhite, and they are determined to eradicate every vestige of the notion that the white race is superior or entitled to special privileges because of race." The United States was engaged in a world struggle for freedom, against the forces of communism. Rusk warned that "in waging this world struggle we are seriously handicapped by racial or religious discrimination in the United States. . . . In their efforts to enhance their influence among the nonwhite peoples and to alienate them from us, the Communists clearly regard racial discrimination in the United States as one of their most valuable assets."[78]

This problem facing the nation would be worse, Rusk argued, if it were not for the progress made to overcome discrimination, and for the role played by the federal government, particularly the executive branch and the judiciary, to protect civil rights. To illustrate the importance of federal action, Rusk cited one example: "The recent meeting of African heads of state at Addis Ababa, condemned racial discrimination 'especially in the United States,' then approved the role of U.S. Federal authorities in attempting to combat it."[79]

Further action was now crucial. Rusk continued, "If progress should stop, if Congress should not approve legislation designed to remove remaining discriminatory practices, questions would inevitably arise in many parts of the world as to the real convictions of the American people. In that event, hostile propaganda might be expected to hurt us more than it has hurt us until now."[80]

While Rusk's testimony was warmly praised by several members of the Commerce Committee, not all senators were sympathetic to the notion that American race discrimination aided communism. The atmosphere was tense in the crowded Senate caucus room as Senator Strom Thurmond took on the secretary of state. Thurmond asked whether Rusk believed that "Congress should be urged to act on some particular measure, because of the threat of Communist propaganda if we don't?" He also wondered whether the secretary, through his testimony, was "lending at least tacit support to, and approval of, this Communist line." Rusk answered that "the primary issue is for us here at home. . . . I don't think we can create an image abroad unless it fairly represents reality at home. And I believe that, because the rest of the world is so closely watching the United States, the reality at home creates its own image abroad."[81]

As to whether he was aiding the communists, Rusk responded that he was present to advise the committee about "the relationships between these problems here at home and our foreign policy." The secretary stressed, "I consider[ed] that relationship to be very grave and I would certainly hope that no committee of the Congress would ever take the view that a Secretary of State can't come before it without having it said he is supporting a Communist line."[82]

Thurmond continued to press him until, as the *New York Times* put it, Rusk "dropped his normal diplomatic manner of speaking." When Thurmond asked repeatedly whether Rusk supported civil rights demonstrations, Rusk finally retorted, "If I were denied what our Negro citizens are denied, I would demonstrate."[83]

For earlier secretaries of state, discrimination was a problem to be managed in order to safeguard the nation's image, and civil rights activism was a threat because it called attention to the nation's Achilles heel. For Dean Rusk, however, the civil rights movement was to be embraced. The moral power of the movement could not be denied. In addition, civil rights activists presented the nation with an opportunity. As each crisis broke, it provided the federal government with an opportunity to demonstrate the nation's resolve. As long as the story told overseas could be a story of U.S. government action against injustice, then civil rights crises provided opportunities to demonstrate that American democracy sided with the champions of justice, and that the American government would use its power in battles, small and large, between freedom and tyranny. In that sense, civil rights crises provided a stage upon which the United States could act out in symbolic form its Cold War commitments.

By August 1963, most Americans agreed with Dean Rusk that race discrimination was a foreign policy matter. A Harris Poll reported that seventy-eight percent of white Americans surveyed thought that race discrimination in the United States harmed the nation abroad. Twenty-three percent of respondents volunteered that the primary reason discrimination harmed the United States abroad was that it gave the communists a valuable propaganda weapon. The second major reason was that it generally gave the country a bad name. As a Kingsport, Tennessee, lawyer put it, "The pictures of dogs attacking colored people in Birmingham have been sent abroad and you know what kind of opinion that gives them about us."[84]

Internationally, there was both progress and the need for continued vigilance. On July 9, 1963, Assistant Secretary of State G. Mennen Williams returned from a trip to Africa, and reported that, on one hand, the nation's position in Africa was "strong because of our past policy and President Kennedy's image." On the other hand, it was "precarious because of the need to realize the promise of the President's civil rights program."[85]

In this context, civil rights leaders' plans to hold a massive civil rights march represented both a threat and an opportunity. A. Philip Randolph had long advocated a march on the nation's capital, and had used the possibility of a march as leverage to pressure President Franklin Roosevelt to address racial discrimination in defense industries during World War II. As Scott Sandage has argued, the site of the March on Washington—the Lincoln Memorial—had symbolic value in the context of the nationalism of this era. Protest at the Lincoln Memorial, a national cultural space, enabled the movement to portray its demands dramatically as claims to full American citizenship, and therefore within the terms of "Americanism." According to Sandage, "Black leaders assembled at the shrine a compelling universe of national symbols . . . which linked the black political agenda to the regnant cultural nationalism of the era."[86]

President Kennedy and his aides were concerned that a large march would erupt in violence and that the message conveyed might be critical of Kennedy civil rights policy. However, if peaceful, the march might also be seen by the world as an example of effective participation in an open, democratic political process. If supportive of Kennedy administration civil rights policy, it also held potential to be seen as a reinforcement of an argument the administration had been making overseas that the federal government was behind civil rights reform. What better evidence of that than a march by civil rights activists themselves reaffirming Kennedy's policies?

For march organizers, of course, the Kennedy administration's commitment to civil rights reform was a matter of concern. Although the objectives of the march went beyond the civil rights bill pending in Congress, one goal was to pressure Kennedy to strongly support a meaningful civil rights bill. March organizers disagreed among themselves over how directly the march should challenge the administration. Internal disagreement continued until the day of the march itself, when SNCC representative John Lewis was pressured to modify his speech. Lewis had planned to call for a recreation of General Sherman's march through the South, saying "We shall pursue our own 'scorched earth' policy and burn Jim Crow to the ground—nonviolently." As for the pending civil rights legislation, Lewis's speech argued that "we cannot support, wholeheartedly" the bill, for "it is too little, and too late." Some civil rights leaders and Justice Department officials objected to the speech. The Justice Department went so far as to draft an alternative, and, ultimately, Martin Luther King Jr. and Randolph, the father of the original March on Washington movement, pressured Lewis to tone down the speech.[87]

Objecting to the content of John Lewis's speech was only one part of the Kennedy administration's efforts to affect the image of the march. The administration was well aware that a civil rights march on the nation's capital would be followed worldwide. The State Department and the United States Information Agency worked to ensure that the "right" message would be conveyed by the march, and that the message would be understood as consistent with the image of democracy the government tried to project. Before and after the event, the story of the march was carefully packaged for foreign audiences.[88]

If the march was peaceful, the speeches moderate in tone, and the story of the march appropriately told, the event might be seen as a symbol of progress, a marker of African American political participation, a fulfillment of a liberal democratic vision. Control over the international image of the march slipped through the government's fingers, however, as the March on Washington became a worldwide event.

The writer James Baldwin took the March on Washington to Paris. Baldwin traveled to that city in August 1963, hoping to find some peace and quiet so that he could complete a play that was soon to enter production. Although he sought isolation in Paris, Baldwin did not wish to disengage from the struggle for racial justice back home. He placed an advertisement in the *Herald Tribune*, calling a meeting about civil rights in the United States, to be held on August 17 at the Living Room, a Paris nightclub. According to Barbara Sargent, wife of the pastor of the American Church in Paris, about one hundred people attended the meeting. Many of them were prominent jazz musicians. While most of the attendees were U.S. citizens, others at the meeting included a leader of the African student movement and a Ceylonese law student.[89]

William Marshall began the meeting, as Sargent reported it, speaking of "the desire of the American negro in Paris to have first hand knowledge of the integration movement in the USA, and to be a part of it, though living and working here." James Baldwin spoke briefly about the march, then "emphasized instead the explosive nature of the situation in Chicago and New York City." According to Sargent,

> [M]any of the negroes asked if there was anything they could do. The pianist . . . Art Simmons spoke movingly of being forced every night to explain to foreigners something about America which he could not really explain to himself. They all felt that as jazz musicians they were *the* most influential unofficial ambassador's [sic] that America had. . . .
>
> So they began to plan.

The group discussed the ideas of a sympathy march on the American embassy in Paris the same day as the March on Washington, and possibly a sit-down strike on the embassy grounds. The purpose of such a protest would be "to make a point. They obviously feel that one reason, if not the main reason, that progress has been made toward equality in our country, has been the pressure of foreign opinion, and the fact that our racial troubles cripple us vis a vis the world." The atmosphere at the meeting was "electric. One after another spoke of their bitterness and grief and frustration, each one urging the other on."[90]

At some point, a drafting committee consisting of Marshall, Baldwin, jazz musician Memphis Slim, actor Anthony Quinn, Barbara Sargent, and Silvia Jerico composed a brief petition in support of the March on Washington, to be placed in the international editions of the *New York Times* and the *Herald Tribune*. The petition stated that

> I, the undersigned, as an American citizen, hereby publicly express my support of the March on Washington Movement, which aspires not only to eradicate all racial barriers in American life but to liberate all Americans from the prison of their biases and fears. I cannot physically participate in this March, but I, like the rest of the world, have been tremendously stirred by so disciplined an exhibition of dignity and courage and persistence and would like to associate myself with it.

Some published copies of the petition indicated that it was sponsored by "a group of Americans in Paris." All copies asked signers to present the petition at "the American Embassy in your city on Wednesday, August 21, between 1 and 3 o'clock." The ad was paid for by donations, with the overall amount guaranteed by Quinn.[91]

Planning continued the next day at a meeting at the American Church. Two hundred attended. The group ultimately did not plan a formal march. Some felt that a march or sit-in would be "irresponsible." According to a U.S. embassy officer, "Another important element in the decision to abandon a 'march' on the Embassy was the fact that an organized demonstration in the streets involved red tape with the French authorities." Instead, many people simply walked from the American Church to the embassy at about the same time on August 21. No "march" happened in Paris that day, but 80 to 100 people left the church for the embassy at the same time, walking alone or in small groups. Others showed up separately at the embassy, and by the end of the day more than 550 petitions had been delivered.[92]

The high point of this "walk" came shortly after one in the afternoon, when the leaders arrived at the embassy. William Marshall headed the delegation, which included James Baldwin, Hazel Scott, Memphis Slim, Mezz Mezroe, and Mae Mercer. They presented a scroll of signatures to Cecil Lyon while approximately 150 others waited in the embassy's main hall.[93]

This effort, begun in a Paris nightclub, quickly spread across the continent. The newspaper petitions appeared in issues of the *New York Times* and the *Herald Tribune* distributed throughout Europe. Readers clipped out and signed the petitions and delivered them to U.S. diplomatic posts in many countries. Forty-seven were delivered in London, thirty-five in Rome, and eight in Madrid. Petitions were delivered to U.S. missions in several German cities. While most of those signing the petition were American citizens, citizens of other nations at times wrote in their own nationality. Those who could not personally deliver their petitions mailed them in. Many wrote personal notes. Richard C. Longworth hoped to emphasize "the heartfelt desire of us Americans living abroad that our nation, which has stood for so long as a symbol of all that is best, will now be able to extend its liberties and opportunities to all its citizens." A small number of petitions did not support the march. A group of unnamed U.S. tourists in London edited their copy of the petition to state that they "*object* to the March on Washington Movement," and "*don't* associate with it." The tourists complained, "We *resent* this kind of attempt to publicize a *minority* group!" and "p.s. The U.S.A. form of gov't stems from '*The Town Hall*' consent, & will, of the *majority* !!"[94]

James Baldwin returned to the United States, and on August 28, 1963, he marched with more than two hundred thousand people to the Lincoln Memorial in Washington, D.C. The news of support from Americans overseas was conveyed to the crowd as the actor Burt Lancaster read the Paris petition. When Martin Luther King Jr. gave the final speech of this historic day, his words echoed across continents, as well as across time. King decried the fact that one hundred years after Emancipation, "the Negro is still languished in the corners of American society and finds himself in exile in his own land." He emphasized the urgency of the moment: "This sweltering summer of the Negro's legitimate discontent will not pass until there is an invigorating autumn of freedom and equality." Yet King was hopeful for the future, for he held to "a dream deeply rooted in the American dream that one day this nation will rise up and live out the true meaning of its creed—We hold these truths to be self-evident, that all men are created equal."[95]

The March on Washington had a worldwide impact, inspiring additional solidarity marches abroad. On the date of the Washington March, in several countries around the world, people marched on American diplomatic posts to express their solidarity with the March on Washington. Others sent telegrams and delivered petitions. The August 28 actions appear to be largely unrelated to the organizing in Paris and uncoordinated with each other. Between twelve hundred and fourteen hundred marched on the U.S. consulate in Amsterdam. This demonstration was organized by the Action Committee for Solidarity with the March on Washington, a local ad hoc group. Approximately twenty-five hundred demonstrated in Kingston, Jamaica, led by the mayor of the city. In Ghana, a smaller, informal group organized a protest at the embassy carrying signs with slogans like "America, Africa is Watching You," and "Stop Genocide in America and South Africa." Students demonstrated at the U.S. legation in Burundi. Another sympathy march occurred in Tel Aviv. In Oslo, one hundred people marched through heavy rain to present a petition to the U.S. embassy supporting President Kennedy's proposed civil rights bill. The actor Al Hoosman led a group of forty to fifty Germans and Americans to the American consulate in Munich. With few exceptions, American diplomatic personnel described these and other demonstrations as peaceful and respectful. A protest in Berlin was marked by disorder, but not due to the actions of the protesters. As the U.S. consulate reported it, while sixty-five people "gathered quietly" outside the U.S. mission in Berlin, "a short scuffle developed" when two men in civilian clothes (later identified as U.S. soldiers) attempted to harass demonstrators until two MPs stepped in.[96]

The orderliness of protest could sometimes be a sign of government suppression. In at least one context, U.S. embassy complicity in confining the scope of a sympathy march was continuing evidence of U.S. government efforts to protect its image abroad by silencing critics.

The U.S. embassy in Cairo anticipated several hundred demonstrators on August 28. The embassy and Cairo police planned accordingly. According to Donald C. Bergus, counselor of the embassy for political affairs, "The police took elaborate precautions not only to see that the 'demonstration' stayed entirely within peaceful bounds but even more to reduce the whole affair to minimal proportions." Preparations included "[s]izeable police contingents" posted at the embassy early in the morning. By the time the march occurred, "[a]bout 200 policemen were stationed in the Embassy area." Only thirteen protesters chose to face these forces. They walked to the center of town, wearing signs that read "Remember Negroes Also Built America," "Down With the Ku Klux Klan," and "Medgar Evers Did Not Die in Vain." As they marched peacefully the thirteen protesters were followed by "a contingent of police." The group had come within one block of the U.S. embassy when "they were intercepted by a strong contingent of police." The group was told that only two of them could approach the embassy. The marchers selected M. A. Makiwame of the African National Congress and R. I. Sibanda of the Simbabwe African Peoples Union. According to Bergus, the two men "approached the Embassy surrounded by policemen and looking rather frightened that they might be arrested if they did or said the wrong thing. Immediately in front of the gate they were again stopped by a police officer who gave them a three-minute lecture about behaving themselves. The two then presented the petition to the waiting Embassy officers." Makiwame and Sibanda gave the officers a memorandum in support of the civil rights movement, signed by representatives of African liberation organizations based in Cairo. They viewed "with great concern the plight of the Negro people in the United States of America. . . . The beastly conduct of Governor Faubus and the intimidations against Negroes in Little Rock and Birmingham, Alabama, are fresh in our minds." American racism "fills us with anger." "For generations, the Governments [sic] of the United States have been fooling the world into believing that everything was going on well in the country, they have shouted at the top of their voices about freedom and democracy, but these have only been on paper and never practiced." The statement quoted the Fifteenth Amendment to the U.S. Constitution, and spoke of the importance of protecting the rights of blacks in the United States to vote. The protesters "strongly condemn[ed] the Kennedy Administration" and called upon the United States government to protect civil rights. The protest was extensively covered on Cairo Radio.[97]

This small but determined protest was met by the full power of the state. The government of Egypt did not support the group's efforts and had "assured the Embassy that it considers African Association attacks on the Kennedy administration grossly mistaken and counterproductive." As Bergus put it, the government's "handling of this protest was in line with the assurances to the Embassy. The action taken by the authorities on August 28 also provided excellent evidence that when the Nasser regime decides it wants to control a demonstration, it knows how to do the job extremely well."[98]

On the same day that two Africans faced the Cairo police, on the other side of the globe hundreds of thousands marched on Washington. The Washington marchers could not have been aware of the extent of support for them by so many people around the world. Great effort and planning had gone into the march, and its success is often measured by the size of crowd and the enduring power of the message of its speakers. Its great success is surely also measured by the thousands abroad, inspired by the march, who made their own personal pilgrimages to register their support.

As expected, the march was a major worldwide news event. In Europe, according to the USIA, "most comment found the Washington March a ringing affirmation of the power of the American

On August 28, 1963, more than two hundred thousand people marched on Washington in support of civil rights. The march was an international event, spawning sympathy marches around the world. (UPI/CORBIS-BETTMANN)

The Soviet Union stepped up its criticism of U.S. racism in 1963. In this cartoon in the Soviet publication *Krokodil*, an African American student is stopped by police from entering an American university. Segregationists in the background carry signs that say: "Nigger Go Away," "Lynch Him," "We Want Segregation," and "Put the Colored on Their Knees." August 24, 1963. (UPI/CORBIS-BETT-MANN)

democratic process." The Cold War implications were evident. "Many papers specifically contrasted the opportunity granted by a free society with the despotic suppression practiced by the USSR." As *Algemeen Dagblad* in Rotterdam put it, "Nowhere in the world has so much been done . . . for the solution of the racial problem as in the US in recent years . . . ; just imagine what would have happened had such a demonstration been planned in East Berlin [or] Moscow." The *Times of India* called the march "a heart-warming reassertion of the dignity of man." In Calcutta, *Jugantar* praised the "freedom fighters," noting that "[i]f Mahatma Gandhi's ideal is living anywhere, it is in the Negro demonstration and in Martin Luther King's goal of life." Meanwhile, the Chinese Communist press, engaged in a "large scale campaign" on the topic of civil rights, found "little to exploit in [the] peaceful nature of [the] march."[99]

In Africa, "[m]uch of the comment hailed [the march] as the greatest event of its kind in history." In Ghana, the *Evening News* called the march one of the "greatest revolutions in the annals of human history." Criticism of the United States was still warranted, however. The *Ghanaian Times* thought that "time is running out." Race discrimination in America "casts much slur on Western civilization championed by the US." A *Times* columnist "urged Negro leaders to 'fuse [their] revolutionary upsurge' with the efforts of the 'victims of U.S. imperialism in other continents.' " In Cairo, *Al-Gomhuriyah* thought that President Kennedy supported the marchers because "he realized the 'disastrous effects' the 'policy of persecuting U.S. Negroes [has] on the general situation inside the United States itself as well as the harm it does to the prestige of the United States in the eyes of all the peoples of the world.' "[100]

There was a lesson in this commentary about the need for federal action to protect U.S. prestige abroad. The USIA reported that most foreign comment agreed "that the meaningful impact of the March would be measured in terms of the response of Congress to the Administration's civil rights proposals and the day-to-day support given to civil rights by the American public." Because of "strong opposition in Congress and the South as well as the indifference of the general public, considerable skepticism prevailed concerning the passage and implementation of civil rights legislation." There was general consensus that the United States still had "a long way to go to achieve racial equality."[101]

Before the March on Washington occurred, the USIA had plans to present the story of the march in an advantageous manner. Foreign posts received a USIA telegraph two days before the march indicating that the British Independent Television network (ITV) planned a fifteen-minute feature. This film was intended to "plac[e] [the] March in proper context within civil rights struggle." It would "highlight positive aspects [of the] March and emphasize its significance as [a] manifestation of public sentiment in support [of] civil rights." Because of the march's importance, ITV planned the "most rapid distribution possible," with copies of the film most likely sent out the day after the event. A USIA documentary was later prepared on the march and distributed in 1964.[102]

Yet, as Donald Wilson had written so presciently, a new crisis erupted even as efforts to spin the story of the march were getting underway. On Sunday morning, September 15, a bomb exploded in the Sixteenth Street Baptist Church in Birmingham, Alabama. Four young girls preparing for Sunday school were killed. David Garrow calls this incident "the greatest human tragedy that had befallen the movement." In the aftermath, "[t]he rage and desperation felt by black Birmingham exploded into the city's streets." Martin Luther King Jr. thought that Birmingham was "in a state of civil disorder" and called upon President Kennedy for a strong federal presence. If the federal government did not act, King telegraphed the president, "we shall see the worst racial holocaust this nation has ever seen." Kennedy issued a statement condemning the bombing, and later would meet with King and other civil rights leaders. In the meantime, SNCC leader Diane Nash Bevel drew up a plan of action to break the back of segregation in Alabama. Among the plans contemplated were "[d]emonstrations at the United Nations to secure the vote."[103]

There had been, and would later be, other deaths. The brutal killing of children, however, seemed especially horrific. The international press condemned the "slaughter of innocents" while also giving prominent coverage to President Kennedy's expression of outrage over the killings. American embassies around the world were flooded with petitions condemning the bombing and calling for civil rights reform. Funds from abroad were sent to rebuild the Sixteenth Street Baptist Church. The deputy premier of Western Nigeria sent a check for the "relatives of [the] deceased as [a] small token of my genuine sympathy for their loss and as an expression of my oneness with them, and their oneness with all people in Africa in our common struggle for equality, justice and democracy." The deputy premier's letter, which was released to the press, noted the "determination and positive action" of the Kennedy administration to fight racism, but nevertheless suggested that "increasing brutalities and bestialities of white men to black men, black women and black children in the United States of America is really becoming unbearable."[104]

The bombing undercut U.S. efforts to play up the March on Washington as an example of racial progress. In Cameroon, the U.S. embassy reported that the march had "captured the local imagination and focused attention on the Negro drive for equality as no other event before it had done." When news of the church bombing broke, it did much to "dissipate any feeling of hopefulness and sympathy evoked by the march." When the embassy public affairs officer invited a top government official to a screening of a March on Washington film, he replied, "Don't you have a film of the church dynamiting, too?"[105]

The narrative of American racial progress was threatened by protest against American racism, so U.S. embassy officers in at least one country took solace in government repression of critics. In Tanganyika, the government "squashed" a demonstration in reaction to the church bombing at the U.S. embassy because, in the words of a Tanganyikan official, the "Tanganyikan government saw no basis for [the] demonstration since [the] policy [of the] U.S. government [is] so firmly against such outrages." The U.S. embassy response was to express "appreciation" for Tanganyikan government confidence.[106]

The Birmingham bombing, coming on the heels of successful efforts to project a positive message about the March on Washington, powerfully underscored the fact that a new era had begun. There were to be no breaks in the international side of the U.S. civil rights crisis. In terms of its impact on foreign affairs, by 1963 civil rights was a constant, critical theme. This meant that President Kennedy's ability to control the place of civil rights on his policy agenda was limited. The moral power of the movement, the brutality of resistance, and the ever present international gaze meant that civil rights could not be subordinated. The circumstances required strong civil rights leadership if the president wished to be seen as an effective statesman at home and abroad.

On November 22, in Dallas, Texas, an assassin's bullet ended Kennedy's life and cast a shadow of uncertainty over the future. Having embraced him so recently as a civil rights hero, many wondered whether his passing would eclipse American civil rights progress. The world deeply mourned the young president—the man, and the ideas he had come to represent.

Shock and despair over Kennedy's assassination swept the globe. Concerned about how these events would affect U.S. standing overseas, the USIA surveyed the international reaction. On December 6, the agency reported that "[n]ations first reacted by relating events to their own preoccupations and predicaments." Western European and Soviet concerns focused initially on "Soviet-American relationships and the prospects for peace." In Africa, in contrast, the focus was on "the fate of the civil rights movement." Overall, "The most damaging aspect of world reaction is to the image of the United States as a nation of laws and morality."[107]

In the Philippines, a commentator eulogized President Kennedy this way:

> A sniper's bullet killed his body. His spirit lives. The legacy is there, for the American government, particularly the American Congress, to accept or reject. . . . [T]he American Congress could kill his spirit by refusing to pass the civil rights bill he fought for, or passing it in meaningless form. There is physical and there is spiritual assassination. Body and soul would be dead then. May the spirit of John F. Kennedy live on.[108]

* * *

By the time of his death, the nation and the world had taken notice of President Kennedy's commitment to civil rights. Even those close to the president had noticed a change. Harris Wofford thought that during Kennedy's last year, "he was not only seeing it straight" on civil rights, "but he was putting it as central—or beginning to put it as really central—to our body politic, the soul of the country and things like that." Wofford said that Martin Luther King Jr. had felt of Kennedy that "he's got the understanding and he's got the political skill and he'll probably bring it about, but the moral passion is missing on this issue." However, after the deaths of the four girls in Birmingham in September 1963, and the other events in Birmingham that year, King "began to feel the moral passion was there, too."[109]

Earlier Kennedy had put off civil rights so that it would not interfere with his other objectives, including foreign affairs. In June 1963, he took bold steps on civil rights and foreign affairs simultaneously. He seemed to be moved by both issues. The human drama in Birmingham was inescapable. At the same time, he had also come to terms with a point Roy Wilkins and Arnold Aaronson had pressed upon him during his first days in office. Civil rights was not a distraction from economic and foreign policy. Rather, it was intertwined with Kennedy's other objectives: "the third leg of the stool."[110] A president who campaigned for office using foreign affairs—Africa policy—to court a domestic constituency—black voters—ultimately understood that questions of justice at home reflected overseas, affecting his role as a world leader.

If the lever was foreign relations, the pressure had been applied by the children of Birmingham, by civil rights leaders, by all those who stood up to racial injustice in the South and who faced the terror of massive resistance. Civil rights activists had generated the worldwide headlines that so troubled Dean Rusk and members of Congress. Africans and African Americans drew strength and inspiration from each other's liberation movements, coming to see their struggles as one. The civil rights movement's global reach was evident in August 1963 when hundreds of thousands marched on

Washington, both directly in the nation's capital and at American embassies all over the world. The international character of the movement and the role of foreign affairs in moving government policy might seem to take civil rights far from the strategy meetings of the SCLC, CORE, and SNCC, and far from the grassroots activism at the heart of the movement. Yet it was the movement that generated this worldwide interest. And the world reciprocated, placing new power in the movement's hands.

CHAPTER 6

Shifting the Focus of America's Image Abroad

[I]t seems probable that we have crossed some sort of watershed in foreign judgments and perspectives on the racial issue in the U.S.

UNITED STATES INFORMATION AGENCY, 1966[1]

As the world grieved for the fallen president, Lyndon Johnson stepped forward to comfort and to heal. Tragedy had enabled him to replace his former rival. This tragedy also shaped the contours of his leadership in the early months of his presidency. Johnson could not cast off the memory of Kennedy, or its hold on the world's emotions. Instead, he embraced it, elevated it, and shaped it. In so doing, he presented himself as the vessel of another's good intentions.

On November 27, two days after John F. Kennedy had been laid to rest, Lyndon Johnson stood before a joint session of Congress and delivered an address to the nation and to the world. "No words are sad enough to express our sense of loss," he said. "No words are strong enough to express our determination to continue the forward thrust of America that he began." Johnson constructed Kennedy as a visionary, with dreams of progress extending to the heavens. These dreams now shaped the obligations of those who followed after him.

The dream of conquering the vastness of space—the dream of partnership across the Atlantic—and across the Pacific as well— . . . the dream of education for all of our children— . . . and above all, the dream of equal rights for all Americans, whatever their race or color—these and other American dreams have been vitalized by his drive and dedication.

"And now," Johnson urged, "the ideas and the ideals which he so nobly represented must and will be translated into effective action." That action would include maintaining a military presence abroad. The nation would "keep its commitments from South Viet-Nam to West Berlin." The country would also "carry on the fight against poverty and misery, and disease and ignorance, in other lands and in our own." Through domestic initiatives and foreign affairs, the nation would not "linger over this evil moment," but would "fulfill the destiny that history has set for us."[2]

In giving life to Kennedy's vision, one initiative stood out in importance. According to Johnson,

[N]o memorial oration or eulogy could more eloquently honor President Kennedy's memory than the earliest possible passage of the civil rights bill for which he fought so long. We have talked long enough in this country about equal rights. . . . It is time now to write the next chapter, and to write it in the books of law. . . . There could be no greater source of strength to this Nation both at home and abroad.

To fulfill this important commitment, Johnson asked for the help of the Congress and the nation. "We meet in grief," he said, "but let us also meet in renewed dedication and renewed vigor. Let us meet in action, in tolerance, and in mutual understanding. John Kennedy's death commands what his life conveyed—that America must move forward." And this progress, now presented as Kennedy's legacy, required especially racial justice. "The time has come for Americans of all races and creeds and political beliefs to understand and to respect one another." It was Johnson's hope that "the tragedy and the torment of these terrible days will bind us together in a new fellowship, making us one people in our hour of sorrow." This unity would give meaning to the tragedy. Johnson urged, "[L]et us here highly resolve that John Fitzgerald Kennedy did not live—or die—in vain."[3]

In embracing civil rights as a legacy of Kennedy's presidency, Johnson laid a cornerstone in the construction of Camelot. Kennedy friends and family would place a heroic gloss on the youthful image of the departed leader. Johnson himself, an outcast during the Kennedy presidency, would aid that construction by elevating civil rights as a Kennedy legacy. Civil rights had not been at the top of Kennedy's agenda while he lived. In death, however, his motives and priorities were transformed. He was now above politics. He became a symbol of the public morality, as well as the youthful vigor, that an anxious nation longed for. This image was a salve to the wounded nation. This image was, as well, a comfort to a saddened world.

In the Near East and South Asia, the USIA reported that "[t]he President's speech to Congress did much to dispel any existing doubts in the area that changes in American domestic or foreign policies were to be expected." "South Asian media were especially pleased to learn that President Johnson was determined to carry through President Kennedy's civil rights program. No memorial could 'more eloquently honor the memory of President Kennedy than the earliest possible passage of the civil rights bill for which he fought,' wrote *The Mail* of Madras."[4] Nevertheless, the USIA reported that "U.S. moral stature has suffered at least a temporary decline in some areas." Some foreign observers had worried that Kennedy's death was in retaliation for his support of civil rights, and "[t]he initial assumption that the assassination was racially inspired continues to receive publicity."[5]

Johnson's message of stability and continuity provided reassurance that the United States would not descend into chaos. Other nations were concerned, of course, about continuity in U.S. foreign policy. The Johnson administration learned quickly that carrying out Kennedy foreign policies would not be enough. Good relations, particularly with African nations, would require a commitment to Kennedy's civil rights policies as well.

According to the USIA, civil rights was "more important to Africans than other U.S. foreign or domestic policies. The depth of concern has been greatly influenced by the belief that Mr. Kennedy was far more prepared than past presidents or many American citizens to push vigorously on this front." The agency was pleased to report that Johnson's address to Congress was met with "relief and gratification" in Africa. The African press focused on the civil rights section of the speech. The *Sudan Daily* noted Johnson's " 'emphatic' stand" on civil rights, and the *Voice of Ethiopia* "said Mr. Kennedy had not 'lived or died in vain' since the new President was 'determined to fight for racial equality.' " Later commentators were more reserved, however. "The *Daily Telegraph* in Nigeria warned that the new Administration would be judged by its success in this field," while others felt that "no one can replace the late President on the civil rights front."[6]

Seeing Kennedy as a civil rights advocate, some African leaders were distressed that his death might be a backlash against civil rights reform. President Azikiwe of Nigeria sent a condolence message that sounded more like an indictment. For Azikiwe, Kennedy's assassination was "a setback in the struggle for fundamental human rights." African nations, he argued, should question whether the United Nations should be headquartered in the United States, since "the slaughter of this typical American reformer shows clearly that among some Americans there is a deep seated hatred of the black man as a human being." Azikiwe felt chastened. "As one who was educated in American universities I am disappointed that for over [a] quarter of a century I had preached to my people to regard the United States of America as 'God's country.' " He now "pray[ed] that all who believed me will forgive me for being such a simpleton." What would the future portend, he wondered. "Who knows whether it would not be in the best interests of Africa if the newly emergent African states were not to be obliged to look elsewhere?"[7]

According to the U.S. embassy in Lagos, Azikiwe and others feared that the "death [of] President Kennedy means [a] strategic set-back [in the] civil rights battle and are rationalizing their fears in terms [of a] racial motivation for [the] assassination." Because of these concerns, the embassy in Lagos emphasized that "assurances re continuity [of] foreign policy . . . will not in themselves reassure Nigerians." More would be needed. The embassy "strongly recommend[ed] that [the] earliest possible opportunity be found for categoric restatement [of the] administrations policy on civil rights and [the] determination [to] carry through [the] Kennedy program." Stressing a commitment to civil rights reform would be essential to United States–Nigeria relations.[8]

In the ensuing weeks, confidence in the new president increased. At the same time, civil rights continued to be a measure of the new administration's effectiveness. The USIA reported that Western Europeans were reassured by Johnson's handling of his first two weeks in office. "The orderly and immediate transfer of power and the President's unquestioned sincerity and firmness in pledging allegiance to the Kennedy policies, both foreign and domestic, gave further assurance to the European public of a continuity of principles and activities plainly desired." Johnson's "unequivocal support of the Civil Rights Bill was widely applauded because it betokened to Europeans the continuation of a forward thrust in domestic affairs, a courageous stand by a President still identified by most Europeans with the South and the realization that a successful outcome of this revolution in American society was basic to its leadership in world affairs."[9]

In the Far East, "opinion on the domestic policies of President Johnson is predominantly concerned with the civil rights issue. Most commentators clearly see the advancement of civil rights as President Johnson's 'first duty' domestically." Some felt that "President Kennedy's death would create an atmosphere conducive to public and Congressional progress" on civil rights. According to a Thai newspaper, "President Kennedy's blood has flowed to wipe out the senselessness of that problem."[10]

Similarly, in December 1963, the U.S. ambassador to the Congo reported that the Congolese prime minister had asked him to convey the following message to Washington: "that Congo along with most [of] Africa does not really care about ideologies . . . but does care deeply about [the] human factor; [the] key to good US relations therefore is how we continue [to] handle [the] race problem." The prime minister had been happy with Kennedy's actions. As far as Johnson was concerned, he was "keeping up [the] good work but we must not lose impetus."[11]

As President Johnson moved forward on civil rights, the Cold War/civil rights conundrum seemed, for a moment, to be resolved. Congress would pass important new civil rights legislation. Other nations would take this as evidence of official U.S. government support for civil rights reform. Yet, on the cusp of resolution, this victory would soon dissolve. The Vietnam War soon pushed domestic civil rights off the table as a major factor determining American prestige abroad, just as shifts within the civil rights movement and among the electorate changed the dynamics and undermined the fragile consensus about civil rights politics at home. By 1965, urban unrest made it clear that the problem of inequality could not be fully solved by the president's civil rights agenda, even if meaningful reform was still within reach under the shadow of Vietnam. At home, the story of race and American democracy became more complex; overseas, American militarism cast a new shadow on the nation's image.

Early in Johnson's first year in office, the image of the United States abroad was in need of repair. A February 1964 statement on "America's Human Rights Image Abroad" painted an unfortunate picture. As Hugh J. Parry explained, for years the USIA had conducted studies of world reactions to specific events in the United States, aspects of U.S. policies, and other factors "that make up the American Image throughout the world." The USIA did not conduct this research simply out of curiosity. Rather, it "found that various attitudes toward aspects of American life are often inter-related with reactions to American foreign policies and to American relations with the people of a nation."[12]

According to the statement, "There are some aspects of American life that appear to have little impact on the man in the street in foreign countries. . . . But there are others to which larger proportions seem to react." The person on the street reacted "above all" to "the status of minority groups in our country." The primary focus of concern about American minority groups was "the American Negro, for he is the focus and symbol of human rights in America to the world as a whole." Parry found that the topic of American race relations attracted "world-wide interest among the most influential segments of the population." In addition, "it is precisely the best educated and best informed groups that judge the United States most harshly on the issue of the status of the American Negro." College students, "the future leaders of many nations," judged the U.S. "most severely." The good news seemed to be that interest in learning about this issue was "at a relatively high level." Underscoring Parry's conclusions, the USIA report found that 85 percent of the educated elite in Asian and African countries described themselves as being aware of recent U.S. racial incidents. The figure was 91 percent in Latin America and Western Europe. A September 1965 study of residents of Lagos, Nairobi, and Dakar found that a "very high proportion" of literate persons had a "bad or very bad opinion of the treatment of Negroes in the U.S." In Dakar, for example, nine out of ten had a negative opinion about U.S. race relations.[13]

In crafting his civil rights strategy, President Johnson was keenly aware that the issue had international as well as domestic repercussions. "As you know," USIA Director Edward R. Murrow advised him in January 1964, "the progress of the civil rights movement in this country is of preeminent interest overseas, particularly in Africa." In 1963, under Secretary of State Dean Rusk's leadership, the Kennedy administration had already made the point that enacting strong civil rights legislation would help ameliorate the impact of race discrimination on the nation's overseas image. It was left to the Johnson administration to carry the bill forward and ensure its passage. Johnson's legendary skills at forging a legislative majority meant that he was particularly well suited to carry out this task. His personal ambition to make his own mark and to set himself apart from his predecessor led Johnson to push for a stronger civil rights bill than had Kennedy.[14]

The international press followed the bill's progress, reporting on committee votes and parliamentary maneuvering. The president's aides kept him abreast of the reactions of other nations. When it initially passed the House, the USIA reported that the French publication *L'Aurore* thought that Johnson was "following in the footsteps of Kennedy."[15]

In the Senate, a vote on the bill was stymied by a filibuster. For that reason, one of the most important votes was the Senate cloture vote on June 10, 1964. When the motion to limit debate passed, this procedural victory was celebrated overseas. In Nigeria, Minister Wachuku told the U.S. ambassador of his "great satisfaction" at the Senate cloture vote. Wachuku thought that "passage of [the] bill would go [a] long way toward decreasing African criticism [of] race relations in [the] US." As the *Philippines Herald* saw it, the Senate vote was "[a]n eloquent reaffirmation of the democratic maxim that 'all men are created equal.'" According to the *Manila Times*, the new law "will be a triumph for the Negro cause, but no less so for the American people as a whole and for their Federal system of government." Some commentators expressed reservations. According to *Paris-Presse*, the act was "'[a] big step for equality,' but a long time will pass before American Negroes become full-fledged Americans." Amid widespread support for American civil rights progress, in the Soviet Union criticism of U.S. race relations increased. The U.S. embassy in Moscow reported that "[t]he newspaper Soveitskaya Rossiya has apparently entered into competition with Ixvestiya recently to see which organ can get in the dirtiest digs at the United States."[16]

After one more week of debate, the Civil Rights Act finally passed the Senate on June 19. The lengthy process did not mean that the final days were anticlimactic. Instead, according to the USIA, "the long debate heightened attention to the racial question and increased the dramatic impact of the Senate's action." On June 23, as the legislation neared a final vote in the House of Representatives, Carl Rowan, Edward R. Murrow's replacement as USIA director, wrote the president that "[a]ll continents hail the imminent passage of the civil rights bill." This was "a great moment in history." The impact of this moment would reverberate around the world. According to Rowan's report to the president, *Chen Hsin Wen Pao* of Taipei proclaimed that the act would "gradually exert an influence over the whole world, just like the Declaration of Human Rights." The Trinidad *Guardian* agreed that "[t]he U.S. bill has advanced the cause of civil rights for men everywhere." In Vienna, *Neues Oesterreich* thought that "[t]he nations of Africa and Asia can now be told convincingly that America takes the equality of all of its citizens seriously." In Tegucigalpa, *El Nacional* wondered whether the United States appreciated "the dignity it has won in the eyes of the whole world."[17]

The act's passage was acclaimed abroad as "an historic advance." According to the USIA,

> Commentators viewed the passage as the most important step forward in the American Negro's struggle for equality since the Emancipation Proclamation; as a 'victory' that will 'shape the future of the United States'; as a 'turning point' in American history; as enhancing the international influence of the United States, reinforcing the moral authority of the United States and its dedication to freedom and social justice.[18]

There were, of course, cautionary notes. In Kenya, the *Daily Nation* thought that the act "will not change overnight the discrimination and prejudice which for so long have been the lot of the Negro in America." In London, the *Sunday Telegraph* questioned whether the role of the government in policing discrimination meant that the act was "a grim recognition by the U.S. that justice for the Negro can be achieved only by un-American methods." Yet overall, as Rowan reported, the Civil Rights Bill was seen as "a vindication of the U.S. democratic system." He told Johnson that "[p]laudits to you, to the political parties, and the Senate leadership continue to come in from all areas." As if to complete the circle, many viewed the upcoming vote as fulfilling the Kennedy legacy, just as Johnson had proposed. As Rowan put it, "The bill as a monument to President Kennedy is a frequent theme."[19]

Johnson's signing of the Civil Rights Act capped this historic moment. The United States Information Agency prepared ahead of time. On June 30, Rowan told the president, "Your signature on the Civil Rights Act will set in motion a worldwide USIA campaign explaining its meaning." The agency had already distributed to seventy-two countries a televised round-table discussion of the act featuring Roy Wilkins of the NAACP and others. The Voice of America was prepared to broadcast the soundtrack of this discussion, and the text had been distributed to all USIS posts. Photographs of

President Johnson signing the bill would be air-expressed abroad, but in the meantime a "backgrounder" on Johnson's role in the act's passage had already been distributed.[20]

Secretary Rusk wrote to Georgia Congressman Charles Weltner to commend him on his support for the Civil Rights Act. Rusk noted that the act's "primary concern" was "how we as citizens deal with each other." Yet other critical national interests were also at stake. As secretary of state, Rusk was "deeply impressed by the connection between this problem here at home and the great struggle for freedom which is being waged throughout the world. . . . [T]his country is looked upon as the leader of those who wish to be free, and what we do here has an importance far beyond our borders."[21]

Meanwhile, the Nigerian National Committee on Civil Liberties wrote Senator Barry Goldwater to express its "disgust" at the senator's opposition to the act. The committee appealed to Goldwater to reverse his stand on civil rights "in the interest of your good name, . . . and in the interest of your nation whose prestige rises or falls with the advancement or retardation of civil rights by its leading men."[22]

Within hours of the bill's passage, Johnson signed it into law. This event provided one more media opportunity that the president was sure to take advantage of. In his televised remarks, Johnson emphasized that the nation had been founded by "a small band of valiant men" who sought "not only to found a nation but to forge an ideal of freedom." While the president challenged Americans to pursue justice within the nation's borders, he also emphasized that the United States had inspired democratic movements worldwide. "Today in far corners of distant continents, the ideals of those American patriots still shape the struggles of men who hunger for freedom."[23]

The signing brought "a further round of congratulations." Some foreign writers commented on "the effects of the event on the U.S. image abroad, seeing gains for U.S. 'moral prestige.' " Congratulations to Johnson poured in from the president of India, the president of the Republic of Guinea, the president of Niger, and leaders of other nations. Prime Minister Obote of Uganda was "overjoyed" upon hearing the news. He thought that "this action happily removes [the] basis for criticism of [the] US which communists have used among Africans with telling effect." A Nigerian leader told the U.S. ambassador to that country that passage of the act "would enhance [the] close association presently existing between Nigeria and the U.S." Nigerian reaction overall, according to the U.S. embassy, was "overwhelmingly favorable."[24]

Passage of the act was front-page news in Dar-es-Salaam. In Bonn, West Germany, the *General Anzeiger* front-page headline announced, "Civil Rights Bill Finally Approved; Colored People Have Equal Status With Whites; Important Success of Johnson Administration." The act's passage was covered prominently on German radio, and a statement by President Johnson was broadcast on German television.[25]

U.S. diplomatic posts put the news to good use. In Addis Ababa, for example, the U.S. mission was "making maximum effort to exploit the signing of the civil rights bill." The results of these efforts were encouraging. The governor of Western Nigeria told Assistant Secretary of State G. Mennen Williams that "Nigerians followed the racial situation in the United States very closely" and "were gratified to see the passage of the Civil Rights Bill." The Nigerian foreign minister thought that the act's passage "would enhance [the] close association presently existing between Nigeria and [the] U.S."[26]

While civil rights problems in the United States had been criticized at the Organization of African Unity (OAU) conference the year before, the 1964 OAU meeting was a marked contrast. The USIA reported that passage of the act was "a major theme" at the 1964 meeting. Guinea President Sékou Touré told the conference that the act was "a great victory" for the struggle for equality in the United States, while Nasser of Egypt thought it was a "promising sign."[27]

The Johnson administration took pride in its success with the Civil Rights Act, and in the act's positive impact on the U.S. image abroad. The Civil Rights Act looked good in American propaganda. It was true evidence of social change. American leaders had long understood that social change itself was the only effective way to convince foreign audiences that the nation was committed to its professed principles of liberty and equality. The administration could not celebrate long, however, or rest on its laurels. Even as

USIA materials heralding the act were on their way overseas, new threats to the image of American democracy were on the horizon.

On August 4, 1964, within weeks of the signing of the Civil Rights Act, U.S. destroyers in the Gulf of Tonkin off the coast of North Vietnam reported that they were under attack. Although these reports may have been erroneous, they provided President Johnson with the political cover he needed for an already anticipated escalation of U.S. involvement in the war in Vietnam. Congress as well as many Americans rallied behind the president and supported an American military response to what was seen as North Vietnamese aggression.[28] During the summer of 1964, the Vietnam War was one of a number of issues affecting American politics and foreign relations. In later years, with the escalation of the conflict and a growing worldwide antiwar movement, the war would have a profound effect on both domestic politics and U.S. standing overseas.

Even as developments overseas set the stage for a new challenge to the worldwide image of American democracy, developments at home threatened to undermine the positive impact of the Civil Rights Act itself. The Civil Rights Act was signed during the summer of 1964: Freedom Summer. The power and strength of the civil rights movement, and the virulence of the backlash, threatened to overcome the federal government's efforts to characterize the passage of the act as the capstone of social change efforts. Events in Mississippi in the summer of '64, and increasing efforts of civil rights leaders to internationalize the civil rights struggle, meant that U.S. racial justice continued to be questioned abroad. The story of race in America would not be easily contained.

During Freedom Summer, students flocked to the South to work in the civil rights movement. Hundreds of college students joined veteran civil rights activists to help with voter registration in Mississippi. The infusion of white college students into the southern civil rights movement brought publicity and resources but did not soften the terms of racial politics in Mississippi. Early in the summer, three young men, one African American and two whites, were missing. Andrew Goodman, James Chaney, and Michael Schwerner had been arrested on their way to investigate the bombing of a black church. When their broken bodies were finally discovered in an earthen dam, a new wave of outrage swept the nation and the world.[29]

President Johnson made sympathetic calls to the young men's families and pressed the FBI and Justice Department about the course of the investigation of this incident. He wanted the matter resolved carefully and was concerned about others "tying it into [the] Little Rock thing." Meanwhile, civil rights groups sent a letter to a large number of United Nations delegations urging them to bring the issue of violence in Mississippi before the Security Council. They wanted the United Nations to send a peacekeeping force to Mississippi.[30]

Brutal as it was, as long as racial violence was confined to the South, the USIA could argue that racism was a regional, not a national, problem. American propaganda always tried to put violent incidents like the Mississippi murders "in context." The context was the structure of American federalism. The *federal* government, the USIA and U.S. diplomats argued, was committed to civil rights reform. States were making progress, but the rate of progress varied. It only made made sense, U.S. propaganda suggested, that southern states—the former slave states—would be slower in achieving racial justice. Problems in the South, it was argued, were to be expected and were a sign that even in the states of the former Confederacy, social change was at hand.[31]

The idea that race discrimination was a regional problem was challenged in July 1964 as a major riot broke out in Harlem. It was touched off when a white police officer shot an African American teenager. A protest march then turned violent, with African Americans battling police. Rioting followed for days.[32]

By July 27, African newspapers and radio were "voicing alarm at the violence." In Cairo, an *al-Akhbar* headline proclaimed, "America is Threatened with Civil War." In Lagos, the *West African Pilot* saw the riots as an indication of the "ineffectiveness" of the new Civil Rights Act.[33] The rights protected by the Civil Rights Act would, at least formally, create a legal regime of equal treatment, yet as race riots continued to plague American cities, formal legal rights could not alleviate the distress in many communities. Congressional action on civil rights did not speak to the poverty, joblessness, and police brutality in the nation's cities. And so, ironically, as the United States achieved one of its greatest milestones in the struggle for racial justice, the nation's grip on race relations seemed to be failing.

In the face of new challenges, the USIA and the State Department tried to bolster the image of American democracy. While the Johnson administration believed that civil rights reform would be the most effective way to placate foreign critics, an information campaign remained a critical component of efforts to improve the image of American race relations abroad. Besides reporting news of American civil rights progress in a positive manner, the USIA also produced films that focused on the civil rights movement. The USIA took a potential threat—racial protest—and turned it into an asset. The movement could be portrayed as an example of democratic politics in action.

The March on Washington was the subject of one important USIA film on civil rights. USIA filmmaker James Blue presented the story of the march using the style of documentary realism. As Nicholas Cull has written, Blue "creates the impression that his film is an authentic filmic record of the events in Washington, presented with the minimum of artifice." Handheld cameras followed marchers on buses as they made their way to Washington. The focus throughout was on participants in the march, African American and white, young and old, men and women. The minimal use of commentary seemed to enable the film's viewers to join in the crowd and experience the event as it unfolded. Yet while the film presented itself as a simple, realistic depiction, Blue's choices in focus told the story of the march from a particular perspective.[34]

Although the march was presented against a backdrop of conflict over civil rights, conflict within the March on Washington movement was written out of the story, as was conflict between the march organizers and the Kennedy administration. Rather than challenging government policy on civil rights, the marchers were seen as fulfilling an American ideal. As the film's brief voice-over suggested,

"The Constitution of the United States guarantees every American the right to protest peacefully. Two hundred thousand Americans, then, are going to use this right." The image of consensus was reinforced by the film's coverage, or lack of coverage, of march speakers. Only Martin Luther King Jr.'s speech was included, and that in an edited form. King's speech had begun with a critique of the state of civil rights, arguing that the U.S. Constitution was a "bad check" whose promise had not been fulfilled, but the film focused only on the forward-looking "dream" segment.[35]

While the film *The March* presented a story of a united, peaceful, interracial movement carrying out the democratic ideals of free speech and political participation, the film generated its own controversy. Dissenting voices within the USIA wondered whether the film's recognition that some civil rights problems remained to be solved meant that too much of the nation's dirty laundry was to be aired overseas. Members of Congress got wind of the project, and some were offended by the film's celebration of protest and the depiction of an interracial couple among those traveling to the march. President Johnson told Senator Richard Russell that he liked the film, though he acknowledged that "[t]here's been some hell raised about" it. "All it shows . . . is marching here—from Washington's Monument to Lincoln's Tomb [sic] and it shows that the Nigra has a right to be heard and is heard and has a voice and can petition and doesn't get shot." The film was popular at many U.S. diplomatic posts. The post in Bonn, for example, found the film to be "an antidote to Little Rock, Oxford and Birmingham." Ultimately, the film was edited in response to its critics. The USIA added an introduction by USIA Director Carl Rowan. He called the march "a moving exercise of one of the most cherished rights in a free society: the right of peaceful protest." Rowan told viewers that he believed "that this demonstration of both whites and Negroes, supported by the federal government and by both President Johnson and the late President Kennedy, is a profound example of the procedures unfettered men use to broaden the horizons of freedom." Rowan's introduction put an explicit spin on the film that James Blue's filmic style had intended to display more subtly. In so doing, Rowan reinforced the fact that the film was a U.S. government–sponsored propaganda message. In this way, efforts to make the film more palatable to domestic critics may well have undercut its persuasiveness overseas.[36]

As if to complete the circle, the Little Rock crisis itself was recirculated overseas as another important USIA film in 1964. The event that had played a defining role in international perceptions of race in America was repackaged into an American success story. *Nine from Little Rock* followed the nine African American students who had integrated Central High School in 1957. All had gone on to college, and with the exception of one who had married early, all contemplated satisfying professional careers.[37]

The film opened with a drumroll and an unsettling musical score as the shadow of a man stretched ominously across the ground. The camera panned upward to the imposing facade of Central High. Yet the shadow belonged to the calm and friendly figure of Justin Thomas, one of the Little Rock Nine.

Little Rock had cast an imposing shadow on the image of American democracy. Thomas's narration of the Little Rock story dissipated its foreboding quality, while the musical score created a sense of comfort, moderating from minor to major tones. This national crisis was characterized as the actions of a racist "few who tried to impose their will on the many." The film focused on what the nine African American students who had integrated Central High were doing with their lives. The film suggested that the difficult experience the students had endured at Central High had been an opportunity for personal growth. They were truly American success stories, enjoying advancement through personal hard work and perseverance. "If Little Rock taught us nothing more," Thomas assured viewers, "it taught us that problems can make us better. Much better." With that, the camera took in the entrance to Central High, until a wider shot of the city of Little Rock focused on the dome of the state capitol building. The implicit message was that this story of personal growth was generalizable. Just as the "problems" in Little Rock had made the students better, out of the crisis of racial conflict improvement had come to Arkansas and the nation.[38]

Nine from Little Rock was acclaimed from Hollywood to Kampala. It was the first USIA film to receive an Academy Award. Translated into seventeen languages and distributed to ninety-seven countries, the film was also a hit overseas. Carl Rowan told the president that "[i]n Africa where it is vitally important that we do our best to keep the United States civil rights struggle in perspective, USIS Nairobi reported that 'Nine From Little Rock' was the 'best film the Agency has yet made on civil rights. . . . [I]t supports the high priority country objective of showing progress in the U.S. to our racial difficulties.' " The USIS post in Kampala, Uganda, reported that "[t]his film closes the book on Little Rock and frees the mind to consider the changed aspects of the struggle." Thanks in part to USIA efforts to recast the story, the shadow of Little Rock on American prestige abroad appeared to be receding.[39]

The March and *Nine from Little Rock* capped U.S. government efforts to manage the stories of these critical events in the civil rights struggle. In the hands of the USIA, the March on Washington was portrayed as an illustration of American democracy rather than a critique of it, and the Little Rock crisis was an episode in the inexorable democratic progress toward equality. By the early 1960s, however, U.S. propaganda competed with proliferating international news sources. News photographs of massive resistance published around the world threatened to overcome the government's story of racial progress. International travel by civil rights leaders meant that Africans, Asians, Latin Americans, and Europeans could get a picture of race in America that they considered more authentic. Efforts to use filmic portrayals of events in the civil rights movement to bolster the government's narrative of race and democracy could not be fully effective as long as the movement, through efforts at home and abroad, contested the government's story.

With the Freedom Rides, Ole Miss, and Birmingham, efforts to secure civil rights—and the violent reaction against them—became a focus of international attention and concern because they were events the world press considered newsworthy. The movement did not need to do anything to generate international interest other than to organize the protests and endure the reaction. By 1964, the movement engaged in more sustained efforts to use international pressure to further domestic civil rights reform through appeals to the United

Nations, international travel by civil rights activists, and international organizing.

During the 1960s, many civil rights advocates traveled overseas. They hoped to spread the word about the U.S. civil rights movement, gain support from citizens of other nations, and encourage independence movements around the world. Many activists saw the struggle for civil rights in the United States and anticolonial movements abroad as different branches of one worldwide human rights movement. Civil rights activists turned especially to Africa, which became a source of support and inspiration.

When civil rights activists traveled overseas, they presented a challenge to USIA and State Department efforts to craft a particular image of civil rights in the United States. African Americans could speak with more authority about race in America. In an earlier era, the State Department had reacted by silencing those who challenged the government's efforts to project a positive vision of race and American democracy. The methods of the early Cold War years would not withstand international scrutiny in the 1960s, however. For that reason, harsh critics of American racism, including Malcolm X and Stokely Carmichael, had a liberty to travel internationally that Paul Robeson had not enjoyed. The challenge these activists posed to the U.S. government narrative about race and democracy would be managed in other ways. Just as Josephine Baker's impact could be moderated through behind-the-scenes efforts in the 1940s and 50s, the response to 1960s activists was also largely indirect. The State Department quietly facilitated the international travel of more moderate and supportive voices. And, ultimately, the best advertisement for American democracy would be continued social change at home.

In December 1964, Martin Luther King Jr. traveled to Norway to receive the Nobel Peace Prize. The award was a sign of worldwide support for the civil rights struggle in the United States. King accepted the award on behalf of the movement as a whole—the leaders and those who would "never make the headlines" yet whose labor was indispensable to the struggle. King saw the award as a "profound recognition that nonviolence is the answer to the crucial political and moral question of our time—the need for man to overcome oppression and violence without resorting to violence and oppression." He proclaimed his "faith in America" and his "audacious faith in the future of mankind." It was not only racial injustice that he rejected, but also militarism. "I believe that even amid today's mortar and whining bullets, there is still hope for a brighter tomorrow." King celebrated what, he suggested, America would eventually become, reinforcing the idea of the inevitability of social justice within the existing form of government. The USIA might have been pleased with this aspect of his message. Yet, intertwined as it was with a critique of militarism, King's address foreshadowed a development that would greatly concern the federal government: his explicit critique of the U.S. role in Vietnam.[40]

U.S. government efforts to present a positive picture of race in America were hampered by African receptivity to the message of Malcolm X. Both at home and abroad, Malcolm X was not about to contain his critique of American racism within the boundaries of Cold War liberal discourse. He called himself "one of the 22 million black people who are the victims of Americanism." Blacks were "victims of democracy." He declared, "I don't see any American dream; I see an American nightmare." Malcolm X argued that the movement should "[e]xpand the civil-rights struggle to the level of human rights," and "take it to the United Nations," where Asians, Africans and Latin Americans could "throw their weight on our side."[41]

Malcolm X traveled extensively in Africa in 1964. He hoped that his popularity in Africa would "forever repudiate the American white man's propaganda that the black man in Africa is not interested in the plight of the black man in America." He sought to give Africans "the *true* picture of our plight in America, and of the necessity of Africans helping us bring our case before the United Nations."[42]

In July 1964, Malcolm X flew to Cairo, hoping to appear and present a petition at the second meeting of the Organization of African Unity. He was admitted as an observer to the conference. At 2:30 one morning he was able to read to the delegates a memorandum on behalf of the Organization of Afro-American Unity. Malcolm X implored the African leaders to take up the cause of African Americans. "[Y]ou are the shepherd of *all* African peoples everywhere," he told them. "We, in America, are your long-lost brothers and sisters." The good shepherd, he reminded them, "will leave the ninety-nine sheep, who are safe at home, to go to the aid of the one who is lost and has fallen into the clutches of the imperialist wolf."[43]

Although the United States had passed civil rights legislation, Malcolm X argued that this should not lead Africans to believe that all was right in America.

> Many of you have been led to believe that the much publicized recently passed civil-rights bill is a sign that America is making a sincere effort to correct the injustices we have suffered there. This propaganda maneuver is part of her deceit and trickery to keep African nations from condemning her racist practices before the United Nations, as you are now doing as regards the same practices in South Africa.[44]

While Dean Rusk had argued that the Civil Rights Act was needed to counter Soviet propaganda, Malcolm X suggested that the act itself was an American propaganda stunt.

Robert E. Lee, State Department Acting Assistant Secretary for Congressional Relations, reported that while in Cairo Malcolm X made "extreme statements to the press." Lee reassured Congressman Charles C. Diggs Jr. that "[t]he leaders of Africa are genuinely concerned with the racial problems in the United States. They were greatly encouraged by the passage of our civil rights legislation and are much too well informed to be taken in by the extreme statements of Malcolm X." Rather than joining Malcolm X in a call to arms against American racism, African leaders approved a resolution commending the United States for passing the Civil Rights Act. Peter Goldman put it this way:

> There was, as Malcolm eventually was forced to recognize, a disparity between the warmth with which Africa welcomed him and the yes-but caution with which it received his call to arms against America. In the end, he discovered that he was bucking not only the vast distance between Harlem and Africa . . . but the great reach of U.S. foreign aid.

Malcolm X came to believe that "as long as you take money from America, you'll have only the external appearance of sovereignty."[45]

In spite of African reticence, the State Department remained concerned about Malcolm X's influence. As Lee put it, "[T]here is no denying that the propaganda which was generated by his extreme statements may have caused some damage to the United States image." Lee believed that the best antidote for such damage was civil rights reform. "The whole episode points up the importance of continuing on the path we have already chosen—to make our nation one in which all the rights of every citizen are guaranteed at all times and in all places." In the meantime, the department kept tabs on Malcolm X, investigating whether he might be in violation of U.S. law. American diplomatic posts reported on his activities, and the State Department contemplated ways to counter his influence.[46]

Malcolm X traveled to Saudi Arabia on September 19. There he was regarded as "Leader of Muslim Negroes in the United States" and was treated as an honored guest of the Saudi government. During his three days in the country, Malcolm X made a pilgrimage to the Holy City of Mecca, where he experienced a spiritual rebirth that convinced him that "perhaps American whites can be cured of the rampant racism which is consuming them and about to destroy" the United States. He developed a new interest in working with others across racial and ideological lines. At a speech at University College in Addis Ababa, Ethiopia, the following month, Malcolm X "emphasized the relative unity between himself and such leaders as Martin Luther King, saying that their differences were primarily differences of method rather than goals. 'The main difference is that he doesn't mind being beat up and I do.' " In spite of Malcolm X's new approach, U.S. diplomats remained wary. Malcolm X may have had more positive things to say about Martin Luther King Jr., but he still had nothing good to say about the state of race relations in America.[47]

On October 18, 1964, Malcolm X flew to Kenya at the invitation of the Kenyan government. He was treated warmly by Kenyan officials, who called him the "leader [of the] whole civil rights movement in America." The U.S. ambassador to Kenya, William Attwood, felt that Malcolm X's warm reception was "disturbing." He feared that Kenyan leaders might be receptive to Malcolm X's "twisted account [of the] U.S. civil rights situation." The ambassador reported that while in Kenya "Malcolm declared that American [sic] will never voluntarily give American Negroes freedom unless forced and that as [a] minority they do not have the force. Africa, he said, has [the] key to [the] Negro problem solution and will determine [the] degree of freedom they get because African leaders hold [the] strategic power balance in world affairs." An objective of Malcolm X's mission to Africa, the telegram continued, "was to make leaders aware of their position of power." He was "surprised by support of African leaders for American Negro cause, they had all shown *unlimited concern and sympathy.*"[48]

The Civil Rights Act had been lauded in Africa, but according to Ambassador Attwood, in a television interview in Nairobi Malcolm X had claimed that the act was "nothing but a calculated propaganda move by the US to impress the peoples of Africa and Asia. He added that nothing had changed for the Negro since passage of the law; that in fact, Negroes were being persecuted more vigorously than before." Malcolm X had come to Nairobi to encourage African leaders to condemn U.S. racism in the United Nations. He felt that "[i]n light of 'no progress' in US and 'mealy-mouthed' American Negro leadership, little can be expected internally in [the] US and internationalization of [the] problem [was] required to bring pressure on [the U.S. government] and on 'good people' in US who would then take action to avoid embarrassment." Malcolm X warned that the more moderate statements of others reflected government actions. "American Negroes who come to Africa are 'well-chosen' not to embarrass the US." The ambassador was concerned that Malcolm X had "considerable success in Kenya in publicizing his views and in getting the ear of Kenyan leaders."[49]

Because of concerns about Malcolm X, U.S. diplomats in Africa were thrilled to learn of CORE president James Farmer's interest in traveling to Africa in 1965. Farmer's trip was sponsored by the American Negro Leadership Conference on Africa. Secretary of State Dean Rusk told U.S. embassies that Farmer would present a "true picture of the progress of civil rights in America" and would "state the true aspirations of most American Negroes as compared with what has been said in Africa by Malcolm X and Cassius Clay." Rusk asked

U.S. missions in Africa to "extend the usual courtesies" to Farmer, and to "facilitate his making contact with government leaders, university students, media representatives, and other influential groups." Embassies should keep their enthusiasm to themselves, however. "It is recognized that in some countries too close an identification with the Embassy may be counterproductive." In preparing for Farmer's visit, "All posts which Malcolm X visited should have [a] file of statements and suggestions re tactics available for Mr. Farmer on arrival." Posts were also to "offer political briefings" to Farmer and to keep the State Department informed about his visits.[50]

Secretary Rusk's belief that Farmer would counter Malcolm X's influence may have stemmed from Farmer's public statements disagreeing with Malcolm X. Farmer had defended the Kennedy administration in a televised debate with Malcolm X. Farmer told Malcolm X, however, that his objective was not to counteract the Black Muslim leader. Rather, his purpose "would be to develop a liaison between the new nations of Africa and the civil rights movement in America." Apparently satisfied with Farmer's explanation, Malcolm X supplied him with names and phone numbers of contacts in Africa.[51]

In Lagos, Nigeria, Farmer told a television audience that he had come to Africa to "develop closer ties between American Negroes and Africans and to interpret the civil rights revolution in the U.S. to Africans." According to an embassy officer, "Farmer praised the role of African nations in bolstering U.S. Negroes' pride." Nigerians responded warmly. The state house released a statement saying that "CORE and Nigerians are partners in the struggle for safeguarding individual freedom under the rule of law." The embassy's only regret was that Farmer was not clearer about the fact that "the Civil Rights struggle in the U.S. is a nation-wide effort in which whites as well as Negroes are participating."[52]

In Ghana, the U.S. embassy thought that Farmer gave an "extremely effective talk on civil rights" at the University of Ghana. Farmer reportedly argued that the "Negro revolution seeks to complete [the] American revolution, not overthrow of govt but full participation in it." He stressed the interracial character of the Freedom Rides and other civil rights movement activities, and cooperation between movement organizations and the U.S. government. As for

Malcolm X and the Black Muslims, they advanced a "racist solution" and represented a small proportion of African Americans. Farmer's visit to Ghana was described by the embassy as "helpful." He was able to "undo in part [the] damage caused by two Malcolm X visits."[53]

Not all of CORE's actions pleased the State Department, however. In December 1964, CORE wrote to U.S. firms doing business in South Africa. CORE wondered whether there was a double-standard. Large U.S. companies would not risk their image by doing business with communist countries, so why South Africa? CORE asked,

> How can your company policy allow its investment to secure apartheid in South Africa and support fair employment here? How can you pay slaves and negotiate with unions here? Your company has put free enterprise and American labor in competition with a slave labor force and a government that scoffs at your system.

CORE noted that U.S. companies could "help to achieve a better way of life for the great mass of repressed peoples of South Africa. Your investment can be used to apply pressure for relief, and withholding of more investment can give added pressure." Attached to the letter was a summary of South African apartheid legislation and a description of conditions. Secretary Rusk described it as "generally devastating." CORE's letter created "quite a stir" among U.S. firms. A Socony Mobil official told American diplomats that he thought this was just the beginning of domestic pressure on the subject of apartheid. Meanwhile, the State Department's policy was that decisions to invest in South Africa "must rest with individual firms."[54]

In later years, the left would continue in its efforts to internationalize the movement. SNCC and the Black Panther Party argued that the movement for black power at home was part of an international struggle against imperialism. For Stokely Carmichael and Huey Newton, the liberation struggle linked unrest in American cities with Vietnam's National Liberation Front, or Vietcong.[55] As radical voices came to play a more important role in the civil rights movement by the mid-1960s, it became more difficult for the U.S. government to argue that activists sought change within the terms of

Martin Luther King Jr. is congratulated by Norway's King Olav and Crown Prince Harald after receiving the Nobel Peace Prize, December 10, 1964. The Nobel Prize was a sign of the strong international support for the U.S. civil rights movement. (UPI/CORBIS-BETTMANN)

Malcolm X at a press conference in New York following his return from Africa, November 24, 1964. The Black Muslim leader sought African support to encourage the United Nations to pressure the United States to end racial discrimination. (UPI/CORBIS-BETTMANN)

American democracy. Increasingly at home, American society itself was under attack.

Within the United States, even as civil rights leaders reported that their efforts to test enforcement of the Civil Rights Act in the South had met with success, race discrimination continued to present challenges to American diplomatic efforts. On September 24, 1964, fifty-five representatives to the United Nations from African and Asian countries submitted a petition to UN Secretary General U Thant expressing "grave concern" about discrimination against UN diplomats in New York. The petitioners were particularly concerned about an attack on Youssouf Gueye, first secretary of the Permanent Mission of Mauritania to the United Nations. Mr. Gueye was assaulted "by a group of New York citizens" while walking near his home on the evening of August 30. According to the petition, "The circumstances surrounding the assault . . . continue to arouse in us most serious misgivings. Obviously, Mr. Gueye, whose identity was not unknown to his attackers, was attacked because he was a diplomat and because he was coloured." The attack was not an isolated event. "A mention of the many similar incidents that have taken place is enough to explain the indignation felt by all the members of our group." Because of the "continued repetition of such incidents," the diplomats had "serious misgivings as to the conditions we require in order to live normal lives and carry out our work as diplomats." The petitioners urged that "effective measures should be taken to ensure the protection of our diplomatic officers against these humiliations."[56]

Foreign leaders were also targeted in the nation's capital. Shaban Kirunda Nkutu, a Ugandan government official, was on his way to his Washington, D.C., hotel following Thanksgiving dinner with an American family when he decided to take a stroll. A group of white teenagers called to him from their car. As the secretary of state later reported it, "Thinking they needed help, Nkutu approached and was deluged by shaving cream thrown by one person. Head, shoulders covered, Nkutu was temporarily blinded by cream. . . . He, in own words, was humiliated by incident." The State Department would gear up after such incidents to convey legions of apologies, but these events could not be erased from the personal memories of foreign leaders. Beyond shaping their attitudes about the United States, they also led them to question statements about racial progress in America. American propaganda characterized civil rights as a sectional problem, residing in the American South, and argued that continuing difficulties were the product of regional differences resulting from U.S. federalism. Racial attacks in the seat of the United Nations and in the nation's capital undercut the validity of these characterizations.[57]

Problems in New York also raised the question of whether that city was an appropriate site for the United Nations. Ambassador Adlai Stevenson reported that at a December 1964 luncheon, S. O. Adebo, Nigeria's ambassador to the UN, "spent almost [the] entire afternoon" discussing U.S. racial problems with G. Mennen Williams. Adebo "seemed bitter." He "describe[d] NY as [a] most inhospitable city for [the] UN site," and "[s]tated that if [a] vote were taken, [the] overwhelming choice would be to remove [the] UN from [the] US." Adebo said that "he feared to go out at night for fear of physical harm." He made "no distinction between violence in Mississippi and in NY." Adebo was "unyielding to any arguments put forward by Williams."[58]

African leaders often took U.S. racial injustice personally, even when they were not the targets. Treatment of African Americans was taken as evidence of American feelings toward Africa as well. When Martin Luther King Jr. was arrested and imprisoned in Selma, Alabama, in February 1965, for example, the U.S. embassy in Luanda, Angola, reported that the arrest had "done more to damage [the] image [of the] US in [the] eyes of literate African people in Angola than any other single event" since the embassy officer had been in his position. Government leaders told him that "Africans can no longer trust US sympathetic statements re: African aspirations. They consider them hypocritical and devoid of any substance." Instead, the "reality is shown by continuing disregard [of the] rights [of] America's Negroes and especially bare faced actions such as [the] arrest [of] Doctor King."[59]

In the face of this criticism, it became clear that there would be no quick fixes for the diplomatic consequences of American race discrimination. A civil rights bill in Maryland might ameliorate difficulties on Route 40, but it could not contain random racist acts on the streets of New York. A federal civil rights bill might express a broad norm of equality, but it would not stymie southern police in their efforts to silence the civil rights movement. The daily life of race in America was experienced by African diplomats residing in the country. Global mass media brought racist incidents into homes around the world. The images of formal legal change broadcast to the world competed with the lived experience of foreign nationals in the United States, and the persistence of international media interest in the story of race in America.

As Lyndon Johnson's first full year as president came to a close, he hoped to turn his attention to matters other than civil rights. He told Martin Luther King Jr. that 1965 would not be the right time for a voting rights act. Voting rights would cost the president white southern votes he needed for other Great Society programs.[60]

Throughout the South, black disenfranchisement remained widespread. In Dallas County, Alabama, half the voting-age population was African American, but only 156 of 15,000 voting-age blacks were registered to vote in 1961. In spite of Justice Department efforts to use litigation to expand voting rights, by 1964 the number of African American voters remained very low. Civil rights leaders decided to stage demonstrations in Selma to focus national attention on the issue. According to David Garrow, King and the Southern Christian Leadership Conference hoped to use a campaign in Selma "to challenge the entire structure of racial exclusion in Alabama politics and to force Lyndon Johnson's hand on a federal voting rights statute."[61]

The Selma campaign began with peaceful marches to the courthouse where African American residents of the city were unable to register to vote. Hundreds were arrested, and as the days went by, police brutality against the demonstrators increased. On Sunday, March 7, the Selma campaign came to a head as civil rights activists began a march from Selma to Montgomery. They got only as far as the Edmund Pettus Bridge across the Alabama River heading out of town. Alabama state troopers and sheriff's officers on horseback blocked the road on the other side. The marchers were ordered to disperse for engaging in an "unlawful assembly . . . not conducive to the public safety." When they refused to do so, troopers descended on the crowd, beating them with nightsticks. Marchers screamed, while white spectators cheered. Officers on horseback then "rode at a run into the retreating mass." Authorities unleashed tear gas. In news reports broadcast to a horrified nation, "night-sticks could be seen through the gas, flailing at the heads of the marchers."[62]

The Selma violence was widely denounced and led many to call for legislation protecting the right to vote. Meanwhile, violence continued, as James Reed, a white clergyman from Boston who had gone to Alabama to support the civil rights movement, was killed in Birmingham. On March 13, as more than a thousand civil rights supporters marched outside the White House, President Johnson told reporters:

> What happened in Selma was an American tragedy. The blows that were received, the blood that was shed, the life of the good man that was lost must strengthen the determination of each of us to bring full and equal and exact justice to all of our people.
>
> This is not just the policy of your government or your President. It is the heart and purpose and meaning of America itself.[63]

For Johnson, the most meaningful way to respond was again to call Congress into action. On the evening of March 15, the president appeared before a joint session of Congress, speaking "for the dignity of man and the destiny of democracy." He saw Selma as "a turning point in man's unending search for freedom." There was "no cause for pride in what has happened in Selma," he said. "But there is cause for hope and for faith in our democracy in what is happening here tonight."[64]

Two decades before, Gunnar Myrdal had argued that the "American Dilemma" was "the Negro problem," and that this problem generated conflict within "the heart of the American." For Johnson as well, taking up the issue of race was to "lay bare the secret heart of America itself." Yet Johnson reconceptualized the nature of the American Dilemma. "There is no Negro problem," he said. "There is no Southern problem. There is no Northern problem. There is only an American problem." To deny equality of rights was "not only to do injustice, it is to deny America and to dishonor the dead who gave their lives for American freedom."[65] America, Johnson suggested embodied freedom and equality. This was the America U.S. troops fought for. As American soldiers risked their lives in Vietnam, those at home bore the responsibility to uphold the values the nation stood for.

Johnson called upon Congress to work overtime to pass a voting rights act expeditiously. "From the window where I sit with the problems of our country I recognize that outside this chamber is the outraged conscience of a nation, the grave concern of many nations, and the harsh judgment of history on our acts." A voting rights act would not end the nation's obligations, however, for "what happened in Selma is part of a far larger movement. . . . It is the effort of American Negroes to secure for themselves the full blessings of American life." Johnson told his audience, "Their cause must be our cause too." The entire nation "must overcome the crippling legacy of bigotry and injustice." And in the words of the movement song, he told them, "[W]e shall overcome."[66]

Civil rights activists reinforced the idea that their struggle was a quintessentially *American* struggle. They continued the march from Selma to Montgomery, Alabama, in a procession cloaked with American flags. Meanwhile, the world press hailed the president's speech as "a firm step forward." In Paris, the *Nation* thought that Johnson's call for a voting rights act "demonstrated—if this was still needed—that the excesses of certain backward racists do not in any way represent the official or the private sentiments of the Americans. . . . The fact is, the responsible Americans have realized the seriousness of racial strife." The paper hoped that "reason will finally prevail over extremism." The London *Daily Mirror* saw aid for the U.S. image abroad. With Selma, an "entirely misleading . . . sombre picture . . . has gone round the world—the clash of black and white in the deep South; the thud of the truncheon; the vile language and viler actions of the extremists." Johnson's speech had "repudiated the racialists in most impressive words." His actions held out a promise. "Out of the American tragedy, President Johnson must now pluck the flower of hope; the promise of a new step forward in liberty for the American Negro; the reality of decisive legislation. What a wonderful achievement that will be for the American image throughout the world." In Mexico City, the *Excelsior* was optimistic.

"Johnson's forceful decision . . . probably will be the beginning of the end for segregation, and this has drawn the attention of the world." Some commentators viewed continuing racial incidents precisely in the terms argued for by the USIA. As *Swadesamitran* of Madras put it, "A handful of whites are mad with color frenzy," and "the U.S. President is now going to take firm action to ensure justice to Negroes." Race discrimination was not seen as a feature of American society. Instead it was the action of the radical fringe. It was contrary to the policies and the values of the nation as a whole.[67]

In spite of the brutality at Selma, the USIA later reported that the "world press comment on Selma has been more calm and restrained than the treatment accorded earlier U.S. racial conflicts, ranging from Little Rock in 1957 to Birmingham in 1963." According to the USIA's analysis, the difference between Selma and earlier crises was "the wide editorial recognition that in one short year the country has moved rapidly forward into an entirely new phase of race relations, marked by Congress' passage of the Civil Rights Bill, President Johnson's uncompromising address to the American conscience, and the unprecedented demonstrations and marches by thousands of Negroes and their white supporters." News coverage of Selma was light to moderate, and there were few editorials. Although photographs and descriptions of police brutality were widely disseminated, editorials "have expressed increased understanding. . . . They see the course of events as leaving little room for doubt that the Negro American is winning his struggle with the strong support of the Federal Government and the great majority of the American people." In contrast to school segregation before *Brown* and earlier events like the Little Rock crisis, Selma was not viewed as an example of the character of American democracy. It was instead "the rearguard action of white supremacists doomed to defeat." Previously, "editorials condemned brutality and condemned the U.S. for permitting it. Today, they condemn the brutality but not the U.S." Because of this, Selma was not the international news story that Little Rock was. Coverage of Selma appeared primarily on the inside pages of the world's newspapers. According to the USIA, it was "overshadowed by other events of more immediate concern such as Vietnam, . . . U.S. and Soviet achievements in space, and matters of strictly local interest."[68]

In India, for example, the Bombay *Free Press Journal* predicted that "Selma may go down in American history as the last great barrier to civilization and freedom in the United States." The federal government's actions were "a great victory for all Americans and for human decency." The *Ethiopian Herald* thought the U.S. government was "doing its best to make all Americans equal before the law." The paper celebrated the civil rights movement and white support for racial justice, believing that "[a]ll America is waging a war against the minority of its citizens who want to turn the clock back." In Western Europe, there was a positive and "overwhelming response" to President Johnson's speech.[69]

Over time, it seemed, the United States had become more immune to criticism. The idea of American racial progress had taken hold. A USIA word-count analysis of news coverage in New Delhi found "a steady falling off both in news and editorial coverage of racial incidents" from Little Rock to Selma. In the Far East as well, the USIA reported that "press interest in America's racial problem has declined steadily in the past year, especially since the passage of the Civil Rights Act of 1964." Limited coverage of Selma in Africa led the agency to conclude that "the Civil Rights Act of 1964 convinced Africans of Federal responsibility for decisive action in advancing civil rights."[70]

Even in the Soviet Union the coverage of Selma, although critical, was "far less extensive than previous coverage of such disturbances." The harshest criticism came from China. Propaganda from Peking criticized the Civil Rights Act and suggested that Johnson's call for voting rights legislation was designed to "paralyze the fighting will of the Negroes." Social change could only happen through struggle against U.S. imperialism. "[T]he law and the court are but instruments of the ruling class for the oppression of the American people."[71]

In spite of the harsh tone of Chinese statements, overall it appeared as if the tenor of international coverage of race in America had changed. Civil rights crises no longer threatened the nation's international prestige. Instead, they had become moments to showcase and reinforce the lessons of the previous twenty years of U.S. propaganda: that the federal government was on the side of justice and equality, that racism was not characteristic of American society but was aberrational, and that democracy was a system of government that enabled social change.

Civil rights violations continued to provoke outrage, but the nature of the outrage was different. The change was illustrated by African news coverage of a new civil rights crisis. Following Selma came the murder of civil rights worker Viola Liuzzo by members of the Ku Klux Klan. This event unleashed a new wave of criticism. On April 1, the Senegalese *Unité Africaine* published an editorial criticizing American racism. The critique, in contrast with earlier editorials of this kind, was not monolithic. While the paper condemned racism, it did not suggest that the federal government was responsible for it. Instead of being part of the problem, the U.S. government was perceived to be part of the solution. According to *Unité Africaine*, in the United States "the Negro's struggle for civil equality is assuming hitherto unequaled proportions." Blame for current difficulties lay with the Klan and with violent reaction to civil rights protest. The paper was "following sympathetically the efforts of the men of good will and of the United States Federal Government to give Negroes the chance to exercise their voting rights."[72] Tragedies like the Liuzzo killing were now occasions for the celebration of federal government resolve.

In response to Selma, Congress acted quickly, passing the Voting Rights Act of 1965 within six months. The act was intended to outlaw the variety of methods used by state and local governments to disenfranchise African American voters. Discriminatory literacy tests, poll taxes, and other voter registration requirements, as well as violence against African Americans who tried to register and vote, had kept large numbers of African Americans from the polls. Under the new law, registration restrictions used to disenfranchise racial minorities were invalidated. The act also required that future voting practices in discriminatory jurisdictions be approved by the attorney general, and it authorized federal examiners to ensure evenhanded application of the law. With these provisions in place, more than 230,000 new African American voters registered within a year after the act was signed.[73]

Leander H. Perez, a Louisiana state judge, told the Senate Judiciary Committee that the voting rights bill was part of a communist conspiracy, "a Stalin Communist plan for the takeover of the Black Belt."[74] The bill's supporters, however, believed it strengthened American democracy by broadening political participation.

As President Johnson put pen to paper to sign the Voting Rights Act, he told Congress and the nation that the act's passage meant that "perhaps the last of the legal barriers is tumbling." This moment was one of his administration's greatest achievements. It occurred, however, at a time when the war in Vietnam was on the verge of undermining Johnson's hold on his domestic political agenda and his leadership of his party. It was strangely fitting that at this moment the president cast his great civil rights victory in the rhetoric of militarism.

Johnson called the Voting Rights Act "a triumph for freedom as huge as any victory that has ever been won on any battlefield." With its achievements, "the struggle for equality must move now toward a different battlefield," that of enforcement and fulfillment of legally protected rights. The "fight for freedom" was a difficult one, but it helped fulfil central American ideals. In that sense, this was "a victory for the freedom of the American Negro. But it is also a victory for the freedom of the American Nation."[75]

With the passage of the Voting Rights Act, a set of formal legal protections were in place that would be of enormous help in U.S. propaganda efforts. Federal statutes now proclaimed equality before the law. Even as difficulties in communities around the nation persisted, the civil rights statutes could be a symbol of the federal government's commitment to equal rights.

A 1965 USIA pamphlet summarized these developments. *For the Dignity of Man: America's Civil Rights Program* opened with a photograph of President Johnson signing the Civil Rights Act of 1964. The pamphlet argued that the Civil Rights Act and Voting Rights Act secured rights proclaimed by the founders of the nation in the

Declaration of Independence, that "all men are created equal." According to the pamphlet, passage of the new laws "represented a determination by the people and the government of the United States to eliminate prejudice and racism." The occasion was momentous, and yet, the pamphlet declared, "As a policy of the national government, this is nothing new." *For the Dignity of Man* was premised on the argument that American democracy, the American people, and the American government were fundamentally good. How could the pamphlet celebrate social *change* without acknowledging past failings? The rhetorical strategy was to isolate the wrongdoing, and argue that it was not a core value of the nation. According to the pamphlet,

> Racial discrimination has been practiced mostly by individuals and by some state and local governments, and as long as the rights of racial minorities were not spelled out in national legislation, it was difficult to check these abuses. The American people, acting through their Congress, have now taken major steps toward fulfilling the national ideal.

The problem of prejudice was reconceptualized as one of clarity. American values had always embraced equality, the pamphlet suggested. What was lacking was a clear statement of those values in federal law.[76]

For the Dignity of Man told the story of the passage of the landmark civil rights legislation of the 1960s. As with earlier examples of U.S. propaganda, the pamphlet was illustrated with interracial photographs that presented a middle-class, integrated world that most African Americans did not actually inhabit in 1960s America. But the text of the pamphlet simply described statutes that had, in fact, been enacted. Compared with fifteen years earlier, when *The Negro in American Life* told the story of race in America, less effort was needed in 1965 to spin the story of American race relations.[77]

In spite of the rosy picture painted in U.S. propaganda, the tumult on the streets of American cities showed no signs of abating. President Johnson hoped that the tale of civil rights in his administration would be a victorious one. Having achieved the passage of landmark civil rights legislation, Johnson expected a pat on the back and the freedom to turn his attention to other matters. Yet within five days of the signing of the Voting Rights Act, the Los Angeles neighborhood of Watts erupted in a major riot. Even as the impact of race on American prestige abroad lessened, the story of race in America changed in a new and troublesome direction. The outpouring of international attention and concern about racial equality from earlier years was replaced by a focus on urban violence.[78]

The community of Watts in Los Angeles had long experienced poverty and segregation. What set off the uprising in August 1965 was the arrest of an African American motorist by white police officers. The incident quickly spiraled out of control. Thousands soon battled police and then turned to looting and burning. After three days the National Guard was called in. When the smoke finally cleared after seven days, thirty-four people had been killed, and Watts had sustained over forty million dollars in property damage. Urban racial conflict would come to many American cities. As Allen J. Matusow has suggested, "Black riots became such a regular feature of the decade that their annual appearance soon ceased to occasion surprise."[79]

At the same time, protest movements became a more common feature in the American landscape. Civil rights, antipoverty, and antiwar activists joined in a cacophony of protest for social change. As the movement became broader and the voices became louder, the impact of race relations on U.S. foreign relations seemed, nevertheless, to be declining. The role of race in U.S. foreign affairs was changing, in spite of continuing civil rights crises. The irony was that the impact of race on U.S. foreign relations, and therefore the Cold War imperative for civil rights reform, would wane even as American racial conflict showed no signs of disappearing.[80]

By 1966, the USIA believed that a significant shift was underway. A USIA report, "Racial Issues in the U.S.," emphasized that "*it seems probable that we have crossed some sort of watershed in foreign judgments and perspectives on the racial issue in the U.S.*" The agency had spent years trying to foster a positive image of American race relations overseas. The mid-1960s watershed was not, however, a widespread shift from negative to positive world reactions. The reaction was more complex. Yet in its complexity, it promised to be more enduring.[81]

According to the report, "It is clear from all sources that foreign peoples have a predominantly bad opinion of the treatment of Negroes in the U.S. On no other issue we have tested is reaction so predictably and uniformly adverse, or so strongly negative." Critical views about race in America were persistent. What was changing was the impact of these views on overall U.S. standing worldwide. "[T]hough this unfavorable view is widespread, strong, and persistent, it appears to be more conspicuous as a blot on our image, and galling to our self-esteem, than as a problem for our influence." In 1963 Secretary Rusk had believed that race discrimination was highly damaging to U.S. foreign affairs. In 1966, however, the USIA report emphasized, "*Awareness of and disapproval of treatment of the Negro seem to have comparatively little effect on general opinion of the U.S.*" Worldwide opprobrium was constant. What had declined was not the condemnation, but rather the perceived impact of that condemnation on U.S. foreign relations.[82]

The reasons for the changing impact of race in America on foreign opinion of the nation seemed to be because a message the United States had been promoting had gotten through. Whether because of U.S. propaganda programs or simply due to press coverage of American developments, "Foreign audiences appear to believe that there has been and continues to be improvement in the treatment of the Negro. . . . The actions of the Federal Government in promoting Negro rights are everywhere approved." There appeared to be "a change in the temper and tendency of foreign editorial comment" on U.S. racial incidents. Foreign reporting was characterized by "greater complexity and sophistication," and "greater calm and restraint." Foreign writers now appeared "to accept to a notable extent the idea that the US is coping with its problems and is determined to assure Negro rights." Significantly, "The target of blame is now largely a white supremacist minority, the barriers established by past practices, and the difficulties inherent in a history of economic, educational, and social deprivation." Overall, the report emphasized, there was a "*general belief that things have changed, will continue to change, and that the change is for the better.*"[83]

As measured by this report, foreign opinion was developing along the lines the USIA and State Department had long hoped for. Racial problems were not going away, but they could now be seen in the light the government had argued for. Racial incidents were not a sign of national moral failure or a compromise of the nation's underlying principles. Rather, they were a product of American federalism and of the tensions inherent in integrating a historically disadvantaged minority into the mainstream. Gradual progress, coupled with education for all, would slowly and peacefully bring about racial justice. Continuing incidents could be seen as out of the mainstream of American life and at odds with the nation's core values. America could be seen as good, even as American racism was abhorrent.

The declining effect of race relations on U.S. foreign affairs raised the question: "*Does the racial issue as a propaganda problem preoccupy us more than the facts warrant?* The answer seems to be, probably *Yes.*" If race no longer undermined the nation's status abroad, the USIA could turn its propaganda efforts to matters of greater strategic importance.[84]

The executive branch had come to believe that it had resolved the Cold War/civil rights dilemma, and that race in America no longer damaged the nations's prestige abroad. Resolving this problem would not, however, leave all foreign observers with benevolent feelings for Uncle Sam. If the United States seemed more legitimately to be the land of the free by the late 1960s, it was also the nation behind an increasingly unpopular war in Vietnam. Concern with justice on the home front was quickly replaced with broad-based worldwide criticism of American militarism. In June 1965, USIA Director Carl Rowan's daily survey for the president of international reactions to U.S. policies found that "[i]ncreasing U.S. involvement in Vietnam brings growing editorial concern and divided opinion, some of it strongly critical." As of 1966, USIA daily reports, formerly on a range of subjects, were increasingly saturated with world reaction to the U.S. role in Vietnam.[85]

By 1967, in the face of mounting casualties, domestic support for the war effort fell apart. A growing antiwar movement led to a protest march of more than two hundred thousand in the nation's capital in October of that year. By November, polls reported that 57 percent of Americans opposed Johnson's Vietnam policies.[86]

Just as at home Vietnam would destroy Johnson's ability to maintain a political coalition to sustain his Great Society programs, abroad Vietnam eclipsed domestic civil rights reform as a defining characteristic of international perceptions of the Johnson administration. Coverage of the war, steady from the early days of the Johnson administration, increased in volume and ultimately overwhelmed all other topics. The war came to define America's image abroad. All other issues paled in significance. In March 1966, for example, a report on Senegalese opinion noted that "American actions abroad were regarded with especially marked disfavor, and opinions on race relations contributed to a lesser degree." By 1966 Vietnam had replaced American race relations as an important matter of international concern.[87]

The shift in focus of the U.S. image abroad coincided with changes on the domestic civil rights front. In the fall of 1966, Senator James Eastland of Mississippi opened his campaign by announcing proudly that "[t]he sentiment of the entire country now stands with the southern people." While Eastland surely overstated his case, the tenor of American politics and public culture had changed. Only two years before, the nation had rallied behind passage of the Civil Rights Act. In the chill of backlash politics leading up to the 1968 presidential campaign, those heady days of civil rights victories seemed a world away.[88]

In 1964, George Wallace and then Barry Goldwater had given voice to the impatience of some white voters with black protest. All along there had been an undercurrent of white opinion, in the North as well as the South, that blacks were seeking too much too soon. Once important new civil rights laws were passed in 1964 and 1965, some whites felt that blacks should be satisfied. Yet the formal equality established in the civil rights acts did not touch pervasive black poverty. Systemic segregation and disenfranchisement over so many years had affected labor patterns, causing race and class in America to be correlated. Formal equality would go a long way toward opening opportunities for the middle class. For the poor, for those living in blighted urban areas now bereft of industry, formal equality would help break down the barrier of race. It would not touch the barrier of class. For urban blacks and other persons of color, as William Julius Wilson has argued, with the easing of overt racial barriers, class became a more central determinant of status.[89]

Class differences had never been something the nation felt the need to apologize for. Instead, capitalism, which assumed an inequality of wealth and power, was championed as an economic system that would best promote economic growth. Class-based inequality did not threaten the nation's core principles. The U.S. Constitution did not address the issue. The Supreme Court, for the most part, treated class and conditions of poverty as a natural phenomenon, as something outside the law, as something that triggered no special constitutional concern.[90]

Out of this dynamic would come a clash of expectations setting whites and people of color along a new path of racial division. Rising expectations coupled with persistent poverty helped fuel urban unrest and the race riots of the 1960s. In July 1967, rioting in Detroit resulted in forty-three deaths and the destruction of thirteen hundred buildings. The Detroit riots received banner headlines around the world. One U.S. embassy reported that the South African Broadcasting Company was having a "field day lately reporting the racial strife in America. . . . The fault with the U.S., gloated the radio, lies in integration." According to the radio commentary, Black Power was "actually a quest by the American Negro to find his own Bantustan-type homeland and culture far removed from any whites— proving that apartheid is the answer to America's racial situation as well." The nation's adversaries in Vietnam also found comfort in the disturbances. Hanoi claimed that "the Afro-Americans' struggle" was "a second front . . . to weaken US imperialism," while Peking hailed the "armed struggle in the U.S."[91]

Radio Moscow used racial violence in renewed propaganda attacks. The United States was "on the brink of civil war," broadcasts claimed in the summer of 1967. Soviet propaganda drew a link between violence in the nation's inner cities and the war in Vietnam, suggesting that the greatest threats might come from the warfare at

Michigan National Guardsmen with bayonets drawn push back African American protesters during rioting in Detroit, Michigan, July, 26, 1967. The Detroit riots and other urban unrest captured headlines around the world. Radio Moscow proclaimed that the United States was "on the brink of civil war." (UPI/CORBIS-BETTMANN)

home. "These days many Negroes [in Vietnam] have stopped receiving letters from their relatives and friends and this is not the fault of the U.S. Army mail service. Many of these relatives and friends have either been killed or wounded in 36 American cities."[92]

Other nations chose not to capitalize on U.S. difficulties but instead reacted with profound concern. Meanwhile, the State Department sent background material to all U.S. diplomatic posts with advice about how to discuss the riots overseas. According to the statement, the "riots involve a small minority of the urban Negro population and are being exploited by extremists." The riots were opposed by "responsible Negro Organizations."[93]

The disorder in the cities was followed by the killing of key national leaders, and then by another wave of rioting. Malcolm X was assassinated in February 1965. In 1968 Martin Luther King Jr. and then Robert F. Kennedy were shot to death. In the international press, the urban violence and assassinations were woven together into one troublesome fabric. The United States, it now seemed, was a nation of violence.[94]

There was an international outpouring of grief over these killings, as well as concern about the state of the nation. According to a USIA report, "The assassination of Martin Luther King and the consequent violence throughout the country have caused serious repercussions throughout Europe. Essentially, these events have caused the average European to question the stability of the American form of government and to cast doubt on our position as the leaders of the free world." The sentiment was not "anti-American." Rather, "there would appear to be a loss of respect in the same way that a child is shaken when he discovers that his parents are fallible." The Soviet media was more harsh, describing the country as "dominated by fear," with murderous conspiracies and uncontrolled use of firearms. One publication suggested that "[t]he possession of two guns in the house has a much longer tradition than the slogan 'two cars in every garage.' "[95]

USIA Director Leonard Marks reported to the president that "[t]he looting and burning in American cities following the assassination of Dr. Martin Luther King drew sensational headlines and lurid press accounts in news centers around the world." Foreign editorial comment reflected "shock and sorrow" at King's death. Some suggested that the nation's turmoil meant that the U.S. "was on the brink of civil war." Among the "typical" comments, *Izvestia* in Moscow reported that "[t]he fatal gun of the murderer of Dr. King was aimed by the same America which is bringing death in Viet-Nam with tens of thousands of bullets." Marks warned that "the events of the past week have seriously shaken the confidence of American allies and friends throughout the world." The nation had suffered "a blow from which it will take a long time to recover."[96]

According to the Soviet press, Robert Kennedy's assassination signaled the breakup of American society. The nation was now governed by "jungle law," and the "myth of wild west violence" was in reality the "American way of life." When violence marred the 1968 Democratic National Convention in Chicago, a British paper reported that it was "exceptionally ugly *even in American terms.*"[97] Student protest and rioting was a worldwide phenomenon in 1968. In the eyes of overseas critics, however, it was as if violence had become quintessentially American. More seemed to be expected of the leader of the free world. If disorder characterized American political culture, then the nation could hardly provide a model of democratic superiority. With disappointment and despair, more than disgust, U.S. allies again questioned the nation's leadership.

Within the United States, coming on the heels of what appeared to be so much social change, many whites responded to urban unrest not with compassion but with derision. Then, in the 1968 presidential campaign, George Wallace and Richard Nixon successfully tapped into this hotbed of white resistance, arguing that what the nation truly needed was "law and order."[98]

This environment bred new forms of oppression. When civil rights leaders joined forces with the antiwar movement, criticizing Johnson's Vietnam policies, the FBI saw in the antiwar posture of civil rights leaders a new element of subversion. J. Edgar Hoover reported to the president that the Communist Party was engaged in a "massive effort to create a united front in opposition to United States military presence in Vietnam" and other activities designed to "exploit racial issues and to create the chaos upon which communism flourishes." Hoover put a special counterintelligence unit,

COINTELPRO, to work on domestic civil rights, antiwar and other progressive groups. It was designed to "expose, disrupt, misdirect, discredit, or otherwise neutralize the activities of black nationalist, hate-type organizations and groupings, their leadership, spokesmen, membership and supporters." Not restricting itself to more militant groups like the Black Panthers, COINTELPRO also targeted leaders advocating nonviolence, including Martin Luther King Jr. The impact of domestic protest on foreign affairs was used as a justification for renewed suppression of progressive movements.[99]

Amid international coverage of assassinations and domestic unrest, Vietnam remained a consistent theme in the international press. Anti-American protest had become a staple. On March 27, 1968, USIA Director Leonard Marks reported that "[t]he headlines of the world press have featured stories on protests against U.S. policies in Viet-Nam, bombs left at embassies, in USIS libraries and other adverse reports." As if to cheer up the beleaguered president, Marks also included some contrary reports. At The Hague, 4,000 had participated in a "*pro-Viet-Nam parade*," carrying signs with slogans such as "U.S. Don't Withdraw." In London, 150 members of the Conservative Party marched to the U.S. embassy to deliver a petition supporting U.S. policy in Vietnam, with 600 signatures.[100]

Four days later, Johnson gave an address to the nation on Vietnam and his hopes for peace. Noting that at this time the presidency must not "become involved in the partisan divisions that are developing in this political year," Johnson announced: "I will not seek and I will not accept the nomination of my party to another term as your President." The speech was promptly reproduced by the USIA in a glossy pamphlet with compelling photos of the president. In bold letters on the cover, the pamphlet's title was a quote from the speech: "an end to this long and bloody war."[101] It was an unusual statement as a U.S. propaganda missive, both in its despair and also in its implicit recognition of the limits of U.S. power. The bloody war would not end soon, either in Vietnam or on the streets of American cities, and Lyndon Johnson's presidency would end on a note of regret.

Advances on civil rights, especially the Civil Rights Act of 1964 and the Voting Rights Act of 1965 would be an important legacy of the Johnson Administration. These statutes laid the groundwork for more effective enforcement of the rights to equal treatment and political participation. They also capped years of effort at recasting the image of race and American democracy. They underscored the idea that the federal government supported racial equality.

Although the new civil rights laws ultimately helped bring an end to some of the most overt forms of segregation and discrimination, racial inequality remained. The formal equality in these statutes and other legal reforms had not touched the poverty and oppression in the inner city. In response to urban unrest, the Kerner Commission issued a report calling for a firmer national commitment to social change. Yet this call for massive, structural reform coincided with a broadening anti–civil rights backlash. No longer a southern phenomenon, resistance to civil rights reform took hold across the nation.[102]

The response to unrest, in the context of a growing civil rights backlash, would not be along the lines recommended by the Kerner Commission report. What was to some a rebellion against unjust conditions was to others simply a matter of "crime in the streets." Law and order, not social change, was demanded by many Americans. Into this new political cauldron stepped Richard Nixon. The Republican presidential nominee would be particularly effective at tapping into backlash politics and marshaling the law-and-order rhetoric that now appealed to so many voters.[103]

Just as Vietnam had eclipsed civil rights as a defining issue affecting U.S. prestige abroad, law and order had eclipsed social justice as a politically popular response to racial conflict. These new imperatives would frame Richard Nixon's policies as president. Civil rights reform, on some level, would continue to be a federal objective, but it was no longer a critical issue in U.S. foreign affairs.[104]

CONCLUSION

The world is white no longer, and it will never be white again.

JAMES BALDWIN, "STRANGER
IN THE VILLAGE" (1953)[1]

On April 9, 1968, as a mule-drawn wagon carried the coffin of Martin Luther King Jr. through the streets of Atlanta, Georgia, flags flew at half staff in Addis Ababa, Ethiopia. The coffin was made of African mahogany. At the front of the funeral procession, marchers carried three flags—of the United States, King's church, and the United Nations. The tens of thousands gathered to pay their respects to King included foreign leaders. It was as if it were the funeral for a head of state. The world had embraced King as an icon of American civil rights progress. His death served as a marker, a moment of closure for an era.[2]

The world came together for a moment to honor King. Amid the shock and the sorrow was a commitment to uphold the ideals he had come to represent. It was a sorrowful moment in a year in which the world seemed perched on a precipice. Civil rights reform, on some level, would survive this moment as a continuing national goal, but the dynamics would change in a new political era. Worldwide interest in U.S. civil rights would not create the leverage it had in the past, as international affairs turned on a new axis.

The Cold War imperative for social change spanned a particular era, and did not survive the length of the Cold War itself. From the immediate postwar years until the mid-1960s, race in America was thought to have a critical impact on U.S. prestige abroad. Civil rights crises became foreign affairs crises. Domestic difficulties were managed by U.S. presidents with an eye toward how their actions would play overseas. In this context, secretaries of state promoted civil rights reform, and progress on civil rights was counted as a foreign affairs achievement.

The story of civil rights and the Cold War is in part the story of a struggle over the narrative of race and democracy. The U.S. government tried to project a story of progress. Having moved from slavery to freedom, surely America had a government that facilitated social change. Democracy, it seemed, was the site of an inexorable march toward justice. Yet as the civil rights movement gained strength, and as the movement faced the brutality of massive resistance, the government would find it impossible to contain the story of race in America. When nine schoolchildren tried to enforce their constitutional right to attend Central High School in Little Rock, their actions, and the outpouring of resistance they engendered, exploded the careful story of American racial progress that the Supreme Court's *Brown* decision was said to symbolize. When demonstrators faced Bull Connor's brutality in Birmingham, the blows they received pushed race in America firmly onto the Kennedy administration's foreign affairs agenda.

Soviet manipulation of American racial problems ensured that race in America would be an important Cold War narrative. U.S. government effort to contain and manage the story of race in America was a component of the government's broader Cold War policy of containing communism. Yet within this framework, the Cold War was simultaneously an agent of repression and an agent of change. The government's response to the movement was driven in part by whether activists supported or detracted from the Cold War/civil rights frame. Those who spoke out of turn, especially to an international audience, were silenced. Struggles in the streets of American cities continually pushed the boundaries and redefined the narrative. The government's inability to control the story forced American leaders to promote stronger civil rights reform. However, just as Cold War ideology limited the federal government's vision of social change, the international referent also limited the nature of the government's commitment to reform. To the extent that reform was motivated by a desire to placate foreign critics, reform efforts that safeguarded the nation's image would best respond to that concern. With *Brown* and Little Rock, formal equality could protect the image of American constitutionalism even if the reforms supported by the federal government would not lead to meaningful social change in the communities affected. It was only when the movement demanded more in the 1960s that more extensive change would be required. When the international gaze later shifted to Vietnam and to civil unrest, the international leverage for civil rights reform receded.[3]

It has been a familiar refrain among historians of American race relations to look back at the 1960s, at that decade's promise of racial reconciliation, and to ask what went wrong. Perhaps a failure of resolve, perhaps a lack of consensus about the means or extent of social change, perhaps the forces of resistance, led to the failure of America's second reconstruction. Amid these notes of despair there seems to be an implicit assumption that if only the historical actors had been good enough, strong enough, or wise enough, perhaps the story might have turned out differently.

The years following the passage of the Voting Rights Act of 1965 are viewed as a time when a national commitment to reform fell apart. Some argue that after critical milestones were achieved, a consensus about social change no longer existed. Others suggest that with the emergence of Black Power and the antiwar turn of civil rights leaders like Martin Luther King Jr., the movement splintered and thereby lost effectiveness. Yet divergent voices had always been present within the movement. And within the nation as a whole, a consensus that social change was necessary never congealed around a unitary vision of racial equality, and always coexisted with a strong and brutal tradition of dissent. One part of the more complex story is that during the mid-1960s, the movement lost a crucial element of leverage. The Cold War, now embodied in the Vietnam War, played a role in the eclipse of the domestic reform agenda as international attention turned to other matters.[4]

While it provided leverage for social change, the Cold War imperative was never static. A continual struggle over the narrative of race in America meant that the terms of debate were always shifting. The movement gained leverage not only by drawing upon international interest but also by helping to generate the international audience and by shaping the international understanding of the story. As liberation struggles in Africa and the United States gained strength from each other, the movement itself took on an international character, so that the March on Washington was literally a worldwide event.

Although the Cold War helped motivate civil rights reform, it limited the field of vision to formal equality, to opening the doors of opportunity, and away from a broader critique of the American economic and political system. Racism might be an international embarrassment. Class-based inequality, however, was a feature of capitalism, an economic system Americans were proud of. The government's commitment to reform was, of course, limited by what it thought was at stake. If what was at stake during the Cold War was the image of American democracy, formal legal equality, carefully described in U.S. propaganda, gave the government what it needed. Once America's image seemed secure, Cold War concerns dropped out as one of the factors encouraging civil rights reform.

This narrative has taken civil rights history from the streets of American cities to the newsstands of the world, and back to the halls of Congress and the offices of presidents and secretaries of state. Although a transnational story, this has been an *American* story. We see that the borders of history are permeable, that American soil cannot contain the story of American history. There is something to be gained by setting American history within an international context, by telling American stories with attention to the world's influence upon them and their influence upon the world.

As historians internationalize the study of American history, as they reconfigure our understanding of domestic events and individual biographies by viewing them in a global context, how will these new histories interface with the older global histories, the histories of international relations? Histories of relations between nations are usually thought of as state-centered histories. The focus is often on struggles between nations over global hegemony and power. Yet, as the history of Cold War civil rights shows us, attention to foreign relations helps us reconsider the role of the state in a domestic context. An international frame need not eclipse a focus on the grassroots. Instead it draws the grassroots and the government together in a new way. The struggles between them are acted out on a world stage, giving new leverage to the movement while restricting the state's options. Government power polices the relationship between the grassroots and the international audience, acting as the border control limiting the international influence of the movement. But under an international gaze, government power itself is subject to restraint.

Internationalizing American history, then, helps us reconfigure our understanding of the boundaries of state power. State power is affected by the mirror of international criticism. Its autonomy over "domestic" matters is limited by its role in the world.

In the American Century, the United States took on a new role as a global power. World events, in that context, were part of the story of *America*. The boundaries of domestic and foreign affairs became blurred. As we write histories of twentieth-century America, an international framework for events at home will not simply serve as window dressing, providing a broader context for an internal event. An international framework helps us discover *what happened* at home. External events affect internal American histories. Even the terms—domestic/foreign, internal/external—seem to collapse. What we are left with is not the natural categories of the domestic and the foreign, but instead angles of vision on one seamless narrative.[5]

Although the Cold War is over, race in America is still an international story. In 1992, when a major riot broke out in Los Angeles following the acquittal of police officers charged with beating Rodney King, it was a major worldwide news event. Banner headlines and front-page photos blanketed the world press, many questioning whether this was a manifestation of what President George Bush called the "New World Order." In 1999, when President Bill Clinton criticized China's human rights record, the Chinese government released a report on human rights in the United States. Other nations decried the United States death penalty. And many questioned the state of racial justice in America when Amadou Diallo, an immigrant from Guinea, was shot nineteen times by New York City police officers as he stood, unarmed, in the doorway of his home.[6]

The international critique has been persistent. What has changed is the perception of whether it has strategic importance. In the absence of immediate strategic advantages there remains, however, the ever-present international gaze, and the questions of new generations about the nature of American democracy. As Locksley Edmundson put it, "Those states best technically equipped to maintain world order are not necessarily the ones whose credentials recommend them as the most appropriate guardians of a global conscience." Edmundson's point was at the center of the international critique of American racism during the Cold War. World politics is no longer structured by Cold War divisions, but one aspect of international relations remains the same. We live, now as then, in a world of color. As Martin Luther King Jr. suggested, the destiny of people of color "is tied up in the destiny of America," and justice at home will have an impact on the nation's moral standing in a diverse and divided world.[7]

Notes

INTRODUCTION

1. Lewis Allan and Earl Robinson, "The House I Live In," (1942), *The Great American Songbook* (Milwaukee: Hal Leonard, 1991), 54. Several artists, including Paul Robeson, recorded "The House I Live In." Frank Sinatra popularized the song in 1945, when he sang it in a wartime short film. Earl Robinson with Eric A. Gordon, *Ballad of an American: The Autobiography of Earl Robinson* (Lanham, Md.: The Scarecrow Press, 1998), 151–157.

2. Consulate General, Toronto, to Department of State, August 25, 1958, RG 59, 811.411/8–2558, National Archives (enclosure: story from *Toronto Star*, August 20, 1958).

3. Ibid.; *Wilson v. State of Alabama*, 268 Ala. 86, 105 So. 2d 66 (Ala. 1958); Janie L. Ellzey, "Criminal Law—Evidence—Proof of other Crimes as Part of *Res Gestae*," *Alabama Law Review* 11 (Fall 1958): 169–173; Dulles to All African Posts, September, 12, 1958, RG 59, 811.411/9–1258; National Archives; American Consul, Edinburgh, Scotland, to Department of State, September 10, 1958, RG 59, 811.411/9–1058, National Archives; American Embassy, Bern, to Department of State, September 16, 1958, RG 59, 811.411/9–1658 HBS, National Archives.

4. American Embassy, Addis Ababa, to Department of State, September 23, 1958, RG 59, 811.411/9–2358 HBS, National Archives; American Embassy, Accra, to Department of State, August 30, 1958, enclosure no. 1, RG 59, 811.411/8–3058, National Archives; Monrovia to Secretary of State, September 3, 1958, RG 59, 811.411/9–358, National Archives; American Embassy, Monrovia, to Department of State, July 1, 1958, RG 59, 811.411/7–158, National Archives.

5. Translator's Summary of Communication, September 12, 1958, RG 59, 811.411/9–1258, National Archives; Members of Israeli Parliament to Government of the United States of America, September 21, 1958, RG 59, 811.411/9–2158, National Archives; Trades Union Congress (Ghana) to Chargé d'Affaires, American Embassy, Accra, September 16, 1958, Enclosure 1 to American Embassy, Accra, to Department of State, September 18, 1958, RG 59, 811.411/9–1858, National Archives; American Consul General, Kingston, Jamaica to Department of State, September 10, 1958, RG 59, 811.411/9–1058, National Archives; The Hague to Secretary of State, September 12, 1958, RG 59, 811.411/

9–1258, National Archives; Perth to Secretary of State, September 5, 1958, RG 59, 811.411/9–558, National Archives.

6. *New York Times*, August 23, 1958, p. 16; *New York Times*, August 25, 1958, p.16; *New York Times*, August 27, 1958, p. 16; *New York Times*, September 13, 1958, p. 9; *New York Times*, September 15, 1958, p. 21; *New York Times*, September 23, 1958, p. 20.

7. Robinson to Dulles, August 22, 1958, RG 59, 811.411/8–2258, National Archives.

8. *New York Times*, September 14, 1958, p. 56; *New York Times*, September 25, 1958, p. 20; *New York Times*, September 30, 1958, p. 1; Circular to All American Diplomatic Posts—Except Taipei, September 9, 1958, RG 59, 811.411/9–958, National Archives; Circular to All American Diplomatic Posts—Except Taipei, September 12, 1958, RG 59, 811.411/9–1258, National Archives; Dulles to Folsom, September 4, 1958, RG 59, 811.411/9–458, National Archives; Montgomery, Alabama, to Secretary of State, September 5, 1958, RG 59, 811.411/9–558, National Archives.

9. Frederick Douglass, *My Bondage and My Freedom* (New York: Dover, 1969), 376–390; Linda O. McMurry, *To Keep The Waters Troubled: The Life of Ida B. Wells* (New York: Oxford University Press, 1998), 188–199. See also Edward P. Crapol, "The Foreign Policy of Antislavery, 1833–1846," in *Redefining the Past: Essays in Diplomatic History in Honor of William Appleman Williams*, Lloyd C. Gardner, ed., (Corvallis: Oregon State University Press, 1986), 85–103, reprinted in *Race and U.S. Foreign Policy from Colonial Times through the Age of Jackson*, Michael L. Krenn, ed., (New York: Garland Publishing, 1998), 345–366.

10. Jonathan Seth Rosenberg, " 'How Far the Promised Land?': World Affairs and the American Civil Rights Movement from the First World War to Vietnam" (Ph.D. diss., Harvard University, 1997), 84, 90–91, 116, 147–148; Carol Elaine Anderson, "Eyes Off the Prize: African-Americans, the United Nations, and the Struggle for Human Rights, 1944–1952" (Ph.D. diss., Ohio State University, 1995), 55–104. The importance of race at the Paris Peace Conference is detailed in Paul Gordon Lauren's masterful work, *Power and Prejudice: The Politics and Diplomacy of Racial Discrimination*, 2nd ed. (Boulder, Colo.: Westview Press, 1996), 82–107.

11. On the impact of World War I on civil rights reform, see Philip A. Klinkner with Rogers M. Smith, *The Unsteady March: The Rise and Decline of Racial Equality in America* (Chicago: University of Chicago Press, 1999), 109–118.

12. David M. Bixby, "The Roosevelt Court, Democratic Ideology and Minority Rights: Another Look at *United States v. Classic*," *Yale Law Journal* 90 (March 1981): 741.

13. Gunnar Myrdal, *An American Dilemma: The Negro Problem and American Democracy* (New York: Harper and Row, 1944), 1004.

14. Ibid., lxix, 4 (emphasis in original).

15. Ibid., 1015–1016.

16. Pearl S. Buck, *American Unity and Asia* (New York: John Day, 1942), 29; Myrdal, *An American Dilemma*, 1016; John W. Dower, *War Without Mercy: Race & Power in the Pacific War* (New York: Pantheon Books, 1986), 5, 26.

17. Paula F. Pfeffer, *A. Philip Randolph, Pioneer of the Civil Rights Movement* (Baton Rouge: Louisiana State University Press, 1990); Herbert Garfinkel, *When Negroes March: The March on Washington Movement in the Organizational Politics for FEPC* (Glencoe, Ill.:

The Free Press, 1959); Lucy Grace Barber, "Marches on Washington, 1894–1963: National Political Demonstrations and American Political Culture" (Ph.D. diss., Brown University, 1996), 251–362; Brenda Gayle Plummer, *Rising Wind: Black Americans and U.S. Foreign Affairs, 1935–1960* (Chapel Hill: University of North Carolina Press, 1996), 86. On domestic civil rights consciousness, see Peter J. Kellogg, "Civil Rights Consciousness in the 1940s," *The Historian* 42 (1979): 18–41.

18. *The House I Live In* (RKO, 1945); Kitty Kelley, *His Way: The Unauthorized Biography of Frank Sinatra* (New York: Bantam Books, 1986), 115–116. I will always be grateful to Steve Wizner for telling me about this film.

19. John Morton Blum, *V Was for Victory: Politics and American Culture During World War II* (New York: Harcourt Brace Jovanovich, 1976). On the impact of the atomic bomb on postwar American culture and politics see Paul Boyer, *By the Bomb's Early Light: American Thought and Culture at the Dawn of the Atomic Age* (New York: Pantheon Books, 1985); Martin J. Sherwin, *A World Destroyed: Hiroshima and the Origins of the Arms Race* (New York: Random House, 1987).

20. "Rabbi on Iwo" (pamphlet), President's Committee on Civil Rights Pamphlets File, Box 28, Papers of the President's Committee on Civil Rights, Harry S. Truman Library, Independence, Missouri.

21. Ibid.

22. On postwar reconversion and domesticity, see Elaine Tyler May, *Homeward Bound: American Families in the Cold War Era* (New York: Basic Books, 1988).

23. Ellen Schrecker, *Many Are the Crimes: McCarthyism in America* (Boston: Little Brown, 1998), 154–200, 359–415; David Caute, *The Great Fear: The Anti-Communist Purge under Truman and Eisenhower* (New York: Simon and Schuster, 1978); Manning Marable, *Race, Reform and Rebellion: The Second Reconstruction in Black America* (Jackson: University of Mississippi Press, 1984); Gerald Horne, *Communist Front?: The Civil Rights Congress 1946–1956* (Rutherford, N.J.: Farleigh Dickinson University Press, 1988); Kenneth O'Reilly, *"Racial Matters": The FBI's Secret File on Black America, 1960–1972* (New York: The Free Press, 1989).

The Cold War turn in American race politics stifled a left-progressive tradition that had existed in the years before the war. See Patricia Sullivan, *Days of Hope: Race and Democracy in the New Deal Era* (Chapel Hill: University of North Carolina Press, 1996); Robin D. G. Kelley, *Hammer and Hoe: Alabama Communists During the Great Depression* (Chapel Hill: University of North Carolina Press, 1990); Thomas J. Sugrue, *The Origins of the Urban Crisis: Race and Inequality in Postwar Detroit* (Princeton, N.J.: Princeton University Press, 1996).

24. Penny M. Von Eschen, *Race Against Empire: Black Americans and Anticolonialism, 1937–1957* (Ithaca, N.Y.: Cornell University Press, 1997), 112–121. See also Thomas Borstelmann, *Apartheid's Reluctant Uncle: The United States and Southern Africa in the Early Cold War* (New York: Oxford University Press, 1993), 56.

25. Rosenberg, " 'How Far the Promised Land?'," 395–475; Klinkner with Smith, *The Unsteady March;* Kenneth R. Janken, "From Colonial Liberation to Cold War Liberalism: Walter White, the NAACP, and Foreign Affairs, 1941–1955," *Ethnic and Racial Studies* 21 (November 1998): 1074–1095; Martin Duberman, *Paul Robeson* (New York: Knopf,

1988), 341–350, 364–372, 388–389; Horne, *Communist Front?*; Victor Navasky, *Naming Names* (New York: Viking Press, 1980); Mary L. Dudziak, "Josephine Baker, Racial Protest and the Cold War," *Journal of American History* 81 (September 1994): 543–570.

26. On approaches to civil rights historiography, see Armstead L. Robinson and Patricia Sullivan, *New Directions in Civil Rights Studies* (Charlottesville: University Press of Virginia, 1991); Steven F. Lawson, "Freedom Then, Freedom Now: The Historiography of The Civil Rights Movement," *American Historical Review* (April 1991): 456–471; Charles M. Payne, *I've Got the Light of Freedom: The Organizing Tradition and the Mississippi Freedom Struggle* (Berkeley: University of California Press, 1995), 413–441; David Chappell, "Introduction," *Arkansas Historical Quarterly* 56 (Fall 1997): 11–16 (editor's introduction to collection of essays on the Little Rock crisis).

The question of the role of the Cold War and foreign affairs in domestic civil rights reform has been noted consistently by some scholars but until recently has been at the margins of civil rights historiography. The work of Gerald Horne, Brenda Gayle Plummer, and others has helped lay a foundation for a broadening literature on race, civil rights, and foreign relations. Derrick Bell has long argued that the Cold War was a critical factor in influencing the development of the constitutional right to equality. Gerald Horne, *Black and Red: W. E. B. DuBois and the Afro American Response to the Cold War* (Albany: State University of New York Press, 1986); Plummer, *Rising Wind*; Derrick A. Bell Jr., "Brown v. Board of Education and the Interest-Convergence Dilemma," *Harvard Law Review* 93 (January 1980): 518, reprinted in Derrick A. Bell Jr., *Shades of Brown: New Perspectives on School Desegregation* (New York: Teachers College Press, 1980); Derrick A. Bell Jr., "Racial Remediation: An Historical Perspective on Current Conditions," *Notre Dame Lawyer* 52 (October 1976): 5, 12. See also Thomas Borstelmann, *Apartheid's Reluctant Uncle: The United States and Southern Africa in the Early Cold War* (New York: Oxford University Press, 1993); Penny Von Eschen, *Race Against Empire: Black Americans and Anticolonialism, 1937–1957* (Ithaca, N.Y.: Cornell University Press, 1997); Michael L. Krenn, *Black Diplomacy: African Americans and the State Department, 1945–1969* (Armonk, N.Y.: M. E. Sharpe, 1999); "Symposium: African Americans and U. S. Foreign Relations," *Diplomatic History* 20 (Fall 1996): 531; Mark Solomon, "Black Critics of Colonialism and the Cold War," in *Cold War Critics: Alternatives to American Foreign Policy in the Truman Years*, Thomas G. Patterson, ed. (Chicago: Quadrangle Books, 1971), 205–239; Mary Francis Berry, *Black Resistance White Law: A History of Constitutional Racism in America* (New York: Penguin Press, 1994), 135, 146; Mary L. Dudziak, "Desegregation as a Cold War Imperative," *Stanford Law Review* 41 (November 1988): 61–120; Richard Lentz and Pamela Brown, " 'The Business of Great Nations': International Coverage, Foreign Public Opinion and the Modern American Civil Rights Movement" (paper presented to the Western Journalism Historians Conference, Berkeley, California, February 28–29, 1992); Yvette Richards, "Race, Gender and Anticommunism i the International Labor Movement: The Pan-African Connections of Maida Springer, International Labor Representative," *Journal of Women's History* 11 (Summer 1999). On race and U.S. foreign affairs, see Michael M. Hunt, *Ideology and U. S. Foreign Policy* (New Haven, Conn.: Yale University Press, 1987), 46–91; *Race and U.S. Foreign Policy from the Colonial Period to the Present*, 5 vols., Michael

L. Krenn, ed., (New York: Garland, 1998). Drawing upon works like these, and looking more broadly across the span of American history, Philip Klinkner and Rogers Smith in their important book argue that periods of conflict, including the Cold War, have been a crucial element in moments of change leading to greater racial equality in the United States. Klinkner with Smith, *The Unsteady March*, 317–351.

27. For powerful critiques of the black/white paradigm, see Robert S. Chang, *Disoriented: Asian Americans, the Law and the Nation-State*; Juan F. Perea (New York: New York University Press, 1999), "The Black/White Binary Paradigm of Race: The 'Normal Science' of American Racial Thought," *California Law Review* 85 (October 1997): 1213–1258.

28. *Recasting America: Culture and Politics in the Age of the Cold War,* Lary May, ed., (Chicago: University of Chicago Press, 1989); E. May, *Homeward Bound*; Stephen J. Whitfield, *The Culture of the Cold War* (Baltimore: Johns Hopkins University Press, 1991). Adolph Reed argues that the Cold War intellectual climate also limited the focus of scholarly inquiry on African American thought. Adolph L. Reed Jr., *W. E. B. DuBois and American Political Thought: Fabianism and the Color Line* (New York: Oxford University Press, 1997), 6–11.

During the early Cold War years, "Americanism" came to be identified with support for the status quo, and unqualified defense of American democracy. This focused Americanism replaced a more diverse set of ideas. During the pre–World War II years, labor activists and civil rights leaders found in the concept of Americanism notions of justice and equality and employed Americanism as rhetoric for social change. Gary Gerstle, *Working Class Americanism: The Politics of Labor in a Textile City, 1914–1960* (Cambridge: Cambridge University Press, 1989), 5–15.

29. For other works that place American history within a transnational framework, see Daniel T. Rodgers, *Atlantic Crossings: Social Politics in a Progressive Age* (Cambridge: Harvard University Press, 1998); David Thelen, "The Nation and Beyond: Transnational Perspectives on United States History," *Journal of American History* 86 (December 1999): 965–975, and other essays collected in "The Nation and Beyond: A Special Issue," *Journal of American History* 86 (December 1999): 965–1307. While the global turn is often seen as a new methodology in American historiography, Robin D. G. Kelley argues that "Black studies, Chicano/a studies, and Asian American studies were diasporic from their inception." Robin D. G. Kelley, " 'But a Local Phase of a World Problem': Black History's Global Vision," *Journal of American History* 86 (December 1999): 1045.

CHAPTER ONE

1. American Embassy, Colombo, Ceylon, to Secretary of State, May 25, 1949, RG 59, 811.4016/5–2549, National Archives.

2. *Congressional Record,* 79th Cong., 2d Sess., 1946, 92, pt. 8:10259 (reprinting article from *New York Herald Tribune*, July 27, 1946). The broader context of these killings is discussed in Wallace H. Warren, " 'The Best People in Town Won't Talk': The Moore's Ford Lynching of 1946 and Its Cover-Up," in *Georgia in Black and White: Explorations in*

the Race Relations of a Southern State, 1865–1950, John C. Inscoe, ed. (Athens: The University of Georgia Press, 1994), 266–288.

3. *Congressional Record,* 79th Cong., 2d Sess., 1946, 92, pt. 8:10259 (reprinting article from *New York Herald Tribune,* July 27, 1946).

4. Ibid.; *New York Times,* July 28, 1946, pp. 1, 25; Warren, "The Moore's Ford Lynching."

5. *Congressional Record,* 79th Cong., 2d Sess., 1946, 92, pt. 8:10259 (reprinting article from *New York Herald Tribune,* July 27, 1946).

6. Ibid.; *New York Times,* July 28, 1946, pp. 1, 25; *The Times* (London), July 27, 1946, p. 3; Lynching—Walton GA/Press Releases & Statements, II-A-400, Frame 588, Papers of NAACP: The Anti-Lynching Campaign 1912–1955, Series A (Frederick, Md.: University Publications of America).

7. Leon F. Litwack, *Trouble in Mind: Black Southerners in the Age of Jim Crow* (New York: Knopf, 1998), 280–325; Charles M. Payne, *I've Got the Light of Freedom: The Organizing Tradition and the Mississippi Freedom Struggle* (Berkeley: University of California Press, 1995).

8. *New York Times,* July 31, 1946, pp. 1,48; *Daily Worker* (New York), August 7, 1946, p. 2, in Lynching—Walton GA/Press Releases & Statements, II-A-400, Frame 530, Papers of NAACP: The Anti-Lynching Campaign 1912–1955, Series A (Frederick, Md.: University Publications of America).

9. *New York Times,* July 31, 1946, pp. 1, 48; U.S. Embassy, Moscow, to Department of State, August 26, 1946, RG 59, 811.4016/8–2646, National Archives.

10. *New York Times,* July 29, 1946, p. 36.

11. *Congressional Record,* 79th Cong., 2d Sess., 1946, 92, pt. 8:10258.

12. Donald R. McCoy and Richard T. Ruetten, *Quest and Response: Minority Rights and the Truman Administration* (Lawrence: University Press of Kansas, 1973), 45–48; Walter White, *A Man Called White: The Autobiography of Walter White* (New York: Viking Press, 1948), 322–323, 327.

13. McCoy and Ruetten, *Quest and Response,* 47–48. While Truman appeared to be acting spontaneously upon Walter White's suggestion that he set up a committee on civil rights, William Berman has written that Truman and his advisors had previously decided to set up such a committee and used the meeting with the National Emergency Committee Against Mob Violence as the vehicle to announce the decision. William C. Berman, *The Politics of Civil Rights in the Truman Administration* (Columbus: Ohio State University Press, 1970), 51.

14. Robert J. Donovan, *Conflict and Crisis: The Presidency of Harry S. Truman, 1945–1948* (New York: Norton, 1977), 32–33.

15. *Off the Record: The Private Papers of Harry S. Truman,* Robert H. Ferrell, ed., (New York: Harper and Row, 1980), 146–147; David McCullough, *Truman* (New York: Simon and Schuster, 1992), 588–589; Alonzo L. Hamby, *Man of the People: A Life of Harry S. Truman* (New York: Oxford University Press, 1995), 364–666.

16. Donovan, *Conflict and Crisis,* 32–33, 114; McCoy and Ruetten, *Quest and Response,* 32–33; A. Philip Randolph, "Call to the March," in *Black Protest Thought in the*

Twentieth Century, 2d ed., August Meier, Elliott Rudwick, and Francis L. Broderick, eds. (Indianapolis: Bobbs-Merrill, 1971), 220–224.

While some historians have viewed Truman's support for FEPC legislation as evidence of his commitment to civil rights, others have considered it an example of his ineffectiveness. According to Louis Ruchames, Truman supported permanent FEPC legislation, which he knew wouldn't get through Congress, and at the same time refused to push for an appropriation for the existing temporary FEPC, which might have been aided by his active support. Louis Ruchames, *Race, Jobs and Politics: The Story of FEPC* (Westport, Conn.: Negro University Press, 1953), 126. See also Berman, *The Politics of Civil Rights in the Truman Administration,* 26–29.

17. Clark Clifford to Truman, November 19, 1947, Political File—Confidential Memo to President, box 21, Clark Clifford Papers, Harry S. Truman Library, Independence, Missouri, pp. 3, 12–13, 19, 40; Harvard Sitkoff, "Harry Truman and the Election of 1948: The Coming of Age of Civil Rights in American Politics," *Journal of Southern History* 37 (November 1971): 597. While Clark Clifford claims authorship for the memo which bears his name, David McCullough has written that the memo was actually drafted by James A. Rowe Jr. and edited by Clifford and George Elsey. According to McCullough, Rowe's authorship was obscured because he was the law partner of a man Truman disliked. Compare Oral History Interview with Clark M. Clifford, vol. 1, Harry S. Truman Library (April 1977), 215–220, with McCullough, *Truman,* 590.

Others also held the view that the black vote was highly important in 1948. That year, Henry Lee Moon published a book arguing that the black vote could play a critical role in the 1948 election and that the black vote was "in the vest pocket of no party," but would have to be earned. Henry Lee Moon, *The Balance of Power: The Negro Vote* (Garden City, N.Y.: Doubleday, 1948), 11–12, 213–214.

18. McCoy and Ruetten, *Quest and Response,* 127, 131–134, 145–146.

19. Sitkoff, "Election of 1948," 610; McCoy and Ruetten, *Quest and Response,* 129, 143.

20. Sitkoff, "Election of 1948," 613–614; McCoy and Ruetten, *Quest and Response,* 143–144, 145–147; Barton J. Bernstein, "The Ambiguous Legacy: The Truman Administration and Civil Rights," in *Politics and Policies of the Truman Administration,* Barton J. Bernstein, ed. (Chicago: Quadrangle Books, 1970), 712–713.

21. Harry S. Truman, "Special Message to the Congress on Greece and Turkey: The Truman Doctrine," March 12, 1947, in *Public Papers of the Presidents of the United States, Harry S. Truman, 1947* (Washington, D. C.: Government Printing Office, 1963), 176–179; Bernard A. Weisberger, *Cold War, Cold Peace: The United States and Russia Since 1945* (New York: American Heritage, 1984), 55–61; Les K. Adler and Thomas G. Paterson, "Red Fascism: The Merger of Nazi Germany and Soviet Russia in the American Image of Totalitarianism, 1930s–1950s," *American Historical Review* 75 (April 1970): 1046; Dean Acheson, *Present at the Creation: My Years in the State Department* (New York: Norton, 1969), 217–219.

22. Ellen Schrecker, *Many Are the Crimes: McCarthyism in America* (Boston: Little, Brown, 1998); David Caute, *The Great Fear: The Anti-Communist Purge Under Truman and Eisenhower* (New York: Simon and Schuster, 1978), 30. On Truman and the origins

of McCarthyism, compare Alonzo L. Hamby, *Beyond the New Deal: Harry S. Truman and American Liberalism* (New York: Columbia University Press, 1973), 86–91 (arguing that McCarthyism as a social phenomenon was due to factors external to Truman administration politics, and that Truman was a strong, although ineffective, denouncer of McCarthyism), with Richard M. Freeland, *The Truman Doctrine and the Origins of McCarthyism* (New York: Knopf, 1972), 5 (arguing that McCarthyism was "the result of a deliberate and highly organized effort by the Truman administration in 1947–48 to mobilize support for the program of economic assistance to Europe"). See also Melvyn P. Leffler, *A Preponderance of Power: National Security, the Truman Adminstration, and the Cold War* (Stanford, Calif.: Stanford University Press, 1992); *The Truman Period As a Research Field, A Reappraisal, 1972,* Richard S. Kirkendall, ed. (Columbia: University of Missouri Press, 1974), 105–108, 129–136, 182–187.

23. *Labor-Management Relations (Taft-Hartley) Act,* § 9(h), Pub. L. 80–101, 61 Stat. 136, 146 (1947); Schrecker, *Many Are the Crimes,* 266–273; Caute, *The Great Fear,* 355–356; *Adler v. Board of Education,* 342 U.S. 485 (1952); 1939 N.Y. Laws § 1318, as amended 1940 N.Y. Laws § 1499; 1949 N.Y. Laws § 1024; Diane Ravitch, *The Troubled Crusade: American Education, 1945–1980* (New York: Basic Books, 1983), 82. See also Ellen Schrecker, *No Ivory Tower: McCarthyism and the Universities* (New York: Oxford University Press, 1987).

24. Wayne Addison Clark, "An Analysis of the Relationship Between Anti-Communism and Segregationist Thought in the Deep South, 1948–1964" (Ph.D. diss., University of North Carolina, 1976), 12, 30, 34.

25. Roy Wilkins, "Undergirding the Democratic Ideal," *The Crisis* 58 (December 1951): 647, 650 (emphasis in original). See also Gloster Current, "The 41st–A Convention of Great Decision," *The Crisis* 57 (August/September 1950): 512, 523; "Resolutions adopted by the Forty-Second Annual Convention of the NAACP at Atlanta, GA., June 30, 1951," *The Crisis* 58 (August/September 1951): 475, 476; Wilson Record, *Race and Radicalism: The NAACP and the Communist Party in Conflict* (Ithaca, N.Y.: Cornell University Press, 1964), 132–141.

26. Robert E. Cushman, "Our Civil Rights Become a World Issue," *New York Times* magazine, January 12, 1948, p. 12.

27. American Consulate General, Suva, Fiji Islands, to Secretary of State, December 27, 1946, RG 59, 811.4016/12–2746, National Archives.

The article was motivated by a *Chicago Tribune* article criticizing Britain for its handling of the Palestine crisis in 1946. The *Fiji Times & Herald* article began by claiming that "many people in the United States seem to enjoy crusading as long as they avoid entanglements and can direct criticism across the Atlantic." Ibid.

The idea that the United States had unclean hands and, accordingly, no standing to criticize Britain on the issue of Palestine was suggested in the British media as well. A cartoon in the June 8, 1947, *London Sunday Express* showed two white men reading a newspaper entitled "Southern Press" and standing in front of a whites-only hotel that was draped with an American flag. Behind them a dead man lay beneath a tree beside a rope. One of the whites remarked to the other, "Shameful the way the British are handling this

Palestine business." American Consul General, Hamburg, Germany, to Secretary of State, June 10, 1947, RG 59, 811.5016/6–1047, National Archives.

28. American Consulate General, Suva, Fiji Islands, to Secretary of State, December 27, 1946. The reference in the *Fiji Times & Herald* is to the denial of Supreme Court Review in a case in which lower federal courts had found Georgia voting laws to be unconstitutional. In this case, Primus E. King sued the Democratic Executive Committee of Muscogee County, Georgia, claiming that he had been denied the right to vote in the July 1944 Democratic primary solely on the grounds of his race. Following *Smith v. Allwright,* 321 U.S. 649 (1944), which abolished the Texas white primary, the district court ruled that the Georgia Democratic primary was an integral part of the state electoral process, and therefore the refusal of Democratic officials to allow King to vote was impermissible state action, violating the Fourteenth, Fifteenth, and Seventeenth Amendments. This victory was short-lived, however. In February 1947 the Georgia legislature repealed all state primary laws. *King v. Chapman,* 62 F. Supp. 639, 649–650 (M.D. GA 1945), affirmed, 154 F.2d 460 (5th Cir. 1946), cert. denied, 327 U.S. 800 (1946); Steven F. Lawson, *Black Ballots: Voting Rights in the South, 1944–1969* (New York: Columbia University Press, 1976), 49.

Instances of racism on the part of the DAR received widespread critical attention in the foreign press. For example, when the DAR refused to permit African American pianist Hazel Scott to perform in Constitution Hall, the American Consul General in Bombay, India, stated that news of the incident "was fully reported in practically all of the local press." The Bombay *Morning Standard* called it a "shameful manifestation of racial intolerance." American Consulate General, Bombay, India, to Secretary of State, October 17, 1948, RG 59, 811.4016/10–1745, National Archives.

29. The dinner was funded by an endowment left by Wendell Willkie, the 1940 Republican presidential candidate, who the *Fiji Times & Herald* described as "a notable fighter against the persecution of negroes." American Consulate General, Suva, Fiji Islands, to Secretary of State, December 27, 1946.

30. Ibid.

31. American Embassy, Colombo, Ceylon, to Secretary of State, December 22, 1948, RG 59, 811.4016/12–2248, National Archives; American Embassy, Colombo, Ceylon, to Secretary of State, December 31, 1948, RG 59, 811.4016/12–3148, National Archives; American Embassy, Colombo, Ceylon, to Secretary of State, May 25, 1949, RG 59, 811.4016/5–2549, National Archives.

32. *New York Times,* May 3, 1948, pp. 1, 12.

33. Chinese Press Review No. 635, American Consulate General, Shanghai, China, May 6, 1948, Enclosure No. 1, American Consulate General, Shanghai, China, to Secretary of State, May 10, 1948, RG 59, 811.4016/5–1048, National Archives (quoting Shanghai *Ta Kung Pao*).

34. Ibid. (quoting *China Daily Tribune*).

35. American Consulate General, Madras, to Secretary of State, May 6, 1948, RG 59, 811.4016/5–648, National Archives (concerning editorial on *Shelly v. Kraemer,* 344 U.S. 1 (1948)); American Embassy, Manila, to Secretary of State, October 5, 1948, RG 59,

811.4016/10–548, National Archives. In *Perez v. Sharp*, 32 Cal. 2d 711, 198 P.2d 17 (1948), an African American man and a white woman had been denied a marriage license by the Los Angeles county clerk. The California Supreme Court held that the state statute forbidding interracial marriage was void on equal protection grounds.

36. Chester Bowles, *Ambassador's Report* (New York: Harper, 1954), 2–3, 31, 99.

37. Frenise A. Logan, "Racism and Indian-U.S. Relations, 1947–1953: Views in the Indian Press," *Pacific Historical Review* 54 (February 1985): 71–79; American Consulate General, Bombay, India, to Secretary of State, March 28, 1947, RG 59, 811.4016/3–2847, National Archives; American Consulate General, Bombay, India, to Secretary of State, July 11, 1945, RG 59, 311.4016/7–1145, National Archives (quoting *Sunday Standard* (Bombay), July 8, 1945); American Consulate General, Bombay, India, to Secretary of State, May 4, 1949, RG 59, 811.4016/5–449, National Archives (quoting *Blitz*, April 23, 1949).

38. American Consulate General, Bombay, India, to Secretary of State, May 4, 1949.

39. American Embassy, New Delhi, "Survey of Communist Propaganda in India," vol. 2, no. 13, July 1–31, 1952, folder 507, box 112, series 2, Chester Bowles Papers, Manuscripts and Archives, Yale University Library, pp. 8–9.

40. American Consulate General, Madras, India, to Secretary of State, May 6, 1948, RG 59, 811.4016/5–648, National Archives (concerning editorial on *Shelley v. Kraemer*, 344 U.S. 1 (1948)).

41. American Embassy, London, to Secretary of State, June 25, 1946, RG 59, 811.4016/6–2546, National Archives (concerning *Manchester Guardian* editorial on Ku Klux Klan); American Embassy, London, to Secretary of State, September 12, 1946, RG 59, 811.4016/9–1246, National Archives (concerning *Manchester Guardian* article "Race Friction in the South: The War and the Negro"); *London Sunday Express* cartoon, American Consul General, Hamburg, Germany, to Secretary of State, June 10, 1947, RG 59, 811.5016/6–1047, National Archives; London, via War Department, to Secretary of State, January 10, 1947, RG 59, 811.4016/1–1047, National Archives (discussing attention given to case in London press and Parliament); London, via War Department, to Secretary of State, January 16, 1947, RG 59, 811.4016/1–1647, National Archives; American Embassy, London, to Secretary of State, February 6, 1947, RG 59, 811.4016/2–647, National Archives; *Lewis v. State*, 201 Miss. 48, 61, 28 So.2d 122, 124 (1946); *Trudell v. State*, 28 So.2d 124, 125 (Miss. 1946); *Trudell v. Mississippi*, 331 U.S. 785 (1947); *New York Times*, January 5, 1947, p. 42.

Publicity from such protests was important in generating outside scrutiny of the criminal justice system in the South. Such protests were often unsuccessful in changing the outcome in a particular case, however. The impact of anticommunism on local politics helped to undercut the effectiveness of mass protest. For example, in the Martinsville Seven case, in which seven African American men were sentenced to death in Virginia for the rape of a white woman, domestic and international protest was in part orchestrated by the Communist Party and the Civil Rights Congress. Eric Rise has written that Virginia Governor John Stewart Battle's refusal to grant clemency to at least some of the defendants was influenced by his desire not to "to appear to be bowing to the radical influence." Eric

W. Rise, *The Martinsville Seven: Race, Rape and Capital Punishment* (Charlottesville: University Press of Virginia, 1995), 99–116.

42. Senator William Benton, *Congressional Record*, 81st Cong., 2nd Sess., May 9, 1950, 6692.

43. James W. Ivy, "American Negro Problem in the European Press," *The Crisis* 57 (July 1950): 413, 416–418. As Richard Lentz and Pamela Brown have written, the American media paid extensive attention to the way American race relations were viewed overseas. Richard Lentz and Pamela Brown, " 'The Business of Great Nations': International Coverage, Foreign Public Opinion and the Modern American Civil Rights Movement" (paper presented to the Western Journalism Historians Conference, Berkeley, California, February 28–29, 1992).

44. Ivy, "American Negro Problem," 416–417.

45. Ibid., 416.

46. Chinese Press Review No. 635, American Consulate General, Shanghai, China, May 6, 1948, Enclosure No. 1, American Consulate General, Shanghai, China, to Secretary of State, May 10, 1948, RG 59, 811.4016/5–1048, National Archives (quoting Shanghai *Ta Kung Pao*); American Consulate General, Bombay, India, to Secretary of State, May 4, 1949, RG 59, 811.4016/5–449, National Archives (quoting *Blitz*, April 23, 1949); American Embassy, Oslo, Norway, to Department of State, August 5, 1947, RG 59, 811.4016/80–547, National Archives; American Embassy, Athens, Greece, to Secretary of State, July 22, 1938, RG 59, 811.4016/7–2248, National Archives.

47. Moscow to Secretary of State, November 20, 1946, RG 59, 811.4016/11–2046, National Archives; American Embassy, Moscow, to Department of State, August 26, 1946, RG 59, 811.4016/8–2646, National Archives.

48. American Embassy, Moscow, to Department of State, August 26, 1946. The *New York Times* reported that John Jones's body was discovered on Dorcheat Bayou in Louisiana by a group of fishermen. He had apparently been beaten to death. Jones and a companion, who was also African American, had been arrested after allegedly trying to break in to a white woman's home. No charges were filed, and the two were released. Soon after their release, the men were picked up by a group of unidentified persons and placed in separate cars. Jones's companion was beaten and survived. Jones was later found dead. The Linden, Louisiana, police chief, B. Geary Gantt, two deputy sheriffs, and three others were later indicted by a federal grand jury for depriving Jones and his companion of their constitutional rights by "causing them to be released and handed over to a mob which then inflicted a beating upon both." Five of the defendants were tried and acquitted by a Shreveport, Louisiana jury. The *Times* did not report the disposition of the charges against Police Chief Gantt. *New York Times*, August 16, 1946, p. 36; *New York Times*, October 19, 1946, p. 22; *New York Times*, March 2, 1946, p. 63.

49. American Embassy, Moscow, to Department of State, August 26, 1946, RG 59, 811.4016/8–2646, National Archives. State laws that continued to allow the system of peonage described in the *Trud* article were overturned by the Supreme Court in the 1940s. *Taylor v. Georgia*, 315 U.S. 25 (1942); *Pollock v. Williams*, 322 U.S. 4 (1949); Pete Daniel, *The Shadow of Slavery: Peonage in the South, 1901–1969* (Urbana: University of Illinois

Press, 1972), 175–192; William Cohen, "Involuntary Servitude in the South, 1865–1940: A Preliminary Analysis," *Journal of Southern History* 42 (February 1976): 31.

50. Moscow to Secretary of State, July 27, 1949, RG 59, 811.4016/6–2749, National Archives; *Congressional Record*, 81st Cong., 2nd Sess., May 9, 1950, 6692. While it criticized the United States, the Soviet Union was not without its own ethnic strife. Largely through conquest, the Soviet Union was an amalgam of different nationalities, yet non-Russian nationalism was often suppressed as "bourgeois." Stalin himself was not Russian but Georgian, yet ironically it was Stalin who pursued a policy of Russian cultural superiority. John S. Reshetar Jr., *The Soviet Polity: Government and Politics in the USSR*, 3rd ed. (New York: Harper and Row, 1989), 9–19, 281–292; Robert Conquest, *Stalin: Breaker of Nations* (New York: Viking Penguin, 1991), 2, 141–300.

51. Moscow to Secretary of State, July 27, 1949, RG 59, 811.4016/6–2749, National Archives.

52. *Congressional Record*, 81st Cong., 2nd Sess., May 9, 1950, 6993.

53. As reported by Senator William Benton, ibid., 6694.

54. Memorandum of Conversation, Department of State, Subject: Alleged Discrimination Against Haitian Agriculture Minister, November 14, 1947, RG 59, FW 811.4016/11–1247, National Archives; H. K. Thatcher to Norman Armour, December 1, 1947, RG 59, 811.4016/12–147, National Archives; Jimmie Love to Robert F. Woodward, November 25, 1947, RG 59, 811.4016/11–2547, National Archives; American Embassy, Port-au-Prince, Haiti, to Secretary of State, November 18, 1947, RG 59, 811.4016/11–1847, National Archives.

55. Ambassador of Haiti to Secretary of State, November 12, 1947, TC No. 46760, Department of State translation, RG 59, 811.4016/11–1247, National Archives.

56. Port-au-Prince, Haiti, to Secretary of State, November 20, 1947, RG 59, 811.4016/11–2047, National Archives (quoting *La Nation*). Representatives from other countries and territories in North and Central America were in attendance and were not segregated. American Embassy, Port-au-Prince, Haiti, to Secretary of State, November 18, 1947.

57. Port-au-Prince, Haiti, to Secretary of State, November 20, 1947 (quoting *Le Nouvelliste*).

58. Memorandum of Conversation, Department of State, Subject: Alleged Discrimination Against Haitian Agriculture Minister, November 14; Holt to Secretary of State, November 28, 1947, RG 59, 811.4016/11–2847, National Archives.

59. John H. Lord to Secretary of State, September 12, 1945, RG 59, 811.4016/9–1245, National Archives.

60. Logan, "Racism and Indian-U.S. Relations," 76 (quoting *Bombay Chronicle*, July 4, 1952).

61. Virginia A. Pratt, *The Influence of Domestic Controversy on American Participation in the United Nations Commission on Human Rights, 1946–1953* (New York: Garland, 1986), 37; Rusk to Hulten, November 4, 1947, RG 59, 501.B.D Human Rights/11–447, National Archives.

62. *New York Times*, June 2, 1946, p. 33; "The First Petition to the United Nations from the Afro-American People," in Herbert Aptheker, *Afro-American History: The Modern Era* (New York: Citadel Press, 1971), 301–311; Abner W. Berry, "Rough, Tough and Angry," *New Masses*, June 18, 1946, pp. 17–19.

63. "An Appeal to the World," reprinted in W. E. B. DuBois, "Three Centuries of Discrimination," *The Crisis* 54 (December 1947): 380; *New York Times*, October 24, 1947, p. 9; *New York Times*, October 12, 1947, p. 52; McCoy and Ruetten, *Quest and Response*, 67; Berman, *The Politics of Civil Rights in the Truman Administration*, 65–66.

64. Walter Frances, White, *A Man Called White: The Autobiography of Walter White* (New York: Viking Press, 1948), 358–359; McCoy and Ruetten, *Quest and Response*, 67; Gerald Horne, *Black and Red: W. E. B. DuBois and the Afro-American Response to the Cold War, 1944–1963* (Albany: State University of New York Press, 1986), 15, 78.

65. Berman, *The Politics of Civil Rights in the Truman Administration*, 66; McCoy and Ruetten, *Quest and Response*, 67; Joanna Schneider Zangrando and Robert L. Zangrando, "ER and Black Civil Rights," in *Without Precedent: The Life and Career of Eleanor Roosevelt*, Joan Hoff-Wilson and Marjorie Lightman, ed. (Bloomington: Indiana University Press, 1984), 88, 101–102.

66. Berman, *The Politics of Civil Rights in the Truman Administration*, 66; White, *Man Called White*, 359; Horne, *Black and Red*, 79–80 (quoting *Des Moines Register* and *Morgantown Post*).

67. Robert Coe, U.S. Embassy, The Hague, The Netherlands, to Department of State, February 13, 1950, RG 59, 811.411/2–1350, National Archives.

68. Ibid.

CHAPTER TWO

1. *The Negro in American Life*, folder 503, box 112, series 2, Chester Bowles Papers, Manuscripts and Archives, Yale University Library.

2. American Embassy, Rangoon, Burma, to Secretary of State, October 7, 1947, RG 59, 811.4016/10–747, National Archives.

3. Ibid.

4. James L. Tyson, *U.S. International Broadcasting and National Security* (New York: Ramapo Press: National Strategy Information Center, 1983), 4–5; Walter L. Hixon, *Parting the Curtain: Propaganda, Culture and the Cold War, 1945–1961* (New York: St. Martin's Press, 1997); Laura Ann Belmonte, "Defending a Way of Life: American Propaganda and the Cold War, 1945–1959" (Ph.D. diss., University of Virginia, 1996); *Congressional Record*, 80th Cong., 2nd Sess., 6560–6561 (1947) (remarks of Representative Everett Dirksen); S. Rep. No. 811, 80th Cong., 2d Sess., reprinted in 1948 U.S. Code Cong. & Admin. News 1011, 1013, 1023; *Expanded International Information and Education Program by the United States: Hearings before a Subcommittee of the Senate Committee on Foreign Relations on S. Res. 243*, 81st Cong. 2d Sess. 39–40 (1950) (statement of Secretary of State Dean Acheson).

5. *The Negro in American Life.* The thirty-three-page pamphlet is undated, but it seems clearly to have been written in 1950 or 1951. The pamphlet relies on 1950 census data. It discusses by name Supreme Court cases that were decided in 1950, and, in particular, does not mention *Brown v. Board of Education*, which was decided in 1954. In addition, the pamphlet is collected with Chester Bowles's papers from his first tenure as U.S. ambassador to India from 1951 to 1953. Chester Bowles, *Promises to Keep: My Years in Public Life, 1941–1969* (New York: Harper and Row, 1971), 248. Laura Belmonte thoughtfully explores a broader range of portrayals of the "American Way of Life" in U.S. propaganda in Belmonte, "Defending a Way of Life." See also Walter L. Hixon, *Parting the Curtain*; Michael Krenn, " 'Unfinished Business': Segregation and U.S. Diplomacy at the 1958 World's Fair," *Diplomatic History* 20 (Fall 1996): 591–612.

6. *The Negro In American Life.*

7. Ibid., 2–3.

8. Ibid., 5.

9. Ibid., 2.

10. Ibid., 9.

11. Ibid., 6.

12. Ibid., 6–7. Importantly, "school age" was not defined. High school enrollment in the South also increased, but the essay makes no mention of percentages of African American youths of high school age enrolled. Rather, only absolute numbers were given, with a rise from 5,232 in 1900 to an estimate of 300,000 in 1950.

13. Ibid., 7.

14. Ibid., 13 (emphasis added).

15. Ibid., closing (unnumbered) pages.

16. Psychological Strategy Board, "Status Report on the National Psychological Effort and First Progress Report of the Psychological Strategy Board," August 1, 1952, file 391.1, box 22, Papers of the Psychological Strategy Board, Harry S. Truman Library, p. 3.

17. Gerald Horne, *Black and Red: W. E. B. DuBois and the Afro-American Response to the Cold War, 1944–1963* (Albany: State University of New York Press, 1986), 280–281. The CAA, co-founded by Paul Robeson, operated from the 1930s to 1955, when, according to Mark Solomon it "was finally dissolved . . . under ferocious McCarthyite attacks." Mark Solomon, "Black Critics of Colonialism and the Cold War," in *Cold War Critics: Alternatives to American Foreign Policy in the Truman Years*, Thomas G. Patterson, ed. (Chicago: Quadrangle Books, 1971), 207–208, 233–234, and n.9; American Consul, Lagos, Nigeria, to Department of State, July 30, 1952, RG 59, 811.411/7–3052, National Archives.

18. American Consul, Lagos, Nigeria, to Department of State, July 30, 1952 (as paraphrased and quoted in press release).

Yergan had previously been associated with the Communist Party, although he claimed, after his break with the Party, that he had never been a member. Wilson Record, *The Negro and the Communist Party* (Chapel Hill: University of North Carolina Press, 1951), 197; *New York Times*, May 14, 1952, p. 12. On May 13, 1952, Yergan testified before the Senate Internal Security Committee that the Party had "used him for ten years to spread Red propaganda among American Negroes." He claimed that "the Reds were 'interested in exploiting undesirable conditions and in preventing a solution of racial problems.' " *New York Times*, May 14, 1952, p. 1; American Consul, Lagos, Nigeria, to Department of State, July 30, 1952.

19. American Consul, Lagos, Nigeria, to Department of State, July 30, 1952 (as paraphrased and quoted in press release).

20. Ibid.

21. Ibid.

22. "Touring Schedule" and "Report of Jay Saunders Redding," September 30, 1952, folder 416, box 111, series 2, Chester Bowles Papers, p. 1 of Report.

23. Ibid, 2–3.

24. Ibid., 3.

25. Ibid., 4; Logue to Wilkins, December 8, 1952, folder 450, box 107, series 2, Chester Bowles Papers. See also "Notes on the Talks of Stephen M. Schwebel to Colleges and Other Institutions in the Calcutta Zone," October 20–November 9, 1952, folder 499, box 111, series 2, Chester Bowles Papers; "Notes on Talks of Stephen M. Schwebel, Bombay Zone," Dec. 1–15, 1952, folder 499, box 111, series 2, Chester Bowles Papers.

26. Logue to Bowles, February 26, 1952, folder 498, box 111, series 2, Chester Bowles Papers, pp. 4–5; "Log of Clifford Manshardt," 28 February-11 March 1952, folder 517, box 114, series 2, Chester Bowles Papers.

27. Bowles to Drew, January 2, 1953, folder 450, box 107, series 2, Chester Bowles Papers. On African Americans in diplomatic posts, see Michael L. Krenn, *Black Diplomacy: African Americans and the State Department, 1945–1969* (Armonk, N.Y.: M. E. Sharpe, 1999).

Bowles also believed that white embassy personnel should not harbor racial prejudice. In a letter to the State Department's Director of the Office of South Asian Affairs, he discussed his concern regarding an American officer in Bangalore, India. "I am afraid that tucked away deep inside him is a prejudice against people with a dark skin. . . . Aren't we taking a serious risk in sending such people to a city like Bangalore to operate without close supervision in an area inhabited by the darkest-skinned people of India?" Bowles to Kennedy, December 28, 1951, folder 501, box 112, series 2, Chester Bowles Papers.

28. William O. Douglas, *Strange Lands and Friendly People* (New York: Harper, 1951), 296.

29. American Embassy, New Delhi, "Survey of Communist Propaganda in India," Vol. 2, no. 14, August 1 to 31, 1952, folder 507, box 112, series 2, Chester Bowles Papers, p. 9.

30. *New York Times*, March 19, 1950, p. 50.

31. "Status Report on the National Psychological Effort and First Progress Report of the Psychological Strategy Board," Aug. 1, 1952, folder 391.1, box 22, Papers of the Psychological Strategy Board, Truman Library, p. 3.

32. W. James Ellison, "Paul Robeson and the State Department," *The Crisis* 84 (May 1977): 185; Martin Duberman, *Paul Robeson* (New York: Knopf, 1989), 341–350, 364–372.

33. Duberman, *Paul Robeson*, 388–389; Alan Rogers, "Passports and Politics: The Courts and the Cold War," *The Historian* 47 (August 1985): 499–502; Paul Robeson, *Here I Stand* (New York: Othello Associates, 1958), 71–81.

34. Duberman, *Paul Robeson*, 398–403.

35. David Cushman Coyle, *The United Nations and How It Works*, rev. ed. (New York: Columbia University Press, 1969), 84–85; Civil Rights Congress, *We Charge Genocide: The Historic Petition to the United Nations for Relief from a Crime of the United States Government Against the Negro People*, 2nd ed., William Patterson, ed. (New York: International Publishers, 1970), 3, 32; William Patterson, *The Man Who Cried Genocide: An Autobiography* (New York: International Publishers, 1971), 178–179.

36. Civil Rights Congress, *We Charge Genocide*, vii, xiv–xvi, xvii–xviii, 58–187; *New York Times*, December 18, 1951, p. 13.

37. Civil Rights Congress, *We Charge Genocide*, xvi.

38. Ibid., 27–28.

39. Gerald Horne, *Communist Front?: The Civil Rights Congress, 1946–1956* (Rutherford, N.J.: Fairleigh Dickinson University Press; 1988), 169–174; Patterson, *The Man Who Cried Genocide*, 193–195, 205–206; Press Analysis Section, United States Information Service, American Embassy, New Delhi, "Survey of Communist Propaganda in India," February 1–15, 1952, folder 415, box 105, series 2, Chester Bowles Papers; United States Information Service, American Embassy, New Delhi, "Survey of Communist Propaganda in India," March 1–15, 1952, folder 507, box 112, series 2, Chester Bowles Papers, p. 6.

40. *New York Times*, December 25, 1951, p. 15; *New York Times*, January 1, 1952, p. 10; *New York Times*, December 27, 1951, p. 11; *New York Times*, January 24, 1952, p. 8; *New York Times*, December 18, 1951, p. 13; Horne, *Communist Front?* 156, 174; Carol Elaine Anderson, "Eyes Off the Prize: African Americans, the United Nations and the Struggle for Human Rights, 1944–1952" (Ph.D. diss., Ohio State University, 1995), 164–174; Patterson, *The Man Who Cried Genocide*, 198–210; Civil Rights Congress, *We Charge Genocide*, vii.

41. Gary Giddins, *Satchmo* (New York: Doubleday, 1988), 160–165; Hugues Panassie, *Louis Armstrong* (New York: Scribner's, 1971), 34–36.

42. James Campbell, "Black Boys and the FBI," *Times Literary Supplement*, November 30–December 6, 1990, pp. 1290–1291; Kenneth O'Reilly, *Black Americans: The FBI Files* (New York: Carroll and Graf, 1994), 17–24, 78–79; Walter White, *A Man Called White* (New York: Viking Press, 1948), 242–261, 271–293; Walter White, *How Far the Promised Land?* (New York: Viking Press, 1956), 3–28; Donald R. McCoy and Richard T. Ruetten, *Quest and Response: Minority Rights and the Truman Administration* (Lawrence: University Press of Kansas, 1973), 261–264.

43. Lynn Haney, *Naked at the Feast: A Biography of Josephine Baker* (New York: Dodd, Mead, 1981), 247–252; Phyllis Rose, *Jazz Cleopatra: Josephine Baker in Her Times*, (New York: Atheneum, 1989), 218–19; *Chicago Defender*, October 27, 1951, pp. 1–2; *Amsterdam News*, July 14, 1951, p. 22.

44. Haney, *Naked at the Feast*, 238, 255–256; *Washington Post*, October 22, 1951, p. 9B; *Washington Post*, October 24, 1951, p. 15B; *Washington Post*, October 26, 1951, p. 15B; *Washington Post*, November 30, 1951, p. 15B; *Washington Post*, November 3, 1951,

p. 9B; "Josephine Baker," files of the Federal Bureau of Investigation, file no. 62–95834; *Counterattack*, letter no. 200, March 23, 1951, pp. 3–4; FBI file, cross-references.

Although Winchell was at the Stork Club at the same time, it is unclear whether he was aware of the discrimination against Baker. Walter White also contacted J. Edgar Hoover about Josephine Baker, but his request was that Hoover protest the Stork Club's refusal to serve her because "such discrimination . . . anywhere in the United States plays directly into the hands of communists and other enemies of democracy. Disapproval of such policy by those who make [the] Stork Club [the] success it is will demonstrate [the] vitality and integrity of democracy." Regarding White's request, Hoover commented, "I don't consider this to be any of my business." Telegram, National Association for the Advancement of Colored People to J. Edgar Hoover, October 19, 1951, FBI file; O'Reilly, *Black Americans*, 5–6.

45. American Embassy, Montevideo, to State Department, September 30, 1952, RG 59, 811.411/9–3052, National Archives.

46. Ibid.

47. American Embassy, Buenos Aires, to State Department, November 13, 1952, RG 59, 811.411/11–1352, National Archives.

48. Department of State translation of *Critica*, Buenos Aires, Argentina, October 3, 1952, TC no. 57594, RG 59, 811.411/10–352, National Archives.

During her travels, Baker sought to establish branches of an organization she founded, the World Cultural Association Against Racial and Religious Discrimination. The organization's purpose was to promote interracial understanding. While Baker sought government support and apparently engaged in fund-raising for the organization in several countries, it is unclear whether it was ever anything more than a paper organization. Ibid.; American Embassy, Buenos Aires, to State Department, October 24, 1952, RG 59, 811.411/10–2452, National Archives.

49. Haney, *Naked at the Feast*, 259–265; American Embassy, Buenos Aires, to State Department, October 6, 1952, RG 59, 811.411/10–652, National Archives; Department of State translation, TC no. 57594, T-19/R-I, Spanish, Source: *Critica*, Buenos Aires, October 3, 1952, RG 59, 811.411/10–352 CS/H, National Archives.

50. Ibid.; Philip Raine to PO—Mr. Haden, October 20, 1952, RG 59, FW 811.411/9–3052 CS/W, National Archives; *Amsterdam News*, November 29, 1952, p. 20.

51. Ibid. By this point, White had already traveled on behalf of the U.S. government, both to help with disputes involving African American troops during World War II and on postwar trips during which he defended American democracy. White, *A Man Called White*; White, *How Far the Promised Land?* 3–28.

52. Raine to Haden, October 20, 1952.

53. American Embassy, Buenos Aires, to State Department, December 29, 1952, RG 59, 811.411/12–2952, National Archives; American Embassy, Santiago to State Department, December 30, 1952, RG 59, 811.411/12–3052, National Archives; American Embassy, Lima, to State Department, December 31, 1952, RG 59, 811.411/12–3152, National Archives, American Embassy, Rio de Janeiro, to State Department, February 2, 1953, RG 59, 811.411/2–253, National Archives.

54. American Embassy, Habana, to Secretary of State, January 27, 1953, RG 59, 811.411/1–2753, National Archives.

55. American Embassy, Habana, to State Department, January 30, 1953, RG 59, 811.411/1–3053, National Archives.

56. Ibid.

57. Ibid.; American Embassy, Habana, to State Department, February 12, 1953, RG 59, 811.411/2–1253, National Archives.

The U.S. embassy thought that failure to arrive at a financial understanding was closer to the true reason Teatro América canceled Baker's performance. Baker had a history of financial disputes with her employers, and at times tried to hold out for more money than had originally been agreed to. Consequently, it is entirely possible that a disagreement over her pay was an element in the cancellation of her Teatro América contract. Nevertheless, it is also clear that the U.S. Embassy took steps to show its displeasure over the possibility that Baker might perform in Cuba. Consequently, it is most likely that any disagreement over finances, like Baker's tardiness, provided the theater with "just the legal loophole they needed to 'get out from under' a ticklish situation." American Embassy, Habana, to State Department, January 30, 1953.

58. American Embassy, Habana, to State Department, February 18, 1953, RG 59, 811.411/2–1853, National Archives; American Embassy, Habana, to State Department, February 19, 1953, RG 59, 811.411/2–1953, National Archives; Josephine Baker and Jo Bouillon, *Josephine*, trans. Mariana Fitzpatrick (New York: Paragon House, 1988), 189.

59. American Embassy, Habana, to State Department, March 3, 1953, RG 59, 811.411/3–353, National Archives.

60. American Embassy, Port-Au-Prince, to State Department, February 3, 1953, RG 59, 811.411/2–353, National Archives.

61. Ibid.

62. Ibid. I found no additional despatches concerning Josephine Baker and travel to Haiti in declassified State Department records from the 1950s. Although there was occasional coverage of Baker's activities in the Haitian press, there are no news stories regarding a visit to Haiti during this period. See *Le Matin*, February 13, 1953, p. 4; *Le Matin*, February 20, 1953, p. 1 (discussing Baker's experiences in Cuba).

63. N. W. Philcox to R. R. Roach, Re: Josephine Baker, December 10, 1954, FBI file, teletype message to FBI, January 28, 1955; G. H. Scatterday to A. H. Belmont, Re: Josephine Baker, February 10, 1960, FBI file.

Hoover sent a one-page document to the INS commissioner regarding Baker, most of which was deleted by the FBI when supplied to me under the Freedom of Information Act on the grounds that it contained "material which is properly classified pursuant to an Executive order in the interest of national defense or foreign policy." Director, FBI, to Commissioner, INS, Re: Josephine Baker, January 6, 1955, FBI file.

In 1952 Baker indicated that she was aware of efforts to ban her from the country. She said that "If my entry into the United States is forbidden, for me this (will be) an honor because it will show that my work for humanity has been successful." American Embassy,

Buenos Aires, to State Department, November 6, 1952, RG 59, 811.411/11–652, National Archives; Scatterday to Belmont, Re: Josephine Baker, February 10, 1960.

64. Chester Bowles, "Racial Harmony—How Much Does it Matter in World Affairs?" 1952, folder 540, box 115, series 2, Chester Bowles Papers. See also Chester Bowles, *Ambassador's Report* (New York: Harper and Brothers, 1954), 31, 216–217, 395–396.

65. Chester Bowles, "Racial Harmony—How Much Does it Matter in World Affairs?" 1952, folder 540, box 115, series 2, Chester Bowles Papers.

66. Ibid.; Bowles, *Ambassador's Report*, 396.

CHAPTER THREE

1. Brief for the United States as Amicus Curiae, p. 6, *Brown v. Board of Education*, 347 U.S. 483 (1954) (filed December 1952).

2. According to the committee, the moral reason was that "the pervasive gap between our aims and what we actually do is creating a kind of moral dry rot which eats away at the emotional and rational bases of democratic beliefs." U.S. failures in the area of civil rights bred "cynicism about democratic values" that was harmful to all. The economic reasons were that "one of the principal economic problems facing us and the rest of the world is achieving maximum production and continued prosperity." Discrimination interfered with economic growth because it led to "the loss of a huge, potential market for goods." Discrimination in the marketplace gave rise to interrelated losses in market and human terms. President's Committee on Civil Rights, *To Secure These Rights* (Washington, D.C.: U.S. Government Printing Office, 1947), 139–148.

3. Ibid., 20, 148.

4. Dean Acheson, "Morality, Moralism and Diplomacy," in *Grapes from Thorns* (New York: Norton, 1972), 125–140. Douglas Brinkley has suggested that since Acheson would at times use moralism in his own arguments about foreign relations, at least while secretary of state, his objections may have been to the moralism of John Foster Dulles, and not to moralism per se. Douglas Brinkley, *Dean Acheson: The Cold War Years, 1953–71* (New Haven, Conn.: Yale University Press, 1992), 24–26.

Acheson's prolific writings do not disclose a strong interest in race relations. He had one important foray into the making of civil rights policy, however. He helped Senate Majority Leader Lyndon Baines Johnson steer the Civil Rights Act of 1957 through the Senate. While the bill had to be watered down so significantly to pass that the civil rights movement contemplated opposing it, the legislation was nevertheless the most significant civil rights bill at that time since reconstruction. Dean Acheson, *Present at the Creation: My Years in the State Department* (New York: Norton, 1969); Dean Acheson, *Power and Diplomacy* (Cambridge: Harvard University Press, 1958; New York: Atheneum, 1970); Dean Acheson, *A Democrat Looks at His Party* (New York: Harper, 1955); Dean Acheson, *A Citizen Looks at Congress* (New York: Harper, 1957); Brinkley, *Dean Acheson*, 204–205.

5. President's Committee on Civil Rights, *To Secure These Rights*, 148 (emphasis in original).

6. Harry S. Truman, "Special Message to the Congress on Civil Rights," February 2, 1948, *Public Papers of the Presidents of the United States: Harry S. Truman, 1948* (Washington, D.C.: Government Printing Office, 1964), 121–126.

7. Louis Ruchames, *Race, Jobs and Politics: The Story of FEPC* (Westport, Conn.: Negro University Press, 1953, 1971), 208; William C. Berman, *The Politics of Civil Rights in the Truman Administration* (Columbus: Ohio State University Press, 1970), 167; Barton J. Bernstein, "The Ambiguous Legacy: The Truman Administration and Civil Rights," in *Politics and Policies of the Truman Administration*, Barton J. Bernstein, ed. (Chicago: Quadrangle Books, 1970), 271–277, 291; Susan M. Hartmann, *Truman and the 80th Congress* (Columbia: University of Missouri Press, 1971); Richard M. Dalfiume, *Desegregation of the Armed Forces: Fighting on Two Fronts, 1939–1953* (Columbia: University of Missouri Press, 1969), 157–174; Mary L. Dudziak, "Desegregation as a Cold War Imperative," *Stanford Law Review* 41 (1988): 61, reprinted in *Race and U.S. Foreign Policy During the Cold War,* Michael L. Krenn, ed. (New York: Garland, 1998), 177–236.

8. Christopher Thorne, "Britain and the Black G.I.s: Racial Issues and Anglo-American Relations in 1942," in *Race and U.S. Foreign Policy from 1900 through World War II,* Michael Krenn, ed. (New York: Garland, 1998), 342–349; Thomas Hachey, "Walter White and the American Negro Soldier in World War II: A Diplomatic Dilemma for Britain," *Phylon* 39 (September 1978): 241–249, reprinted in Krenn, *Race and U.S. Foreign Policy from 1900 through World War II*, 333–341.

9. Walter White, Broadcast over Columbia Broadcasting System from Cincinnati, Ohio, July 7, 1945, NAACP Papers, part 9, series B, reel 26, F0188. The text of the broadcast indicated that it was "[a]pproved by War and Navy Departments."

10. President's Committee on Civil Rights, transcript of meeting, April 17, 1947, p. 20, Papers of the President's Committee on Civil Rights, Reel 6, Harry S. Truman Library, Independence, Missouri; President's Committee on Civil Rights, transcript of meeting, June 30, 1947, Papers of the President's Committee on Civil Rights, Reel 6, Truman Library.

11. Randolph to Truman, December 28, 1947, Digitalization: Project Whistlestop, Desegregation of the Armed Forces, Truman Library; *Blacks and the Military in American History: Basic Documents*, Bernard C. Nalty and Morris J. MacGregor, eds. (Wilmington, Del.: Scholarly Resources, 1977), 182.

12. Dagen and Dagen to Truman, June 15, 1948, Digitalization: Project Whistlestop, Desegregation of the Armed Forces, Truman Library. Andrea Champlin's well-researched paper drew my attention to this correspondence. Andrea Champlin, "The Desegregation of the Armed Services," (paper, University of Southern California Law School, March 1999).

13. Harry S. Truman, "Special Message to the Congress on Civil Rights," February 2, 1948, *Public Papers of the Presidents of the United States: Harry S. Truman, 1948*, 126; Harry S. Truman, "Special Message to Congress on the Threat to the Freedom of Europe," March 17, 1948, *Public Papers of the Presidents of the United States: Harry S. Truman, 1948*, 182–186; Dalfiume, *Desegregation of the Armed Forces*, 167; Jack D. Foner, *Blacks and the Military in American History: A New Perspective* (New York: Praeger, 1974), 182.

14. President Harry S. Truman, executive order, "Establishing the President's Committee on Equality of Treatment and Opportunity in the Armed Services, Executive Order 9981," *Federal Register* 13 (July 26, 1948): 4313; David McCullough, *Truman* (New York: Simon and Schuster, 1992), 587.

15. Bernard C. Nalty, *Strength for the Fight: A History of Black Americans in the Military* (New York: Free Press, 1986), 241–242.

16. McCullough, *Truman*, 712–713; Bernstein, "Ambiguous Legacy," 291–292; Foner, *Blacks and the Military*, 185; Michael J. Klarman, "*Brown*, Racial Change and the Civil Rights Movement," *Virginia Law Review* 80 (February 1994): 32–35; Harry S. Truman, "Address in Harlem, New York, Upon Receiving the Franklin Roosevelt Award," *Papers of the Presidents of the United States: Harry S. Truman, 1948*, 924.

17. Nalty, *Strength for the Fight*, 241; Michael S. Sherry, *In the Shadow of War: The United States Since the 1930s* (New Haven, Conn.: Yale University Press, 1995), 147.

18. Jacob K. Javits, press release, January 12, 1950, Digitalization: Project Whistlestop, Desegregation of the Armed Forces, Truman Library.

19. Nalty, *Strength for the Fight*, 255–269.

20. *Congressional Record*, 81st Cong., 2nd Sess., 1950, 96: 6692.

21. Ibid., 6692–6693.

22. Ibid., 6694–6695. Opposition to civil rights reform was also cast in anticommunist terms when legislation to fund the temporary FEPC was before Congress in 1944. Representative John Rankin of Mississippi called it "the beginning of communistic dictatorship. . . . They want to dictate to you who shall work in your factory, who shall work on your farm, who shall work in your office, who shall go to your schools, and who shall eat at your table, or intermarry with your children." Ruchames, *Race, Jobs and Politics*, 94.

23. *Congressional Record*, 81st Cong., 2nd Sess., 1950, 96: 6694–6695; Ruchames, *Race, Jobs and Politics*, 94.

24. Truman administration scholars have different perspectives on whether the civil rights briefs should be thought of as an important part of Truman's civil rights program. Since an understanding that they *should* be viewed that way underlies this chapter, I will consider this issue at some length. Some scholars pay little attention to the court efforts, focusing instead on legislative efforts and executive orders, the traditional subject matter of works on civil rights politics. In such accounts, the legal battle is simply a different story and revolves instead around the organizations and individuals supporting and opposing legal change, as well as focusing on the courts. As an account of civil rights politics, this approach is incomplete, missing the critical political judgements about whether the government should participate in these high-profile cases.

Some writers do take up the amicus brief strategy but conclude that it should not be understood as high-level, Truman administration policy. Barton J. Bernstein has argued that the briefs were filed as a result of the efforts of members of the solicitor general's staff and that the administration simply acquiesced in them. Bernstein's analysis of the amicus briefs is in keeping with his view that Truman was a "reluctant liberal" who left an "ambiguous. . .legacy" in the area of civil rights. Bernstein's primary source for this interpretation appears to have been a 1966 interview with Philip Elman, a former attorney in the solicitor general's office who was involved in writing the amicus briefs. Bernstein, "Ambiguous Legacy," 296–297, 303, 312 n. 49, 314 n. 60; Barton J. Bernstein, "Commentary," in *The Truman Period as a Research Field: A Reappraisal, 1972,* Richard S. Kirkendall, ed. (Columbia: University of Missouri Press, 1974), 105–108, 161, 187; Barton J. Bernstein, "The Truman Administration and Minority Rights: A Review Essay," *Journal of Ethnic Studies* (Fall 1973): 66, 70–71. For contrary views, see Alonzo L. Hamby, *Beyond the New Deal: Harry S. Truman and American Liberalism* (New York: Columbia University Press, 1973), 189–190; Donald R. McCoy and Richard T. Ruetten, *Quest and Response: Minority Rights and the Truman Administration* (Lawrence: University Press of Kansas, 1973), 211–212, 218–221; John T. Elliff, *The United States Department of Justice and Individual Rights, 1937–1962* (New York: Garland, 1987), 254–259.

A later Elman interview published in the *Harvard Law Review* undercuts Bernstein's argument. While Elman views his role as pivotal, he also provides enough information to show that the amicus briefs were not simply the effort of an isolated and committed group of lawyers in the solicitor general's office but can appropriately be described as Truman administration actions. Philip Elman, "The Solicitor General's Office, Justice Frankfurter and Civil Rights Litigation, 1946–1960: An Oral History," *Harvard Law Review* 100 (February 1987): 817–818, 826–830 (interview conducted by Norman Silber). See also Randall Kennedy, "A Reply to Phillip Elman," *Harvard Law Review* 100 (June 1987): 1938–1948 (questioning the importance of Elman's role).

The first amicus brief, filed in *Shelley v. Kraemer,* was signed by attorney general Tom C. Clark, as well as Solicitor General Perlman. As Elman noted, it was unusual for the attorney general to sign Supreme Court briefs. Clark's name was placed on the brief so that it would be "as authoritative a statement of the position of the United States as possible." Although Elman does not say whether Clark personally approved having his name on the brief, it is unlikely that such a departure from Justice Department policy involving the use of his name in such a high-profile case would have happened without his knowledge. The fact that the very filing of the brief was an innovation in Department policy reinforces the likelihood that Clark knew about and approved the fact that his name was being placed on the brief. Further, Clark and Perlman were so pleased with the *Shelley* brief that they published it as a book. President Truman himself identified the government's participation in *Shelley* as one of his administration's civil rights accomplishments in a 1948 campaign speech in Harlem. Elman, "Oral History," 254–259, 819–820; Tom C. Clark and Philip Benjamin Perlman, *Prejudice and Property: An Historic Brief Against Racial Covenants* (Washington, D.C.: Public Affairs Press, 1948); Harry S. Truman, "Address in Harlem, New York Upon Receiving The Franklin Roosevelt Award," October 29, 1948, *Public Papers of the Presidents of the United States: Harry S. Truman, 1948,* 924; Berman, *Politics of Civil Rights,* 127.

According to Elman, pressure from within the administration to file a brief in *Shelley* first came from Phineas Indritz, an attorney in the Department of the Interior, and Oscar Chapman, the secretary of the interior. The State Department assisted Elman's efforts on the brief by sending a letter to the attorney general regarding the effect of race discrimination on foreign policy. Although Elman did not know who finally approved the filing of a brief, his best guess was that "probably Tom Clark made the decision after checking with Truman." Elman, "Oral History," 818.

Attorney General J. Howard McGrath considered the segregation cases *Henderson v. United States, Sweatt v. Painter,* and *McLaurin v. Oklahoma* to be among "some of the most important cases in this generation." In a departure from Justice Department practices, he participated in oral argument in *Henderson. Henderson v. United States,* 339 U.S. 816, 817 (1950). Attorney General James P. McGranery unsuccessfully petitioned the Court for permission to present an oral argument in *Brown.* Notwithstanding his argument that Truman was disinterested and uninvolved in the amicus briefs, Bernstein has written that Truman "specifically approved the filing of a brief in *Brown.*" McGrath to Truman, June 6, 1950, Papers of J. Howard McGrath, Truman Library; Bernstein, "Minority Rights," 71 (apparently relying on an interview with Elman); Daniel M. Berman, *It Is So Ordered: The Supreme Court Rules on School Segregation* (New York: Norton, 1966), 61. See also Berman, *Politics of Civil Rights,* 232 (arguing that the *Brown* brief was filed on the Justice Department's own initiative).

This record of high-level participation in the desegregation cases makes it appropriate to characterize the amicus briefs as consciously adopted Truman administration policy. Cabinet-level advisors were involved in the cases. Even if, as is likely, Truman did not personally approve all of the briefs, high-level members of his administration charged with furthering his interests and desires participated in the cases. Truman's advisors were so attuned to the political consequences of civil rights efforts that it is hard to imagine government participation in such well-publicized civil rights cases as being anything other than a deliberate policy decision made at the highest levels of the Truman Administration. William Berman's work is consistent with this analysis. Berman, *Politics of Civil Rights,* 239–240.

25. The amicus briefs were also helpful for domestic political purposes. Truman referred to them in his 1948 campaign speeches before African American audiences. McCoy and Ruetten, *Quest and Response,* 134–135.

26. On Justice Department policy, see Elliff, *The United States Department of Justice and Individual Rights,* 254–259.

27. *Shelley v. Kraemer,* 334 U.S. 1, 6–7 (1948); *Hurd v. Hodge,* 334 U.S. 24 (1948); *Mitchell v. United States,* 313 U.S. 80 (1941); *Taylor v. Georgia,* 315 U.S. 25 (1942); Brief for the United States as Amicus Curiae, *Shelley v. Kraemer,* 334 U.S. 1 (1948).

28. Oral argument of Solicitor General Perlman, *United States Law Week* 16 (January 20, 1948): 3219 (paraphrased account of argument); Clement E. Vose, *Caucasians Only: The Supreme Court, The NAACP, and the Restrictive Covenant Cases* (Berkeley: University of California Press, 1959), 200; Elliff, *The United States Department of Justice and Individual Rights,* 254–259 (quoting address by Perlman to the National Civil Liberties Clearing House (February 23, 1950)); Brief for the United States as Amicus Curiae, p.19, *Shelley v. Kraemer,* 334 U.S. 1 (1948).

Because my purpose is to examine the Truman administration's participation in these cases, this study does not dwell on the crucial role in the cases played by the NAACP. For excellent treatments of the NAACP's litigation efforts, see Mark V. Tushnet, *NAACP's*

Legal Strategy Against Segregated Education 1925–1950 (Chapel Hill: University of North Carolina Press, 1987); Richard Kluger, *Simple Justice: The History of Brown v. Board of Education and Black America's Struggle for Equality* (New York: Knopf, 1976); Jack Greenberg, *Crusaders in the Courts: How a Dedicated Band of Lawyers Fought for the Civil Rights Revolution* (New York: Basic Books, 1994).

29. *Shelley*, 334 U.S. at 20; *Congressional Record*, 81st Cong., 2nd Sess., May 9, 1950, 96: 6694.

30. Elliff, *The United States Department of Justice and Individual Rights*, 323–329; *Henderson v. United States*, 339 U.S. 816, 820–822 (1950); Brief for the United States, pp. 9–11, *Henderson v. United States*, 339 U.S. 816 (1950).

The Interstate Commerce Act provided that "it shall be unlawful for any common carrier . . . to make, give, or cause any undue or unreasonable preference or advantage to any particular person . . . in any respect whatsoever; or to subject any particular person . . . to any undue or unreasonable prejudice or disadvantage in any respect whatsoever." *Interstate Commerce Act*, ch. 722, § 5(a), 54 Stat. 898, 902, 49 USCA § 3(1) (1946).

31. Brief for the United States, pp. 60–61, *Henderson v. United States*, 339 U.S. 816 (1950) (quoting United Nations, General Assembly, *Ad Hoc* Political Committee, Third Session, Part 2, Summary Record of the Fifty-Third Meeting (May 11, 1949)), 6, 12. The brief also quoted from the same letter from Dean Acheson that the Department had relied on in *Shelley*.

32. Ibid., 61 n. 73 (quoting Frantsov, "Nationalism—The Tool of Imperialist Reaction," *The Bolshevik* (U.S.S.R.), no. 15 (1948), and Berezko, "The Tragedy of Coloured America," *The Literary Gazette* (U.S.S.R.), no. 51 (1948)).

33. Ibid., 59–60 (quoting *Hearings Regarding Communist Infiltration of Minority Groups—Part I*, 479). On Jackie Robinson, see Jules Tygiel, *Baseball's Greatest Experiment: Jackie Robinson and His Legacy* (New York: Oxford University Press, 1983).

34. *Henderson*, 339 U.S. at 825–826.

35. Memorandum for the United States as Amicus Curiae, pp. 1–2, *McLaurin v. Oklahoma*, 339 U.S. 637 (1950), and *Sweatt v. Painter*, 339 U.S. 629 (1950); *McLaurin*, 339 U.S. at 638–640; *Sweatt*, 339 U.S. at 631–634.

36. Memorandum for the United States as Amicus Curiae, pp. 11–13, *McLaurin v. Oklahoma*, 339 U.S. 637 (1950), and *Sweatt v. Painter*, 339 U.S. 629 (1950).

In 1949, the solicitor general's office also filed a brief in *Graham v. Brotherhood of Locomotive Firemen*, 338 U.S. 232 (1949), a case involving noncompliance by a railroad and a union with a previous Supreme Court decision, *Steele v. Louisville & Nashville R.R. Co.*, 323 U.S. 192 (1944), forbidding racially discriminatory collective bargaining agreements. Elliff, *The United States Department of Justice and Individual Rights*, 323.

37. *Sweatt*, 339 U.S. at 636; *McLaurin*, 339 U.S. at 638, 642.

38. Brief for the United States as Amicus Curiae, p. 4, *Brown v. Board of Education*, 347 U.S. 483 (1954). American critics of U.S. race discrimination focused on the contradictions of segregation in the capital as well. National Committee on Segregation in the Nation's Capital, *Segregation in Washington* (Chicago: National Committee on Segregation in the Nation's Capital, 1948).

39. *Brown v. Board of Education*, 347 U.S. 483, 486 (1954); *Briggs v. Elliott*, 103 F. Supp. 920 (E.D.S.C. 1952), reversed, *Brown v. Board of Education*, 349 U.S. 294 (1955) (*Brown II*); *Davis v. County School Board*, 103 F.Supp. 337 (E.D. Va. 1952), reversed, *Brown v. Board of Education*, 349 U.S. 294 (1955) (*Brown II*); *Brown v. Board of Education*, 98 F. Supp. 797 (D. Kan. 1951), reversed, *Brown v. Board of Education*, 359 U.S. 294 (1955) (*Brown II*); *Belton v. Gebhart*, 32 Del. Ch. 343, 87 A.2d 862, affirmed, *Gebhart v. Belton*, 33 Del. Ch. 144, 91 A.2d 137 (Del. 1952), affirmed, *Brown v. Board of Education*, 349 U.S. 294 (1955) (*Brown II*); *Bolling v. Sharpe*, 347 U.S. 497, 498 (1954).

40. Brief for the United States as Amicus Curiae, pp. 4–6, *Brown*, 347 U.S. 483 (quoting Truman, "Special Message to the Congress on Civil Rights," 124, and quoting President's Committee on Civil Rights, *To Secure These Rights*, 89, 95).

41. Ibid., 3 (emphasis in original).

42. Ibid., 6.

43. Brief for the United States as Amicus Curiae, p. 7, *Brown*, 347 U.S. 483 (quoting letter from the secretary of state (December 2, 1952)).

44. Ibid.

45. Ibid., 8.

46. Ibid., 31–32 (quoting Truman, "Special Message to the Congress on Civil Rights," 126).

47. Brief for Appellants on Reargument, p. 194, *Brown v. Board of Education*, 347 U.S. 483 (1954); The Hague, Netherlands, to Department of State, December 30, 1952, RG 59, 811.411/12–3052 LWC, National Archives.

48. *Brown*, 347 U.S. at 493–495; *Bolling*, 347 U.S. at 500. In *Brown* the Court ruled that public school segregation by states violated the equal protection clause of the Fourteenth Amendment, and in *Bolling* the Court found that such segregation in the District of Columbia violated the due process clause of the Fifth Amendment.

49. *Minersville v. Gobitis*, 310 U.S. 586, 595 (1940); *West Virginia Board of Education v. Barnette*, 319 U.S. 624, 641 (1943); *Hirabayashi v. United States*, 320 U.S. 81, 100–101 (1943); *Korematsu v. United States*, 323 U.S. 214, 219 (1944); Mary L. Dudziak, "The Supreme Court and Racial Equality During World War II," *Journal of Supreme Court History* 1996 (November 1996): 35–48. On the Court and the internment cases, see Peter H. Irons, *Justice at War* (Berkeley: University of California Press, 1993); Jacobus tenBroek, Edward N. Barnhart, and Floyd W. Matson, *Prejudice, War and the Constitution* (Berkeley: University of California Press), 68–184. For works on the role of totalitarianism in Supreme Court caselaw, see David M. Bixby, "The Roosevelt Court, Democratic Ideology and Minority Rights: Another Look at *U.S. v. Classic*," *Yale Law Journal* 90 (March 1981): 741; Richard Primus, "A Brooding Omnipresence: Totalitarianism in Postwar Constitutional Thought," *Yale Law Journal* 106 (November 1996): 423–457; Margaret Raymond, "Rejecting Totalitarianism: Translating the Guarantees of Constitutional Criminal Procedure," *North Carolina Law Review* 76 (April 1998): 1193–1263. A classic treatment of the impact of war on the Constitution is Edwin S. Corwin, *Total War and the Constitution* (New York: Knopf, 1947).

50. *Hirabayashi*, 320 U.S. at 101; *Dennis v. United States*, 341 U.S. 494, 554–555 (1951), concurring opinion of Justice Frankfurter (citing George F. Kennan, "Where Do You Stand On Communism," *New York Times* magazine, May 27, 1951, pp. 7, 53, 55).

51. On the contextuality of thought, see Karl Mannheim, *Ideology and Utopia: An Introduction to the Sociology of Knowledge*, trans. Louis Worth and Edward Shils (New York: Harcourt, Brace, and World, 1968), 2–4. For excellent works on the Court's deliberations in the desegration cases, see Dennis Hutchinson, "Unanimity and Desegregation in the Supreme Court, 1948–1958," *Georgetown Law Journal* 68 (October 1979): 1; Mark V. Tushnet with Kayta Lezin, "What Really Happened in *Brown v. Board of Education*," *Columbia Law Review* 91 (December 1991): 1867–1930.

52. William O. Douglas, *Strange Lands and Friendly People* (New York: Harper, 1951), 296.

53. Ibid., 296, 321, 326 (emphasis in original).

54. William O. Douglas, *Beyond the High Himalayas* (Garden City, N.Y.: Doubleday, 1953), 317, 321–323.

55. *New York Times*, June 29, 1954, collected in Papers of the United States Information Agency, Reel 42, John F. Kennedy Library, Boston Massachusetts; *New York Times*, August 20, 1954, collected in Papers of the United States Information Agency, Reel 42, Kennedy Library. On Warren's trip to India, see *New York Times*, July 27, 1956, p. 1; *New York Times*, September 1, 1956, p. 3; *New York Times*, August 29, 1956, p. 12. On Warren's European travel the year before *Brown* was decided, see Earl Warren, *The Memoirs of Earl Warren* (Garden City, N.Y.: Doubleday, 1977), 265–269.

56. Justice Robert Jackson took a leave from his Court duties to serve as a prosecutor at the Nuremburg trials in Germany. J. Woodford Howard Jr., *Mr. Justice Murphy: A Political Biography* (Princeton, N.J.: Princeton University Press, 1968), 354.

57. *New York Times*, May 18, 1954, p. 1. The Voice of America's ability to use the decision effectively was enhanced by the fact that the opinion was short and easily understood by lay persons. As Chief Justice Earl Warren described it, *Brown* was "not a long opinion, for I had written it so it could be published in the daily press throughout the nation without taking too much space. This enabled the public to have our entire reasoning instead of a few excerpts." Warren, *Memoirs*, 3.

58. U.S. Embassy, Rio de Janeiro, to Department of State, June 2, 1954 (embassy translation), RG 59, 811.411/6–254, National Archives.

59. U.S. Consul, Dakar, French West Africa, to Department of State, May 26, 1954, RG 59, 811.411/5–2654, National Archives.

60. U.S. Embassy, Cape Town, South Africa, to Department of State, June 9, 1954, RG 59, 811.411/6–954, National Archives.

61. Carl T. Rowan, *The Pitiful and the Proud* (New York: Random House, 1956), 19; "Chief Justice Warren In India," *Baltimore Sun*, October 1, 1956, India 1956 Correspondence, Clippings, Photographs Folder No. 1, Foreign File, Personal Papers, Papers of Earl Warren, Library of Congress.

62. National Security Council, "Status of United States Program for National Security as of June 30, 1954," NSC 5430, *Foreign Relations of the United States, 1952–1954* (Washington, D.C.: Government Printing Office, 1984), 11:1777, 1785–1786.

63. National Security Council, "Status of United States Program for National Security as of December 31, 1954," NSC 5509, *Foreign Relations of the United States, 1955–1957* (Washington, D. C.: Government Printing Office, 1987), 9:504, 516; The Historical Background of the Nehru Visit, December 16–20 (1956), State, Dept. of (1956) (Briefing Book—Nehru's Visit) (2), Confidential File, Records as President, White House Central Files, Dwight D. Eisenhower Library, Abilene, Kansas.

64. Republican National Committee, News Release, May 21, 1954, p. 3, White House Files—Civil Rights—Republican National Committee 1954, box 37, Philleo Nash Papers, Truman Library; Robert Frederick Burk, *The Eisenhower Administration and Black Civil Rights* (Knoxville: University of Tennessee Press, 1984), 144, 162, 165–166; Michael S. Mayer, "With Much Deliberation and Some Speed: Eisenhower and the *Brown* Decision," *Journal of Southern History* 52 (February 1986): 43. Eisenhower criticized "foolish extremists on both sides" of the school desegregation controversy, and, in an effort to distance his administration from the Supreme Court's ruling, he "rebuked Vice President Nixon for referring to Earl Warren as the 'Republican Chief Justice.' " Chief Justice Warren was angered by the President's stance. He believed that if Eisenhower had fully supported *Brown*, "we would have been relieved . . . of many of the racial problems that have continued to plague us." Burk, *The Eisenhower Administration and Black Civil Rights*, 162–163; Warren, *Memoirs*, 291; J. Harvie Wilkinson III, *From Brown to Bakke: The Supreme Court and School Integration* (New York: Oxford University Press, 1979), 24.

65. *New York Times*, May 18, 1954, p. 2 (quoting *New York Herald Tribune* and the *Pittsburgh Courier*); *San Francisco Chronicle*, May 18, 1954, p. 18.

66. *Birmingham Post-Herald*, May 18, 1954, p. 5 (quoting *Charlotte News*); *New York Times*, May 18, 1954, pp. 1, 20; *Atlanta Daily World*, May 18, 1954, p. 1.

67. John Barlow Martin, *The Deep South Says Never* (New York: Ballantine Books, 1957), 1–4, 24. On anticommunism in segregationist thought, see Wayne Addison Clark, "An Analysis of the Relationship Between Anti-Comunism and Segregationist Thought in the Deep South, 1946–1964" (Ph.D. diss., University of North Carolina, 1976).

68. Herman E. Talmadge, *You and Segregation* (Birmingham, Ala.: Vulcan Press, 1955), vii, 1. Talmadge's book was popular. The first printing of ten thousand copies sold out in one week, and a second printing of fifty thousand copies was ordered. *Time*, November 14, 1955, p. 31.

69. *Brown v. Board of Education* (*Brown II*), 349 U.S. 294, 301 (1955); Stephen L. Wasby, Anthony A. D'Amato, and Rosemary Metrailer, *Desegregation from Brown to Alexander: An Exploration of Supreme Court Strategies* (Carbondale: Southern Illinois University Press, 1977), 162–173; Jack Bass, *Unlikely Heroes* (New York: Simon and Schuster, 1981); J. W. Peltason, *Fifty-eight Lonely Men: Southern Federal Judges and School Desegregation* (New York: Harcourt, Brace and World, 1961); Hutchinson, "Unanimity and Desegregation," 60.

It was not until *Goss v. Board of Education* in 1963 and *Griffin v. County School Board* in 1964 that the Court reentered the fray, invalidating state plans, including the closing of public schools in Virginia that were intended to directly circumvent the Court's ruling in *Brown*. The Court suggested in *Griffin* that "the time for mere 'deliberate speed' has run out." Then, in 1968, in *Green v. County School Board*, the Court insisted that "[t]he burden on a school board today is to come forward with a plan that promises realistically to work, and promises realistically to work now." *Goss v. Board of Education*, 373 U.S. 683 (1963); *Griffin v. County School Board*, 377 U.S. 218, 234 (1964); *Green v. County School Board*, 391 U.S. 430, 439 (1968) (emphasis in original); *Covington v. Edwards*, 264 F.2d 180 (4th Cir. 1959); *Shuttlesworth v. Birmingham Board of Education*, 162 F. Supp. 372 (N.D. Ala. 1957), *affirmed* 358 U.S. 101 (1958); Wasby, D'Amato, and Metrailer, *Desegregation from Brown to Alexander*, 194–195.

Also in 1963, the Court required immediate desegregation of municipal recreational facilities in *Watson v. City of Memphis*, 373 U.S. 526, 530 (1963). In *Watson* the Court noted that "*Brown* never contemplated that the concept of 'deliberate speed' would countenance indefinite delay in elimination of racial barriers in schools."

70. American Consul General, Madras, India, to Department of State, February 28, 1956, RG 59, 811.411/2–2856, National Archives.

71. American Embassy, Bern, to Department of State, October 6, 1955, RG 59, 811.411/10–655, National Archives (enclosure no. 2, translation of "If Shame Could Kill," *La Sentinelle* (La Chaux-de-Fonds, Switzerland), October 4, 1955); Enclosure no. 2, American Embassy, Bern to Department of State, September 30, 1955, RG 59, 811.411/9–3055, National Archives (translation of Charles-Henri Favrod, "The Verdict in Sumner," *Gazette de Lausanne*, September 29, 1955). On the international reaction to the Till case, see Stephen J. Whitfield, *A Death in the Delta: The Story of Emmett Till* (New York: The Free Press, 1988), 46.

CHAPTER FOUR

1. American Consulate, Lourenço Marques, to Department of State, September 30, 1957, RG 59, 811.411.9–3057 HBS, National Archives.

2. Jack Greenberg, *Crusaders in the Courts: How a Dedicated Band of Lawyers Fought for the Civil Rights Revolution* (New York: Basic Books, 1994), 229–230; *Aaron v. Cooper*, 143 F. Supp. 855, 866 (E.D. Ark 1956); *Little Rock, U.S.A.*, Wilson Record and Jane Cassels Record, eds. (San Francisco: Chandler Publishing, 1960), 36.

3. *Faubus v. United States*, 254 F.2d 797, 799–801 (8th Cir. 1958).

4. *Arkansas Gazette*, September 5, 1957, p. A1, reprinted in Record and Record, *Little Rock, U.S.A.*, 40.

5. Record and Record, *Little Rock, U.S.A.*, 209; Orval Faubus, *Down from the Hills* (Little Rock, Ark.: Pioneer, 1980), 211; Herbert Brownell and John P. Burk, *Advising Ike: The Memoirs of Attorney General Herbert Brownell* (Lawrence: The University Press of Kansas, 1993), 207.

6. Faubus, *Down from the Hills*, 19–20, 55; Robert Fredrick Burk, *The Eisenhower Administration and Black Civil Rights* (Knoxville: University of Tennessee Press, 1984), 154–156; Tony Allan Freyer, *The Little Rock Crisis: A Constitutional Interpretation* (Westport, Conn.: Greenwood Press, 1984), 63–68.

7. Record and Record, *Little Rock, U.S.A.*, 37.

To his last days, Faubus maintained that his decision to use the National Guard to block integration was motivated by reports of impending violence. He was never forthcoming, however, with evidence to back up his assertions about such reports. An FBI report concluded that his allegations were groundless. Scholars have generally concluded that Faubus was instead motivated by a desire to court segregationist voters as massive resistance polarized southern politics. This was Attorney General Herbert Brownell's view as well. *Arkansas-Democrat Gazette*, November 21, 1993, p. 63; *Arkansas-Democrat*, October 17, 1993, p. 1A; Freyer, *Little Rock Crisis*, 113 n. 65; Michael Klarman, "*Brown*, Racial Change, and the Civil Rights Movement," *Virginia Law Review* 80 (February 1994): 110, 118–119; Brownell and Burk, *Advising Ike*, 209.

8. Record and Record, *Little Rock, U.S.A.*, 38, 41–42; *Thomason v. Cooper*, 254 F.2d 808, 809 (8th Cir. 1958); Freyer, *Little Rock Crisis*, 102.

9. Record and Record, *Little Rock, U.S.A.*, 39; Eisenhower to Faubus, September 5, 1957, microformed in series D, reel 1, frame 358 (U.S. Government Printing Office) NAACP Papers, Collections of the Manuscript Division, Library of Congress.

10. Record and Record, *Little Rock, U.S.A.*, 51–53.

11. Faubus, *Down from the Hills*, 205 (quoting *Arkansas Gazette*).

12. *Arkansas Gazette*, September 11, 1957, p. 2A, reprinted in Record and Record, *Little Rock, U.S.A.*, 48–49; Dwight D. Eisenhower, *The White House Years: Waging Peace, 1956–1961*, (Garden City, N.Y.: Doubleday, 1965), 162, 168.

13. See, for example, American Consul General, Nairobi to Department of State, October 2, 1957, RG 59, 811.411/10–257, National Archives; American Consul, Curitiba, to Department of State, October 1, 1957, RG 59, 811.411/10–157, National Archives; American Embassy, Brussels, to Department of State, October 8, 1957, RG 59, 811.411/10–857, National Archives; *New York Times*, September 27, 1957, p. 12; *New York Times*, September 26, 1957, p. 14; *New York Times*, September 7, 1957, p. 9; *New York Times*, September 10, 1957, p. 10. See also Faubus, *Down from the Hills*, 205–328 (discussing international coverage).

The international reaction to Little Rock is discussed in Mary L. Dudziak, "The Little Rock Crisis and Foreign Affairs: Race, Resistance, and the Image of American Democracy," *Southern California Law Review* 70 (September 1997): 1641–1716; Cary Fraser, "Crossing the Color Line in Little Rock: The Eisenhower Administration and the Dilemma of Race for U.S. Foreign Policy," *Diplomatic History* (Spring 2000); Azza Salama Layton, "International Pressure and the U.S. Government's Response to Little Rock," *Arkansas Historical Quarterly* 56 (Fall 1997): 257–272; Harold R. Isaacs, "World Affairs and U.S. Race Relations: A Note on Little Rock," *Public Opinion Quarterly* 22 (Autumn 1958): 364–370. See also Martin M. Teasley, "Promoting a 'Proper Perspective' Abroad: Eisenhower Administration Concern with Domestic Civil Rights as an Overseas Image Problem" (unpublished paper, 1990).

14. *Times of India*, September 6, 1957, p. 1; *Tanganyika Standard*, September 6, 1957, p. 1; *East African Standard*, September 6, 1957, p. 1; *East African Standard*, September 7, 1957, p. 1; *Daily Mail* (Sierra Leone), September 11, 1957, p. 1; *Egyptian Gazette*, September 5, 1957, p. 1; *Egyptian Gazette*, September 10, 1957, p. 1; *Egyptian Gazette*, September

11, 1957, p. 1. *Egyptian Gazette* was the English-language newspaper in Egypt with the largest circulation. The paper covered the crisis on almost a daily basis, usually with front-page stories, from September 5 to October 5, 1957. Coverage continued after that date but was more sporadic.

The international press coverage cited in this chapter helps provide detail and texture in describing the international reaction to Little Rock, but the newspaper stories are not a representative sample of international media coverage. State Department despatches and records from the Eisenhower administration are the best evidence of the extent and nature of the international reaction, at least as it appeared to the administration, and such records are relied on extensively throughout this work.

15. *Times* (London), September 4, 1957, p. H10.

16. *Montreal Star,* September 25, 1957, microformed in series D, reel 2, frame 114, NAACP Papers, Collections of the Manuscript Division, Library of Congress; *Times* (London), September 23, 1957, p. C6; *Austrian Information,* November 22, 1957, p. 5, microformed in series D, reel 2, frame 189, NAACP Papers (discussing letter from Association of Austrian Socialist Secondary School Students); Seligmann to Wilkins, October 24, 1957, microformed in series D, reel 1, frame 625, NAACP Papers (letter of support to be forwarded to Little Rock students from Présidente de la 7ème section et membre du comité central de la Ligue des droits de l'homme); Francis to Wilkins, September 9, 1957, microformed in series D, reel 1, frame 458, NAACP Papers.

17. The Hague to Secretary of State, September 25, 1957, RG 59, 811.411/9–2557, National Archives; Stockholm to Secretary of State, September 25, 1957, RG 59, 811.411/9–2557, National Archives; American Embassy, Dublin, to Department of State, September 23, 1957, RG 59, 811.411/9–2357, National Archives; Bern to Secretary of State, September 12, 1957, RG 59, 811.411/9–1257, National Archives. See also *Star* (Johannesburg, South Africa), September 25, 1957, p. 1; American Consul General, Amsterdam, to Department of State, September 16, 1957, RG 59, 811.411/9–1657, National Archives.

18. Harry S. Ashmore, "The Easy Chair," *Harper's Magazine,* June 1958, microformed in series D, reel 2, frame 60, NAACP Papers; Ross to Faubus, October 14, 1957, microformed in series D, reel 1, frame 796, NAACP Papers.

19. *New York Times,* September 26, 1957, p. 14.

20. *Izvestia,* September 13, 1957, p. 4, reprinted in *Current Digest of the Soviet Press* 9 (October 23, 1957): 25.

21. *Current Digest of the Soviet Press* 9 (October 23, 1957): 25–26.

22. Faubus, *Down from the Hills,* 221.

23. "The Commies Trained Gov. Faubus of Arkansas," *Confidential,* December 16, 1958, pp. 19–21, 62, microformed in series D, reel 2, frames 230–235, NAACP Papers.

The magazine played up the fact that during the 1930s Faubus attended Commonwealth College, which would later be listed on the attorney general list of subversive organizations. Faubus was elected student body president at Commonwealth, the magazine reported, and gave a speech on "The Story of May Day." When he ran for governor in 1954, Faubus was evasive about his Commonwealth ties. His past and current activities left the magazine questioning whether Faubus was a dupe or a conspirator. Ibid.

24. Faubus, *Down from the Hills*, 33–37; "The Commies Trained Gov. Faubus of Arkansas," 1–2; Hearing Before the Special Education Committee of the Arkansas Legislative Council, December 16, 1958, pp. 4–9, microformed in series D, reel 2, frames 196–229, NAACP Papers.

25. Copenhagen to Secretary of State, September 5, 1957, RG 59, 811.411/9–557, National Archives; American Consul, Lourenço Marques, to Department of State, September 30, 1957; American Consul General, Amsterdam, to Department of State, September 16, 1957, RG 59, 811.411/9–1657, National Archives; American Consul General, São Paulo, to Department of State, September 23, 1957, RG 59, 811.411/9–2357, National Archives.

26. American Consul, Paramaribo, to Department of State, September 18, 1957, RG 59, 811.411/9–1857, National Archives.

27. Bonn to USIA, October 5, 1957, RG 59, 811.411/10–557, National Archives; American Consul General, Johannesburg, to Department of State, December 5, 1957, RG 59, 811.411/12–557, National Archives. In his careful study of West German perceptions of African Americans, David Braden Posner finds that Little Rock did raise concerns among West Germans about such matters as the ability of the United States "to win the allegiance of the non-white peoples in a decolonizing world," and raised doubts about the nation's stability. David Braden Posner, "Afro-America in West German Perspective, 1945–66" (Ph.D. diss., Yale University, 1997), 216.

28. Burk, *The Eisenhower Administration and Black Civil Rights*, 178–179; Telegram, Eisenhower to Faubus, September 10, 1957, *Public Papers of the Presidents of the United States: Dwight D. Eisenhower, 1957* (Washington, D. C.: Government Printing Office, 1958), 673–674; Dwight D. Eisenhower, *The White House Years: Waging Peace, 1956–1961* (Garden City, NY: Doubleday, 1965) 166–167; Statement by President Eisenhower following meeting with Governor Faubus, September 14, 1957, *Public Papers: Dwight D. Eisenhower, 1957*, 674–675.

29. *Asahi Shimbun* (Tokyo), September 15, 1957, p. 1 (photo of Eisenhower and Faubus); Eisenhower, *The White House Years*, 166; Burk, *The Eisenhower Administration and Black Civil Rights*, 182, 193. I am grateful to Noriko Takuma for help with Japanese language materials.

30. *The Times* (London), September 20, 1957, p. F10.

31. *The Times* (London), September 23, 1957, p. C6.

32. *Race Relations Law Reporter* 2 (1957): 957–963.

33. Record and Record, *Little Rock U.S.A.*, 56–57.

34. Ibid., 60–62 (reprint of Relman Morin article in the *Sacramento Bee*).

35. Ibid., 63; Melba Pattillo Beals, *Warriors Don't Cry* (New York: Pocket Books, 1994), 117–119.

36. Proclamation no. 3204, 22 Fed. Reg. 7628 (1957), reprinted in *Race Relations Law Reporter* 2 (1957): 963–964; Eisenhower, *The White House Years*, 169–172.

37. Mann to Eisenhower, September 24, 1957, DDE Dictation (1), Whitman File, DDE Diary Series, Dwight D. Eisenhower Library, Abilene, Kansas; Dwight D. Eisen-

hower, *The White House Years*, 170; *Congressional Record* 90 (1958) (remarks of Congressman Winstead).

38. Eisenhower, *The White House Years*, 170.

39. Earl Warren, *The Memoirs of Earl Warren* (Garden City, N.Y.: Doubleday, 1977), 291; Burk, *The Eisenhower Administration and Black Civil Rights*, 142–145; "War and Peace in Ike's Favor," *Washington Post*, August 7, 1955, OF 142-A-4(I), Central Files, Official File, Dwight D. Eisenhower Papers as President, Eisenhower Library; Max Rabb to Governor Pyle, August 8, 1955, OF 142-A-4-(I), Central Files, Official File, Dwight D. Eisenhower Papers as President, Eisenhower Library; President's Press Conference, May 19, 1954, Integration—Little Rock, Football Games, A. C. Powell, Harlow Records, Eisenhower Library; Stanley L. Kutler, "Eisenhower, the Judiciary, and Desegregation: Some Reflections," in *Eisenhower: A Centenary Assessment*, Gunter Bischof and Stephen E. Ambrose, eds. (Baton Rouge: Louisiana State University Press, 1995), 87.

40. Eisenhower, *The White House Years*, 171. For discussions of the president's decision to send in troops that focus principally on domestic factors, see Burk, *The Eisenhower Administration and Black Civil Rights*, 185–186; James C. Durham, *A Moderate Among Extremists: Dwight D. Eisenhower and the School Desegregation Crisis* (Chicago: Nelson-Hall, 1981), 143–172; Stephen A. Ambrose, *Eisenhower: The President* (New York: Simon and Schuster, 1984) 2:417–422; Klarman, "*Brown* and the Civil Rights Movement," 28.

41. Lodge to Eisenhower, September 25, 1957, Henry Cabot Lodge, 1957–58 (3), Whitman File, Administrative Series, Eisenhower Library. Lodge was referring to a United Nations General Assembly vote on September 24, 1957, rejecting India's proposal to substitute Communist China for Taiwan in the General Assembly. G.A. Res. II 35, U.N. GAOR, 12th Sess., Supp. No. 18, p. 53, U.N. Doc. A/3805 (1957).

42. Telephone call, Knowland to Eisenhower, September 24, 1957, Memo Tel. Conv. Gen., 9/2/57–10/31/57 (2), Dulles Papers, Telephone Call Series, Eisenhower Library; Telephone call, Dulles to Brownell, September 24, 1957, Memo Tel. Conv. Gen., 9/2/57–10/31/57 (3), Dulles Papers, Telephone Call Series, Eisenhower Library.

43. Telephone call, Dulles to Eisenhower, September 24, 1957, Memo Tel. Conv., W.H. 9/2/57–12/26/57 (3), Dulles Papers, Telephone Call Series, Eisenhower Library; Dulles to Eisenhower, September 24, 1957, second draft, Memo Tel. Conv., W.H. 9/2/57–12/26/57 (3), Dulles Papers, Telephone Call Series, Eisenhower Library.

44. Eisenhower, *The White House Years*, 172; Dwight D. Eisenhower, "Radio and Television Address to the American People on the Situation in Little Rock," September 24, 1957, *Public Papers of the Presidents of the United States: Dwight D. Eisenhower, 1957*, 690–694.

45. Dwight D. Eisenhower, "Radio and Television Address to the American People on the Situation in Little Rock," September 24, 1957, *Public Papers of the Presidents of the United States: Dwight D. Eisenhower, 1957*, 690–694.

46. Ibid.

47. Telephone call, Dulles to Eisenhower, September 25, 1957, Memo Tel. Conv., W.H. 9/2/57–12/26/57 (3), Dulles Papers, Telephone Call Series, Eisenhower Library; Telephone call, Dulles to Brownell, September 24, 1957.

48. The Hague to Secretary of State, September 26, 1957, RG 59, 811.411/9–2657, National Archives; American Consul General, Cardiff, Wales, to Department of State, September 27, 1957, RG 59, 811.411/9–2757, National Archives; American Consul, Salvador, Bahia, Brazil, to Department of State, September 30, 1957, RG 59, 811.411/9–3057, National Archives; American Consul General, São Paulo, to Department of State, September 27, 1957, RG 59, 811.411/9–2757, National Archives; Quito, to Secretary of State, September 27, 1957, RG 59, 811.411/9–2757, National Archives; *South China Morning Post*, September 26, 1957, p. 10; *Egyptian Gazette*, September 30, 1957, p. 4; American Embassy, Bogotá, to Department of State, October 7, 1957, RG 59, 811.411/10–757, National Archives (enclosure, *El Tiempo*, October 3, 1957, favorable editorial on Eisenhower's order to send in the troops in Columbia's leading newspaper). For coverage of Eisenhower's address, see, for example, *Tanganyika Standard*, September 26, 1957, p. 1; *East African Standard*, September 26, 1957, p. 1; *Asahi Shimbun* (Tokyo), September 25, 1957, p. 1; *Le Monde*, September 26, 1957, p. 1. See also *Atlanta Constitution*, September 25, 1957, p. 12 (discussing international coverage).

49. U.S. Embassy, Luxembourg, to Department of State, September 30, 1957, RG 59, 811.411/9–3057, National Archives; American Consul, Lourenço Marques, to Department of State, September 30, 1957, RG 59, 811.411/9–3057 HBS, National Archives; American Consul, Salvador, Bahia, Brazil, to Department of State, September 30, 1957, RG 59, 811.411/9–3057, National Archives.

50. American Consul, Kampala, to Department of State, October 4, 1957, RG 59, 811.411/10–457 HBS, National Archives; American Embassy, San José, to Department of State, October 4, 1957, RG 59, 811.411/10–457, National Archives (enclosure, translation of Manuel Mora Valverde, "La Actitud del Pdte. Eissenhower [sic] Frente a los Negros Merece Nuestro Aplauso," *Adelante*, September 29, 1957); *Renmin Ribao (People's Daily)* (China), September 29, 1957, p. P7. I am grateful to Kevin Gao for his help with Chinese language materials.

51. U.N. GAOR 3d Comm., 12th Sess., 768th mtg., 27, U.N. Doc. A/3613, A/C.3/L.609 (1957); Dulles to U.S. Embassy, Paris, September 30, 1957, RG 59, 811.411/9–3057, National Archives.

52. *Atlanta Constitution*, Sept. 25, 1957, pp. 1, 5.

53. *South China Morning Post*, September 28, 1957, p. 11; *Times of India*, September 30, 1957, p. 6; *Eyes on the Prize—America's Civil Rights Years, Fighting Back 1957–1962*, produced by Blackslide, Inc., for PBS-TV, 1986.

54. The Hague to Secretary of State, September 27, 1957, RG 59, 811.411/9–2757, National Archives.

55. *Hindustan Times*, September 29, 1957, p. 1.

56. Ibid.

57. Ibid.

58. *South China Morning Post*, October 4, 1957, p. 1.

59. Larson to Eisenhower, September 30, 1957, USIA (1), Whitman File, Administrative Series, Eisenhower Library.

60. *Aaron v. Cooper*, 163 F. Supp. 13, 21–27 (E.D. Ark. 1958).

61. Goodenough to Lemley, June 30, 1958, microformed in series D, reel 1, frame 892, NAACP Papers.

62. Randolph, Granger, King, and Wilkins to Eisenhower, June 23, 1958, microformed in series D, reel 1, frames 855–861, NAACP Papers.

63. Ibid.

64. Greenberg, *Crusaders in the Courts*, 232–238; Faubus, *Down from the Hills*, 388–395; Record and Record, *Little Rock, U.S.A.*, 105 (reprint of July 30, 1958, *New York Times* article); *Aaron v. Cooper*, 257 F.2d 33, 40 (8th Cir. 1958) (emphasis in original).

65. *Sacramento Bee*, September 12, 1958, p. 14A, reprinted in Record and Record, *Little Rock, U.S.A.*, 118–119.

66. The survey sampled opinions of people in Great Britain, West Germany, France, Italy, and Norway. All these countries except Norway were also included in the April 1956 survey. Office of Research and Intelligence, United States Information Agency, "Post-Little Rock Opinion on the Treatment of Negroes in the U.S.," January 1958, p. 1, P.M.S. 23, Records as President, White House Central Files, Confidential File, Eisenhower Library.

67. In Italy, 18 percent had a "fair" opinion of the treatment of African Americans in the United States, and 36 percent had no opinion. See also Michael L. Krenn, " 'Unfinished Business': Segregation and U.S. Diplomacy at the 1958 World's Fair," *Diplomatic History* 20 (Fall 1996): 593.

68. United States Information Agency, "Post-Little Rock Opinion," 1.

69. Ibid., 4.

70. Oren Stephens to Albert P. Toner, September 24, 1957, USIA 1–350, WHO, Staff Research Group (Toner and Russell), Eisenhower Library.

71. Department of State Instruction no. CA-3382, October 10, 1957, RG 59, 811.411/10–1057, National Archives (to U.S. diplomatic posts in sub-Saharan Africa); Instruction from the Department of State to Belgrade, et al., October 10, 1957, CA-3390, RG 59, 811.411/10–1057, National Archives (instruction was directed to Belgrade, Bucharest, Budapest, Moscow, Prague, and Warsaw).

72. Department of State Instruction no. CA-3382, October 10, 1957; Instruction from the Department of State to Belgrade, et al., October 10, 1957.

73. American Consulate, Port Elizabeth, South Africa, to Department of State, October 10, 1957, RG 59, 811.411/11–1357, National Archives; American Consul General, Johannesburg, South Africa, to Department of State, December 5, 1957, RG 59, 811.411/12–557, National Archives.

74. *The Report of Operation Crossroads—Africa*, p. 27, Africa, Morrow Files, Eisenhower Library; American Embassy, Canberra, to Department of State, October 8, 1957, RG 59, 811.411/10–857, National Archives. See also Rio de Janeiro to Secretary of State, September 26, 1957, RG 59, 811.411/9–2657 HBS, National Archives; American Embassy, Accra, to Department of State, November 15, 1957, RG 59, 811.411/11–1557, National Archives.

Another important effort at spin control was the U.S. exhibit "Unfinished Business" at the 1958 World's Fair. The exhibit acknowledged problems such as Little Rock and put them "in context" to present American democracy as a process leading to greater freedom and justice. Krenn, " 'Unfinished Business,' " 597–599.

75. U.S. Information Agency, *9th Report to Congress: July 1–December 31, 1957*, pp. 7–8, USIA-1958, Harlow Records, Eisenhower Library.

76. Robert W. Smith, "Large-Scale Scientific Enterprise," in *Encyclopedia of the United States in the Twentieth Century*, Stanley L. Kutler et al. eds. (New York: Charles Scribner's Sons, 1996): 2:754–755; David Halberstam, *The Fifties* (New York: Villard Books, 1993), 624–628; Allen to Eisenhower, December 13, 1957, USIA (1), Whitman File, Administrative Series, Eisenhower Library (including attached report: The Significance Assigned the "Sputniks" by Western Europeans); American Consul General, Genoa, to Department of State, undated, RG 59, 811./411/10–2157 (REC'D), National Archives; American Consulate, Port Elizabeth, South Africa, to Department of State, October 10, 1957, 811.411/11–1357, National Archives.

77. *Cooper v. Aaron*, 358 U.S. 1 (1958).

78. *Eyes on the Prize, Part 2: Fighting Back 1957–1962*; Beals, *Warriors Don't Cry*, 241, 299–305.

79. Freyer, *Little Rock Crisis*, 148.
On August 4, the Eighth Circuit Court of Appeals convened a special session to hear an appeal from the district court order delaying implementation of desegregation in Little Rock. Two weeks later, the appellate court reversed the district court's order but subsequently stayed its own judgment to enable the school board to seek review in the U.S. Supreme Court. At that point, the NAACP petitioned Supreme Court Justice Whittaker, as circuit justice for the Eighth Circuit, for a stay of the orders of the courts below. Justice Whittaker referred the matter to the entire Court, and the Supreme Court scheduled its own extraordinary summertime session. Transcript of Oral Argument, *Cooper v. Aaron*, 358 U.S. 1 (1958), pp. 46–47 (no. 1, 1958 August Special Term) (oral argument of Thurgood Marshall on behalf of the African American students), reprinted in Philip B. Kurland and Gerhard Kasper, *Landmark Briefs and Arguments of the Supreme Court of the United States* (Washington, D.C.: University Publications of America, 1975) 54:711–712; *Cooper*, 358 U.S. at 13–14 (1958).

80. Dennis J. Hutchinson, "Unanimity and Desegregation: Decisionmaking in the Supreme Court, 1948–1958," *Georgetown Law Journal* 68 (October 1979): 78; Bernard Schwartz with Stephen Lesher, *Inside the Warren Court* (Garden City, N.Y.: Doubleday, 1983), 162; *Cooper*, 358 U.S. at 5.

81. "Governor's School Closing Proclamation," *Race Relations Law Reporter* 3 (1958): 869; "Act No. 4 of the 1958 Extraordinary Session of the Arkansas Legislature," *Race Relations Law Reporter* 3 (1958): 1048–1049; Freyer, *Little Rock Crisis*, 154–156. Following the school closing, a group of parents organized themselves as the Little Rock Private School Corporation. They hoped to lease public school buildings and operate "private" schools on a segregated basis. The school board petitioned to the district court for a declaration of the legality of the leasing plan, and the NAACP sought a restraining order against it. The Eighth Circuit Court of Appeals enjoined the leasing arrangement, finding the actions of

the school board to be contrary to the requirements of *Cooper v. Aaron* and to violate the board's court-imposed duties. "Private School Charter," *Race Relations Law Reporter* 3 (1958): 870–872; "Petition for Order Against Leasing," *Race Relations Law Reporter* 3 (1958): 875–877; "*Aaron v. Cooper*" (8th Cir.), *Race Relations Law Reporter* 3 (1958): 1135, 1142–1143.

82. 358 U.S. 11 (1958); Mark V. Tushnet, *Making Civil Rights Law: Thurgood Marshall and the Supreme Court, 1936–1961* (New York: Oxford University Press, 1994), 264; Schwartz with Lesher, *Inside the Warren Court*, 162; Hutchinson, "Unanimity and Desegregation," 78–80.

83. *Cooper*, 358 U.S. at 19–20.

84. *Times* (London), September 30, 1958, p. 9; *Times* (London), September 15, 1958, p. 8; *Times* (London), September 18, 1958, p. 8; *Times* (London), September 23, 1958, p. 7; *Times* (London), September 17, 1958, p. 10; *Times* (London), September 19, 1958, p. 9; *Times* (London), September 16, 1958, p. 8; *Times* (London), September 22, 1958, p. 9.

85. *South China Morning Post*, August 30, 1958, p. 14; *South China Morning Post*, September 10, 1958, p. 6. The *South China Morning Post* covered Little Rock in the fall of 1958 in the context of other civil rights developments, including the arrest of Dr. Martin Luther King Jr., during a civil rights protest. *South China Morning Post*, September 15, 1958, p. 10; *South China Morning Post*, August 27, 1958, p. 12; *South China Morning Post*, August 28, 1958, p. 9; *South China Morning Post*, August 29, 1958, p. 13; *South China Morning Post*, August 30, 1958, p. 12.

Times of India, October 1, 1958, p. 6. With the exception of an August 28 front-page story on the U.S. government's brief in *Cooper v. Aaron*, the *Times of India*'s coverage was on the inside pages and was relatively brief. *Times of India*, August 29, 1958, p. 1; *Times of India*, August 30, 1958, p. 5; *Times of India*, September 14, 1958, p. 9.

86. Coverage in the *Egyptian Gazette*, for example, was extensive but was on the inside pages. See *Egyptian Gazette*, September 30, 1958, p. 2. The paper published only one front-page article on Little Rock in the fall of 1958—on an October 4 federal court order finding the privatization of Little Rock public schools to be unlawful. *Egyptian Gazette*, October 5, 1958, p. 1.

In contrast to the *Egyptian Gazette* coverage, the *Tanganyika Standard* carried brief Little Rock stories but placed them on the front page. *Tanganyika Standard*, August 23, 1958, p. 1; *Tanganyika Standard*, September 1, 1958, p. 1.

87. Daisy Bates, *The Long Shadow of Little Rock: A Memoir* (New York: David McKay, 1962), 163; Greenberg, *Crusaders in the Courts*, 242.

88. Act 461 of the 1959 Session of the Arkansas General Assembly (March 30, 1959), *Race Relations Law Reporter* 4 (1959): 747–749. There was one direct reference to race in the statute: "no child shall be compelled to attend any school in which the races are commingled with a written objection of the parent or guardian has been filed with the Board of Education [sic]." This provision appeared to enable parents to pull their children out of integrated schools notwithstanding Arkansas' school attendance requirements. Ibid., 749.

89. Greenberg, *Crusaders in the Court*, 242. The Supreme Court denied certiorari in 1959 in *Covington v. Edwards*, a Fourth Circuit case upholding North Carolina's pupil placement plan, following a narrow, summary affirmance of a district court opinion upholding an Alabama plan in 1958. *Covington v. Edwards*, 264 F.2d 180 (4th Cir. 1959), cert. denied, 361 U.S. 840 (1959); *Shuttlesworth v. Birmingham Bd. of Educ.*, 162 F.Supp. 372 (N.D. Ala. 1957), *affirmed* 358 U.S. 101 (1958); Stephen L. Wasby, Anthony A. D'Amato, and Rosemary Metrailer, *Desegregation from Brown to Alexander* (Carbondale: Southern Illinois University Press, 1977), 194–195.

90. Although the Court's denial of certiorari in *Covington* gave southern states the green light to go ahead with pupil placement schemes, the Court's action was not reported in the *Tanganyika Standard, Egyptian Gazette, South China Morning Post, Times of India*, or *Times* (London). The Court's affirmance of a pupil placement plan in *Shuttlesworth* was also not reported in these papers. All of these papers had carried very detailed coverage of other legal developments pertaining to the desegregation crisis.

The pupil placement cases were front-page news in the United States, although without the banner headlines that attended the *Brown* and *Cooper* rulings. *New York Times*, November 25, 1958, p. 1; *New York Times*, October 13, 1959, p. 1.

CHAPTER FIVE

1. American Embassy, Niamey, to Department of State, May 21, 1963, RG 59, Central Foreign Policy File 1963, SOC 14–1 US, National Archives.

2. Report of Incident Involving Ambassador Malick Sow of Chad, (undated), Folder: Chad, General, 1961–1962, Papers of President Kennedy, President's Office Files, Countries, Box 113a, John F. Kennedy Library, Boston, Massachusetts: Battle to O'Donnell, June 19, 1961, Folder: Chad, General, 1961–1962, Papers of President Kennedy, President's Office Files, Countries, Box 113a, Kennedy Library.

3. Report of Incident Involving Ambassador Malick Sow; Battle to O'Donnell, June 19, 1961; Harris Wofford, *Of Kennedys & Kings: Making Sense of the Sixties* (New York: Farrar, Straus and Giroux, 1980), 126–128.

4. H. S. Wilson, *African Decolonization* (London: Edward Arnold, 1994), 177.

5. Dean Rusk, *As I Saw It* (New York: W. W. Norton, 1990), 581; Remarks of Louis Martin, April 3, 1963, Folder: Civil Rights Press Releases, Papers of Arthur M. Schlesinger Jr., Writings File, Box W-4, Kennedy Library. The importance of civil rights to Rusk's role as secretary of state is illustrated by the fact that he devoted an entire chapter of his memoir to the issue. Rusk, *As I Saw It*, 579–592.

6. William H. Chafe, *Civilities and Civil Rights: Greensboro, North Carolina and the Black Struggle for Freedom* (New York: Oxford University Press, 1980), 71–100.

7. John Lewis Gaddis, *We Now Know: Rethinking Cold War History* (Oxford: Oxford University Press, 1997), 260–280; Jennifer Whitmore See, "US–Soviet Entente?: John F. Kennedy and the Pursuit of Peace, 1963" (paper presented at annual meeting of the Society for Historians of American Foreign Relations, June 1996).

8. Ellen Schrecker describes the McCarthy era as extending through the 1940s and 1950s. Ellen Schrecker, *Many Are the Crimes: McCarthyism in America* (Boston: Little, Brown, 1998), x. On the Supreme Court and individual rights during the 1960s, see Milton R. Konvitz, *Expanding Liberties: Freedom's Gain in Postwar America* (New York: Viking Press, 1966). On DuBois' later years, see Gerald Horne, *Black and Red: W. E. B. DuBois and the Afro-American Response to the Cold War, 1944–1963* (Albany: State University of New York, 1986).

9. David Garrow, *Bearing the Cross: Martin Luther King, Jr., and the Southern Christian Leadership Conference* (New York: William Morrow, 1986); Taylor Branch, *Parting the Waters: America in the King Years, 1954–1963* (New York: Simon and Schuster, 1988).

10. Harris Wofford, recorded interview by Berl Bernhard, November 29, 1965, pp. 7, 31, John F. Kennedy Library Oral History Program, Kennedy Library.

Carl M. Brauer describes Kennedy's posture toward civil rights during his years in the Senate as that of a moderate. For example, Kennedy supported the Civil Rights Act of 1957 but also voted for an amendment favored by Southern Democrats that weakened the act. He was criticized for this and other votes by the African American press. During the same period, when asked about school desegregation while speaking in Mississippi, Kennedy said that "he accepted it as the law of the land." According to Brauer, "Kennedy's moderate stand on civil rights allowed and even encouraged Southern politicians to embrace him." Carl M. Brauer, *John F. Kennedy and the Second Reconstruction* (New York: Columbia University Press, 1977), 20–23.

11. Richard D. Mahoney, *JFK: Ordeal in Africa* (New York: Oxford University Press, 1983), 20–33.

12. Brauer, *Second Reconstruction*, 43, 127, 205–210, 212–213; Branch, *Parting the Waters*, 586–587; Wofford, *Of Kennedys and Kings*, 124; Arthur Schlesinger, *A Thousand Days: John F. Kennedy in the White House* (Boston: Houghton Mifflin, 1965), 847–849, 853.

13. Aaronson/Wilkins, Confidential Memorandum, February 6, 1961, Papers of Theodore C. Sorensen, Subject Files, 1961–64, Box 30, Kennedy Library; Roy Wilkins with Tom Mathews, *Standing Fast: The Autobiography of Roy Wilkins* (New York: Viking Press, 1982), 280–282.

Carl Brauer noted in 1977 that "the foreign implications of America's race problems" were "especially significant" for the Kennedy administration. Brauer's important book was written long before the records to fully explore the impact of foreign affairs on civil rights were declassified or otherwise made public. As a result, an issue that Brauer recognized but was unable to develop more fully remains to be more thoroughly considered using the diplomatic and other materials made available in the twenty years since his work was published. Brauer, *Second Reconstruction*, 76.

14. Aaronson/Wilkins, Confidential Memorandum, February 6, 1961.

15. Elisabeth Cobbs Hoffman, *All You Need is Love: The Peace Corps and the Spirit of the 1960s* (Cambridge: Harvard University Press, 1998), 29.

16. Chafe, *Civilities and Civil Rights*, 71; Garrow, *Bearing the Cross*, 127–136; Clayborne Carson, *In Struggle: SNCC and the Black Awakening of the 1960's* (Cambridge: Har-

vard University Press, 1981), 9–30; *Eyes on the Prize: America's Civil Rights Years*, Clayborne Carson, David J. Garrow, Vincent Harding, Darlene Clark Hine, eds., (New York: Penguin Books, 1987), 78–79, 83–88.

17. August Meier and Elliott Rudwick, *CORE: A Study in the Civil Rights Movement* (New York: Oxford University Press, 1973), 135–158; Garrow, *Bearing the Cross*, 158–161.

18. Meier and Rudwick, *CORE*, 136–138; Garrow, *Bearing the Cross*, 155–157.

19. Schlesinger, *A Thousand Days*, 854–855; Meier and Rudwick, *CORE*, 138.

20. *Eyes on the Prize-America's Civil Rights Years, Ain't Scared of Your Jails, 1960–1961*, produced by Blackside, Inc., for PBS-TV, 1986.

21. Richard Reeves, *President Kennedy: Profile of Power* (New York: Simon and Schuster, 1994), 123; Wofford, *Of Kennedys and Kings*, 125.

22. United States Information Agency, "Worldwide Reactions to Racial Incidents in Alabama," pp. 7–15, May 29, 1961, Folder: S-17-61, RG 306, Records of the USIA, Office of Research, Special "S" Reports, 1953–63, National Archives.

23. Ibid., 1.

24. Ibid.

25. Ibid., 2.

26. Meier and Rudwick, *CORE*, 139.

27. Battle to Dutton, September 19, 1961, Folder: Foreign Policy, 4/1/61–10/8/63, Papers of Theodore C. Sorensen, Subject Files, 1961–64, Box 34, Kennedy Library.

28. *Meredith v. Fair*, 305 F. 2d 343 (5th Cir., 1962); *Fair v. Meredith*, 371 U.S. 828 (1962); Schlesinger, *A Thousand Days*, 858–859; Reeves, *President Kennedy*, 354–364.

29. United States Information Agency, "Media Comment on the Mississippi Crisis," October 5, 1962, p. 5, Folder: R-109-62, RG 306, Records of the USIA, Office of Research, "R" Reports, 1960–63, Box 10, National Archives; U.S. Information Agency, "Student Reaction in Bogota to the Mississippi Crisis," October 1962, Folder: Mississippi Situation 10/1/62–1/26/63 and undated, Papers of Arthur M. Schlesinger, Jr., White House Files, Box WH-15, Kennedy Library.

30. United States Information Agency, "Media Comment on the Mississippi Crisis," October 5, 1962, pp. 9–12.

31. Bowles to R. Kennedy, October 10, 1962, Folder: Bowles, Chester 10/62–11/62, Papers of Robert F. Kennedy, Attorney General's General Correspondence, Box 5, Kennedy Library.

Long after the crisis was resolved, James Meredith remained on the minds of people around the world. When Chester Bowles traveled through thirteen African countries, at each stop "one question was inevitable, urgent, and recurrent: What about James Meredith at the University of Mississippi?" Chester Bowles, "Emancipation: The Record and the Challenge," February 15, 1963, Folder: Bowles, Chester, 1963, Papers of Robert F. Kennedy, Attorney General's General Correspondence, Box 6, Kennedy Library.

32. Schlesinger, *A Thousand Days*, 866.

33. United States Information Agency, "Media Comment on the Mississippi Crisis," October 5, 1962, p. ii; United States Information Agency, "Racial Prejudice Mars the

American Image," October 17, 1962, Folder: R-136-62, RG 306, Records of the USIA, Office of Research, "R" Reports, 1960–63, Box 5, National Archives.

34. Wilson to Lincoln, October 11, 1962 (and attached report), Folder U.S.I.A. 7/62–12/62, Papers of President Kennedy, President's Office Files, Departments and Agencies, Box 88a, Kennedy Library.

35. Rusk, *As I Saw It*, 582.

36. Ibid., 583–584.

37. Report of Incident Involving Ambassador Malick Sow of Chad (undated); Battle to O'Donnell, June 19, 1961; Meeting with Representatives of State Governors (transcript), p. A-5, June 16, 1961, Folder: Second Meeting with Representatives of State Governors, Papers of Pedro Sanjuan, MS 78–21, Kennedy Library; Wofford, *Of Kennedys and Kings*, 126–128.

38. Wofford, *Of Kennedys and Kings*, 127–128; Brauer, *Second Reconstruction*, 77.

39. Pedro Sanjuan, "Address to the Legislative Council of the General Assembly of Maryland," September 13, 1961, Folder: Campaign in Maryland for Passage of Public Accommodations Bill, 9/1/61, Papers of Pedro Sanjuan, MS 78–21, Kennedy Library. Pedro Sanjuan and the Office of Special Protocol Services are discussed more fully in Renee Romano, "No Diplomatic Immunity: African American Diplomats and the Dilemma of American Racism during the Cold War, 1961–1964," *Journal of American History* (forthcoming); Timothy P. Maga, "Battling the 'Ugly American' at Home: The Special Protocol Service and the New Frontier, 1961–63," *Diplomacy and Statecraft* 3 (1992): 126–142. Discrimination in housing in Washington, D.C., was another source of particular embarrassment. Nonwhite foreign diplomats and their staffs regularly faced discriminatory landlords, turning simple apartment searches into diplomatic crises. United States Commission on Civil Rights, *Civil Rights U.S.A.: Housing in Washington, D.C.* (Washington, D.C.: Government Printing Office, 1962), 21–26.

40. Sanjuan, "Address to the Legislative Council of the General Assembly of Maryland," September 13, 1961 (emphasis in original); Progress Report, April 2, 1962, Folder: Progress Report, 4/2/62, Papers of Pedro Sanjuan, MS 78–21, Kennedy Library; Progress Report, June 16, 1963, p. 6, Folder: Progress Report, 6/16/63, Papers of Pedro Sanjuan, MS 78–21, Kennedy Library; R. Kennedy to Sanjuan, March 28, 1963, Folder: Sanjuan, Pedro: 9/1961, Papers of Robert F. Kennedy, Attorney General's General Correspondence, Box 51, Kennedy Library.

41. Branch, *Parting the Waters*, 758–763.

42. Garrow, *Bearing the Cross*, 267–268; Branch, *Parting the Waters*, 764–785; U.S. Information Agency, "Reaction to Racial Tension in Birmingham, Alabama," May 13, 1963, R-85-63 (A), RG 306, National Archives; John Walton Cotman, *Birmingham, JFK and the Civil Rights Act of 1963: Implications for Elite Theory* (New York: P. Lang, 1989), 100–102.

43. Wilson to J. F. Kennedy, May 14, 1963, Folder: USIA (Classified) 1/63–11/63, Box 133, Papers of Pierre Salinger, Background Briefing Material, Kennedy Library; Accra to Secretary of State, May 17, 1963, RG 59, Central Foreign Policy File 1963, SOC 14–1 US,

National Archives; Richard Lentz, "Snarls Echoing 'Round the World: The 1963 Birmingham Civil Rights Campaign on the World Stage," *American Journalism* (forthcoming).

44. Cotman, *Birmingham, JFK and the Civil Rights Act*, 35.

45. Burke Marshall Oral History Interview, May 29, 1964, pp. 98–99, Kennedy Library; Cotman, *Birmingham, JFK and the Civil Rights Act*, 21–60.

46. King Hassan II of Morocco was absent out of concern that his presence would be construed as recognition of Mauritania. Mauritania's president was present at the meeting, and Morocco had previously claimed sovereignty over Mauritania's territory. According to *Keesing's Contemporary Archives*, Togo's president was absent because "no agreement had been reached on the question of his country's admission." *Keesing's Contemporary Archives* (London: Longman, 1963–64), 14:19463. South Africa was not invited to the meeting. Brubeck to Bundy, May 27, 1963, Folder: Africa, General, 6/63, Box 3, National Security Files, Countries, Africa, Kennedy Library.

47. *Keesing's Contemporary Archives*, 14:19463; Brubeck to Bundy, May 27, 1963.

48. Ibid. The United States and the Soviet Union are obviously different models of nationhood. In invoking them, however, Selassi illustrated his general goal of political unification, without embracing any particular model of national organization.

49. Addis Ababa to Secretary of State, May 23, 1963, Folder: Civil Rights, 6/19/63–7/9/63, National Security Files, Subjects, Box 295, Kennedy Library (quoting Obote letter); *Keesing's Contemporary Archives*, 14:19465. At the State Department's urging, President Kennedy had sent a congratulatory message to the conference. It was expected that many other nations, including the Soviet Union, would send such messages. Obote's letter was in response to Kennedy's message. Brubeck to Bundy, May 11, 1963, Folder: Africa, General 5/63, Box 3, National Security Files—Countries—Africa, Kennedy Library; Department of State to American Embassy, Addis Ababa, May 17, 1963, Folder: Africa, General 5/63, Box 3, National Security Files—Countries—Africa, Kennedy Library.

50. Addis Ababa to Secretary of State, May 23, 1963 (quoting Obote letter).

51. Addis Ababa to Secretary of State, May 27, 1963, RG 59, Central Foreign Policy File 1963, SOC 14–1 US, National Archives. The despatch identified the "American Negro black Muslim" as Akbar Mohammad, a student living in Cairo. Elijah Muhammad's son Akbar was living in Cairo at the time, and attended the OAU meeting as a reporter for *Muhammad Speaks*. In an e-mail to the author, however, Dr. Akbar Muhammad indicated that he was not the source of the Obote letter. Akbar Muhammad to Mary Dudziak, March 6, 2000 (e-mail correspondence). It is unclear whether another American helped generate the Obote letter, or whether the embassy was mistaken on this point.

52. Quoted in Monrovia to Secretary of State, May 22, 1963, Folder: Africa, General 5/63, Box 3, National Security Files—Countries—Africa, Kennedy Library.

53. Addis Ababa Resolutions, p. 5, Folder: Africa, General 6/63, National Security Files, Countries, Ghana, Box 99, Kennedy Library.

54. Brubeck to Bundy, May 27, 1963; Nyerere to J. F. Kennedy, June 18, 1963, Folder: Tanganyika, 1961–1964, Box 124a, Papers of President Kennedy, President's Office Files, Countries, Kennedy Library.

55. Youlou to J. F. Kennedy, May 17, 1963, Folder: Congo, General, 1963, Box 114, Papers of President Kennedy, President's Office Files, Countries, Kennedy Library; J. F. Kennedy to Youlou, June 4, 1963, Folder: Congo, General, 1963, Box 114, Papers of President Kennedy, President's Office Files, Countries, Kennedy Library.

56. Rusk to All American Diplomatic and Consular Posts, Circular 2177, June 19, 1963, Folder: Civil Rights, 6/19/63–7/9/63, National Security Files, Subjects, Box 295, Kennedy Library; Rusk, *As I Saw It*, 581–583.

57. Rusk to All American Diplomatic and Consular Posts, Circular 2177, June 19, 1963.

58. Donald Wilson, "Racial Strife: The Overseas Impact," June 10, 1963, attached to Jordan to G. Mennen Williams, June 12, 1963, Folder: Civil Rights Folder, RG 59, Classified Records of Assistant Secretary of State for African Affairs G. Mennen Williams, 1961–66, Box 3, National Archives; White to Jordan, June 11, 1963 attached to Jordan to Williams, June 12, 1963.

59. Gardner to Cleveland, October 31, 1963, Folder: Civil Rights Folder, RG 59, Classified Records of Assistant Secretary for African Affairs G. Mennen Williams, 1961–1966, Box 3, National Archives.

60. Reeves, *President Kennedy,* 514–522.

61. Cotman, *Birmingham, JFK and the Civil Rights Act*, 147.

62. John F. Kennedy, "Radio and Television Report to the American People on Civil Rights," June 11, 1963, *Public Papers of the Presidents of the United States: John F. Kennedy, 1963*, (Washington, D. C.: U.S. Government Printing Office, 1964), 468.

63. Ibid., 469.

64. Ibid.

65. Ibid., 470.

66. John F. Kennedy, "Special Message to the Congress on Civil Rights and Job Opportunities," June 19, 1963, *Public Papers of the Presidents: John F. Kennedy, 1963*, 483.

67. Brauer, *Second Reconstruction*, 247.

68. John F. Kennedy, "Commencement Address at American University in Washington," June 10, 1963, *Public Papers of the Presidents: John F. Kennedy, 1963*, 459–464. The juxtaposition of Kennedy's civil rights and arms control speeches is discussed at greater length in Jennifer Whitmore See's thoughtful paper for the 1999 meeting of the Society for Historians of American Foreign Relations. See, "US–Soviet Entente?," 14–15.

69. Cited in see, "US–Soviet Entente?"

70. Read to Bundy, July 7, 1963, Folder: Africa, General 7/63, Box 3, National Security Files—Countries—Africa, Kennedy Library.

71. Korry to J. F. Kennedy, June 28, 1963, Folder: Africa, General 7/63, Box 3, National Security Files—Countries—Africa, Kennedy Library; Addis Ababa, to Department of State, June 29, 1963, Folder: Africa, General 7/63, Box 3, National Security Files—Countries—Africa, Kennedy Library; *Ethiopian Herald*, June 25, 1963, in Folder: Africa, General 7/63, Box 3, National Security Files—Countries—Africa, Kennedy Library; "Soviet Media Coverage of Current US Racial Crisis," June 14, 1963, Folder: Civil Rights, 6/

11/63–6/14/63, National Security Files, Subjects, Box 295, Kennedy Library; USIA to J. F. Kennedy, June 14, 1963, Folder: Civil Rights, 6/11/63–6/14/63, National Security Files, Subjects, Box 295, Kennedy Library.

72. *NAACP v. Button*, 371 U.S. 415 (1963); *Gibson v. Florida Legislative Investigation Committee*, 372 U.S. 539 (1963).

On public versus private discrimination, see *The Civil Rights Cases*, 109 U.S. 3 (1883). In that ruling, the Supreme Court overturned the Civil Rights Act of 1875 in part because it regulated private behavior. The Court ruled that the Fourteenth Amendment's equal protection clause only applied to "state action."

73. The Supreme Court upheld the Civil Rights Act of 1964, as applied to private enterprises that had an impact on interstate commerce, in *Heart of Atlanta Motel, Inc. v. United States*, 379 U.S 241 (1964); and *Katzenbach v. McClung*, 379 U.S. 294 (1964). Prior to the enactment of the Civil Rights Act, Congress's power under the commerce clause was extensive, reaching even private activities with a very small impact on interstate commerce, as long as, taken together with other similar activities, the "cumulative effect" on interstate commerce was substantial. Wickard v. Filburn, 371 U.S. 111 (1942).

74. *Congressional Record*, 88th Cong., 1st Sess., 1963, 109, pt. 6: 8293.

75. Rusk, *As I Saw It*, 586–588; U.S. Senate Committee on Commerce, Hearings on S. 1732, A Bill to Eliminate Discrimination in Public Accommodations Affecting Interstate Commerce, 88th Cong., 1st Sess., 1963, 281.

In his memoirs and oral history interview, Rusk recalled that his testimony on July 10, 1963, was before the Senate Judiciary Committee. Senate records, however, indicate that his testimony was before the Commerce Committee. The reason the civil rights bill came before the Commerce Committee was that one source of constitutional power relied on by Congress as authority for the Civil Rights Act was Congress's power to regulate interstate commerce. U.S. Const. Art. I, Sec. 8; U.S. Senate Committee on Commerce, Hearings on S. 1732.

76. Reeves, *President Kennedy*, 527–528; Hugh Davis Graham, *The Civil Rights Era: Origins and Development of National Policy, 1960–1972* (New York: Oxford University Press, 1990), 125–152; Biography—Pedro A. Sanjuan (undated), Folder: Sanjuan, Pedro: 6/1963, Box 51, Personal Papers of Robert F. Kennedy, Attorney General's Papers, General Correspondence, Kennedy Library; Sanjuan to Attorney General, June 28, 1963, Folder: Sanjuan, Pedro: 6/1963, Box 51, Personal Papers of Robert F. Kennedy, Attorney General's Papers, General Correspondence, Kennedy Library; "Living Conditions of New Diplomats in Washington and Vicinity and Suggestions for Easing of Tensions by the Office of Protocol," February 23, 1961, Folder: Living Conditions, New Diplomats, Box 1, Papers of Pedro Sanjuan, Kennedy Library.

77. U.S. Senate Committee on Commerce, Hearings on S. 1732, 281; Rusk, *As I Saw It*, 586.

78. U.S. Senate Committee on Commerce, Hearings on S. 1732, 281–282.

79. Ibid., 282–283.

80. Ibid., 283.

81. Ibid., 311; *New York Times*, July 11, 1963, p. 1.

82. U.S. Senate Committee on Commerce, Hearings on S. 1732; *New York Times*, July 11, 1963, p. 16.

83. U.S. Senate Committee on Commerce, Hearings on S. 1732; *New York Times*, July 11, 1963, p. 16.

84. *Washington Post*, August 26, 1963, p. 1, attached to Sanjuan to R. Kennedy, August 26, 1963, Folder: Sanjuan, Pedro: 8/1963, 10/1963, Box 51, Personal Papers of Robert F. Kennedy, Attorney General's Papers, General Correspondence, Kennedy Library.

85. Memo for Bundy, Status Report of African Reactions to Civil Rights in the United States, Week Ending 7/12/63, Folder: Africa, General 7/63, Status Report of African Reactions to Civil Rights in the United States, Box 99, National Security Files, Countries, Kennedy Library.

86. Scott A. Sandage, "A Marble House Divided: The Lincoln Memorial, the Civil Rights Movement, and the Politics of Memory, 1939–1963," *Journal of American History* 80 (June 1993): 137–138, 159.

There are many sources on the March on Washington. A particularly helpful recent account appears in Lucy Grace Barber, "Marches on Washington, 1894–1963: National Political Demonstrations and American Political Culture" (Ph.D. diss., Brown University, 1996), 363–465. See also Garrow, *Bearing the Cross*, 265–286; Branch, *Parting the Waters*, 846–887; Paula F. Pfeffer, *A. Philip Randolph, Pioneer of the Civil Rights Movement* (Baton Rouge: Louisiana State University Press, 1990), 240–280. For accounts of the earlier march on Washington Movement, see Herbert Garfinkle, *When Negroes March: The March on Washington Movement in the Organizational Politics for FEPC* (Glencoe, Ill.: Free Press, 1959); Barber, "Marches on Washington," 251–362.

87. Barber, "Marches on Washington," 444–447.

88. USIA to Curaçao, Dhahran, Kuwait, Dublin, August 26, 1963, RG 59, Central Foreign Policy File, 1963, SOC 14–1 US, National Archives.

89. Sargent to Fales, August 28, 1963, enclosure to American Embassy, Paris, to Department of State, September 17, 1963, RG 59, Central Foreign Policy File, 1963, SOC 14–1 US, National Archives. The embassy reported that only thirty people attended the meeting at the Living Room, but its estimate was not based on a firsthand account. American Embassy, Paris, to Secretary of State, August 28, 1963, RG 59, Central Foreign Policy File, 1963, SOC 14–1 US, National Archives.

90. Sargent to Fales, August 28, 1963.

91. Ibid.; American Embassy, Paris, to Secretary of State, August 28, 1963; Enclosures to American Embassy, London, to Department of State, August 28, 1963, RG 59, Central Foreign Policy File 1963, SOC 14–1 US, National Archives.

92. Sargent to Fales, August 28, 1963; American Embassy, Paris, to Secretary of State, August 28, 1963; Paris to Secretary of State, August 21, 1963, RG 59, Central Foreign Policy File 1963, SOC 14–1 US, National Archives; Paris to Secretary of State, August 19, 1963, RG 59, Central Foreign Policy File 1963, SOC 14–1 US, National Archives.

93. Paris to Secretary of State, August 21, 1963; Sargent to Fales, August 28, 1963.

94. American Embassy, The Hague, to Department of State, August 24, 1963, RG 59, Central Foreign Policy File 1963, SOC 14–1 US, National Archives; Enclosure to

American Embassy, London, to Department of State, August 28, 1963 (emphasis in original).

95. David Leeming, *James Baldwin* (New York: Alfred A. Knopf, 1994), 227–228; Branch, *Parting the Waters*, 878–883; Maxwell R. Brooks, "The March on Washington in Retrospect," *Journal of Human Relations* 12 (1964): 80; Martin Luther King Jr., "I Have a Dream," in *A Testament of Hope: The Essential Writings and Speeches of Martin Luther King, Jr.*; James M. Washington, ed. (New York: Harper Collins, 1986), 217–220.

96. American Embassy, London, to Secretary of State, September 5, 1963, RG 59, Central Foreign Policy File 1963, SOC 14–1 US, National Archives; American Embassy, The Hague, to Department of State, September 5, 1963, RG 59, Central Foreign Policy File 1963, SOC 14–1 US, National Archives; American Embassy, Accra, to Department of State, September 1, 1963, RG 59, Central Foreign Policy File 1963, SOC 14–1 US, National Archives; American Embassy, Kingston, to Department of State, August 30, 1963, RG 59, Central Foreign Policy File 1963, SOC 14–1 US, National Archives; Oslo to Secretary of State, August 29, 1963, RG 59, Central Foreign Policy File 1963, SOC 14–1 US, National Archives; American Consulate, Munich, to Department of State, August 30, 1963, RG 59, Central Foreign Policy File 1963, SOC 14–1 US, National Archives; Berlin to Secretary of State, August 29, 1963, RG 59, Central Foreign Policy File 1963, SOC 14–1 US, National Archives; United States Information Agency, "Worldwide Comment on the Washington Civil Rights March," September 6, 1963, pp. 6–8, RG 306, Records of the USIA, Office of Research, "R" Reports, 1960–63, Box 17, Folder R-172–63, National Archives.

97. American Embassy, Cairo, to Secretary of State, August 31, 1963, RG 59, Central Foreign Policy File 1963, SOC 14–1 US, Records of the Department of State, National Archives; U.S. Information Agency, "Worldwide Comment on the Washington Civil Rights March," September 6, 1963, p. 14.

98. American Embassy, Cairo, to Secretary of State, August 31, 1963.

99. United States Information Agency, "Worldwide Comment on the Washington Civil Rights March," September 6, 1963; Hong Kong to Secretary of State, September 5, 1963, RG 59, Central Foreign Policy File 1963, SOC 14–1 US, National Archives; Brooks, "The March on Washington in Retrospect," 83.

100. United States Information Agency, "Worldwide Comment on the Washington Civil Rights March," September 6, 1963.

101. Ibid.

102. USIA to Curaçao, Dhahran, Kuwait, Dublin, August 26, 1963.

103. Garrow, *Bearing the Cross*, 292–293. See also Spike Lee, *4 Little Girls* (1997: 40 Acres and a Mule Filmworks).

104. American Embassy, Rome, to Secretary of State, September 17, 1963, RG 59, Central Foreign Policy File 1963, SOC 14–1 US, National Archives; American Embassy, The Hague, to Department of State, September 24, 1963, RG 59, Central Foreign Policy File 1963, SOC 14–1 US, National Archives; American Embassy, Lagos, to Department of State, September 20, 1963, RG 59, Central Foreign Policy File, SOC 14–1, National Archives; Bern to Secretary of State, September 20, 1963, RG 59, Central Foreign Policy

File 1963, SOC 14–1 US, National Archives; American Embassy, Lagos, to Secretary of State, September 19, 1963, RG 59, Central Foreign Policy File 1963, SOC 14–1 US, National Archives; Kampala to Secretary of State, September 18, 1963, RG 59, Central Foreign Policy File 1963, SOC 14–1 US, National Archives, American Embassy, The Hague, September 17, 1963, RG 59, Central Foreign Policy File 1963, SOC 14–1 US, National Archives; American Embassy, New Delhi, to Secretary of State, September 17, 1963, RG 59, Central Foreign Policy File 1963, SOC 14–1 US, National Archives.

105. American Embassy, Yaounde, to Department of State, September 23, 1963, RG 59, Central Foreign Policy File 1963, SOC 14–1 US, National Archives.

106. Dar-es-Salaam to Secretary of State, September 28, 1963, RG 59, Central Foreign Policy File 1963, SOC 14–1 US, National Archives (telegram no. 344); Dar-es-Salaam to Secretary of State, September 28, 1963, RG 59, Central Foreign Policy File 1963, SOC 14–1 US, National Archives (telegram no. 342).

107. U.S. Information Agency, "Foreign Reaction to the Presidential Succession," December 6, 1963, pp. i–ii, Folder: United States Information Agency Vol 1 [3 of 3], National Security File, Agency File, Box 73, Lyndon Baines Johnson Library, Austin, Texas.

108. U.S. Information Agency, "Foreign Reaction to President Johnson and his Policies," December 4, 1963, pp. 5–6, Folder: United States Information Agency Vol 1 [3 of 3], National Security File, Agency File, Box 73, Johnson Library.

109. Harris Wofford, Oral History Interview, Kennedy Library, 50, 63.

110. Aaronson/Wilkins, Confidential Memorandum, February 6, 1961, Theodore C. Sorenson Papers, Subject Files, 1961–64, Box 30, Kennedy Library.

CHAPTER SIX

1. "Racial Issues in the U.S.: Some Policy and Program Indications of Research," March 14, 1966, RG 306, Records of the United States Information Agency, Office of Research, Special "S" Reports, 1964–82, S-3-66, National Archives.

2. Lyndon B. Johnson, "Address Before a Joint Session of the Congress," November 27, 1963, *Public Papers of the Presidents of the United States: Lyndon B. Johnson, 1963–64* (Washington, D. C.: U.S. Government Printing Office, 1965), 1:8–9.

3. Ibid., 9–10.

4. United States Information Agency, "Worldwide Reaction to the First Month of the Johnson Administration," December 24, 1963, p. 15, Folder: United States Information Agency Vol I [3 of 3], National Security File, Agency File, Box 73, Lyndon Baines Johnson Library, Austin, Texas.

5. United States Information Agency, "Foreign Reaction to the Presidential Succession," December 6, 1963, p. 18, Folder: United States Information Agency Vol I [3 of 3], National Security File, Agency File, Box 73, Johnson Library.

6. Ibid., 19–20.

7. Department of State to American Embassy, Lagos, Nigeria, November 24, 1963, RG 59, Central Foreign Policy File 1963, SOC 14–1 US, National Archives.

8. American Embassy, Lagos, to Secretary of State, November 24, 1963, RG 59, Central Foreign Policy File 1963, SOC 14–1 US, National Archives.

9. United States Information Agency, "Foreign Reaction to the Presidential Succession," December 6, 1963, p. 18; United States Information Agency, "Worldwide Reaction to the First Month of the Johnson Administration," December 24, 1963.

10. United States Information Agency, "Foreign Reaction to the Presidential Succession," December 6, 1963.

11. Brazzaville to Secretary of State, December 14, 1963, RG 59, Central Foreign Policy File 1963, SOC 14–1 US, National Archives. Johnson's emphasis on civil rights and world peace was also praised by government officials in Burundi. Usumbura to Secretary of State, December 2, 1963, RG 59, Central Foreign Policy File 1963, SOC 14–1 US, National Archives.

12. Hugh J. Parry, "America's Human Rights Image Abroad," February 26, 1964, p. 1, Folder: S-3-64, RG 306, Records of the United States Information Agency, Office of Research, Special "S" Reports, 1964–82, Box 1, National Archives.

13. Ibid.; "Attitudes of Lagos, Nairobi, and Dakar Residents Toward U.S. Race Relations," September 23, 1965, RG 306, Records of the United States Information Agency, Office of Research, Special "S" Reports, 1964–82, Box 2, S-13-65, National Archives.

14. Murrow to Johnson, January 17, 1964, FG 296 US Information Agency 11/22/63 –1/31/64, White House Central Files, Subject File, Federal Government, Johnson Library; Robert Dallek, *Flawed Giant: Lyndon Johnson and His Times, 1961–1973* (New York: Oxford University Press, 1998), 111–118; Paul R. Henggeler, *In His Steps: Lyndon Johnson and the Kennedy Mystique* (Chicago: Ivan R. Dee, 1991), 113–115; Doris Kearns, *Lyndon Johnson and the American Dream* (New York: St. Martin's Griffin, 1976), 190–193; James C. Harvey, *Black Civil Rights During the Johnson Administration* (Jackson: University and College Press of Mississippi, 1973), 3–7.

15. United States Information Agency, "Foreign Reaction to Senate Passage of Civil Rights Bill," June 29, 1964, Folder: FG 296 U.S. Information Agency 5/22/64–6/30/64, White House Central Files, Subject File, Federal Government, Box 314, Johnson Library; Thomas C. Sorensen to Malcolm Kilduff, February 13, 1964, Folder: United States Information Agency Vol I [1 of 3], National Security File, Agency File, Box 73, Johnson Library.

16. Lagos to Department of State, June 26, 1964, RG 59, Central Foreign Policy Files, 1964–66, SOC 14–1 US, National Archives; Rowan to Johnson, June 22, 1964, Folder: United States Information Agency Vol. 2 [2 of 2], National Security File, Agency File, Box 73, Johnson Library; American Embassy, Moscow, to Department of State, June 19, 1964, RG 59, Central Foreign Policy Files, 1964–66, SOC 14–1 US, National Archives; Hugh Davis Graham, *The Civil Rights Era: Origins and Development of National Policy, 1960–1972* (New York: Oxford University Press, 1990), 151–152.

17. United States Information Agency, "Foreign Reaction to Senate Passage of Civil Rights Bill," June 29, 1964; Rowan to Johnson, June 23, 1964, National Security File, Agency File, Box 73, Folder: United States Information Agency Vol. 2 [2 of 2], Johnson Library. Deliberation on the Civil Rights Act "was the longest continuous consideration of a single measure in the history of the United States Senate" at that time. Peter Evans

Kane, "The Senate Debate on the 1964 Civil Rights Act" (Ph.D. diss., Purdue University, 1967), 59.

18. United States Information Agency, "Foreign Reaction to Senate Passage of Civil Rights Bill," June 29, 1964.

19. Rowan to Johnson, June 23, 1964.

20. Rowan to Johnson, June 30, 1964, Folder: United States Information Agency Vol 2 [2 of 2], National Security File, Agency File, Box 73, Johnson Library. See also Department of State Circular to Bucharest, Budapest, Moscow, Prague, Sofia, Warsaw, July 2, 1964, RG 59, Central Foreign Policy Files, 1964–66, SOC 14–1 US, National Archives; Department of State Circular to Curaçao, Dhahran, Kuwait, July 2, 1964, RG 59, Central Foreign Policy Files, 1964–66, SOC 14–1, US, National Archives; American Embassy, Addis Ababa, to Department of State, July 8, 1964, RG 59, Central Foreign Policy Files, 1964–66, SOC 14–1 US, National Archives.

21. Rusk to Weltner, July 2, 1964, RG 59, Central Foreign Policy Files, 1964–66, SOC 14–1 US, National Archives.

22. National Committee on Civil Liberties to Goldwater, June 19, 1964 (attached to William C. Trimble to S. A. Aluko, July 7, 1964), RG 59, Central Foreign Policy Files, 1964–66, SOC 14–1, National Archives.

23. Lyndon B. Johnson, "Radio and Television Remarks Upon Signing the Civil Rights Bill," July 2, 1964, *Public Papers of the Presidents of the United States: Lyndon B. Johnson, 1963–64*, 1: 842–844.

24. Lyndon B. Johnson, "Radio and Television Remarks up on Signing the Civil Rights Bill," July 2, 1964, *Public Papers of the Presidents of the United States: Lyndon B. Johnson, 1963–64*, 2: 842–844; Carl Rowan to Johnson, July 6, 1964, Folder: FG 296, 7/1/64–9/30/64, White House Central File, Subject File, Federal Government, Johnson Library; Nehru to Johnson, July 3, 1964, RG 59, Central Foreign Policy Files, 1964–66, SOC 14–1 US, National Archives; Touré to Johnson (State Department translation), July 18, 1964, RG 59, Central Foreign Policy Files, 1964–66, SOC 14–1 US, National Archives; American Embassy, Niamey, Niger, to Secretary of State, July 9, 1964, RG 59, Central Foreign Policy Files, 1964–66, SOC 14–1 US, National Archives; Kampala to Department of State, July 7, 1964, RG 59, Central Foreign Policy Files, 1964–66, SOC 14–1 US, National Archives; Lagos to Department of State, July 10, 1964, RG 59, Central Foreign Policy Files, 1964–66, SOC 14–1 US, National Archives; American Embassy, Tananarive, to Department of State, July 7, 1964, RG 59, Central Foreign Policy Files, 1964–66, SOC 14–1 US, National Archives.

25. Dar-es-Salaam to Department of State, July 24, 1964, RG 59, Central Foreign Policy Files, 1964–66, SOC 14–1 US, National Archives; American Embassy, Bonn, to Secretary of State, July 3, 1964, RG 59, Central Foreign Policy Files, 1964–66, SOC 14–1 US, National Archives.

26. Addis Ababa to Department of State, July 8, 1964; Memorandum of Conversation, July 23, 1964, Folder: 1964—Memos of Conversation—1964, RG 59, Classified Records of Assistant Secretary of State for African Affairs G. Mennen Williams, 1961–66, Box 2, National Archives; Lagos to Department of State, July 10, 1964.

27. United States Information Agency, "African Reactions to Recent U.S. Civil Rights Developments," July 21, 1964, Folder: FG 296, 7/1/64–9/30/64, White House Central File, Federal Government, Johnson Library. See also Cairo to Department of State, July 18, 1964, RG 59, Central Foreign Policy Files, 1964–66, SOC 14–1 US, National Archives.

28. George C. Herring, *America's Longest War: The United States and Vietnam, 1950–1975*, 2nd ed. (Philadelphia: Temple University Press, 1986), 119–123; William Chafe, *The Unfinished Journey: America Since World War II* (New York: Oxford University Press, 1986), 278–280.

29. Clayborne Carson, *In Struggle: SNCC and the Black Awakening of the 1960s* (Cambridge: Harvard University Press, 1981), 111–115.

30. Tape WH6406.16, June 23, 1964, Recordings of Telephone Conversations—White House Series, Johnson Library; Tape WH6406.17, June 25, 1964, Recordings of Telephone Conversations—White House Series, Johnson Library (conversation with George Reedy); U.S. Mission, United Nations, New York, to Secretary of State, June 30, 1964, RG 59, Central Foreign Policy Files, 1964–66, SOC 14–1 US, National Archives. Thirty members of the Youth Section of the Danish Women's Society marched through the snow to present a petition to the U.S. embassy in Copenhagen later in the year. They felt that the failure to prosecute suspects in the killings showed "silent acceptance of the lynching of the youths, whose fight for Civil Rights we feel ourselves fully in accord." They protested this "violation of human rights . . . in so terrible and dangerous a manner," and urged the governor of Mississippi to see that the men were prosecuted. American Embassy, Copenhagen, to Department of State, December 30, 1964, RG 59, Central Foreign Policy Files, 1964–66, SOC 14–1 US, National Archives.

31. American Embassy, Bamako, to Department of State, June 29, 1964, RG 59, Central Foreign Policy Files, 1964–66, SOC 14 US, National Archives; American Consulate, Milan, to Department of State, November 25, 1964, RG 59, Central Foreign Policy Files, 1964–66, SOC 14 US, National Archives; American Embassy, Rabat, to Secretary of State, July 14, 1964, RG 59, Central Foreign Policy Files, 1964–66, SOC 14 US, National Archives.

32. Allen J. Matusow, *The Unraveling of America: A Story of Liberalism in the 1960s* (New York: Harper and Row, 1984), 139.

33. Rowan to Johnson, July 27, 1964, White House Central File, Federal Government, Folder: FG 296, 7/1/64–9/30/64, Johnson Library.

34. *The March* (1964), RG 306.765, National Archives; Nicholas J. Cull, "Auteurs of Ideology: USIA Documentary Film Propaganda in the Kennedy Era as Seen in Bruce Herschensohn's *The Five Cities of June* (1963) and James Blue's *The March* (1964)," *Film History* 10 (1998): 298–310. I am very grateful to Nick Cull, who kindly took time from his own research at the National Archives to help me locate and copy USIA films, including *The March*.

35. *The March* (1964).

36. Johnson conversation with Russell, January 20, 1964, Tape WH6401.17, PNO 13, Recordings of Telephone Conversations–White House Series, Johnson Library; Cull, "Auteurs of Ideology," 306 United States Information Agency to Johnson, February 19,

1964, Folder: FG 296 U.S. Information Agency 2/1/64–3/31/64, White House Central Files, Subject File, Federal Government, Box 314, Johnson Library.

37. Charles Guggenheim, *Nine from Little Rock* (1964), RG 306.05160, National Archives.

38. Ibid.

39. Rowan to Johnson, April 8, 1965, Folder: FG 296 U. S. Information Service 1/1/65 –6/1/65, White House Central Files, Subject File, Federal Government, Box 314, Johnson Library.

40. Martin Luther King Jr., "Nobel Prize Acceptance Speech," December 10, 1964, in *A Testament of Hope: The Essential Writings and Speeches of Martin Luther King, Jr.*, James M. Washington, ed. (New York: HarperCollins, 1986), 224–226; David Garrow, *Bearing the Cross: Martin Luther King, Jr., and the Southern Christian Leadership Conference* (New York: William Morrow, 1986), 364–365; Taylor Branch, *Parting the Waters: America in the King Years* (New York: Simon and Schuster, 1988), 540–543.

41. Malcolm X, "The Ballot or the Bullet," April 3, 1964, in *Malcolm X Speaks: Selected Speeches and Statements*, George Breitman, ed. (New York: Pathfinder Press, 1965), 26, 35.

42. Malcolm X, letter from Lagos, Nigeria, May 10, 1964, in Breitman, *Malcolm X Speaks*, 61; Malcolm X, letter from Accra, Ghana, May 11, 1964, in Breitman, *Malcolm X Speaks*, 62; Ibadan to Department of State, May 12, 1964, RG 59, Central Foreign Policy Files, 1964–66, SOC 14–1 US, National Archives (emphasis in original). See also Taylor Branch, *Pillar of Fire: America in the King Years, 1963–65* (New York: Simon and Schuster, 1998), 385–386.

43. Malcolm X to African Heads of State, July 1964, and Malcolm X interviewed by Milton Henry, in Breitman, *Malcolm X Speaks*, 73, 79 (emphasis in original).

44. Malcolm X to African Heads of State, July 1964, in Breitman, *Malcolm X Speaks*, 76.

45. Peter Goldman, *The Death and Life of Malcolm X*, 2nd ed. (Urbana: University of Illinois Press, 1979), 217–218.

46. Robert E. Lee to Charles G. Diggs, September 9, 1964, attachment to Department of State to American Embassy, Jidda, Cairo, Beirut, Algiers, Rabat, September 10, 1964, RG 59, Central Foreign Policy Files, 1964–66, SOC 14–1 US, National Archives; American Embassy, Cairo, to Department of State, November 7, 1964, RG 59, Central Foreign Policy Files, 1964–66, SOC 14–1 US, National Archives; Department of State to American Embassy, Jidda, Cairo, Beirut, Algiers, Rabat, September 10, 1964, and attachments, RG 59, Central Foreign Policy Files, 1964–66, SOC 14–1 US, National Archives.

47. American Embassy, Jidda, to Department of State, September 29, 1964, RG 59, Central Foreign Policy Files, 1964–66, SOC 14–1 US, National Archives; Breitman, *Malcolm X Speaks*, 58–59; Goldman, *The Death and Life of Malcolm X*, 208–217; American Embassy, Addis Ababa, to Department of State, October 6, 1964, RG 59, Central Foreign Policy Files, 1964–66, SOC 14–1 US, National Archives; American Embassy, Addis Ababa, to Department of State, November 6, 1964, RG 59, Central Foreign Policy Files, 1964–66, SOC 14–1 US, National Archives.

48. American Embassy, Nairobi, to Secretary of State, October 20, 1964, RG 59, Central Foreign Policy Files, 1964–66, SOC 14–1 US, National Archives; American Embassy,

Nairobi, to Secretary of State, October 19, 1964, RG 59, Central Foreign Policy Files, 1964–66, SOC 14–1 US, National Archives; Nairobi to Secretary of State, October 22, 1964, RG 59, Central Foreign Policy Files, 1964–66, SOC 14–1 US, National Archives (emphasis in original).

49. Nairobi to Department of State, November 2, 1964, RG 59, Central Foreign Policy Files, 1964–66, SOC 14–1 US, National Archives; Nairobi to Secretary of State, October 22, 1964; Nairobi to Department of State, October 20, 1964; Addis Ababa to Department of State, October 6, 1964. See also Dar-es-Salaam to Secretary of State, October 13, 1964, RG 59, Central Foreign Policy Files, 1964–66, SOC 14–1 US, National Archives.

50. Department of State (Rusk) to Accra, Addis Ababa, Dar-es-Salaam, Kampala, Lagos, Leopoldville, Lusaka, Nairobi, Salisbury, December 9, 1964, RG 59, Central Foreign Policy Files, 1964–66, SOC 14–1 US, National Archives.

51. James Farmer, *Lay Bare the Heart: An Autobiography of the Civil Rights Movement* (New York: Arbor House, 1985), 228; Goldman, *The Death and Life of Malcolm X*, 218–219.

52. American Embassy, Lagos, to Department of State, February 5, 1965, RG 59, Central Foreign Policy Files, 1964–66, SOC 14–1 US, National Archives.

53. American Embassy, Accra, to Secretary of State, February 6, 1965, RG 59, Central Foreign Policy Files, 1964–66, SOC 14–1 US, National Archives; American Embassy, Accra, to Secretary of State, February 3, 1965, RG 59, Central Foreign Policy Files, 1964–66, SOC 14–1 US, National Archives.

54. Department of State (Rusk) to American Embassy, Pretoria, December 30, 1964, RG 59, Central Foreign Policy Files, 1964–66, SOC 14–1 US, National Archives.

55. American Embassy, Rome, to Department of State, October 30, 1967, RG 59, Central Foreign Policy Files, 1967–69, SOC 14 US, National Archives; U.S. Mission, Geneva, to U.S. Mission, United Nations, New York, August 31, 1967, RG 59, Central Foreign Policy Files, 1967–69, SOC 14 US, National Archives; American Embassy, Montevideo, to Secretary of State, March 15, 1968, RG 59, Central Foreign Policy Files, 1967–69, SOC 14 US, National Archives; Yohuru R. Williams, "American Exported Black Nationalism: The Student Nonviolent Coordinating Committee, the Black Panther Party, and the Worldwide Freedom Struggle, 1967–1972," *Negro History Bulletin* 60 (July 1997): 13–20; James Forman, *The Making of Black Revolutionaries* (Seattle: University of Washington Press, 1995), 481–492.

56. U.S. Mission, United Nations, New York to Department of State, October 5, 1964, and attached translation of petition to H.E. U Thant, September 24, 1964, RG 59, Central Foreign Policy Files, 1964–66, SOC 14–1 US, National Archives.

57. Department of State (Rusk) to American Embassy, Kampala, November 27, 1964, RG 59, Central Foreign Policy Files, 1964–66, SOC 14–1 US, National Archives.

58. U.S. Mission, United Nations, New York to Secretary of State, December 29, 1964, RG 59, Central Foreign Policy Files, 1964–66, SOC 14–1 US, National Archives.

59. Luanda to Secretary of State, February 10, 1965, RG 59, Central Foreign Policy Files, 1964–66, SOC 14–1 US, National Archives; Garrow, *Bearing the Cross*, 382.

60. Garrow, *Bearing the Cross*, 368.

61. David J. Garrow, *Protest at Selma: Martin Luther King, Jr., and the Voting Rights Act of 1965* (New Haven: Yale University Press, 1978), 31–36; Garrow, *Bearing the Cross*, 380.

62. Garrow, *Bearing the Cross*, 394–399.

63. Ibid., 400–407; Lyndon B. Johnson, "The President's News Conference of March 13, 1965," *Public Papers of the Presidents of the United States: Lyndon B. Johnson, 1965* (Washington, D. C.: Government Printing Office, 1966), 1:275.

64. Lyndon B. Johnson, "Special Message to the Congress: The American Promise," March 15, 1965, *Public Papers of the Presidents of the United States: Lyndon B. Johnson, 1965*, 1:281.

65. Gunnar Myrdal, *An American Dilemma: The Negro Problem and Modern Democracy* (New York: Harper and Row, 1944), lxix; Johnson, "Special Message to the Congress," *Public Papers of the Presidents of the United States: Lyndon B. Johnson, 1965*, 1: 281–282.

66. Johnson, "Special Message to the Congress," *Public Papers of the Presidents of the United States: Lyndon B. Johnson, 1965*, 1:284.

67. Rowan to Johnson, March 16, 1965, White House Central Files, EX FO, Box 2, Folder: FO 3/2/65–6/10/65, Johnson Library.

68. United States Information Agency, "World Press Reaction to Selma," March 29, 1965, pp. 1–2, Folder: R-35-65, RG 306, Office of Research "R" Reports, 1964–74, National Archives.

69. Ibid., 1–2, 7.

70. Ibid., 5–8.

71. Ibid., 9–10.

72. American Embassy, Dakar, to Department of State, April 12, 1965, RG 59, Central Foreign Policy Files, 1964–66, SOC 14–1 US, National Archives.

73. *Voting Rights Act of 1965*, U.S. Statutes at Large 79 (1965): 437–446; Steven F. Lawson, *Black Ballots: Voting Rights in the South, 1944–1969* (New York: Columbia University Press, 1976) 307–321, 334; Steven F. Lawson, *In Pursuit of Power: Southern Blacks and Electoral Politics, 1965–1982* (New York: Columbia University Press, 1985), 14–15; Graham, *The Civil Rights Era*, 171–173. On violence toward African Americans who tried to register to vote, see Kay Mills, *This Little Light of Mine: The Life of Fannie Lou Hamer* (New York: Dutton, 1993), 163.

74. Hearings before the Committee on the Judiciary, U.S. Senate, on S. 1564, *To Enforce the 15th Amendment to the Constitution of the United States*, 89th Cong., 1st sess., 1965, 356. To emphasize his point, Perez introduced the entire Constitution of the Soviet Union into the hearing record, noting similarities between that constitution and the Voting Rights Bill. Ibid., 324–354.

75. Lyndon B. Johnson, "Remarks in the Capitol Rotunda at the Signing of the Voting Rights Act," August 6, 1965, *Public Papers of the Presidents of the United States: Lyndon B. Johnson, 1965*, 2: 840–843. On militaristic rhetoric related to other Johnson initiatives, such as the "War on Poverty," see Michael S. Sherry, *In The Shadow of War: The United States Since the 1930s* (New Haven, Conn.: Yale University Press, 1995), 259–266.

76. U.S. Information Agency, *For the Dignity of Man: America's Civil Rights Program* (undated), Folder: United States Information Agency 1965, Papers of Lyndon Baines Johnson, Papers as President, 1963–1969, Confidential File, Box 135, Johnson Library.

77. Ibid.

78. Graham, *The Civil Rights Era*, 174–175; Kenneth O'Reilly, *Nixon's Piano: Presidents and Racial Politics from Washington to Clinton* (New York: The Free Press, 1995), 256.

79. Gerald Horne, *Fire This Time: The Watts Uprising and the 1960s* (New York: Da Capo Press, 1997), 45–133; Matusow, *The Unraveling of America*, 362; Lester A. Sobel, *Civil Rights 1960–66* (New York: Facts on File, 1967), 306.

80. Todd Gitlin, *The Sixties: Years of Hope, Days of Rage* (New York: Bantam Books, 1987), 242–260.

81. "Racial Issues in the U.S.: Some Policy and Program Indications of Research," March 14, 1966, RG 306, Records of the United States Information Agency, Office of Research, Special "S" Reports, 1964–82, S-3-66, National Archives (emphasis in original).

82. Ibid. (emphasis in original).

83. Ibid. (emphasis in original).

84. Ibid. (emphasis in original).

85. Rowan to Johnson, June 10, 1965, White House Central Files, EX FO, Box 2, Folder: FO 3/2/65–6/10/65, Johnson Library.

86. Herring, *America's Longest War*, 170–185; Chafe, *The Unfinished Journey,* 296–297.

87. Chafe, *The Unfinished Journey,* 273; U.S. Information Agency, "Senegalese Opinion on Selected African and International Issues," March 1966, RG 306, Records of the United States Information Agency, Office of Research, "R" Reports, 1964–74, Folder R-68-66, National Archives.

88. Dan T. Carter, *The Politics of Rage: George Wallace, the Origins of the New Conservatism, and the Transformation of American Politics* (New York: Simon and Schuster, 1995), 306–307.

89. William Julius Wilson, *The Declining Significance of Race* (Chicago: University of Chicago Press, 1978), 144–154; Horne, *Fire This Time*, 280–281. On white discomfort with the pace of social change, see, for example, Robert Penn Warren, *Segregation: The Inner Conflict in the South* (Athens: University of Georgia Press, 1994); George Gallup, *The Gallup Poll 1935–1971*, vol. 3 (New York: Random House, 1972), 1828, 1908, 1933–1938.

90. For Supreme Court cases refusing to recognize class as a cognizable category in U.S. constitutional law, see *Rodriguez v. San Antonio School District*, 411 U.S. 1 (1973); *Harris v. McCrae*, 448 U.S. 297 (1980); *City of Akron v. Akron Center for Reproductive Health, Inc.*, 462 U.S. 416 (1983). An exception to this general trend was a line of Warren Court era cases: *Griffin v. Illinois*, 351 U.S. 12 (1956) (held that under equal protection clause states needed to provide trial transcripts or their equivalents to indigent criminal appellants); *Harper v. Virginia State Board of Elections*, 383 U.S. 663 (1960) (held that a state law conditioning voting on payment of poll taxes violated equal protection); *Douglas v. California*, 372 U.S. 353 (1963) (held that indigents must be provided counsel by the state in a first appeal to challenge criminal convictions); *Cipriano v. City of Houma*, 395 U.S. 701 (1969) (invalidated a state statute restricting voting rights to property owners in an election to approve issuance of a municipal utility's revenue bonds); *Shapiro v. Thomp-*

son, 394 U.S. 618 (1969) (suggested that strict scrutiny analysis applied when the state failed to provide the poor with "necessities").

91. Matusow, *The Unraveling of America*, 363. See, for example, American Embassy, Brussels, to Department of State, July 28, 1967, RG 59, Central Foreign Policy Files, 1967–69, SOC 14 US, National Archives; American Embassy, Beirut, to Secretary of State, July 27, 1967, RG 59, Central Foreign Policy Files, 1967–69, SOC 14 US, National Archives; Thomas L. Hughes to Secretary of State, August 11, 1967, RG 59, Central Foreign Policy Files, 1967–69, SOC 14 US, National Archives; Thomas C. Hughes to Secretary of State, July 27, 1967, RG 59, Central Foreign Policy Files, 1967–69, POL 23–8 US, National Archives.

92. Marks to President, September 1, 1967, Folder: United States Information Agency 1967–, Papers of Lyndon Baines Johnson, Papers as President, 1963–1969, Confidential File, Box 135, Johnson Library.

93. Department of State to All Diplomatic Posts, July 31, 1967, RG 59, Central Foreign Policy Files, 1967–69, POL 23–8 US, National Archives.

94. Goldman, *The Death and Life of Malcolm X*, 275–278; Garrow, *Bearing the Cross*, 392–393, 623–624; Gitlin, *The Sixties*, 305–313.

95. Marks to President, April 30, 1968, Folder: United States Information Agency 1967–, Papers of Lyndon Baines Johnson, Papers as President, 1963–1962, Confidential File, Box 135, Johnson Library; Marks to President, June 19, 1968, Folder: United States Information Agency, 1967–, Papers of Lyndon Baines Johnson, Papers as President, 1963–1962, Confidential File, Box 135, Johnson Library.

96. Marks to President, April 10, 1968, Folder: United States Information Agency 1967–, Papers of Lyndon Baines Johnson, Papers as President, 1963–1962, Confidential File, Box 135, Johnson Library.

97. American Embassy, Kathmandu, to United States Information Agency, June 22, 1968, RG 59, Central Foreign Policy Files, 1967–69, POL 23–8 US, National Archives; London to Department of State, August 30, 1968, RG 59, Central Foreign Policy Files, 1967–69, POL 23–8 US, National Archives (emphasis added).

98. Carter, *The Politics of Rage*, 362–364.

99. O'Reilly, *Nixon's Piano*, 270–272.

100. Marks to President, March 27, 1968, Folder: United States Information Agency 1967–, Papers of Lyndon Baines Johnson, Papers as President, 1963–1962, Confidential File, Box 135, Johnson Library (emphasis in original).

101. U.S. Information Service, "An End to this Long and Bloody War" (undated), Folder: United States Information Agency 1967–, Papers of Lyndon Baines Johnson, Papers as President, 1963–1962, Confidential File, Box 135, Johnson Library.

102. United States Kerner Commission, *The Kerner Report: The 1968 Report of the National Advisory Commission on Civilian Disorders* (New York: Pantheon Books, 1988).

103. Lewis Chester, Godfrey Hodgson, Bruce Page, *An American Melodrama: The Presidential Campaign of 1968* (New York: Viking Press, 1969), 294, 265; O'Reilly, *Nixon's Piano*, 273–275.

104. On civil rights during Richard Nixon's presidency, see Graham, *The Civil Rights Era*, 301–449.

CONCLUSION

1. James Baldwin, "Stranger in the Village," in *Notes of a Native Son* (Boston: Beacon Press, 1955), 175.

2. *New York Times*, April 10, 1968, pp. 1, 34; *Newsweek*, April 22, 1968, pp. 26, 31; Andrew Young, *An Easy Burden: The Civil Rights Movement and the Transformation of America* (New York: HarperCollins, 1996), 477–478.

3. For a discussion of international affairs as leverage for civil rights reform, see John David Skrentny, "The Effect of the Cold War on African–American Civil Rights: America and the World Audience, 1945–1968," *Theory and Society* 27 (1998): 237–285; Doug McAdam, "On the International Origins of Domestic Political Opportunities," in *Social Movements and American Political Institutions*, Anne Costain and Andrew McFarland, eds. (Lanham, Md.: Roman and Littlefield, 1988); Philip A. Klinkner with Rogers M. Smith, *The Unsteady March: The Rise and Decline of Racial Equality in America* (Chicago: University of Chicago Press, 1999), 317–351.

4. For a discussion and critique of standard interpretations of civil rights politics in the 1960s, see Adolph Reed Jr., "The 'Black Revolution' and the Reconstitution of Domination," in *Race, Politics and Culture: Critical Essays on the Radicalism of the 1960s*, Adolph Reed Jr., ed. (New York: Greenwood Press, 1986), 61–95.

5. David R. Campbell, *Writing Security: United States Foreign Policy and the Politics of Identity*, rev. ed. (Minneapolis: University of Minnesota Press, 1998).

6. On international press coverage of the Los Angeles riots, see Mary L. Dudziak, "Cold War Civil Rights: The Relationship Between Civil Rights and Foreign Affairs in the Truman Administration" (Ph.D. diss., Yale University, 1992), 201–209. On China and U.S. human rights, see "Human Rights Records in the United States," *Xinhua News Agency*, March 1, 1999; Jackie Sam, "Human Rights Violations Acceptable Except Outside the United States," *Hong Kong Standard*, March 6, 1999, p. 11; *Los Angeles Times*, April 20, 1996, p. A16. On international criticism of the death penalty, see *The Guardian* (London), April 13, 1999, p. 12; *Soering v. United Kingdom*, 11 EHRR 439 (1989) (European Court of Human Rights). On Amadou Diallo's killing, see *New York Times*, February 9, 1999, p. B4; *New York Times*, February 16, 1999, p. B1; "Adams Isn't Boxing Clver [sic]," *Belfast Telegraph*, March 3, 1999.

7. Locksley G. E. Edmundson, "Africa and the African Diaspora: The Years Ahead," in *Africa in World Affairs: The Next Thirty Years*, Ali A. Mazrui and Hasu H. Patel, eds. (New York: The Third Press, 1973), 18; Martin Luther King, Jr., "Remaining Awake Through a Great Revolution," *A Testament of Hope: The Essential Writings and Speeches of Martin Luther King, Jr.*, James Melvin Washington, ed. (New York: HarperCollins, 1986), 277.

Acknowledgments

A book of this sort invariably takes a span of years, a part of a life-time. Within a few pages, it is impossible to say enough to thank all of those who have supported this project in one way or another, and those who have helped maneuver around life's obstacles along the way.

Robert Cover's simple words of encouragement made it possible for me to imagine that perhaps I could write history worth reading. Pam Green countless years ago took my short stories seriously, and sent me off to become a writer. In the American Studies Program at Yale, Jean-Christophe Agnew opened a window for me on how to think about studying American culture. David Montgomery, with his patient and persistent questions, helped me to see the promise in the finest details in the archives. Adolph Reed challenged me to think critically about race and American politics. David Brion Davis inspired me through his example, and his support kept me on track. Burke Marshall at Yale Law School provided kind and thoughtful counsel even as he seemed skeptical that an episode he lived through would, for me, count as history.

Brenda Gayle Plummer and Gerald Horne, my most frequent conference copanelists, helped expand my thinking in immeasurable ways, and often provided indispensable advice. Derrick Bell's efforts to find new ways to reconceptualize questions of race in America provided inspiration, and his interest and support made me feel as if it mattered to do this work. There is a growing fold of scholars interested in domestic race politics and foreign affairs, including Tim Borstelman, Penny Von Eschen, Cary Fraser, Phil Klinkner, Michael Krenn, Jon Rosenberg, Rogers Smith and John David Skrentny, and I have benefitted from their work and helpful conversation. Doug McAdam and Martin Teasley generously shared their unpublished work. I enjoyed discussions with Azza Layton as she pursued similar questions. Nick Cull, in an unexpected act of kindness, took time away from his own research at the National Archives to help me with USIA films. David Garrow offered wise advice and suggested research leads on more than one occasion. Linda Kerber was there with great ideas and with flowers when times were rough. Robert Max Jackson, who in a previous life was my undergraduate honors thesis advisor, reemerged at just the right moment to give me exactly the advice I needed as I struggled to bring this project to a close.

Colleagues at the University of Iowa and the University of Southern California, and friends at other schools, have shaped this project through their questions, their criticism and their support. I am particularly grateful to Devon Carbado, Erwin Chemerinsky, Catherine Fisk, Barry Friedman, Colin Gordon, Ariela Gross, Herb Hovenkamp, Carolyn Jones, Dan Klerman, Ellen Schrecker, Rip Smith, Ray Soloman, Clyde Spillenger, Allen Steinberg, Nomi Stolzenberg, Chris Stone, Mark Tushnet, and Adrien Wing. Howard Gillman and Bob Chang were true friends toward the end, particularly in helping me rethink the introduction and conclusion. Richard Fox arrived at USC in time to help with, of all things, the copyediting. Participants in workshops at Iowa, USC, Princeton, Yale, Tulane and UCLA, and my copanelists and members of the audience at countless history conferences have raised new questions and sharpened my thinking.

A number of people read the entire manuscript and gave me detailed comments, and to them I am especially grateful. Brenda Gayle Plummer, Gerald Horne, Cary Fraser, and Phil Klinkner pushed me in helpful directions. Laura Kalman raised questions that I had not thought of, and Richard Lentz caught errors I would not have noticed. Elaine Tyler May's comments buoyed me in time to help me persevere through the final rounds of revisions. Gary Gerstle's comments enabled me to step back and view the manuscript from a fresh perspective. My editor at Princeton, Brigitta van Rheinberg, graciously prodded me in the right directions. Her support and the assistance of her staff, have greatly enhanced the final product. I also thank Karen Fortgang, Carol Roberts, and Willa Speiser.

A project that requires multiarchival research is a physical journey as well as an intellectual one. This research could not have been done without generous financial support from many sources. Dean N. William Hines at the University of Iowa College of Law and Dean Scott Bice at the University of Southern California Law School have supported this project in many ways. Summer stipends and other research support were provided by the University of Iowa Law Foundation, the University of Iowa Old Gold Fellowship program, and the University of Southern California Law School. Critical research funds included a Scholars Development Award from the Harry S. Truman Library Institute, a Travel Grant from the Eisenhower World Affairs Institute, the Theodore C. Sorenson award from the John F. Kennedy Library Foundation, a Moody Grant from the Lyndon Baines Johnson Library, and support from the Nellie Ball Trust. My first trip to the National Archives for research on this project was supported by a Littleton-Griswold Research Grant from the American Historical Association.

I would be nowhere, of course, without librarians and archivists. At both the University of Iowa and the University of Southern California law schools I have been very lucky to work with librarians who have faced an endless stream of unusual requests with good cheer. John Bergstrom at Iowa and Hazel Lord at USC seemed to perform magic tricks to make obscure sources quickly appear, and many others at both schools graciously endured my relentless queries. A long list of archivists have provided simply indispensable help along the way at the National Archives, Library of Congress, the Truman, Eisenhower, Kennedy and Johnson Presidential Libraries, and other collections. Freedom of Information officers at the Department of Justice and the U.S. Information Agency provided the help they could within an unduly restricted system. Special thanks go to Mike McReynolds at the National Archives who has been a friendly and extremely helpful source of advice since my first National Archives visit in graduate school, and Sally Marks who was most patient and helpful as I made my first foray into State Department records years ago. The Manuscripts and Archives staff at the Yale University Library redirected me toward the Chester Bowles Papers when I had my sights set on a different collection, and that has had a longstanding impact on my work.

Many hands have helped with typing revisions and other tasks, and I am especially grateful to Mary Sleichter at Iowa and Maria Medrano at USC for their dedicated efforts. Jackie Reynoso helped keep things on track and Vicki Brown seemed to perform minor miracles when needed. Thanks go to every law student who worked with me, checking sources and following up on research ideas. Special thanks go to Frieda Martin who met me in Washington and worked with me one summer at the National Archives.

For Virginia Woolf, "a room of one's own" is a precondition for writing. For parents, especially single parents, child care certainly matters as much as the room. This book would simply not have been completed without the friends, relatives and babysitters who helped with my daughter, Alicia, during crunch times, and on our trips to the archives. I am especially grateful to my sister, Diane Salerno, and her family; my mother Barbara Dudziak; Alicia's aunt, Tracy Dean, and her family; and to Amy Corriea, Cheryl and Cam Davis, Miranda Johnson Haddad, Kathy and Joe Hartley, Keiko Masubuchi, Celia and Andrew McDonald, and Susan Farnsworth and Tom Sargentich.

My most faithful companion during this journey has been my daughter, Alicia, who will be nine years old when these pages are in print. Although parenthood certainly led this book to take longer to find its way to a close, it also made the path so much more joyful. Alicia accompanied me on many trips to archives around the country, and to meetings where I presented papers. Trips to the National Archives always included visits to the National Zoo, and we found that there is a lot to do in Abilene, Kansas when the Eisenhower Library is closed if you're two years old.

While she thinks it is pretty cool to have a book coming out by her mom and with her name in it, Alicia's tolerance of this project has its limits. While vacationing in Maui the summer I was finishing the manuscript, we visited a park celebrating the heritage of different groups that had immigrated to the island. When we came upon a Filipino house, I told her that my next book might begin with something that happened in the Philippines. I thought she would be interested, but instead she looked at me in horror. "Another book?" she asked. After a pause, she continued, sternly, "Well, Mommy, you can write another book, as long as you promise that it's the last one."

This book is dedicated to Alicia, with infinite love, and no promises.

Index

Burundi, 192, 300n. 11
Bush, President George, 253
Byrnes, James F., 110, 130

CAA (Council on African Affairs), 56, 268n. 17
Cairo, 193, 194
California, 32–33, 264n. 35
capitalism, 243, 252
Careful, the Walls Have Ears, *122*
Carey, James, 84
Carmichael, Stokely, 220, 226
Carnegie Corporation, 60
Castro, Fidel, 154
Central High School. *See* Little Rock desegregation incident (Arkansas)
Ceylon, 31
Chaney, James, 214–15
Chapman, Oscar, 276n. 24
Charlotte News (North Carolina), 110
Chen Hsin Wen Pao (Taipei), 210
Chicago Tribune, 262n. 27
children, killing of, 198–99
China: on Freedom Rides, 159–60; human rights in, 253; media focus on American racism, 31–32; on Selma incident, 235
China Daily Tribune, 32
Churchill, Winston, 83
Cipriano v. City of Houma, 307n. 90
civil disobedience, 154, 157
Civil Rights Act (1875), 296n. 72
Civil Rights Act (1957), 273n. 4
Civil Rights Act (1963), 16, 184
Civil Rights Act (1964): and Congress, 183, 296n. 73; and equality, 248; Johnson on, 209–14, 215–16, 301n. 17; Malcolm X on, 222, 224; Rusk on, 167, 212, 222; State Department support of, 167
Civil Rights Act (1965), 167
civil rights activists/movement: African support sought by, 220; antiwar stance of, 246–47, 251; and civil disobedience, 154, 157; college students join, 214; international attention on, 219–20; John F. Kennedy's response to, 155; on Mississippi murders, 215; radical elements of, 226, 228; as subversive, 11, 12, 246–47; travel by activists, 61–63, 65–66, 154, 219–20; United Nations appealed to, 11–12; use of foreign reaction to racism, 43, 252
Civil Rights Congress. *See* CRC (Civil Rights Congress)

civil rights legislation. *See specific legislation*
civil rights reform, 79–114; Acheson on, 80–81, 92, 100–101, 273n. 4; and African American radicalism, 93–94; anticommunist opposition to, 88–89, 94, 111–12, 275n. 22; *Bolling v. Sharpe,* 99, 102, 279n. 48; *Brown v. Board of Education II,* 112, 138; commitment to, decline of, 251; Committee Against Jim Crow in Military Service, 85; and communist propaganda, 87; by Congress vs. Supreme Court, 182–84; and democracy, 81–82, 85, 86–87, 99–102; Democratic Party's platform of, 86; demonstrations vs. judicial forum, 179; desegregation of the military, 83–86, 87–88, 90; economic reasons for, 79–80, 273n. 2; Executive Order 9981, 86; and FEPC vote, 88–90, 275n. 22; and Fifth Amendment, 99, 279n. 48; foreign comment on Congress on, 197–98; foreign relations as requiring, 80–81, 82, 87, 91–93, 96, *97,* 100, 153–54; and Fourteenth Amendment, 92, 95, 112, 147, 279n. 48; *Goss v. Board of Education,* 281n. 69; *Graham v. Brotherhood of Locomotive Firemen,* 278n. 36; *Green v. County School Board,* 281n. 69; *Griffin v. County School Board,* 281n. 69; *Henderson v. United States,* 92–94, 96, 277n. 24; ICC, 92; Interstate Commerce Act, 92, 278n. 30; Justice Department/amicus briefs, 79, 90–92, 95–96, 99–102, 275–77n. 24, 277n. 25; *McLaurin v. Oklahoma,* 53, 94–96, *98,* 277n. 24; moral reasons for, 79, 153–54, 179–80, 186, 273n. 2; NAACP work on, 95, 96, 99, 102, 156, 277n. 28; and national security, 87, 88–89, 102, 104; *Plessy v. Ferguson,* 92, 94; President's Committee on Civil Rights, 79–80, 81–82, 84, *97,* 99, 273n. 2; and racism in the military, 87–88; Rusk on, 167, 175, 184–87, 291n. 5, 297n. 75; and segregation in District of Columbia, 96, 99, 278n. 38, 279n. 48; *Shelley v. Kraemer,* 91–92, 276n. 24; Southern protests against, 25–26; *Steele v. Louisville & Nashville R.R. Co.,* 278n. 36; *Sweatt v. Painter,* 94–96, 277n. 24; *To Secure These Rights,* 79–80, 81, 92; Truman on, 82, 86–87; Truman's desegregation initiatives, 83, 85–86, 90; world peace promoted by, 82, 106. *See also specific court cases and legislation*
Clark, Tom, 20, 45, 276n. 24

POLITICS AND SOCIETY IN
TWENTIETH-CENTURY AMERICA

*Civil Defense Begins at Home: Militarization
Meets Everyday Life in the Fifties*
by Laura McEnaney

*The Politics of Whiteness: Race, Workers, and
Culture in the Modern South*
by Michelle Brattain

*Cold War Civil Rights:
Race and the Image of American Democracy*
by Mary L. Dudziak

*Divided We Stand: American Workers and the
Struggle for Black Equality*
by Bruce Nelson

*Poverty Knowledge: Social Science, Social Policy, and
the Poor in Twentieth-Century U.S. History*
by Alice O'Connor

State of the Union: A Century of American Labor
by Nelson Lichtenstein

*Suburban Warriors: The Origins of the
New American Right*
by Lisa McGirr

*American Babylon: Race and the Struggle
for Postwar Oakland*
by Robert O. Self

*Changing the World: American
Progressives in War and Revolution*
by Alan Dawley

*Dead on Arrival: The Politics of Health Care
in Twentieth-Century America*
by Colin Gordon

*For All These Rights: Business, Labor, and the Shaping of America's
Public-Private Welfare State*
by Jennifer Klein

White Flight: Race and Place in Atlanta
by Kevin Kruse

*Troubling the Waters: Black-Jewish Relations in the
American Century*
by Cheryl Lynn Greenberg

*In Search of Another Country: Mississippi
and the Conservative Counterrevolution*
by Joseph Crespino

*The Shifting Grounds of Race: Black and Japanese Americans
in the Making of Multiethnic Los Angeles*
by Scott Kurashige

*School Lunch Politics: The Surprising History of
America's Favorite Welfare Program*
by Susan Levine

*Trucking Country: The Road to America's
Wal-Mart Economy*
by Shane Hamilton

*Americans at the Gate: The United States and Refugees
during the Cold War*
by Carl J. Bon Tempo

*The Straight State: Sexuality and Citizenship
in Twentieth-Century America*
by Margot Canaday

Little Rock: Race and Resistance at Central High School
by Karen Anderson

Debtor Nation: The History of America in Red Ink
by Louis Hyman